the war
MAGICIAN

David Fisher is the author of more than forty books on a wide variety of subjects. His work has appeared on bestseller lists around the world. He lives in New York City with his wife Laura, two sons, two cats and one small but confident dog.

the war MAGICIAN

the man who conjured victory in the desert

DAVID FISHER

CASSELL

Cassell Military Paperbacks

Cassell
Wellington House, 125 Strand
London WC2R OBB

1 3 5 7 9 10 8 6 4 2

Copyright © David Fisher 2004

First published in the USA by Coward-McCann, Inc., New York

This Cassell Military Paperbacks edition 2005

British Library Cataloguing-in-Publication Data.
A catalogue record for this book is available
from the British Library.

ISBN 0 304 36709 5

Printed and bound in Great Britain
by Cox & Wyman Ltd, Reading, Berkshire

www.orionbooks.co.uk

This book is dedicated to
Richard Curtis
Bob and Catherine Carlen Forgione
Joyce Heiberger
Paul Heller
Rosemary Rogers
for their support
while I wandered in my own desert.

The outbreak of the 1939 war, foretelling inevitable misery to everyone, meant different things to different people. To me, it involved something very strange and rather alarming – the focusing of my whole imagination and knowledge on the problem of how best to mobilize the world of magic against Hitler.

JASPER MASKELYNE

INTRODUCTION

During the sixteenth century, it is said, a stocky English farmer named John Maskelyne served the Cheltenham district as justice of the peace. He was called one day to preside at the trial of a stranger, a small, twisted black man who had appeared mysteriously in the district, clad in an unusual black silk suit. Called by the name Drummer of Tedworth, he stood accused of the practice of black magic. The evidence given against him was such that John Maskelyne declared him guilty of witchcraft and banished him to the American plantations.

Soon thereafter great misfortune befell the Maskelyne farm. Crops inexplicably failed. Cattle became bloated and died. A barn fire destroyed the sparse corn harvest. And at night, on the darkest eves, a little black man was seen limping about the fields.

Suddenly, however, the farm once more blossomed. Crops grew high and straight in the fields. The cattle were fat with milk. During a local famine the Maskelyne barn alone burst with corn, and soon the farmer's pockets clinked with gold coins.

So the tale was told throughout the land that farmer John Maskelyne had purchased, at the price of his mortal soul, the powers of black magic for himself and ten generations of his descendants.

Through the years that followed, the Maskelyne family did indeed seem to possess extraordinary powers. The line is ripe with scientists, magicians and men of standing. Nevil Maskelyne, of the third generation, served as royal astronomer in the court of King George III. He was the first to measure time to tenths of a second, to figure the weight of the earth, and he made great discoveries about the movement of stars in the heavens.

About Peter Maskelyne, the fifth generation, it was said he practised alchemy. Upon his death his notebooks were burned in a public bonfire, and the flames were supposedly many and unusual colours.

In the eighth generation came John Nevil Maskelyne, a remarkable inventor and the man considered to be the father of modern magic. He created the famed Box Trick, in which two people seemingly change places in an instant, learned to fly from the stage to a perch on a crystal chandelier, and was able to cause full-bodied spirits to materialize from his own body and converse. He founded the elite magicians' organization, the Magic Circle, and presented the first edition of *Maskelyne's Magical Mysteries* at London's famed Egyptian Theatre. He also perfected the standard typewriter keyboard and invented Psycho, the marvel of the 1870s, a mechanical man that played flawless whist.

The tenth generation was Jasper Maskelyne, the war magician. To him would fall the greatest challenge of all: to pit the powers of magic against the most evil foe in history. And at the end of the titanic battle he would have added the strangest and most significant page to the family legend.

ONE

Jasper Maskelyne was drinking a glass of razor blades when the war began. It was an old trick, first made popular by his grandfather, the legendary John Nevil Maskelyne, and often performed by his father, Nevil Maskelyne, but it always delighted the audience. As he began withdrawing from his mouth the six sharp blades, conveniently knotted to a cotton string like tiny steel sheets on a clothesline, he first noticed the young army captain moving anxiously down the centre aisle. He was careful not to stare at the officer, lest he divert attention to him, but still managed to watch him scanning the rows. The captain finally stopped near the front and leaned over a handsome woman to whisper something to a colonel. By the time Jasper had discovered the live rose sprouting from the stageboards, and picked it, the colonel was walking briskly out of the theatre. He did not look back.

Jasper sniffed the scarlet flower, briefly luxuriating in its fragrance, then tossed it into the air. Suddenly, it burst into smoke and vanished. The audience cheered this trick, and he bowed and accepted their applause, but even as he did he thought of the two soldiers, and realized it was peace that had disappeared.

Earlier that day, April 9, 1940, German shock troops had stormed into Norway and Denmark, signalling the end of the nine-month 'Bore War,' or 'Phoney War.' The long winter spent waiting for the fighting to begin was over. Finally the Army would meet the enemy.

War had officially been declared against Germany on September 3, 1939, when the Nazi blitzkrieg overran Poland, but had thus far been limited to naval battles. After an immediate flurry of excitement, restaurants, theatres and cinemas had reopened, and life in England had continued much as it had been. But Hitler's invasion of Scandinavia on April 9 marked the beginning of the land war, and a patriotic fervour gripped the nation. Long lines formed in front of enlistment centres throughout the country. Maskelyne dressed in his finest Harry Hall suit, put a fresh flower into his lapel, and joined the queue at the Reserve Officers' Enlistment Centre at Hobart House. But while the other men were volunteering to take up conventional weapons against the Germans, he harboured a much more unusual and daring plan. It was his intention to mobilize the world of magic against Hitler.

Jasper Maskelyne had been born into the world of magic. For sixty-six years, since watchmaker John Nevil Maskelyne had turned the murky Egyptian Theatre in Piccadilly into 'England's Home of Mystery,' the Maskelynes had been Europe's first family of conjuring. The fabled John Nevil, the 'Father of Modern Magic,' had introduced the Box Trick, in which an assistant vanished from a sealed and inspected cabinet and Eye of the Needle, in which one person seemingly passed through a tiny hole in a steel plate to exchange places with another who had been sealed inside a case, as well as numerous other illusions that have become magic-show standards. In addition, he had perfected Psycho, the whist-playing, cigarette-smoking mechanical man that dazzled Europe, had originated the matinée performance, had designed the accepted typewriter keyboard and had founded the exclusive magician's society, the Magic Circle.

His son, Nevil Maskelyne, had carried on the family trade at the opulent St. George's Hall, in Regent Street in the West End. During his reign at the top of the bill, *Maskelyne's Magical Mysteries* remained one of London's most popular attractions, and the Continent's most famous illusionists had astounded audiences from the St. George's stage. In the Great War, Nevil Maskelyne had served England by developing a paste that protected naval gunners' hands from searing gun flashes, and trained magician-spies for T. E. Lawrence in Arabia. Upon Nevil's death in 1926, twenty-four-year-old Jasper Maskelyne stepped into the spotlight.

It was a role for which he had been carefully groomed. His was a childhood spent watching reality turned topsy-turvy. He had grown up in the workshop beneath the stage learning how to make objects materialize or vanish, float in midair and appear to be precisely what they were not. From his grandfather he learned that, with imagination and knowledge, fantasies could be made to come alive. Given the proper equipment, anything was possible.

He was only nine when he made his stage debut, assisting the famed magician David Devant in a royal command performance at the Palace Theatre, and thereafter often worked backstage at St. George's Hall. So he was well prepared to take his place centre stage when it became his turn.

Jasper rapidly became one of London's most celebrated performers. He was almost six feet four inches tall and was handsome in the most dashing manner of the times. His hair was black and gleaming and was worn pulled back passionately, and his brush moustache was always neatly trimmed. His deep green eyes and furrowed dimples, set off by the manly cleft in his chin, made him a proper rival to the swashbuckling matinée idols.

His good looks, and the sophisticated presence that enabled him to charm sceptical patrons into believing that a simple sleight was a feat of great difficulty, made him a natural for the talking pictures, and he made a series of them, starring as a detective who used magic to solve crimes.

But when the world mobilized for war in 1939 he put show business aside and began conceiving of means to adapt the techniques of stage magic to the battlefield. He firmly believed, as he had been taught by his grandfather, that with imagination and knowledge anything was possible.

The prospect of military service thrilled him. Although his fame had spread throughout Europe, he had spent much of his life feeling as if he were a character cast into someone else's play. As a Maskelyne his life had been carefully planned for him, and he had diligently followed that plan. The war represented a chance to finally step out of the historic shadows cast by his grandfather and father. The Maskelyne name would have no meaning on the battlefield. Family contacts could not deflect Nazi bullets. The carpenters in the workshop could not create illusions for him. He would be on his own, dependent entirely upon his own skills.

Ironically, his fame worked against him. He had no difficulty arranging appointments with enlistment officers, but they refused to take him seriously. Time and again they politely explained that the Army needed fighting boys, not thirty-eight-year-old magicians. Then, nearly always, they casually asked how a favourite bit of magic they had seen performed at St. George's Hall had been accomplished.

Jasper admitted he was too old to leap from the trenches into no man's land and acknowledged that he occasionally suffered from motion sickness, but he insisted he could offer something far more valuable than cannon fodder. 'If I can stand in the focus of powerful footlights and deceive an audience only the width of an orchestra pit away, I can certainly deceive German observers fifteen thousand feet in the air, or miles away on land.'

But as desperately as he fought to get a commission, so did the Army seem determined to keep him out, as if there were some shame in allowing a music-hall performer to partake in the serious killing business. It was proving easier for him to levitate an entire chorus in midverse than convince a single ranking officer that his concepts had merit. Although Maskelyne's qualifications included an expertise in optics and applied mechanics, and practical skills in fields ranging from electronics to counterfeiting and forgery, to Army recruitment officers the thought of a magician at war conjured up images of Merlin turning young King Arthur into a bird and Moses parting the Red Sea. A battle for the survival of England was being fought in the skies, and brave boys lacking adequate weapons to defend themselves were dying on the battlefields, and it did not seem a time for magic wands or threatening spells.

While the Nazi blitzkrieg raced through the spring of 1940, Maskelyne laid siege to enlistment offices. He waited impatiently at the Hobart House recruitment centre as the Low Countries fell, paced long grey corridors while the Chamberlain government resigned in disgrace and was replaced by the bulldog Churchill, and sat in outer offices in Whitehall through the fall of Belgium and the disaster at Dunkirk. On June 22, the dark night of the French surrender, he shared a last bottle of claret with Mary, his wife of fourteen years, and said bitterly, 'It's beginning to look as though I won't have to go to the war after all. It seems to be coming to me.'

In September, as more than a thousand Luftwaffe aircraft roared across the Channel every day and Mussolini's Italian Army in Libya marched across the western desert toward lightly defended Egypt, Maskelyne decided to join the Home Guard. But before he could sign up, H. Hendley Lenton, a well-placed family friend, contacted Prime Minister Churchill. 'I have had conversations with Mr Jasper Maskelyne ("The Maskelyne"),' he wrote, 'and he has persuaded me that there are great possibilities (he says certainties) that some of his so-called "tricks" if harnessed to greater "power" or utilised in other form would be valuable assets in the present war conditions and in particular against aircraft.'

The Prime Minister referred this suggestion to his personal assistant on scientific matters, Professor Frederick Alexander Lindemann, and an appointment was arranged.

Maskelyne sat opposite the staid professor in a comfortable Whitehall office and outlined his plan. Lindemann listened with fascination, but remained sceptical. It was one thing to fool a receptive audience under prepared conditions, he pointed out, and quite another to trick the most sophisticated military machine in history. Eventually, their conversation came round to specifics. 'What sort of things do you propose to do?' he asked.

Jasper replied in an even voice. 'Given a free hand, there are no limits to the effects I can produce on the battlefield. I can create cannon where they don't exist and make ghost ships sail the seas. I can put an entire army in the field if you'd like, or make aircraft invisible, even project an image of Hitler sitting on the loo a thousand feet into the sky...'

Lindemann's initial reaction had been to dismiss Maskelyne's claims as a performer's malarkey, but for some reason he had hesitated, and now found himself actually imagining the impossible. Hitler on the loo? The corners of his mouth hinted at a smile. 'It does sound a bit far-fetched, you know. How do you propose to go about doing these things?'

'Look over there,' Jasper responded, pointing to a spot on the whitewashed ceiling behind the professor.

Lindemann spun around in his chair and stared at the general area indicated by Maskelyne. There seemed to be nothing there. He leaned forward a bit and adjusted his eyeglasses, but still did not see anything on the ceiling. 'I don't see anything,' he said.

'Exactly, because there's nothing there to see. But you reacted precisely as would anyone else. Actually, I didn't even have to say a word. If I had just stared at that spot, eventually you would have turned around. That's human nature. And stage magic, the work I do, is nothing more than a bit of suggestion, a touch of knowledge about human nature and the rather elementary use of scientific principles. The fulfilment of carefully planted expectation. It's not all that different than military camouflage, actually. I can make the Nazis see guns where they expect to see guns and soldiers where they believe soldiers might be. It's quite simple, really.'

Lindemann crossed his arms across his chest, leaned back in his chair and stared at the magician. Well, why not? he wondered. Hitler's outlaws had pretty much shattered all the traditional concepts of warfare – there was nothing to be lost by trying something new. 'All right,' he finally agreed. 'Right now a hearty dose of magic might be just the tonic. I'll make some inquiries on your behalf.'

After sending Maskelyne off to fill out the necessary forms, Lindemann closed his eyes and tried to imagine the Führer on the loo. The thought made him chuckle mischievously.

It was growing dark by the time Jasper left Whitehall, and London was beginning to settle in for the night. Thousands of people were retreating to the subterranean tube stations, armed with mattresses, blankets, and games and powdered milk for those children too young to be sent to safety in the country. Maskelyne waited at a tram stop for a decent interval, but the Luftwaffe raids had forced most above-ground transport to stop running after dusk. Finally he settled for the less convenient underground, from which he would still have a long trek home.

He walked the last few blocks in a protective fog, finding his way by following the white stripes that had been painted on tree trunks and curbs.

When he reached the house on Albany Street, he paused outside, wondering how he would tell his Mary he was finally going to the war. For the fourteen years of their marriage they had been inseparable: they had taken Maskelyne magic to the mining towns of Australia and the African bush, they had played the grand opera houses of Europe, and they had performed throughout England always together. Mary had designed the sets and settled the bills and solved the problems, and on occasion she had vanished from boxes and been shot out of a cannon to land in the rafters, but mostly she had been his friend and confidante, and the thought of leaving her was a frightening one.

The Maskelyne house was a sturdy two-storied red-brick-and-mortar construction, topped with a sloping gabled roof. Ivy vines that for some reason never climbed above the first level gave the house the appearance of having a dark beard. Viewed against the night in its blacked-out dress it appeared dark and empty, but inside it was ablaze. A wood fire warmed the parlour, and lights were on in the dining room and kitchen. The black velvet curtains taken from the theatre effectively covered each window, absorbing light rather than reflecting it or allowing it to pierce through. Jasper's thirteen-year-old son, Alistair, and twelve-year-old daughter, Jasmine, had been evacuated to the safety of a reception zone, so Mary waited alone.

When he entered she was loudly preparing dinner, banging pots and pans, clanking the wedding silver normally reserved for special occasions, and humming a popular melody. Evelyn Enid Mary Home-Douglas Maskelyne, Mary, was a small woman with short black hair and a round face, and eyes that seemed perpetually amused by some bit of private whimsy. She turned around to greet him with a kiss, and he immediately realized she knew. She knew in the mystical way women learn of distant realities.

'I'm so proud of you,' she responded when he told her the details of his meeting.

They tried to laugh. Sometimes a single tear would betray her fine act, but she nonchalantly brushed away each one. 'You'll be such a dashing officer,' she boasted. 'Wait till that Hitler hears you're in the war. That might even be enough to send him tramping.'

She was careful not to tell him how much she would worry about him. She knew he would not have an easy time in the services. It was not his age, nor his physical condition, that would cause him the most problems, but rather his basic optimism. He was a man who chased his dreams and worked to turn them into reality. To him a question mark was a challenge, and his greatest joy came with the solution of a troublesome problem. The Army would not nurture him as she had done, there would be no time to indulge his fantasies, and no one nearby to support him when failure seemed inevitable. Mary was terrified he would be wounded in battle, but she worried just as much that he would lose his ability to dream.

He was just as careful not to tell her he would worry about her every minute of every day, and would never feel whole until they were together once again.

The night was given to the past, and it was warm and tender. After dinner they sat close together on the flowered couch in the parlour, remembering a lifetime. Mary had joined Maskelyne's as an assistant in 1925; less than a year later they had married. 'Remember the night you were trying to make a motorbike disappear and the curtain caught fire,' she chided, 'and you were so brave, you grabbed the hose from the stagehand and proceeded to soak everyone in the audience.'

He countered, 'And what about the night I made you vanish from that old Chinese cabinet? You were supposed to reappear at the rear of the theatre, but someone had locked the door in the hallway beneath the auditorium. I can still hear you screaming for someone to open it while I was up there trying to figure out some way to explain exactly what you were doing.'

Later, they disdained the bulky steel-and-wood Morrison indoor shelter and slept on their marriage bed. The German bombers did not dare interrupt them.

Three days later a buff envelope was hand-delivered, ordering Jasper to report to the Royal Engineers Camouflage Training and Development Centre at Farnham.

'Camouflage?' Mary asked.

'Hiding things,' he explained.

She nodded. 'Perfect.'

It had long been a family maxim that a Maskelyne never left, he simply disappeared. But this was not a time for humour. Mary scoured the neighourhood for rationed goods and cooked a Woolton pie, a mixture of carrots, parsnips, turnips and potatoes, moistened with white sauce and covered in pastry. 'It's delicious,' Jasper said as he forced it down.

'It's awful,' she corrected.

'It is awful.'

'Damn that Hitler,' she said, reducing the war to a domestic problem. 'They should make him eat it.'

After dinner Jasper went upstairs to pack his kit. The old leather case was plastered with cheery travel stickers from around the world. He packed one suit from Hall's, five small hard balls with which to exercise his fingers, some shirts, socks, his toilet items and under-garments. After debating it briefly, he decided to take his battered ukulele, then closed the bag.

Mary had been standing in the doorway watching him. He turned and saw her there and started to speak, but stopped midsentence. She was wearing the white silk robe she'd worn on their wedding night. 'You look beautiful,' he said.

'I love you, Jay.'

He took her in his arms and first kissed her sweetly as a friend, then warmly as his wife and companion, and finally passionately as his lover. They made love tenderly and fiercely and both of them laughed and cried and whispered enduring promises, and he caressed her and tried to memorize the feel of her soft skin and the sound of her breathing and the scent of her hair and the touch of her lips, and finally they slept, sweetly cupped together, a most lovely way to say goodbye. Sometime in the middle of the night he arose and neatly hung up the wrinkled white silk robe and then, in keeping with family tradition, silently disappeared.

The village of Farnham was located in the Home County of Surrey, some forty minutes by rail from Waterloo Station. It was a place thick with history, and moved in the present at its own pace. During peacetime it had served as a dormitory town for well-heeled London commuters, and day-trippers often visited for a respite from the hectic pace of city life, but the war had changed all that.

Boards now covered the windows of the small shops on High Street, and the familiar humps of Anderson shelters popped out of backyard gardens. The stately iron picket fences had been torn down and shipped to factories to be smelted into munitions. Each morning long lines formed in front of the greengrocer's. Visitors quickly passed through on their way to the safer outlying districts. And at dusk each night, from the crumbling mullioned windows of Farnham Castle the residents of the town could be seen scurrying home carrying their gas masks in little brown boxes and glancing nervously at the sky. The war had reached Farnham.

It was to Farnham Castle that Jasper Maskelyne came to learn how to march correctly, stand at rigid attention, salute properly, and create illusions that might fool the greatest conquering army in history.

The first class of the Royal Engineers Camouflage Training and Development Centre assembled there on October 14. Thirty men exchanged their civilian clothes for natty Austin Reed uniforms and Sam Browne chest belts, raised their hands and swore to defend Crown and country, then stood around sipping tea, adjusting their starched uniforms and trying to sound as militarily astute as possible. Basically, this consisted of punctuating every few sentences with a crisp 'Damn Jerries.'

The centre had been organized and was commanded by Lieutenant Colonel Frederick Beddington, but the chief instructor was Major Richard Buckley. During the Great War Buckley had served as a camouflage officer under Solomon J. Solomon, the painter who literally wrote the book on wartime camouflage. It was a thin book, however. Camouflage in that war consisted primarily of stringing garnished nets over artillery pieces to hide telltale shadows and flash burns from observers in gas bags, of stretching large pieces of canvas between treetops so that command posts could safely operate beneath them, and of concealing snipers inside blasted trees and setting them out in no man's land. But this experience was far more than anyone else could offer, so the Army had plucked Buckley out of Eton's Tuck Shop and made him chief instructor.

'You are here to learn the art of camouflage,' he boomed as he inspected the scraggly line the first day. 'Camouflage means disguising things so the enemy doesn't know what you're doing, or hiding them so he can't see you doing it. Now, am I going too fast for anyone?'

No one responded.

'Splendid,' he said. 'I can see we're going to get along just fine.'

It was ironic that Buckley was a camouflage officer, because he would have stood out in any crowd. He was as tall as Maskelyne, and broader, and shocks of bright ginger hair sprouted wildly from his head. His green eyes were deepset and dominated by a single brow that rolled casually across his forehead. This combination of flaming hair and lively green eyes against perpetually pale skin gave him an uncanny resemblance to the Irish flag, a fact of which he was extremely proud. But the most Irish thing about him was his legendary temper. 'I lost it once when I was a lad,' he warned the class, 'and haven't found it yet.' And, while it was true he would on occasion express his displeasure by hurling a telephone or a desk across the room, he was also capable of quoting the better poets at length, or musing late into the night about the banality of a war passed in Farnham.

Buckley understood that camouflage was a visual art, and so he helped Beddington recruit men from applicable fields. Some future camoufleurs he found himself and talked into accepting commissions. Others, like Maskelyne, were routed to him by officers who couldn't figure out where else they rightly belonged. The end result was a curious collection. Besides the magician Maskelyne, the group included Victor Stiebel, a well-known couturier, painters Blair Hughes-Stanton, Edward Seago, Frederick Gore and Julian Trevelyan, designers Steven Sykes, James Gardner and Ashley Havindon, sculptor John Codner, Oxford don Francis Knox, at forty-two the oldest recruit and an animal-camouflage expert, circus manager Donald Kingsley, zoologist Hugh Cott, art expert Fred Mayor, who decorated his room at the castle with Rouaults and Matisses from his London gallery, and Jack Keefer, a West End set designer. Among their other classmates were a restorer of religious art, an electrician, two stained-glass artisans, a magazine editor, a *Punch* cartoonist and a Surrealist poet.

Teaching the King's Regulations to this group of creative officers proved to be a considerable challenge for Buckley. During the first weeks of the course he unflinchingly returned some of the most unusual salutes in military history. To his relief, no one suffered any serious injuries in close-order marching drills, although there were a great many banged-up limbs. He finally compromised on the Manual of Arms, telling his men, 'If you can pretend those sticks of wood on your shoulders are rifles, I can pretend you know what you're doing with them.'

The course was divided into general military instruction, theory and application of camouflage and deception, and physical training. It quickly became obvious to Buckley that some of his students knew more about certain aspects of camouflage than he did, so he let them teach their own subjects. Maskelyne, for example, had spent much of his life using light and shadow to deceive, and thus made a fine instructor.

As naturally occurs when men are forced together for a prolonged period, firm friendships were born at the school. Professor Frank Knox preceded Maskelyne in the alphabet, and thus in most lines, and they spent the waiting time getting to know each other. Their friendship was further strengthened by Knox's ability to play a dandy mouth organ in accompaniment to Jasper's efforts on the ukulele.

In appearance, he was quite the opposite of the dapper Maskelyne, and most resembled an unmade bed. Although he was a quite ordinary five feet seven inches tall and pleasantly chubby, he was a man fated to live his life between sizes. Everything he wore was too long or too short, too loose or too tight. Bits of shirttail were always popping from his trousers, which were always baggy; and his belt was either too long, which caused the tongue to drift away from his body and slap his stomach as he walked, or too tight, so that a wave of belly flowed over it. His face was round, his cheeks were almost perfect circles, and he had carefully cultivated a walruslike moustache, so that people often commented that he looked like Theodore Roosevelt. When he was issued his equipment at Farnham he made an attempt to substitute his taped-together black horn-rims for the regulation wire-rimmed glasses, but the army glasses sat ridiculously low on is nose, forcing him to raise his entire face skyward to see straight ahead, so he returned to his horn-rims. Buckley did not object.

Perhaps the only thing that ever fitted Frank Knox perfectly was his contagious smile. Maskelyne grew very fond of the man very quickly.

Some men are cast into lifelong supporting roles, and Frank Knox was the pick of this type. He was a man of constant good cheer, gentle and amiable, content with his own situation and thus able to live free of envy. 'There are few things that really make any difference in life,' he once explained to Jasper. 'Love and friendship are the most important, then honesty and loyalty, a few pounds to get along, and time. Time is precious.'

'Is that all?'

'That's plenty.'

'There's got to be more than that,' Maskelyne insisted.

'If you say so,' Knox readily agreed. Although essentially a private man, he began to confide in Jasper as he got to know him better. He dated his life of accommodation from the death of his wife. She had given him two daughters before dying in the minor pneumonia outbreak of 1932. Eight years later he still grieved. The impact of her loss had set everything else forever in its proper place.

The camouflage course progressed without incident into the winter, much of it being improvised by Buckley and this first class as they moved along. Although Jasper's stage experience had made him an expert in the basic camouflage techniques of colouring, shading, blending, perspective and the use of decoys, the application of these principles to military situations was new to him. Among the many things he had to learn was how to 'read' air reconnaissance photographs, how to fool enemy air recce cameras and how to determine if the enemy was attempting to mislead British surveillance. Eventually, he was able to determine the calibre of a heavy weapon by its muzzle flash or the type and size of a vehicle by the depth of its tyre track; he could estimate the strength of an enemy force by the garbage left in an abandoned bivouac area or pick out a concealed unit by distorted shadows.

'I'm now perfectly able to hide an entire battalion in an open field,' he said to Knox one afternoon as they huffed around the castle to fulfill Buckley's daily exercise requirement. 'Unfortunately, with all the Nazi bombing, we haven't got any open fields.'

'For that matter,' Knox pointed out, 'we've no full battalions either.'

Even more impressive than the fact that Buckley had turned this group of square-peggers into camoufleurs was that he had successfully transformed them into a facsimile military unit, capable of responding to the elementary commands without hazard. On occasion, the class would be trucked to the sprawling army base at Aldershot for specialized training, but Buckley did his best to keep these field days to a minimum, fearful that close exposure to the regular military might spoil his officers. But even though the men were physically isolated from the Army, they could not get away from the war.

The news was bad. German troops occupied most of continental Europe, and half of Hitler's army was poised on the French beaches waiting for his signal to launch the first invasion of Britain in nine hundred years. In the air, Reichsmarshal Hermann Goering's Luftwaffe was flying almost fifteen hundred sorties every day against the heroic but outgunned RAF. By September, German bombers had shifted their primary targets from military bases to cities. London was being devastated, but every city suffered. On November 14, in retaliation for minor bomb damage inflicted by the RAF on the Munich beer hall in which Hitler had begun his 1923 putsch, five hundred Nazi bombers attacked the small historical-industrial city of Coventry. In ten hours, 554 people were killed and fifty thousand homes were destroyed. A week after the raid the fires of Coventry still burned.

In the Middle East, Mussolini, desperate to placate Hitler, had ordered Marshal Graziani's 300,000-man Italian Tenth Army to drive the English out of Egypt. Il Duce coldly estimated that one thousand casualties during the campaign would enable him to sit with the Führer at the conference table. Only the thirty thousand British Tommies of

General Archibald Wavell's Western Desert Force stood between Graziani and the Suez Canal, and beyond that the oil fields of Persia. If the Italian offensive succeeded, England would lose its primary source of gasoline.

The small group of camouflage officers training at Farnham were anxious to get out of their classrooms and into the field while they still might be of some use. But the course had followed no formal schedule, so no one knew for certain when it would officially end. 'Soon,' Buckley promised, but 'soon' passed and was replaced by 'shortly.' Meanwhile, postings became the main topic of conversation.

Jasper said he expected to be sent to Egypt. 'It's the most logical thing. I've toured the Nile Basin with my show. I speak passable Arabic. They're desperately short of supplies there. And my father served there during the Great War.'

'Makes complete sense,' Knox concurred, 'which is precisely why you won't be sent there.' On the night of December 9 the men were sitting around the castle's great stone fireplace, sipping mess-allotment cognac, when the normally placid industrial designer James Gardner rushed into the hall. 'Wavell's on the move,' he announced. 'It's on the BBC.'

That could have only one meaning. Graziani was attacking, and the vastly outnumbered British Army was retreating. Another Dunkirk was shaping up. The disheartened group drifted into the wireless room just in time to hear an astonishing report from news reader John Snagg. Wavell was attacking. The Italians were in retreat. 'The War Office announced that General Wavell's troops began their assault on Italian fortifications at seven-fifteen this morning, Egyptian Standard Time. Twenty enemy vehicles were destroyed in the initial advance and two thousand prisoners taken. Marshal Graziani's soldiers were apparently taken by complete surprise...'

'Comes as a bit of a surprise to me too,' Gardner said.

Incredibly, Wavell's thirty thousand troops were charging headlong across the desert, halted more often by sandstorms and uncharted soft sand seas than by the enemy. What had begun as a limited advance had turned into a rout. Entire towns and forts surrendered without resistance. Tens of thousands of Italian troops were abandoning their weapons and boots and fleeing toward the Libyan border. One British battalion commander estimated his bag of prisoners as 'five acres of officers, two acres of other ranks.'

Maskelyne's Farnham class celebrated this first land victory of the war at the local pub, the Ivy. The publican actually served rounds on the house and the toast 'To the thirty thousand' resounded through the night.

At first Maskelyne held his own in the celebration, even strumming a few patriotic tunes on the ukulele, but after a while he grew quiet and sombre.

Frank Knox noticed the change immediately. They were squeezed into a corner booth and by tucking their heads together could talk in reasonable tones. 'You certainly don't seem too chipper.'

'It shows?'

'Like a peacock on a winter spruce.'

A pensioner standing on top of the bar was claiming to have served in the desert during the last war. Asked to describe the place, he said, 'Hot. Very hot.'

Maskelyne shook his head. Initially the news from the desert had filled him with joy, but during the celebration the joy had slowly drained, and left him feeling empty. The war was passing him by. Great battles were being fought while he was sipping cognac by the fireside. The agreeable surroundings had lulled him into passivity, and he had lost sight of his original intention. But as he sat in the Ivy celebrating the desert victory, his anger was aroused. He had worked too long and too hard fighting his way into the services to spend the war in Farnham. It was time to take control of his own fate. 'You're right, Frank, what you said the other day,' he said firmly. 'If we don't do something right now to make them notice us, we're going to end up stringing nets in Brighton for the duration.'

Knox shrugged. 'Oh, I wouldn't pay too much attention to what I said, Jay. I was just spouting off. We're supposed to complain, you know, we're soldiers.'

'But you were right, we just can't take the chance.' Maskelyne paused, and suddenly the solution to the problem became clear. He smiled in anticipation. 'That's why we're going to do something so startling at Lord Gort's inspection next week that they can't possibly overlook us.'

Frank blanched. 'Us?' he mumbled weakly.

On a gothic morning in mid-December, John Standish Surtees Prendergast Vereker, sixth Viscount Gort, or simply Lord Gort, Commander-in-Chief of the Army, stood at the edge of a rolling field with his aides and a very nervous Buckley. The air was crisp, and dark foreboding clouds hid the sun.

'At your pleasure, sir,' Buckley said smartly.

Gort nodded. To demonstrate their skills, teams of camouflage officers had been assigned a weapon, vehicle or fortification to conceal. The Commander-in-Chief was to walk the field and attempt to uncover their efforts.

Maskelyne and Knox had been given a machine-gun bunker to hide. Jasper attacked the project with relish, as if he were creating a show-stopping illusion for St. George's Hall. He carefully sketched every detail. Then, once the various pieces were fashioned and put in place, each of them was tested and retested until there existed virtually no chance for error. While their classmates packed it in at dusk, Jasper and Frank worked into the freezing night on details Knox was certain no one would ever notice. When it finally got too cold they would return to the castle, and Maskelyne would work on the scale-model battleship that would enable him to turn an ordinary machine gunners' nest into a magic theatre.

They finished the night before the inspection, and the next morning they lay flat on their stomachs inside the cramped position as Lord Gort began his first tour of the field. Gort immediately spotted the dummy tank disguised as a three-ton truck, the papier-mâché twenty-five-pounder poorly silhouetted against the bleak horizon, two snipers' trees, and a number of bunkers covered with garnished netting. Footprints in the soft earth led him to four broom-armed riflemen lying under dirt-encrusted canvas.

Inside the bunker, Maskelyne tensed each time Gort so much as sniffed in his direction, as if the outcome of the war depended upon the General's being fooled.

Eventually, Lord Gort managed to ferret out every piece and position except number four, the Maskelyne-Knox machine-gun nest. The General regarded the exercise as a game, but he was a serious gamesman. 'Don't tell me where it is,' he snapped, and began stalking through the field for the third time.

He failed to find the bunker. Turning to Buckley, he asked, in tiny cloudbursts of cold breath, 'All right, Major, where is it?'

The answer came from a hump of earth no more than thirty-five feet away. 'Here we are, sir!' a muffled voice shouted. Gort squinted at the gentle rise and began walking toward it, but stopped when he spotted a narrow rectangular slit almost completely hidden beneath overhanging clumps of field grass. A broomstick handle popped out. 'This is a machine gun,' the voice yelled playfully. 'Bang.'

Buckley winced.

The machine-gun nest had been made by laying sheets of plywood over a natural depression, then covering the plywood with dirt and grass so that it blended into the field. Irregularly cut pieces of mirror had been placed in front of the bunker to reflect the ground in front of it, and false tyre tracks, supposedly made by the dummy truck that was parked nearby, passed directly over the mound and added to the impression that it was a natural feature of the field.

Lord Gort nodded appreciatively. This time he'd been fooled. 'Well done, chaps,' he shouted.

'Come in and have a look around,' Maskelyne's deep voice invited from within the nest. 'There's some pretty interesting sights to see in here.'

The bunker was barely three feet high, damp and cramped. Its dirt floor had been covered with canvas. After Maskelyne slithered out, Lord Gort and Buckley crawled in beside Knox.

'A bit touchy in here, eh?' the General said.

'A bit, sir,' Knox agreed, sliding away from the viewing slit. The temperature was below freezing, but he was sweating. He'd been in the Army only a few months, and he was about to play a trick on the Commander-in-Chief. He covered his eyes with a glove, not wanting to see what was going to happen next.

Lord Gort scanned the field with his binoculars. To his right the morning frost still blanketed a distant valley. Directly before him the shivering camouflage class waited to be dismissed. And on his left, the Nazi pocket battleship *Admiral Graf Spee* was sailing peacefully down the Thames. 'My word,' he whispered in amazement.

'Sir?' Buckley questioned in an alarmed voice.

On top of the mound Jasper manipulated his scale-model battleship and the intricate glass-and-mirror arrangement used to produce the illusion. The setup was based on an illusion devised by John Nevil Maskelyne in which a spirit appeared to 'grow' right out of his own body. An assistant tilting mirrors in the orchestra pit could make the spirit appear or disappear; Jasper was doing the same thing with his model ship.

Lord Gort lowered his field glasses and tried to blink the image out of his mind. Obviously, the *Graf Spee* could not be sailing down the Thames. That ship had been hunted down and scuttled exactly a year earlier. Besides, the river flowed nowhere near Farnham.

Buckley pushed in next to him. He saw the frost-covered valley and the freezing camouflage class and, to his left, some Jersey cows grazing on winter grass. 'Sir?'

'Who prepared this position?'

'Lieutenants Maskelyne and Knox.'

'Maskelyne? Maskelyne the magician?'

Knox answered. 'Yes, sir.' He no longer had any doubts they would be stringing nets in Brighton for the duration.

By the time Lord Gort had twisted around and wriggled outside, Jasper had stowed his props. He stood there looking as innocent as a politician during a campaign. 'Have a nice look, sir?'

'It was a trick, wasn't it?'

Jasper's eyes twinkled. 'What did you expect, sir? Magic?'

The purpose of the demonstration was not lost on the General. Later, as the class feasted on prime ribs and Yorkshire pudding at Farnham Castle, be quizzed Maskelyne on the real potential of magic on the battlefield. 'That was a nice show and I shan't soon forget it, but conditions in the field are quite different. It's not a stage, and the audience won't be sitting still.'

'And I'm not going to be sawing women in half and making pianos disappear,' Jasper responded. 'General, I don't intend to do hocus-pocus. What I mean to do is apply the same principles used in stage magic to the battlefield.'

Lord Gort sipped a rich burgundy. 'What sort of things do you propose?'

'Almost anything can be done, but I can produce equipment where shortages exist.'

Knox recognized his cue. 'Egypt, for instance.' Wavell's lack of men and equipment had forced him to halt his offensive short of enemy headquarters in Libya. The reinforcements and supplies he had been expecting had been diverted to Greece, and his army was left to bake in the desert.

'Everywhere, right now,' the General replied, then pressed Maskelyne for details.

'It's quite simple,' Jasper explained. 'The one thing Major Buckley has been drumming into us is that a show of force can be nearly as effective as the actual weapons. The enemy can be made to respond precisely as you want them to, perhaps change the direction of an advance, pause before attacking, even waste their ammunition on worthless targets. Well, I can create those targets. I've spent my entire adult life making things appear to be precisely what they are not. You want tanks, I can give you tanks. Guns? How many? Soldiers – just give me some paste and cardboard and I'll build an army for you.'

Frank Knox coughed his way into Jasper's attention, and the magician paused. 'I can be effective, General, if they give me a chance.'

Gort looked at Buckley, who had watched the magician's performance in stunned silence. 'You've certainly managed to instil the necessary confidence in your people, Major.'

'Yes, sir, thank you, sir,' Buckley responded.

The Inspector General was admittedly intrigued by Maskelyne's proposal and promised to give it serious consideration. 'But there's no substitute for good men and machines,' he reminded them, then added, 'unless, of course, you haven't got any.'

Lord Gort's inspection passed for graduation, but there was a long waiting list for transportation overseas, so the new camoufleurs moved to Aldershot and began applying their skills to the greatest deception ever attempted.

The Army was desperately trying to convince Hitler they were ready to meet his invasion, relying on many of the same concepts Maskelyne had proposed to Gort. To replace the 100,000 men, 120,000 vehicles and 2,300 heavy artillery pieces lost at Dunkirk, factories throughout the English countryside were turning out an entire dummy army. Countless cloth and cardboard soldiers, and canvas guns that cast realistic shadows were slipped into real formations to impress Nazi Intelligence.

If the Germans came anyway, they would pay a bloody price. The English countryside had been transformed into a lethal trap. The precious few real heavy weapons had been carefully concealed behind the plywood walls of hastily constructed 'country pubs' and 'thatched-roof cottages.' Sheep grazing in meadows suitable for glider landings were in reality packages of high explosives stuffed into sheepskins and pulled about on wires. Other potential landing fields were mined, or hidden beneath artificial forests. Thirty-foot-tall trees were felled and hollowed out to hold a gun post or a tank trap or a high-explosive package, then replanted in a strategic position. Seemingly innocent 'berry patches' hid elephant traps, which were simply large pits covered with foliage or a thin layer of dirt. In addition, false signposts were erected to make prewar maps useless, and new, inaccurate maps were circulated. Major roads, as indicated on these maps, would end suddenly in overgrown woods and other roads led into bogs. Numerous lakes were drained or covered with nets to further harass the Nazis.

While his classmates helped create the scenery for this show, Maskelyne worked at his drawing board. Creating the illusions for the magic stage had always appealed to him more than performing, and the floor of the workshop at St. George's Hall was usually littered with pages of his discarded ideas. But now, instead of devising a means to run a flaming sword through a villain in full view of the audience, he began designing war machinery. Among these were balloons capable of carrying bombs over the invasion fleet, and a gun, fired from shore, that would lay naval mines. He also improved the camouflage of entrenched gun positions, pillboxes, using reflectors just as he had done during the Farnham demonstration and invented the 'octopus mine.' This was an ordinary nautical mine, but eight long lengths of cable had been attached to its detonator. An invasion barge or a motorboat passing over would snare one of the cords in its propeller, causing the mine to explode. This vastly increased the area protected by the limited number of available mines.

One afternoon in early January 1941, Frank Knox walked into Maskelyne's room and found him hard at work on the octopus mine. He watched over his shoulder for a few minutes, then said, 'That's splendid, Jay, it really is. You know, over the last months I've watched you come up with all these ideas, and I wish … I wonder …' He shrugged. 'Where do they all come from?'

Jasper began shading in the nautical mine. Where indeed? It was a question he had often pondered himself. Where was the beginning of creation? 'It's sort of a skill,' he said. 'Some people are clever at figures, others pick up languages easily. I just see things a bit differently than other people, that's all.' The real answer, he knew, was that there was no answer. Creativity was a gift. Ideas were the toys of gods.

'Used to come up with a few clever ones myself, you know. But lately I don't seem to get the good ones anymore.'

Jasper glanced over his shoulder. 'You've got to keep working at it. Developing it and sharpening it. I've been doing it all my life. The family business, you know.'

Frank nodded. 'Are you ever afraid you'll lose it?'

Jasper hesitated before answering, then admitted, 'Every minute Frank. And I'm frightened that if I do I won't know how to find it again. There's not much I can do about it, though, is there? Trying to hold on to creativity is like trying to draw water with a pitchfork. I just appreciate the gift, and try not to worry about losing it.'

'I see. Not much fun in that, is there?' Frank patted him on the shoulder, and turned to leave. He stopped. 'Oh, almost forgot the big news. Postings are up. We're shipping next week.'

The magician was finally going to war.

TWO

The Nazi invasion did not come. Day and night throughout the winter, coast watchers scanned the empty seas, but Hitler's fleet remained on the French beaches. The raw and bitter weather was greeted by the English as an old ally, and the Channel grew mean. An invasion before spring was considered most unlikely. For the first time in almost a year, England breathed.

At last there was hope. The Churchill government had taken firm control and managed to instil a sense of purpose in the nation. General Charles de Gaulle had 35,000 trained Free French soldiers and 1,000 pilots ready to fight. In North Africa, Wavell's brave 30,000 commanded Egypt and the western desert. And, although America remained officially neutral, its recently reelected President, Franklin D. Roosevelt, declared that the United States 'must be the arsenal of democracy,' a message signalling that substantial aid would be made available.

So it was with some optimism that Jasper Maskelyne and Frank Knox sailed from the Liverpool docks aboard the converted ocean liner *Sumaria* on Sunday, January 19, 1941. For security, their destination was officially 'Area J,' but as they had been ordered to prepare semitropical kits, 'J' was obviously North Africa or the Far East. Most of the shipboard betting pools favoured Egypt.

To ensure total secrecy, all leaves had been cancelled when the postings went up. Telephone calls were not permitted, and letters were collected to be posted after the convoy was safely at sea. Jasper wrote this in his letter to Mary: 'As you read this I shall be at sea. Finally, I will be part of it. I love you more than I had ever hoped to love anyone.' To his children he wrote pages of wishes. It was a joyful letter, it included no mention of his fears, and ended with a promise of reunion.

The *Sumaria* had been built to carry seventeen hundred passengers across the Atlantic in prewar luxury, but its days as a romantic cruise ship were over. On this voyage six thousand troops and their equipment were squeezed onto the decks and into the holds. Its black hull had been camouflaged with broken patterns of khaki and ocean-blue paint. Thirty-six Bren guns were mounted on concrete scaffolding secured to its sides. The main-deck swimming pool now housed a 40mm antiaircraft gun, and large canvas awnings had been stretched across the deck to shade additional bunk space.

There were no bands playing and no one tossed confetti as the *Sumaria* slipped quietly out of the harbour in the night, past scores of seized contraband ships, past the rusting hulks of bombed-out transports and freighters, past the blacked-out buildings of Liverpool, and joined the twenty-one-ship convoy to destination 'J.'

To avoid German submarine wolf packs, Royal Navy escorts led the convoy on a route-of-opportunity. The course was set on a daily basis. The convoy lay off the coast of Iceland for a few days, then steamed south, anchoring so close to New York City that the men aboard could see its night lights twinkling on the horizon, then farther south, past Buenos Aires.

The *Sumaria* sailed through the weeks. To help relieve the tedium aboard the cramped ship, a wide range of esoteric courses was offered to the troops. Jasper taught model-boat building. Frank Knox lectured on animals of the Middle East. Engineer Captain Peter Proud, a well-known film-set designer, demonstrated techniques of individual camouflage. Among many other classes offered were archaeology, music appreciation (without music), cooking with rations, first aid, military history, French, English literature, drawing and magazine writing.

Mandatory calisthenics drills were conducted three times a day. Boxing rings were set up on each deck, and the soldiers had at each other all afternoon. Unfortunately, the wagering on the bouts caused more fights outside the rings than took place inside.

For entertainment, a group of strolling players was organized. These included a violin prodigy, who would later die in the bombing of Crete, two singers, a ventriloquist whose dummy was made in Hitler's image, a sound mimic, and Maskelyne. Jasper did a comedy turn as an inept magician named Nozmo King, a none-too-subtle reminder that smoking regulations had to be obeyed.

After the seventh week at sea Maskelyne began producing a nightly variety. His own contribution to the show was a makeshift version of the Aladdin story, in which he was assisted by Frank Knox, who donned a yellow mop wig to become a blonde temptress. By rubbing a ship's lantern, Jasper conjured up a turbanned djinn floating on a cloud of white smoke. This genie offered to grant three wishes. Jasper took suggestions from his audience and, in response to the inevitable requests, materialized Knox as a ghostly pin-up girl, a turkey dinner and, most popular, a kettle that supplied an endless variety of beverages upon request.

Several original songs were written for the show by Army Captain Page. One of these so impressed Maskelyne that he suggested it be sent to an acquaintance of his at Feldman's, the London music-publishing house. The song written for this variety, 'White Cliffs of Dover,' eventually became a standard.

No contact was made with the enemy during the zigzagging first leg of the voyage, although one night Officer-of-the-Deck Proud ordered the New Zealand Bofors crew to fire at an approaching aircraft. After a few seconds of embarrassed silence, one of them softly informed him the plane was a friendly bomber.

The *Sumaria* finally made landfall in Freetown, Sierra Leone, Africa, in early March. Although the convoy's destination had supposedly been 'most secret,' sacks of mail were waiting on the docks for the men. They were so happy to receive the letters and packages they did not question this serious breach of security. Besides a stack of letters from Mary, Jasper received an expensive box of chocolates. The return address on the package had been smudged beyond legibility, but he assumed it was from his family or a friend.

Within hours of sampling the box his stomach was gripped by excruciating cramps. At first he tried to joke about it, suggesting to Knox, 'The chocolate was probably sent to me by an enemy agent.'

'More likely someone who saw your show,' Frank replied.

Their joking stopped a few hours later when Maskelyne began running a high fever. By the time the *Sumaria* sailed, he was slipping in and out of consciousness. The ship's doctor did everything he could, but Jasper's condition continued to deteriorate. Knox stood by his bunk applying ice blocks to his body, but the fever wouldn't break. During one of his lucid periods, Jasper asked Frank to bring him a bottle of whisky. 'So thirsty,' he pleaded.

Knox reluctantly got the bottle from the ship's steward. Just as Maskelyne was about to pour the first shot, the *Sumaria*'s captain arrived to pay his respects. The captain was nervously clutching his white hat in his hands and avoided looking directly at Jasper as he spoke. In a sombre voice he thanked him for his efforts during the voyage, then did a poor job reassuring him that the doctor predicted a rapid recovery.

Jasper nodded at all the proper pauses, meanwhile trying to keep the open whisky bottle hidden without spilling its contents. Even in his half-stupor, he didn't want to ruin the captain's sincere farewell address by producing a bottle of spirits.

After the captain's departure he downed eight shots and collapsed into a deep sleep. When he woke up almost a full day later Knox was still sitting by his bunk. 'Fever's broken,' Frank said casually.

'I've got a splitting headache,' Jasper moaned.

'It's better than being dead,' Frank said.

Jasper looked at him through bleary eyes. 'That's easy for you to say.' Two days later he was wobbling around the deck.

The chocolate incident was reported to the intelligence section and promptly forgotten. Months later, in an intelligence office beneath a brothel, Jasper would learn that his brief report had sparked a major investigation, which led to the discovery of an Axis spy ring operating throughout the Middle East.

From Freetown the convoy had looped around the Falkland Islands, near Antarctica, causing them all to shiver in their tropical weights, then north again, by Cape Town, finally making land at Durban, South Africa. The convoy had been at sea three months, scurrying around the world avoiding areas in which U-boats had been spotted. Tempers aboard the transports were razor-thin, and many of the ships began logging serious injuries sustained in fights and, more ominously, suicides. One man aboard the *Sumaria* killed himself by drinking a bottle of brass cleaner, and another simply disappeared and was presumed lost overboard.

The convoy darted from Durban to Madagascar, then up the Red Sea toward the Suez Canal. There was no longer any doubt that 'Area J' was the Middle East, but the situation there had changed drastically while they were at sea.

To save his Italian ally from a disgraceful defeat in North Africa, Hitler had offered military assistance to Mussolini. Unknown to the Italians, since 1936 the Nazis had been training officers for an elite desert army inside two huge hothouses in the district of Schleswig-Holstein in the north and in Bavaria in the south. The soldiers lived inside these buildings under desert conditions for weeks at a time. They ate desert rations, drilled in breath-sucking heat, slept in bone-chilling cold and trained on a sand-covered floor. By 1940, the spine of the Afrika Korps had been hardened.

Mussolini had no choice but to accept the offer. The German force was officially under the command of Italian General Garibaldi, but was in fact led by Hitler's favourite general, tank warfare expert Erwin

Rommel. Two months after he arrived in the desert Rommel was crashing his way into history.

The British convoy reached the Suez Canal just as the alcohol stores were exhausted, and the men congratulated themselves on the accuracy of their calculations. But hours before they were to dock in Suez, Luftwaffe bombers were spotted nearby and the convoy turned around and fled back down the Red Sea. It was another week before they finally dropped anchor in Suez.

The *Sumaria* had sailed into chaos. The distressing reports that had been received at sea had not prepared anyone for the situation that greeted them. Suez was a city in shock. Soldiers from every force of the Commonwealth army, from all divisions, all units – tankers, cooks, clerks, riflemen, sappers, drivers, engineers, soldiers of every rank – had crammed into the tiny city and made camp on its pavements or wandered dazed through its streets. The city seemed to ache from the confusion. Its aged and limited public services could not cope with the massive influx of Tommies; the sewage system had backed up and puddles of stagnant water pocked the paved streets and the dirt alleys; piles of garbage lay uncollected and most public transportation had been halted. There was not enough food or water and almost no functioning sanitation facilities. At Port Tewfik mountains of equipment lay untouched on the docks. Unopened boxes of rations, medical supplies, summer uniforms, petrol cans, even weapons and ammunition, spilled down the sides of the man-made slopes. In the harbour countless ships, transports and freighters and small warships as far as it was possible to see, lay drifting at anchor. Waiting. Waiting as the soldiers waited in the streets, for orders that did not come.

Western Desert Force, only months earlier the pride of the Empire, Wavell's gallant thirty thousand, was in a shambles. The chain of command had broken down. Communications facilities were destroyed. Units were scattered helter-skelter over the entire Nile Basin.

'It's another bloody Dunkirk,' Frank whispered in horror as they walked through a crowded street, looking grotesquely out of place in their sparkling uniforms.

'No,' Jasper corrected in a shaken voice, 'it's Suez.'

Presently they joined a knot of officers standing in the middle of the road and asked what had happened.

An Australian captain looked them over suspiciously, then took a long drag on a malodorous Egyptian cigarette, dropped it into the gutter and ground it dead, and said respectfully, 'Rommel.'

General Erwin Rommel had landed at Castel Benito airfield, outside

Tripoli, Libya, on February 12, 1941, to command the *Sperrverband,* or blocking detachment, ordered to halt the British advance into Cyrenaica. Two days later, Afrika Korps arrived. Throughout the afternoon and into the floodlit night an endless stream of haughty soldiers, muzzled artillery pieces, and desert-camouflaged twenty-five-ton panzer tanks, European victory pennants colouring the stark scene, had paraded off their transports through the streets of Tripoli. They were greeted by thousands of cheering Libyans, among them British agents feverishly trying to keep count of the mighty force.

Rommel stood in the blistering sun all afternoon reviewing the troops. But this show of force had actually been staged for the dozens of English spies in the crowds. In his first brilliant deception in North Africa, Rommel had transformed two battalions into an entire army, for as each unit completed the parade it was trucked back to the docks and rejoined the end of the line.

Within hours Wavell had been informed that a mammoth German detachment had landed in Libya. Surveillance efforts in the desert were immediately intensified, but failed to spot any evidence of the German force. Rommel's army seemed to have disappeared into the desert wastelands as suddenly as it had arrived.

Little more than a month later, the officers and troops of the British garrison at El Aghelia were playing a rough-and-tumble football match. The most recent intelligence signals mentioned some minor enemy activity to the southeast, but indicated nothing major brewing. The ball was booted out of bounds over a small dune, and Lance Corporal Richard Duckworth ran to retrieve it. As he began trotting back to the field he glanced over his shoulder – and froze in horror. His mouth opened and he tried to scream a warning – but no words came out. Lumbering through the waves of rising heat, a vast armada of panzer tanks was bearing down on the post.

By nightfall, the stunned football players were dead, prisoners of war, or fleeing toward the outpost at Mersa Brega. Duckworth suffered a superficial foot wound and was captured. As he sat under guard watching the Nazi tank force roll into town, he received another great shock. Following close behind the front rows of panzers were dozens of wooden tank shells mounted on Volkswagen chassis, followed by trucks pulling sweepers to raise dust clouds.

A week later Mersa Brega was overrun. The British retreat began in earnest.

Western Desert Force was not prepared to counter Rommel's offensive. Intelligence Branch had been certain the Germans would not attack. Most of Wavell's veteran troops and their equipment had been shipped to Greece and replaced on the front lines by wet, or newly arrived, soldiers and their inexperienced officers. Then, early in the fighting, General O'Connor, commander of British troops in Egypt, and General Neame, Desert Force commander, drove into a German patrol and were captured. After that, British resistance simply fell apart.

'He's got this special power, see,' the Australian captain explained. 'The Jerries call it *Fingerspitzengefühl*, it's like a feeling in his fingers. He knows things before they happen.'

A New Zealand lieutenant nodded agreement. 'He's got something up his sleeve, that's for damn sure. If it wasn't for the boys at Tobruk, we'd still be runnin'.'

Rommel's blitzkrieg across the western desert had paused outside the deep-water port of Tobruk in early April. Afrika Korps consumed fifteen hundred tons of rations and water daily, and its supply lines were badly overextended. If Tobruk was not captured, those vitals would have to be trucked across a thousand miles of open desert, and this thin lifeline would be extremely vulnerable. If the British broke out of Tobruk, they could conceivably slice it in half, thus isolating most of Afrika Korps. Tobruk became the key to Rommel's entire campaign.

Wavell rushed reinforcements to the beleaguered fortress. Rommel attacked its thirty-mile perimeter on April 14 and was repulsed after heavy fighting. Two days later he attacked again. The defensive line sagged in numerous pockets but never snapped, and Rommel pulled back. His wounded Afrika Korps dug in just outside the city. 'He's like a bloody vulture, just waiting there,' the Aussie said. 'Mark me, if he breaks into Tobruk...'

A young British captain finished the thought. 'Hope you chaps can swim.'

As Maskelyne and Knox walked away from the group, Frank asked, 'You don't really believe any of that stuff about special powers, do you?'

Jasper smiled enigmatically.

Army Command in Suez had set up temporary headquarters inside an abandoned cannery. Jasper and Frank spent the next few days there trying to turn up their orders, which had evidently been lost in the confusion. The colonel to whom Lord Gort had forwarded his personal recommendation was somewhere 'on the Blue,' a localism meaning somewhere on the desert. And with standby plans hourly being superseded by emergency plans, which were subject to contingency plans, while everyone awaited official orders, no officer of sufficient rank was willing to take responsibility for them. In fact, some of the regulars found Maskelyne's mere presence in the war zone embarrassing. They knew that Rommel could never be outwitted by music-hall chicanery, and they could not understand why the Army had allowed Maskelyne to be commissioned.

One ranker thought he might remove the blemish by posting Maskelyne and his chum to Greece, but the day before their orders could be cut the Greek resistance collapsed. Had the clerks been more efficient, Jasper and Frank would have arrived there just in time to be interned. Saved, they continued wandering about Suez.

The sticky heat and filth and incessant flies and never-ending clatter magnified Jasper's frustration. Anger coiled inside him like a snake, and he felt as though he was one careless bump or foul word away from snapping. He had finally got close enough to the fighting to hear the artillery thunder resounding off the desert at night, yet he was even more useless than he had been in London. At home, at least he could have boosted morale. But in Suez he was just another junior officer without a function, another mouth to feed, another number to be evacuated should the rumoured withdrawal be ordered.

It bruised his ego. After living in the centre spot for so long, he found it difficult to accept a place in the audience. Even during the voyage across, his simple pantomime had earned him a celebrity of sorts. So, by the end of the eighth day of waiting at the cannery, he had had enough. Lacking orders, they were officially assigned nowhere; so they were free to go anywhere. He told Knox to get his kit, and they hitched a ride to Cairo.

The eighty-three-mile-long highway from the Red Sea to the Nile Basin was clogged with military traffic and refugees. Egyptian peasants walked steadily along both shoulders of the road, carrying their belongings on hand-pulled wooden carts, or on burros, or tied in bundles balanced on their heads. The jeep driver, a corporal in supply, explained that those on the right were fleeing the expected German attack on Cairo, while those on the left were Nazi sympathizers or beggars, going into the capital to claim the houses abandoned by those on the right.

Maskelyne sat in the rear seat staring beyond the straggling lines into the desert. Between Suez and Cairo it appeared to be docile, drifting casually like a summer ocean. But even on this calm spring day particles of sand dust peppered his eyes and ears and lips, and got into his mouth and his nose and under his clothes, and served to remind him of its raw power.

The desert looked benign, not capable of brutal, slow murder; yet it was, and Jasper had learned during a tour of Egypt in the early 1930s that everything one did there was determined by the mood of the desert. He had been told tales of men who strolled over small dunes to relieve themselves and were never seen again, of great caravans that disappeared without a trace, of cars that strayed a few yards off the thin ribbon roads and were swallowed. It was said that after five days of the Khamsin, the great desert storm, the Bedouins, the wandering tribes, forgave a man for killing a wife; after eight days, his camel.

Frank interrupted his reverie with a sneeze. 'Hope I'm not allergic,' he said cheerfully.

It was quite a jolt to come out of the desert into springtime Cairo. Green palms and almond and olive trees swayed sensuously along the broad boulevards. Traffic was snarled for miles, and drivers of limousines and barely chugging heaps and taxis and buses and trucks and military vehicles of every type were playing their horns like drum sets. Street vendors were hawking everything from fly whisks to hard drugs in screeching voices. Dogs were yelping at the din. Every small shop and café had a radio out front blasting Arabic music from different stations at competing volume. The pavements were jammed by city soldiers wearing proper uniform, and serving soldiers in parodies of that uniform, and Egyptians in jellabas, and European businessmen in finely tailored spring suits, and women in traditional Eastern dress or the latest Western fashion. The intense normalcy of the city belied the fact that Rommel and his Afrika Korps were on the march.

By twilight Maskelyne and Knox had settled into a crumbling rooming house off Sharia Kasr el Nil, and Jasper was standing at the window of his room watching Cairo ease into the night. A carpet of shimmering golden dust was settling over the day. In the distance, the minarets of the elegant mosques stood poised like lances ready to prick the flaming sky. Between buildings, he could see just a bit of the Nile, and the local ships, lateen-sailed feluccas, drifting on the evening breezes. Suddenly, across the road, an apartment burst into light. Then, to his right, another window flared up. Directly below, streetlights flickered on. Neon signs began flashing. Cars and trucks snapped on their headlights. The blast of lights startled him, and it took him a moment to remember that Egypt was not officially at war, so blackout regulations were not enforced. After eighteen months of darkness in England, where striking a match outdoors at night was considered a traitorous act, and three months aboard a ship that ran black after dusk, the sight of a great capital lighting up for a normal evening was utterly dazzling.

In celebration, he took his pipe from his jacket pocket and lit it, boldly allowing the match to burn until it nearly singed his fingers.

The next morning, armed with the arrogance of righteousness, he assaulted the complex of grand houses in the suburb of Garden City that served as British Headquarters for the Middle East. After showing his identification at the sentry box, he marched into Gray Pillars, the heart of the complex, determined to force the military establishment to finally pay attention. He had wasted too much time loitering in too many corridors, pleading with too many cocksure officers. He had been cold-shouldered, downtalked and diverted too long. This time he would make no gracious retreat. He would either walk out of GHQ with an assignment or be carried out with a court-martial.

Gray Pillars had once been the elegant mansion of a pasha, a wealthy Egyptian businessman, but the British Army had successfully turned it into a drab office building. A reception desk had been set up in the foyer, manned by a stern corporal bookended by armed red-capped military policemen standing easy. 'I'm Lieutenant Maskelyne,' Jasper said, handing over his identification. 'I'd like to see someone who knows something about camouflage. My orders were forwarded...'

The corporal squinched up his face as if trying to recall an elusive fact. Then he snapped his fingers and smiled at the solution. 'Maskelyne. Of course.' He leafed through the papers on his desk until he found what he was searching for. 'Here it is,' he said holding a manila folder. 'Knew I'd seen your name somewhere. Colonel Beasley in Ops has been waiting for you. I expect he'll want to see you straightaway.' Handing Jasper a yellow building pass, he pointed to the main staircase. 'One up and to your right, 207-D.'

The plump Colonel Beasley, one of a number of deputy directors of operations, greeted Maskelyne as if he were an elderly rich cousin. 'Thank goodness you're here,' he gushed, energetically pumping Jasper's hand. 'We've been desperate for a magician.'

Maskelyne had been primed to battle his way to an assignment, so this unexpectedly warm reception made him wary. But Beasley's effusive greeting made things clear. He was expected to do his show for the troops. He bristled. 'Excuse me, Colonel,' he said coldly, 'but I'm a soldier now.'

'Yes, yes, I know that. No offence intended. But you see, Maskelyne,

right at this moment a magician is precisely what we need. Look here.'
Beasley picked up a fly swat and plodded over to a large map of the
entire Middle East propped on a table. Numerous coloured stick pins
representing combat units had chewed up its centre, and a sinuous
black line, black as a mourning ribbon, had been drawn on it, stretching
east from Cairo across the canal, through Palestine and Transjordan,
into Syria, Turkey and beyond.

The black line, Beasley explained, was the planned route of evacuation should a withdrawal become necessary. 'As you can clearly see,'
he continued, tracing the route with his swat handle, 'it goes directly
through Arab territories. That, I'm afraid, is the rub.'

Over tea and cakes he outlined the situation. The Imam of the
Whirling Dervish tribe, an aged and revered leader, had threatened to
declare a jihad, a holy war, if one British soldier set foot on Dervish
territory. This was a serious problem. The Imam was a god to his
well-armed people, and if he was harmed in any way his fanatical
followers would carry out his declaration. But if he was not convinced
to withdraw this threat, the evacuation column would come under
murderous Arab fire.

Jasper listened carefully, but did not immediately understand how
his magic could solve the problem.

'The Imam claims to possess true magical powers,' the colonel
continued. 'So we thought perhaps you could go and see him and
convince him to be a good fellow. One magician to another, that sort
of thing. Offer him some trinkets if necessary, those people like the
shiny jinglies. Well, what do you think? Can you help us?'

Maskelyne hesitated. The magic of the religious leaders of the
Middle East was thousands of years old. With it, they had controlled
civilizations. His puny stage tricks could not be compared with it. The
Imam would hardly be impressed by the Endless Silks when his chants
could move a stone wall. But Jasper knew he had no choice. The
Army was finally giving him an opportunity to prove his ability, and
he could not turn it down. Taking a deep breath, he replied, 'I can't
promise anything...'

After thoroughly briefing Maskelyne on the situation, Colonel
Beasley escorted him to the head of the main stairway. All around
them frowning senior officers were racing from one office to the next.
'If nothing else works,' Beasley said sombrely, 'offer him gold. If the
Germans are paying him, we'll pay more. We simply can't risk him
causing us problems right now. Good luck.'

Jasper snapped a salute that would have made Major Buckley proud.

The next day, April 26, while Afrika Korps was readying another strike at Tobruk, and GHQ was issuing instructions for destroying sensitive documents to officers in Cairo, Maskelyne was landing in Damascus, Syria, clutching his bag of stage props. He was wearing a civilian bush jacket and his last pair of fine trousers from Hall's, and he thought it particularly ironic that his first assignment in uniform required him to be out of uniform.

As he pushed through the crowds on the clamorous biblical street called Straight, waiting to be contacted by a British undercover agent, a young Syrian boy begged him for some coins. He ignored the boy and moved on, as he had been warned was necessary and proper, and continued to search for his contact.

The boy followed him through the marketplace at a cautious distance. Once they had broken free of the crowds, he approached him again, but this time he said in clear English, 'Good day, Lieutenant Maskelyne.'

Jasper halted in his tracks and stared at the boy. He could not possibly have been more than eight years old. 'How do you know my name?' he demanded.

The boy looked up at him with much older eyes. 'We have our intelligence, too,' he said, then added, 'I have been made to bring you. Please come.' Without waiting for a response, he spun around and walked away.

Maskelyne hesitated, then followed him through a maze of narrow alleys until, at the end of one of them, they came upon a storybook carriage drawn by two white stallions. The boy opened its door and told him to get in. 'The Prince is expecting you,' he said.

Jasper dutifully climbed in, and the door closed behind him. The Prince. What prince? He had no idea what the boy was talking about, and it was too late to ask. The coach horses started up and made a good pace through the city. He peeped through the drawn curtains, trying to track the route, but the carriage made numerous turns and that proved impossible. They drove through the marketplace, past 'Out of Bounds' warnings, up wide streets, then down alleyways so narrow the Arabs had to push into doorways to give passage.

His fears grew with each street. He had no idea where he was being taken or even in whose coach he was riding. It was one thing to face the predictable dangers of battle, it was quite another to be alone among the fanatical Dervish people. Stories of their bizarre rituals had long chilled hearts in civilized European circles. More than one innocent person had disappeared while in their charge. At that moment he sincerely wished he had packed a real pistol rather than the pathetic stage prop in his sack.

The carriage halted directly beside a set of massive arched doors set in an otherwise solid, high stucco wall. The door was opened from outside, and a bearded Arab urged, 'Move quickly.' Jasper scrambled out of the cab and into another world.

The doors were bolted behind him, shutting out the hubbub of the streets, and he found himself standing in the tranquil courtyard of a great villa. A spreading pomegranate tree shaded one corner, and beneath it sat an Arab playing dulcet melodies on a wooden flute. In another corner a group of veiled women were spinning yarn. In the centre of the yard a fountain splashed lightly into a cloverleaf-shaped lily pond, and above this fountain was the most remarkable sculpture he had ever seen.

Inside what appeared to be a large wooden wheel, four women sat motionless and silent at the quarter-hour positions while the fountain slowly drove the wheel. Jasper guessed this strange human sculpture had some religious significance, and knew for sure he was among the Dervish.

As he followed the bearded servant through the tiled courtyard he had the uneasy sensation he was being observed from above, but scanning the windows of the interior walls he saw no one. They entered a large room, lit mostly by shafts of bright sunlight pouring through cathedral windows. At the far end of this room an elegant throne was raised on a dais, and on it sat a handsome white-haired old man in flowing white robes. The guide bowed and backed out of the room.

Maskelyne walked the length of the room on quaking legs. About six feet from the throne he stopped and, having no idea what was proper, saluted smartly and announced, 'Lieutenant Maskelyne, His Majesty's Royal Engineers.'

The old man beckoned him forward. 'Leftenant Maskelyne,' he said in a raspy voice, 'I am Prince Hassan. It is a pleasure to meet you. Du you know my name?'

Jasper thought he heard a distant echo in his mind, but couldn't quite make it out. He shook his head. 'I'm sorry.'

'It doesn't matter. You see, I knew your father well.' Jasper stood there dumbfounded while the Prince repeated a story he had first heard so many years ago by a London fireside. 'I was with Lawrence in the Turkish campaigns.'

During the Great War Colonel T. E. Lawrence, the famed Lawrence of Arabia, had asked the British government to supply magicians who would live among the wandering tribes masquerading as holy men. Nevil Maskelyne had trained three Arabs, a Frenchman and an Englishman in the conjuring arts. Equipped with a few simple sleights and some technological marvels unknown in that part of the world, these men convinced the tribesmen that they were ascetic marabouts, the strange holy men often attributed with supernatural powers. Then they foretold the future – using advance information conveniently provided by Lawrence. After gaining the confidence of the desert people with their accurate predictions, they prophesied that anyone serving the Turks would suffer the wrath of Allah. Gradually, the Turks lost all their native support.

Two of the magicians disappeared in the desert and were never seen again. Their fate remained a mystery.

When Prince Hassan finished his story, Jasper stammered a few silly sentences. They repaired to a smoking den and lounged on pillows while a servant prepared a nargileh, a hashish pipe. The Prince apologized for having had Jasper 'dumped off at the rear entrance,' but explained that the Imam was in residence at the villa and three of his blackguards were at the front gate. 'The relationship between my family and the leaders of the Dervish can be traced through many centuries,' he continued. 'There is trust between us, and respect. The Imam has agreed to meet you because I requested it and such things are not easily refused, but he does not want it known that he is meeting a white man, particularly an Englishman.'

Jasper politely refused the hashish, instead lighting his own briar pipe. 'But why is he against us?'

Hassan shrugged. 'Perhaps some slight of many years ago that he has never forgotten. His motive is not important. As you English say, the gun is often fired without reason.'

'Is it possible the Germans are paying him?'

'Yes, but not with gold. He has all the wealth he will ever need. If they are whispering in his ear, it is promises of authority when the war is finished.'

Maskelyne shook his head in bewilderment. 'How do I deal with a man like that?'

Prince Hassan dragged deeply on his pipe and savoured the smoke before replying. 'The Imam is not an educated man. He will not listen to arguments of logic, nor will he be agreeable to flattery. There is but one thing. The Imam truly believes his magic is greater than any white man's. And since I learned a Maskelyne would be coming here, I have

been boasting of your abilities.' He smiled sheepishly. 'I am afraid I
have infuriated him on your behalf. Somehow, you must convince him
your powers are the equal of his. Otherwise, I fear ...' He shook his
head, and his voice trailed off.

The marriage of Eastern and Western scents filled the room as
Jasper tried to figure out some means of matching Dervish magic with
his own bag of tricks. It would take a grand performance to make the
Imam back down, and he was barely prepared for a children's show.
He reluctantly began taking his props out of the small bag and slipping
them into various pockets.

A short time later a servant entered and announced that the Imam
had awakened and was prepared to see the visitor.

Jasper looked to the Prince for direction. Hassan had a beneficent
smile on his face. 'Be bold, Maskelyne. Don't let him bluff you. You
too know the real secrets of magic.'

'Right,' Jasper replied, a good deal more confidently than he felt.
Then he stood up and went off to do magic battle.

As he followed the servant through the long corridors, he checked
to make sure he knew where his props were hidden. He might not
have anything up his sleeve, but at least he'd be able to pull something
out of his pocket.

The walk gave him time to fortify his confidence. The Imam's tricks
would undoubtedly be clever, but they would still be tricks. It was
vital that he remember that. Even the belief of the entire Dervish
nation in the Imam's powers did not make them real. The Maskelyne
family had spent a considerable fortune seeking proof of true magic
without uncovering the slightest evidence that such a thing existed.

His heart was pounding. He was about to match illusions with one
of the few men in the world ruling by dint of his magical powers.
And in this contest the Maskelyne family name could not help him.
This time he would be on his own.

The Imam was waiting alone in a small corner room. Its whitewashed
walls were bare, and it was lit by a small hanging lamp. The Dervish
leader was a much smaller man than Jasper had expected, and much
older. His leathery face was cracked and wrinkled like a baked desert
plain and bordered by a brush of scraggly grey beard. Instead of the
traditional robes of a religious leader, he was wearing a blousy green
sateen shirt and white pantaloons, a velvet skullcap, and sandals,
looking altogether like an Eastern mystic created by Noël Coward. He
was in a nasty mood when Maskelyne arrived, and greeted him with a
barrage of harsh words.

The servant immediately bowed, and Jasper followed his lead, catching up with him at the bottom of his dip. 'Tell him I apologize for making him wait,' he commanded. 'Tell him it was not intended as a sign of disrespect.'

As the servant did so, Maskelyne glanced around the room, and his practised eye noted it had been carefully prepared for this encounter. Too many common objects had been set too casually out of position. A dirt-filled clay planter without a plant in it was placed out of range of the sunlight that shafted through the single window in the room. A cabinet with no discernible purpose was pushed into a corner. A sharpened lance leaned against a wall. An Oriental area rug, perhaps covering a trapdoor, was laid badly off centre. Jasper thought he could just barely make out the shadow of a transparent string running along the moulding at the base of the wall. He had no doubt about it; the room had been salted.

The servant translated Maskelyne's apology, which momentarily soothed the Imam. Then the aged leader replied, through the interpreter, 'I have heard of the many wonders you have produced, and I am honoured with your presence.' Belying his words, however, he spat them out in distinctly hostile tones.

Jasper nodded. 'And the greatness of your powers is known to people all over the world,' he lied.

The Imam grinned, exposing gaping holes between his teeth, then spoke again. When he had finished the servant translated. 'The Imam says he is sorry a man with great powers such as yours has travelled such a long way to see him, but there is nothing he can do to change the ... the ... situation. No heathen soldier can be permitted to trespass on Dervish land. It is not his will. It is the will of Allah.' The servant bowed again. Jasper bowed. The Imam bowed.

'Surely there must be some compromise,' Jasper responded when they had finished. 'Ask him if there is not some way my people can show their appreciation for his generosity and understanding.'

The wizened old man listened patiently, then suddenly launched into a bitter anti-British tirade, speaking so rapidly that all the servant could do was summarize. 'He does not like the British at all,' he explained.

'So I gather. Ask him why.'

Ignoring the question, the Imam continued spewing threats as the courtyard fountain splashed water. 'The Imam says your problems with the Germans and the Italians do not concern him. He says that if one English soldier marches on sacred Arab soil he will declare a jihad.'

Jasper began explaining that the proposed withdrawal, which probably would never be necessary, posed no danger to the Arab people, whom the British respected as brothers. 'However,' he repeated, 'my government is prepared to show its respect—'

The Imam suddenly ended the discussion by moving spryly to the clay planter. Positioning himself directly in front of it, he began waving his arms and chanting. Maskelyne watched with fascination. After a bit, the old man stepped aside. A shrivelled but blossoming miniature orange tree had sprouted in the pot.

Jasper had seen the trick done before. And better. This was more an example of how to hide a tiny tree up the sleeve of a blouse than a demonstration of divinely inspired magic. In response, he casually took his pipe from his pocket, snapped his fingers into flame, and lit it. If that was the best the fakir could do, he thought, he could certainly match him.

The Imam's green eyes seethed with anger. Holding open his hands to show they were empty, he placed them over his eyes. Then, very deliberately, he pulled them away. An egg had materialized in each hand.

He stared at the eggs as if to crack them open with the intensity of his glare, then abruptly smacked them together. A dove sat in his cupped hands. He tossed it into the air and it fluttered onto a ceiling beam.

Jasper was feeling quite confident. The Imam would barely make the bill at St. George's Hall with these basic sleights. Then, in response to the dove production, he pulled a multicoloured handkerchief out of his trouser pocket. He swirled it about freely, then poked it into his clenched fist. An instant later he opened his hand, and a butterfly of the kerchief colours flew out the door, disappearing down the hallway.

The Imam responded by elevating a small vase from the top of the cabinet.

Maskelyne produced a flow of trinkets from his mouth.

The Imam faced the cabinet and held out a beckoning hand. Slowly, he drew his hand to his body, and, as he did, the door creaked open as if being pulled by a string. But no string was visible. He paused; the door stopped moving. He clapped his hands; the door slammed shut. Jasper assumed that the string was attached to the Imam's sandal, or toe, and was hidden beneath the Oriental rug.

Jasper was enjoying this duel. The small whitewashed room made a strange battlefield, but his body was alive with the mixture of exhilaration and fear he'd been told a soldier feels in combat. Although the idea of battling with sleights that both men knew were simply stage tricks, and pretending it was real magic, might seem as ridiculous as armies warring with water guns to sophisticated westerners, illusions identical to those being performed in this room had enabled the Imam and his ancestors to rule a great, superstitious people for uncounted decades.

How would he counter the cabinet trick? The old man would not be impressed by more handkerchiefs, no matter how deftly performed. Cards were inadequate. The ropes too obvious. He remembered the prop pistol tucked into his waistband. The Magic Bullet?

The Imam was growing impatient.

Jasper palmed a bullet as he reached into his pocket for the razor blades. The blades might give him a chance to set up the Bullet. After nicking his wrist until a tiny blood bubble proved the sharpness of the razor, he opened his mouth and swallowed six of them. After downing the last one, he rubbed his stomach in delight.

Then he reached into his mouth and began pulling out the blades, knotted to a length of cotton.

The Imam grabbed one of the blades from his hand. He bit down hard on its metal edge, then angrily threw it onto the floor.

Jasper smiled arrogantly. 'Glad you liked that one.'

The servant dared not translate that remark.

The Imam turned toward the Oriental rug and extended his arms. He began raising his hands, and the carpet, rigid as a board, lifted off the floor. Jasper looked for the ceiling wires but couldn't see them. He started moving backward in apparent captivation.

The Imam lifted the rug to waist level.

Jasper was impressed. Although this levitation and perhaps the cabinet were undoubtedly the work of a hidden assistant, it was an extremely effective illusion. He continued backing up until he felt the plaster wall against his back.

The Imam held the carpet at chest level with his fixed gaze.

Jasper began carving a tiny hole in the wall with one of the razor blades, catching the specks of plaster in his palm. When the hole was deep enough, he pressed the bullet into it. If the bullet didn't fall out, he knew he would be able to top the flying carpet.

The Imam lowered the Oriental rug onto the floor.

Maskelyne nodded appreciatively. Then he reached under his shirt and pulled out the prop pistol.

The Imam misunderstood, and begun backing away fearfully.

'No, no, it's all right,' Jasper said, but the old man didn't seem to understand. His eyes began to bulge as he stared at the gun. Just as the Imam opened his mouth to shout for his guards, Maskelyne wisely turned the barrel of the gun on himself.

The Dervish leader relaxed, but maintained his distance and watched cautiously.

Maskelyne took six blank cartridges from his bush-jacket pocket and loaded the gun. Then he raised his open left hand, held the gun in his right hand about eight inches from the centre of his palm, took a deep breath, closed his eyes, grimaced, and fired.

The translator fell onto his knees and began praying.

Jasper held out his left hand for inspection. Apart from a nasty red welt in the centre of his palm, there seemed to be no damage. The bullet appeared to have passed right through it. The Imam moved toward the wall, but Maskelyne beat him to the spot and made an exaggerated show of prying the planted bullet out of the plaster. Holding it out to the Imam for inspection, he said, 'A souvenir of my performance, perhaps?'

The Imam slapped his hand, sending the bullet skittering across the floor. His face contorted in rage and he began muttering in a guttural tone.

Jasper realized he'd gone too far.

The Imam pointed at him and screamed shrilly.

The petrified servant translated in a trembling voice. 'The Imam … the great Imam says you are an impostor. You must go now, taking … taking with you his anger. But before you go, the Imam will show you real magic … so you will never forget him.'

Maskelyne gritted his teeth. He'd bungled the assignment. His blasted ego had messed up the mission.

The Imam picked up the long steel lance and held it above his head. Then he closed his eyes and began an almost hypnotic, monotonic chant.

When he finished, he opened his eyes and glared at Maskelyne. Without taking his eyes off the frustrated magician, he lowered the lance and turned it, placing its sharpened spike against his stomach. Then his gaze softened, as if in pity for the white man's innocence.

In that instant, his intention became horrifyingly clear.

Suddenly, he roared savagely and ran at the wall.

'No!' Jasper screamed, and dived to stop him.

The spear butt rammed into the wall, driving the spike deep into the old man's fragile body. He groaned and was skewered on the lance as it ripped through his stomach. The point of the spike tore through the back of his sateen shirt.

Jasper was paralysed, his hands frozen in midair.

The servant fell to his knees, crying.

Maskelyne was shaken. Now he believed the legends. Years earlier he had heard a fiendish tale: that male children born to high priests were ceremoniously pierced through their bodies, but carefully so that the organs were not disturbed, the way European women had their ear lobes pierced. Those children who survived had a scarred channel through which they could twist sharp objects. He had dismissed the barbaric tale then, but in front of him stood living proof that it was true.

It was not magic in the traditional sense, but it was a far greater feat than anything he had ever seen. None of his stage tricks could compare with it.

The servant translated through worshipful sobs. 'Here is magic no white man can perform, the Imam says. He says that even as this spear has pierced his body, so will your armies be struck through if they dare – if they touch Arab land.' He paused for a quick prayer for deliverance. 'The Imam wants you to withdraw the lance.'

Jasper tried to hide his discouragement. He'd been beaten. If the retreat was ordered, British blood would flow into the sands. All he could do was hope to get away safely and pray the defenders of Tobruk held Rommel in place. He grabbed hold of the shaft and pulled hard. The spear moved sluggishly. He twisted it and yanked it and it moved another few inches.

The Imam was sweating and grunting, but seemed to be in no pain.

An inch at a time, as if it were being dragged out of a blubbery vice, the spear wrenched free. Finally, the last foot of it glided smoothly out of the old man's body.

Jasper hefted it uncomfortably and examined it. Odd, he thought, not a speck of blood on it. He glanced at the Imam's torn shirt. No bloodstains there either. Suddenly, his memory began to itch. There was something ... something he'd once heard about. Another story told by his grandfather. The details were sketchy, but he remembered bits of it. A turn-of-the-century music-hall performer claiming to be a desert marabout had achieved some success with a similar illusion in the outer cities, but had been exposed us a fraud in London. Something about a leather belt.

The Imam held his hand over his wound and triumphantly lectured Maskeleyne.

Jasper obediently held out the spear to the Dervish leader and, as the old man accepted it, he casually brushed the Imam's side.

The old man jumped back as if he had been touched by the hand of the devil.

It was too late. Jasper had felt something much too firm to be flesh. It was the music-hall trick. It had been performed to perfection, and, given the setup, it was entirely believable, but it was nothing more than an old variety turn. After all his years on the stage, after countless performances, he'd fallen for it. He bit down hard on his lip to keep himself from laughing out loud at his foolishness.

The Imam rattled on.

Maskelyne ignored the chatter, trying to decide what to do next. He couldn't do better than the spear bit, not with the props on hand, but he knew that there was much more to a good act than the illusion. There was the bluff.

Turning to the servant, he ordered, 'Tell the Imam I am not impressed by his silly tricks.'

The servant's mouth fell open. 'I cannot,' he pleaded. 'Please ...'

'Tell him. Tell him or I will tell the Prince you have disobeyed me.'

The terrified man stared at the floor as he translated Maskelyne's insult. When he finished he cringed, as if expecting to be struck down by the wrath of the great wizard.

The Imam's eyes boiled with hatred and he hurled curses at Maskelyne.

Maskelyne folded his arms defiantly and stood his ground. Then he loudly commanded, 'Tell him I know he is wearing a leather channel around his waist. Tell him I know the lance will bend around this belt.'

The servant was only a few words into this explanation when the Imam stopped him. Like winter mellowing into spring, then summer, his glare softened into a stare, then a gaze. He replied in a voice soft and respectful.

The astonished interpreter stuttered through the Imam's surrender. 'He says ... he says you are a man of great magic.' Jasper nodded appreciatively. 'He says you have passed his test. That ... that you too belong to a higher circle...'

Jasper knew he had him. The old scallywag couldn't risk being exposed as a fraud to his people. If they discovered that his powers were based upon chicanery...

'... between great men there must be a bond of friendship...'

Jasper laid down his terms. 'I know the Imam will welcome my countrymen, who respect him as I do, to his lands, and provide food and water to them if necessary.'

The Imam knew he had no choice. The two magicians clasped hands and pledged eternal friendship, though neither dared take his eyes off the other.

Jasper turned and walked triumphantly out of the room. He was elated, his mission accomplished. Halfway down the corridor he bent down and retrieved his mechanical butterfly.

That night the delighted Prince Hassan made Jasper tell the story in its entirety three times. Hassan ignored the hard-working dancing girls and laughed harder at each retelling. 'I am afraid my poor interpreter will never recover,' he said, and the image of that sombre man on his knees in fright made him laugh until tears flowed.

Jasper slept safely under the watch of Prince Hassan's guard that night.

He departed the following morning through the rear gate. As he walked through the courtyard with Hassan, he asked about the religious significance of the wooden ring over the fountain.

The Prince looked at him quizzically. Then he understood. 'Oh, I see, the mysterious Dervish practices. Well, my friend, I don't believe in that mumbo-jumbo any more than you do. The ring is an experiment of mine. I'm convinced that if I can figure out the proper balance of weights in relationship to the energy generated by the fountain waters, I can produce a perpetual-motion machine. Thus far, unfortunately . . .'

Jasper was driven back to the reality of war in the story-book carriage.

THREE

Maskelyne's debut as a war magician came just in time. At 6:30 P.M. Egyptian Standard Time, April 30, just as the defenders of Tobruk were climbing out of the concealed dugouts in which they had sweltered through the day, Afrika Korps suddenly launched its most ferocious attack. Behind waves of screeching Stuka dive-bombers and a massive artillery barrage, panzer tanks smashed a hole three miles wide and two miles deep through the southwest perimeter. Only the heroic resistance of the troops commanded by Australian Major General Leslie 'Ming the Merciless' Morshead prevented Rommel from capturing the city that night.

In Cairo, Gray Pillars prepared for the evacuation of Egypt. Hundreds of transport vehicles moved to staging areas. Rations were distributed. Water cans were filled and sealed. All dependants and female personnel were ordered to pack their belongings and prepare to leave. On May 2, British agents in Syria reported that the Imam of the Dervish had withdrawn his threat and offered cooperation. With the escape corridor finally cleared, there was nothing more to do but await the outcome of the fighting at Tobruk. The retreat would begin with its surrender.

In anticipation of the forthcoming battle for the Nile Basin, prices crashed on the local stock exchange and skyrocketed in food markets. Europeans sold their automobiles for whatever cash they were offered. Shopkeepers scribbled signs in German, but kept them temporarily hidden beneath their counters. And at secret meetings of the anti-British Free Officers movement inside the Egyptian Army, young officers Gamal Nasser and Anwar el-Sadat prepared to welcome the Germans.

The battle for the vital deep-water port of Tobruk raged through five days and nights. By May 4, both armies had been badly worn down; Afrika Korps had suffered one thousand casualties and was unable to break out of its salient, while Morshead's counterattacking troops were too weak to dislodge them. Finally, Rommel was ordered by his superiors to dig in, and the British launched the 'Tobruk Ferry,' a nightly supply run from Alexandria harbour employing swift Royal Navy and Australian destroyers. The siege of Tobruk had begun.

For the first time, Rommel had been stopped. His growing legend had been tarnished. The immediate threat to the Nile Delta was alleviated. Europeans were forced to buy back their cars at inflated prices, the stock market began rising, shopkeepers put away their German signs for safekeeping, and officers of Western Desert Force felt secure making plans to attend the horseraces or cricket matches on fashionable Gezira Island. Once again, it was war as usual.

Sniffing Rommel's blood scent, Prime Minister Churchill urged General Wavell to attack him before Afrika Korps could be reinforced. Wavell hesitated, knowing that his own denuded army would not be capable of mounting an offensive until a naval convoy carrying two hundred tanks that was en route from England arrived and these Matilda tanks were fitted for desert warfare. But to mollify Churchill he agreed to Operation Brevity, a limited drive designed to secure a desert staging area from which a major attack could be launched in the future.

There was certainly no place for a magician in this offensive. Colonel Beasley had been extremely pleased with the success of Jasper Maskelyne's mission to Damascus, although privately unhappy at the conjuror's refusal to reveal how various illusions had been done. Although Beasley had become enchanted by the potential of war magic, he realized that most regular military types would find the concept absurd. So, rather than fighting a futile battle against tradition, he obtained Maskelyne permission to form his own unit by suggesting it would be a sure means of removing the commissioned magician from normal army channels. In return, Jasper agreed to produce a number of variety shows, in which he would star, for British troops in Egypt.

Officially, the unit was designated a 'Camouflage Experimental Section' and placed under the command of Major Geoffrey Barkas, head of camouflage in the Middle East. Unofficially, Maskelyne would be free to try to create some of the incredible illusions he had so often proposed.

During the first week of May, Jasper and Frank Knox set up in a field tent in the Cairo suburb of Abbassia. It was distant enough from Gray Pillars as to be almost nonexistent. Knox uncovered the roots of the gossip grapevine that twined throughout the Basin and put onto it the word that the magician Jasper Maskelyne was forming a unit unlike anything in existence in the Army. To make it enticing, the professor hinted there would be no desert fighting, no scheduled formations, no inspections, proper mess facilities, and no Regular Army officers muddling about. Personally, he intended to make much of this true.

Maskelyne was hoping to attract men who had not allowed army standardization to squeeze initiative and creativity out of their minds. Respect for discipline, therefore, was not among the prerequisites. The people he wanted would not have to know how to march or salute, as long as they had ideas and were willing to work.

On the appointed day seventy-two of the Army's motliest soldiers showed up to volunteer. Some came out of curiosity, but many more came out of necessity: they simply did not fit in where they were currently assigned. Among these men were a motion picture daredevil, a perfumer, an optician, a test cricketer, a comic-book illustrator, two politicians, and a sergeant who claimed to have the ability to read minds. Knox politely dismissed the sergeant, saying, 'Then I won't have to explain why we can't use you.' One corporal thought he was on line for the latrine.

After all the applicants had been interviewed, five of them were invited to transfer into the Experimental Section. Jasper had decided to keep the original group small enough to be easily manageable, knowing he could quickly expand when it became necessary.

Maskelyne's first recruit was Private Michael Hill, a streetwise infantryman who had described his civilian occupation as 'doing anything that needed being done what somebody was willing to pay for.' Hill was twenty years old and handsome in a roughneck way. He was about five feet seven inches tall and compact, as if a load of steel nails had been stuffed into a sack and sculpted into manly proportions. His features were sharp, but managed to complement each other, and his greenish blue eyes were nicely set off by sandy-coloured hair much longer than regulation length.

'What does that mean, exactly?' Frank Knox had asked him.

Hill drew a thoughtful breath. He enjoyed sparring with officers. 'Well, sir,' he boasted, 'what that means, exactly, is that on certain occasions I borrowed things. Permanent like. A pair of shoes, a bicycle. I was a man of opportunity. Anyways, that's what got me into this mess here. They gimme a choice of this or the workhouse.'

The young soldier spoke with a dash and swagger that delighted Maskelyne. Life would never settle comfortably on his shoulders, Jasper knew, but he would make the good fight for it, and the bout would be a long and grand one and there would never be a verdict. Although the brash trooper made Knox uncomfortable from the start, the section would need someone tenacious enough to get the job done without regard for proper forms and procedure, and Hill certainly appeared to be a lad who would not be stopped by rules or regulations.

Hill explained that he had arrived in Egypt in early April but was still in a holding company. The unit to which he had been scheduled to report had been smashed up during Rommel's drive and had not yet reorganized. 'Funny thing about that,' he said. 'I'm here, but the company I'm s'posed to be with ain't. First time I ever heard of an army desertin' a soldier.'

Knox had sighed deeply when Maskelyne put the cocksure Private Hill on the list. Some men have a way of squeezing trouble out of the most beautiful day, and he had the depressing feeling this soldier was one of them.

Twenty-eight-year-old carpenter Theodore Albert 'Nails' Graham was serving as a wrench hand at a tank repair depot when he heard the 'syb,' or rumour, about Maskelyne's unit. He hurried right over to Abbassia. Graham hated working on the 'Iron Coffins,' protesting, 'I'm a maker, not a fixer.' Like Jasper, Graham was the third generation to work at the family trade and was extremely proud of his craft. 'Working with wood is just as much an art as painting or stained glass,' he explained. 'I work with my hands and mind, same as they do. Only difference is that the things I make you can use.'

Nails was a burly man, about five feet ten inches tall, with flat, plain features and a short, no-nonsense haircut. Although his shoulders looked broad enough to carry much of Wavell's army, it was his hands that most impressed Maskelyne. They were huge, and calloused, but oddly enough tapered into long slender fingers. Unexpectedly delicate fingers. His were the hands of a workingman and the fingers of a craftsman. Knox thought he looked, appropriately enough, like a reliable tool.

Jasper knew Nails would be a vital addition to the section. It was one thing to make grandiose plans and conjure up incredible weapons; it was quite another to turn drawings into finished products. Graham would be in charge of production.

The plans from which Graham's people would work would be done by bespectacled William Robson, a pacifist artist whose cartoons had often appeared in *Punch* before the war. Maskelyne knew the twenty-nine-year-old artist's work and was attracted by his ability to quickly turn rough sketches into clear renderings.

Bill Robson was tall, over six feet, and so very thin that when he walked the various parts of his body seemed to be operating independently, and only vaguely moving in the same direction. Added to that was the fact that his eyesight was very poor, and although he wore corrective lenses thick as porthole glass, he still walked with his head craned forward as if he were trying to spot objects in front of him before crashing into them. Still he always seemed in danger of stumbling over whatever was in his path.

During the interview Knox had asked him how, as a pacifist, he had managed to find himself in the middle of the most savage land battle of the war. Robson replied in a voice so soft that Jasper had to ask him to speak up. 'I didn't want to be here,' he explained, 'and I don't want to hurt anybody. But I want to be a German subject even less.' That was the only time his beliefs were questioned.

The only fine artist in the original group was Lance Corporal Philip Townsend, a painter who worked mostly in oils in civilian life. 'I know all there is to know about colour,' he said confidently. 'I know pigment, I know mixing and I know hard work.' He wanted to transfer into the unit he told them, 'because my major's a topflight ass. All he knows is scrub floors and kill Germans. You want to kill a Nazi with a mop, he's the bloke to see. Can't take much more of him. So you take me in here and leave me alone to do my work and we'll get along just fine and I'll do a bang-up job for you.'

Townsend had the essence of the brooding artist about him. His dark, handsome Mediterranean features so totally lacked any hint of warmth that they just as easily might have been sculpted out of Roman marble. Maskelyne wondered aloud how well he worked with other men. 'Quietly,' he replied. 'I just want to be left alone to do my work. I'm not here by choice and I'm not here to make pals.' Although Jasper was reluctant to enlist the sullen artist, Townsend was the only applicant with a thorough knowledge of paints and perspective and would therefore be extremely useful. When his sketchbook confirmed his talent it was decided to take a chance with him. 'He'll ease up after a while,' Jasper predicted hopefully.

Knox doubted it. 'That's the only chap I've ever met who has to make an appointment with his face to smile.'

Sergeant Jack Fuller was one of the few regular soldiers to apply for a place. Fuller had enlisted on his twenty-first birthday and served nineteen years, the last seven in the Middle East. After spending most of his career regretting that he had missed out on the Great War, he found himself trapped in a supply room for this one. His dedication to rules and procedure, as well as his military driver's licence, made him invaluable to his commanding officer, who refused to forward his request for a transfer to a combat unit. When Fuller heard that Maskelyne had connections at GHQ, he dressed in a uniform so thickly starched that he walked with an audible *shush*, and reported for an interview.

Although Fuller would be as out of place in the motley section as a whale on the desert, Jasper realized that his knowledge of Cairo, the local dialects and military procedure would be extremely helpful and agreed to initiate a transfer request. 'We'd like to have you join us if we can work it out,' he said, extending his hand in congratulations.

Fuller stood at rigid attention, snapped his shoulders back until his shoulder blades nearly touched, and saluted smartly. 'Suh!' he shouted.

Somewhat sheepishly, Jasper returned his salute. After Sergeant Fuller completed a perfect about-turn and marched out of the tent, Knox asked unhappily, 'How could you let the Army into our unit?'

As soon as Colonel Beasley's office had processed their paperwork, the five recruits moved into the Abbassia encampment and prepared to begin work. The first thing they discovered was that there was nothing for them to do. Every request for supplies or assistance had to be made through normal channels at GHQ – and there was no slot in that channel for a unit that created magic tricks. In another place at another time some junior officer might have been willing to entrust a minor job to Maskelyne, but with the German juggernaut only one battle away from the Basin, the thought of a magician accomplishing anything worthwhile seemed even more improbable than it had in sedate Farnham.

Once again Maskelyne attacked Gray Pillars. As before, his fame worked against him. No one would take him seriously. Those few officers who agreed to see him usually asked him to perform a simple sleight for their amusement.

It was a difficult time for the new members of the Camouflage Section. While units all around them were eagerly preparing for Operation Brevity, they passed the boiling days sitting in front of the field tent talking and tanning, and keeping careful record of the number of flies killed. 'No probables,' Hill had declared at the outset of the contest. 'We only count bodies.'

Frank Knox made a sound of disgust.

'It's us or them, Frank,' the private said seriously.

Jasper did his best to mollify his men. 'I know you're all anxious to get to work,' he said. 'Believe me, so am I. But we're brand new and it'll take some time to spread the word that we're here. We just have to be patient for a bit.'

'Remember,' Knox added in support, 'Rome wasn't built in a day.'

'Leastwise,' quipped Robson, 'not if Marshal Graziani had anything to do with it.'

The men spent the time getting to know one another, learning about their backgrounds, testing each other's sense of humour, comparing experiences, and a rough sort of camaraderie was established. They weren't doing anything at all, but they weren't doing it together. The wiry Hill emerged as the prankster of the unit, while Nails Graham became its serious foreman. Contrary to Bill Robson's fragile appearance, he proved to be a willing participant in whatever mischief Hill proposed, and at times he was actually the instigator. Fuller, serving as unit quartermaster, found himself fighting a losing battle trying to maintain a semblance of Regular Army discipline within the group. Only the painter Townsend kept to himself, making it quite clear that he didn't care what the others thought of him.

Although their conversations covered the range of men's subjects, most eventually came round to the war and women. None of them were really enthusiastic about Churchill as military commander, but agreed it was their patriotic duty to support him. On the subject of women, however, there was no such easy accord. 'A man needs a loyal woman standing right behind him,' Fuller declared firmly one afternoon. 'It's natural.'

'Right,' Hill cracked, 'bringing him his supper on a tray. I'll tell you, given the choice between a woman and a motorcar, I'll take the motorcar every time.'

'You don't really mean that?' Graham challenged.

'I do,' Hill replied, 'I do. Way I see it, a good motorcar takes you where you want to go, while a woman tells you where you want to go.'

After the pleasant laughter had faded, Robson complained, 'Talking to Hill is like talking to a blank wall, only sometimes you get the feeling the wall could at least talk back.'

'Don't get me wrong, I love women,' Hill corrected, then added in a lecherous voice, 'as many of 'em as I can, every chance I get.'

Townsend however chose to remain aloof. If it was possible to be part of a seven-man group yet still be alone, he was. Occasionally, he would volunteer a slip of information about himself. He was married to a dark-haired girl and they had a baby boy. Once he passed around a cracked photograph of this wife and child. It was his most pleasant moment. The woman was attractive. She was holding the boy in her arms and standing in front of white-fenced cottage. Neither of them was smiling. The woman looked as though posing for this photograph was a burdensome chore. Knox looked at the photograph when it was passed around and properly admired it, but he knew this was not the memory a man should carry with him at war.

On May 10, while Maskelyne was at Gray Pillars pleading for an assignment for the Camouflage Section, and his men were bantering the day away, one of the most bizarre events of the war took place. Rudolf Hess, deputy leader of the Nazi Party and second in the line of succession to Hitler, took off from Augsburg airport in Germany and flew a specially equipped Messerschmitt 110 across the North Sea to Petersfield, near Glasgow, Scotland, purportedly to try to arrange a peace treaty between England and Germany. Captured after parachuting safely from his failing plane, he claimed that his name was Alfred Horn, but soon admitted his true identity.

At first Churchill refused to believe that the pilot was actually the Nazi Party's deputy leader, telling aides as he walked to a motion picture screening room, 'Even if it is Hess, I'm going to watch the Marx Brothers.' Even after the Reichsführer's identity had been confirmed, the Prime Minister did not seriously consider his peace proposal. Hess was interned as a prisoner of war.

Hitler's response to the strange episode was to order the Gestapo to arrest most of Germany's astrologers and occultists and prohibit all forms of fortunetelling.

In the days following the announcement of Hess's capture everyone in Egypt tried to guess the motive for his actions. Hitler's response clearly indicated that the flight had some basis in astrology, which caused people to wonder about the relationship between the Nazis and the occult. Maskelyne was suddenly barraged with questions, as officers easily made the giant leap from stage magic to the supernatural and assumed he was an expert on both subjects. Jasper was in fact well versed in the occult and the supernatural, as both his grandfather and father had spent fortunes debunking myths, but he knew very little of the importance of mysticism to the Nazis. In reality, no one did.

Ever since Hitler's meteoric rise to power behind the symbolic swastika there had been speculation about the importance of magic and the occult in his National Socialist movement. There could be no question that the Nazi Party had its roots in the quasi-occult, secret Thule Society, an anti-Semitic, anti-Communist movement, or that many members of the party hierarchy believed in the mystic arts. It is also absolutely certain that Hitler had considerable knowledge of black and white magic and occultism, but whether he actually believed in these powers or simply used them to manipulate others has never been satisfactorily established.

Hitler believed in the use of overwhelming force to achieve his aims, and the magician Jasper Maskelyne had no counterpart in the Nazi ranks. But after the German Army stormed into Austria in 1938, the Führer spent several hours alone in a room with the Spear of Destiny, the lance supposedly used by the German soldier Longinus to pierce Christ's side and end his suffering on the cross. He was obviously aware of the legend that the man who controlled the spear would rule the destiny of the world, and he had it secretly removed from the Hofburg Palace and placed in a vault beneath the streets of Nuremberg.

Before the war, British Intelligence had reported that the Führer employed five astrologers and never made an important decision without consulting this group. In an attempt to infiltrate this circle, the War Office commissioned Ludwig von Wohl, a well-known German astrologer who had emigrated to London in 1935. Captain von Wohl was asked to predict what advice these advisers would give Hitler. In the darkest days of 1940 he accurately forecast that the Germans would not invade England, pointing out that other astrologers would see the stars positioned against such an undertaking. Later in the war he edited a bogus astrological magazine that contained subtle propaganda, but German Intelligence easily uncovered this fraud.

Although little is known about Hitler's astrologers, the existence of this group is not surprising. Belief in magic and the supernatural has long been part of German history. In the sixteenth century the three hundred autonomous states of the Holy Roman Empire tortured and burned more than 100,000 people for the practice of witchcraft. Among the methods of torture used was the 'prayer stool,' a rectangular bench studded with sharpened nails. The prisoner was forced to kneel on this until he confessed his crime. Once one was accused, resistance was futile. A Bamberg city official wrote to his daughter that he had confessed at the advice of his sympathetic jailer, who pleaded, 'Invent something, for you cannot endure the torture you will be put to ... One torture will follow another until you say you are a witch.'

At the end of the First World War almost every type of occult practitioner could be found working successfully somewhere in Germany. The defeated German people were willing to look almost anywhere for an answer to their social and economic problems. Hypnosis, clairvoyance, tarot reading, palmistry, fortunetelling and particularly astrology all flourished, and the best-known mediums and readers were able to fill large concert halls for their demonstrations. Telepathic acts swept the nation, and huge advertisements promising miraculous feats decorated the walls of every major city.

There was also widespread belief in such esoteric phenomena as animal magnetism, the I Ching, voodoo and alchemy. General Erich Ludendorff, commander of the German armies in the Great War, attempted to manufacture gold from base metal. Another high-ranking general claimed to have discovered a death ray capable of destroying aircraft and tanks. A steamship line fired a corporate officer on the advice of a graphologist who noted certain dangerous traits in his handwriting. A road between Hamburg and Bremen was scrupulously avoided because certain 'mysterious rays' supposedly emanated from Milestone 113. A magus who claimed to be able to summon forth the spirit of the dead Chancellor Otto von Bismarck, and who healed the sick by the application of white cheese, managed to attract enough followers to found a city.

In Hanover, a butcher named Fritz Haarman was convicted of vampiric acts. After biting young people to death, he had sold their flesh in his shop. And, in a small village outside Mannheim, a farmer beat his wife to death after a local sorcerer accused her of bewitching the family cattle.

Adolf Hitler took full advantage of the willingness of the German people to believe in the supernatural when creating the National Socialist movement. The Nazi Party symbol, the swastika, had been used by many civilizations as everything from a good-luck charm to a fertility sign. The red, white and black party colours were those of the priestly vestments of the occult-based Manichaean religion. The 'SS' worn by the party's elite soldiers was styled from the mythical Runic alphabet. Nazi concentration-camp officers wore the devil's skull-and-crossbones insignia.

This symbolism only reflected the beliefs of top party officials. Heinrich Himmler, Reichsführer of the dreaded SS and the second most powerful man in Nazi Germany, believed he was the reincarnation of tenth-century German King Heinrich I, the Fowler, with whom he communicated in his sleep. In 1937 he had the monarch's bones excavated and reinterred in a crypt at Quedlinburg Cathedral after a holy procession. Each year on July 2, the date of the King's death, he held a midnight ritual in the crypt.

Himmler also believed in visualization. During the trial of General Werner von Fritsch on trumped-up charges of homosexuality, he gathered twelve SS officers in a room next to the interrogation room in which the General was being questioned and ordered them to try to exert an influence over von Fritsch to tell the truth about his actions. To give credence to his own convictions, he established the *Ahnenerbe* (Ancestral Research) branch of the SS to investigate occult theories of the origins of Aryanism, and eventually supported an expedition to Tibet to search for the fossilized remains of giants.

Rudolf Hess was an even more fervent believer in the occult than Himmler. Hess based all his important decisions on advice given to him by soothsayers and astrologers, which led Hitler to conclude that his flight to Scotland had been suggested by one of these fortunetellers. In addition, before he would sleep in a room he would test it with a divining rod to be sure no subterranean waters ran beneath it; once he was certain it was safe, he arranged magnets above and beneath his bed to draw any harmful substances out of his body while he slept.

Propaganda Minister Joseph Goebbels was also aware of the potential powers of the occult, although he was not a believer himself. Among other things, he had the prophecies of the French seer Nostradamus reinterpreted to foretell German victory and published the results throughout occupied nations.

One of the favoured practitioners of the occult arts in Germany was Erik Jan Hanussen, known as both the 'Magician of Berlin' and the 'Prophet of the Third Reich.' Although the so-called Witchcraft Act of 1933 had specifically prohibited 'the divination of the present or the past, and all other forms of veneration not based on natural practices or perception, including the reading of cards, the casting of horoscopes, the explanation of the stars and interpretation of dreams and omens,' Hanussen was allowed to continue staging elaborate seances in his popular Palace of Occultism, during which he faithfully forecast victory for the Nazi army. Among his other predictions was that the Reichstag, the home of the legal government, would be burned – an event which allowed Hitler to consolidate his power – the night before it occurred.

Hanussen's Palace of Occultism was the forerunner of a very real experiment in magic and the occult. In 1939 the individual German armed forces set up research centres to test suggestions or inventions submitted by civilians which might be of military value. Eventually, these institutes began investigating the supernatural forces. The German Navy's centre housed representatives from most of the occult areas, including spiritualists, mediums and sensitives, astronomers and astrologers, pendulum practitioners, experts in the Indian pendulum theory of Tattwa, as well as legitimate scientists. The object was to isolate the powers of the supernatural and apply them to modern warfare, but the results were predictably disappointing.

With this pseudoscientific work being given official approval, the German military command ridiculed the use of simple stage magic in warfare. Soon after Jasper Maskelyne had arrived in Egypt, British Intelligence showed him a copy of a Turkish newspaper that contained a rough cartoon drawing of him dressed in ancient wizard's robes. The caption revealed he was on the *Sumaria* and named the date on which it was scheduled to arrive in Egypt, then concluded that Hitler was the only real war magician, for he had made the British and French armies disappear from Europe.

The unflattering cartoon bothered Jasper much less than the fact that the enemy had been able to track his movements. This knowledge suddenly made the chocolates incident seem far more ominous than he had originally believed. British agents in Ankara, Turkey, began investigating the newspaper, trying to pinpoint the source of its information. Although the situation made Maskelyne uneasy, he did not have time to worry about it. On May 11, his Camouflage Experimental Section received its first assignment.

Ten days earlier a convoy had delivered 238 new tanks to Alexandria harbour. 'Behold,' the Bible-quoting Churchill had signalled Wavell, 'now is the day of salvation.'

Looking over the tanks, the General doubted that. Many of them had been damaged in transit and all of them lacked sand filters, without which their engines would burn out after a few hours of operation in the desert. In addition, like most of the equipment arriving in Egypt, the tanks had been coated with forest-green camouflage. They would stand out against the monochromatic desert like a bonfire in a blackout. 'They were originally supposed to go to Greece,' Major Geoffrey Barkas explained as he outlined the problem to Maskelyne and Knox, 'but were sent here instead when the government fell. Unfortunately, there isn't a pint of desert camouflage paint in North Africa. Wavell wants us to try to whip up a batch, and I thought it might be something your section could handle. I know it's not much of an assignment...'

'How much of a batch?' Knox asked cautiously.

Barkas hesitated, then replied in a voice much too soft for his bulk, 'Ten thousand gallons.'

Frank laughed.

Without the desert camouflage paint the new tanks – even when they were mechanically sound – could not be used effectively on the desert, and it would be weeks before an emergency paint request could be fulfilled. If most other units hadn't been involved in Brevity preparations, Maskelyne's section might not have been given the job, but no one else was available to do it.

Manufacturing ten thousand gallons of sand-coloured camouflage paint tough enough to withstand the extreme temperature fluctuations peculiar to the desert proved to be a challenging problem. As the painter Philip Townsend carefully explained, making paint was not in itself difficult. All that was needed was a substrate, or base, to hold fast the colour, and a pigment to provide it. 'Almost anything that hardens can be used as a base,' he told the group. 'All we really need to find is a liquid or powder that is soluble to whatever pigment we use and is capable of withstanding intense heat and bitter cold. Then we'll need some colouring substance too, some pigment, of course.'

'So all we need is everything,' Nails Graham interpreted.

Hill had been silent during the discussion, but the thought of making paint, or perhaps having to paint, upset him greatly. 'Bloody paintmakers,' he finally spat out. 'This is the most fouled-up outfit I've ever seen. I should've stayed in the Army!'

Knox reminded him that he was sort of in the Army.

Jasper sat puffing on his pipe as he listened to Townsend's explanation. It was certainly an unusual assignment – precisely the type of queer work he had expected his unit to attract. But if the section wasn't able to produce something as elementary as light-brown paint, it would be difficult to convince anyone they could fulfil more exotic requests. It was a basic equation: the future of the Camouflage Experimental Section depended on its ability to produce ten thousand gallons of paint out of thin air.

The seven men scoured Cairo and its environs for a suitable substrate. Bill Robson nearly tripped over a pile of abandoned Italian cement. Hill uncovered a cache of damp and matted sawdust. Either would serve, but supplies of both were limited, and the search continued.

It was Townsend who discovered the dump. A chap in his old outfit suggested that it was the one place in Cairo where anything might be found. Like everyone else serving in the Nile Basin the painter had been vaguely aware of its existence, but until he hitched a ride there and saw it for himself he never appreciated it.

The dump was spread over acres of desert just north of the city. Occasionally, a shifting breeze would pick up its rough scent and carry it into Cairo proper, but other than those bothersome times few people paid it any attention. It existed; it seemed to have always existed, since the Great War and perhaps even earlier, and like some insatiable monster it grew and grew.

It was more than a dump, really. It was perhaps the largest military junk pile in the world. Here the refuse of war was abandoned helter-skelter in dark ragged piles. Among the mounds of scrap it was indeed possible to find almost anything. The dump was that place where anything that belonged nowhere truly belonged. Entire waterlogged cargoes salvaged from sunken ships could be found in this dump, and hulks of vehicles even Wavell's desperate mechanics couldn't restore, and metal piping of all lengths and circumference, and wooden deck timbers, corrugated-tin sheets, smashed typewriters and broken desks, thousands of bald tyres and ruined tank treads, millions of shell casings, discarded uniforms and issue underwear, outdated and rusted tin helmets, countless cartons of spoiled rations, bags of plaster, broken pens and combs and women's hair clips, endless boxes of papers too worthless to burn, and much more.

The dump stood as a monument to the gluttony of modern warfare. No one knew what had been left there to rot beneath the desert sun. No records were kept because no one had the time or the interest or the need to know. What was here was worthless. As scrap it might have fetched a small fortune, but none of it could support an army, or keep a tank in operation, or help a man stay alive in the desert, or kill an enemy, so in the very real terms of warfare it was all worthless.

Narrow, shadowed alleys ran among the heaps, starting and ending randomly and creating the walls of an eerie, dark maze in which it was possible to get frighteningly lost. The only visible clue to location was the depth of sand dust; the piles in the rear were covered with a thick shroud of the stuff, while more recent additions to the dump sported only a thin covering mist of sand. The area was casually patrolled, and at dusk each day Arab scavengers moved in to climb the steel and cardboard mountains in search of products for the street bazaar. Occasionally a pile would shift and crush a child, or crates would collapse and someone would die under the weight of garbage, but other than these hunters the dump was left to decay, and within a blink of time it would disappear forever beneath mammoth dunes.

Under the circumstances, it was one of the most beautiful sights Jasper Maskelyne had ever seen.

'It goes on for acres,' Townsend said as the men stood near the front. 'Nobody even seems to know how big it is.'

Jasper could barely restrain himself from diving in and exploring it. 'Do we need permission?'

Hill laughed.

Townsend shook his head. 'Doesn't look like anybody cares what goes on around here. The gyppies seem to have free run of the place.'

Jasper looked to Frank Knox for advice. Knox shrugged. So the entire Royal Engineers Camouflage Experimental Section at Abbassia, seven strong, marched into the dump and began ripping it apart. They tore open boxes, pried the lids off crates, smashed containers, crawled through stripped hulks and in general had a jolly good time. At first they found nothing of any practical use to them. Robson unearthed eight large cartons of military-issue brassieres. Fuller discovered thousands of pairs of broken eyeglass frames. Hill uncovered a ton of waterlogged leather boot heels. And, later, Townsend found the paint substrate.

While rooting through the cargo raised from a torpedoed freighter, he chanced upon rows of sealed tin drums. He split the seal on one of them and watched curiously as a thick brown substance oozed out. He dubbed a bit on his finger and tasted it. It had a bitter but familiar taste, and it took him a moment to properly identify it. Worcester sauce. Thick Worcester sauce. Rows and rows and rows of tin drums filled with slightly rancid Worcester sauce. Hundreds of gallons of Worcester sauce. It tasted awful. It was wonderful. He knew he had the paint base.

Additional searching turned up tons of spoiled flour and another load of cement. Enough of everything was carried back to Abbassia to allow Townsend to experiment until he was able to work out the proper mix of cement, flour and sauce. The mix would serve as the paint substrate. Unfortunately, it was mud red in colour, making it as useless in the desert as the original forest green. A pigment was needed to turn the paste a proper sand colour. Two days had already gone by.

Paintmaster Townsend threw every colouring substance he could find into the pot, including various inks and soap powders and melted crayons. He even tried, without success, to scald the dye out of desert camouflage uniforms. Nothing worked. The resulting colour was too light or too dark, failed to hold, flaked in the afternoon sun, peeled in the evening cold, or proved insoluble in the gloppy paste. Two more days passed.

The men were so absorbed in their search for a pigment they barely felt the tremble in the air.

At 5:45 A.M. on May 15, the 22nd Guards Brigade Group rolled out of its staging area toward Halfaya Pass, a strategically important entrance to the escarpment, a high ridge that divided the desert. Control of the western pass was absolutely necessary if a later campaign was to be a success. South of the 22nd Guards, 4th Royal Tank Regiment and 1st Durham Light Infantry advanced on occupied Fort Capuzzo, and along the coast elements of 7th Armoured Division rolled toward beleaguered Tobruk.

At 6:15 Operation Brevity commenced with a brief tank barrage. Afrika Korps was caught completely by surprise and was unable to properly respond. By the end of the afternoon 22nd Guards, supported by 2nd Battalion Scots Guards and part of the 4th Royal Tanks, had captured Halfaya Pass. Fort Capuzzo had been taken after bitter fighting. The 7th Armoured Division was in control of the coastal flank.

News of Brevity's initial success blazed through the Delta. In Cairo, soldiers gathered on every corner to trade snippets of gossip. On the crowded deck of the great Shepheards Hotel, in the steamy barracks, in the illegal houses, at the secret meeting of the Muslim Brotherhood, nothing was discussed except the battle. The collapse of enemy resistance was reminiscent of Wavell's first drive across the desert. No one had expected Rommel to be so easily defeated.

Stuck out in Abbassia, Maskelyne's men followed the battle mostly by rumour. All of their efforts were devoted to concocting a light-brown pigment. Compared to the fighting going on a few miles away the work seemed trivial, but it served to keep their minds occupied and bolstered their spirits.

Rommel had raced to the crumbling front line the moment the fighting began. He mistakenly concluded that Wavell intended to lift the siege around Tobruk, and knew that Afrika Korps would be forced to withdraw to Libya if that objective was achieved. Earlier than he thought prudent, he committed his heavy reserves to the fighting. 7th Panzer and 5th Panzer, dragging 88mm antiaircraft guns behind tank tenders, sped to the threatened fronts. When Wavell's Matilda tanks, the lumbering queens of the battlefield, came within range, the Germans levelled their 88s and opened fire. From as far as a mile away, the antiaircraft shells ripped through the Matildas' flimsy steel hulls as easily as nails being hammered into water.

Wavell had not anticipated such resistance to his modest offensive, and Western Desert Force was not prepared to meet it. By the afternoon of the sixteenth, Afrika Korps had recaptured Fort Capuzzo and stopped 7th Armoured's drive along the coast. Efforts were made in Cairo to show a confident front, but the steady flow of ambulances racing in from the desert made that difficult. From all reports it was obvious that the attack had turned sour.

After two days of brutal fighting, Western Desert Force still maintained a tenuous grip on Halfaya Pass. If they could hold it, Wavell's offensive could be considered successful. But with Fort Capuzzo once again in German hands and the siege troops surrounding Tobruk no longer threatened, Rommel was able to bring his full attention to that position.

Twenty-second Guards began making preparations to withdraw. Wavell's limited attack had been a total failure, and he realized that a much larger and better-equipped force would be needed to dislodge Rommel. Even before 22nd Guards was driven out of Halfaya Pass, GHQ was drawing up plans for that massive offensive. Code-named Operation Battleaxe, it was scheduled for mid-June, before the enemy would be able to replace its Brevity losses. By that time Wavell expected to have his tanks fully operational.

The pigment for the camouflage paint had been right under the noses of Jasper Maskelyne's men the entire time. Under their feet too. After spending a week testing with every colouring substance he could think of, the frustrated Townsend was ready to quit. But as he walked down a dirt path with Jasper, discussing the problem, he stepped into a pile of the answer. 'Camel chips,' he said, reaching down and picking up one of the dried, hard sandy-brown pats. 'Of course, camel droppings.'

Sun-dried camel dung was the perfect colour. It even turned different shades of desert colours depending on the length of time it was exposed to the sun. It was cheap, and plentiful. After a few attempts, Townsend figured out how to make it soluble in Worcester sauce paste. Testing proved that it held fast in heat and cold. Camel dung made a perfect, albeit malodorous, desert camouflage paint pigment.

Thus the 'Dung Patrol' was born. 'We stand behind every camel,' Maskelyne joked, but in fact it was almost true. One of his men or an Egyptian worker recruited for the harvest trailed every caravan leaving the city. Nearby oases were cleaned daily. The streets were swept each dawn for night leftovers. Private Hill grumbled through his duties, complaining, 'That a man of my ability should be reduced to this.' Graham fashioned a little metal scooper for each man. Professor Knox explained that animal faeces had been used throughout history for everything from constructing shelters to currency.

'If I never see another bloody camel again it'll be too bloody soon,' Hill grumbled late one afternoon as the men relaxed at the station.

'Guess that means you're breakin' your date tonight, eh?' Robson said. The young private's social life had become the subject of a thousand nasty jokes.

'Now, now,' Graham said calmly, 'we don't have to make fun of Michael's ladies – I think we should let their looks speak for themselves.' The carpenter was carving a small block of wood, and paused and looked up. 'Besides, I heard he was very good to them. Even took one of 'em to the dog show on Gezira the other day.'

Robson knew the joke. 'She win?' he asked on cue.

'Nah,' Graham finished, 'came in second.'

Hill heaved a sack of dried chips at him.

The Dung Patrol not only provided raw material for the paint, it helped the section attract valuable attention. The ludicrous sight of soldiers waiting patiently behind camels with open burlap bags did much to boost morale in the depressing days following Brevity. Everyone in Cairo wanted to know what possible use a tiny camouflage unit had for thousands of camel chips. The fact that the group was commanded by Maskelyne the magician increased their curiosity. There was considerable and creative speculation. When asked what his people were doing, Major Barkas simply smiled enigmatically. Jasper knew the value of active curiosity, and so he did his best to keep the truth secret. Eventually it leaked out, to the delight of some and the disappointment of many others who had entertained far more exotic possibilities.

The Arab community watched the Dung Patrol with less amusement. Dried camel pats had fuelled their bread ovens for thousands of years, and the increased demand for the limited supply resulted in the creation of a flourishing camel-chip market. Maskelyne's people had to hustle to beat angry Arab men and women as well as mercenary children to the suddenly valuable droppings.

The Worcester sauce paste and the camel pats were mixed in huge washing tubs that had previously been utilized by a laundry unit. Once production got under way, as much as two thousand gallons of paint was mixed each week. The finished product was stored in petrol tins and delivered to a transportation company, which did the actual tank camouflage painting. After a few days of exposure to the sun, the foul scent of the paint wore off.

The Camouflage Experimental Section celebrated this initial success with a boisterous party in Cairo. Jasper dusted off his ukelele and, accompanied by Frank Knox on the harmonica, played some music-hall ditties. Hill recited some bawdy limericks. Even Townsend joined in, singing a loud, off-key version of the local hit 'Here Comes Farouk in His Fifty-Bob Suit.'

Many choruses into the night, Jasper toasted his men. 'I want to thank each one of you,' he offered, 'for lowering your sights for me.'

They jeered him good-naturedly.

'This success has gained us a good deal of attention,' he continued, 'and I suspect we'll be getting requests to perform some pretty absurd tasks. Remember, when someone asks you if we can do a job, the answer is yes. Don't think about it, don't worry about it, the answer is yes. We'll work out the details later. Everybody understand?'

The answer was yes.

Maskelyne spent most of the days of May working on the paint project, but after sundown he gave his attention to things magic. Although he had reluctantly agreed to produce a variety show in return for permission to form the Camouflage Section, the thought of appearing before an audience again excited him. He missed the limelight. He quickly discovered that his skills were badly dulled. He had done his shows on the *Sumaria* and when time allowed had been exercising with steel balls, but his hands had to be practised back into form. The success of a magic act depends on the dexterity of the magician, and Jasper's hands were no longer faster than the eyes. He spent hours standing in front of a dusky mirror, repeating the basic sleights time and again until they once again felt natural. By the time he put away his tools each night his fingers were aching, but gradually each nuance came back to him, old friends showing up at a reunion of special skills. Each was welcomed, and appreciated, and fit back into its proper position, and eventually their individual existence was forgotten and they blended into the smooth, splendid whole.

Actually, the enforced layoff had been beneficial. He had been working hard at the business of magic for fifteen years. In front of countless patrons in numerous countries he had levitated ladies and sawed them in half, made everything from a sparrow to an elephant disappear, conjured ghosts, slipped in and out of impossible spaces, and even managed to cut off his own head! Life for him had become an endless cycle of performing and packing and performing. He had made so many tours the princes and the pashas had become confused in his memory. At home he had to promote the shows at St. George's Hall, help plan the bill, audition and engage new talent, continue to develop new illusions in the shops and worry about the bills. What little spare time he had was spent with Mary and their children, or working in related fields. At some point prior to the war it had all proven too much for him. The joy he had once derived from entertaining had been lost, and magic had become a difficult job. But standing before a cracked mirror outside Cairo, and making promises of wonders to his own reflection, it was different. His limbs tingled with energy. Sometimes, when the kerchiefs popped up just right and the dice disappeared in perfect synchronization with his nonsense patter, he felt romanced. An old and deep and long-lost love had come back to him and made him glow with a comfortable warmth. That the Army had forced him to perform no longer disturbed him, for once again he was in love with illusion.

There was an additional problem to be solved, and for this he turned to Michael Hill. Frank Knox had been a capable assistant aboard ship, but something more than a chunky professor in a mop wig was needed to draw audiences in Cairo. Jasper broke the news to Frank gently. 'Your legs are terrible,' he said.

Setting loose Private Michael Hill on the women of Cairo was similar to placing an unconquered European nation before Hitler. He roamed the streets and bazaars of Cairo during the off hours for almost a week, stopping every attractive woman he passed to offer the opportunity to be in show business. Finally, exhausted, he settled on a winsome, dark-haired club dancer. Save for the fact that she was missing a front tooth, she was an extremely attractive woman. 'Don't smile,' Hill warned her as he took her home to meet his magician.

'Hookay,' she said, smiling.

Jasper was finishing the design of an illusion he tentatively named 'The Mummy's Curse' when they arrived. It was a simple variation of the disappearing box, but he felt it gave desirable local flavour to his act. Hill introduced the girl, and Jasper politely offered his hand. 'How do you do?'

She smiled. She said nothing.

Hill whispered in her ear, then she said, 'I am fine very much thank you.'

Jasper looked sceptically at the soldier. 'She doesn't speak English, does she?'

'I know that's a problem,' Hill admitted, 'but I'm willing to work with her and—'

Maskelyne was astonished. 'You've actually brought me an assistant who doesn't speak English?'

She beamed. Aware that the men were discussing her, she said, 'Fine thank you very much five buns please.'

'I think you should get her out of here.'

'But, sir, she's an orphan and—'

'Out. Now.'

Hill's quest ended with his discovery of Corporal Kathy Lewis, a staffer in Brigadier Dudley Clarke's 'A-Force' deception organization. Brigadier Clarke had created the elite Desert Rats commando group while working at Whitehall in London, and had been brought to Egypt by Wavell to head covert operations for the Mediterranean area. His modest A-Force office occupied the lower floor of a two-storey building in Kasr el Nil. The top floor had long housed one of the city's most popular brothels, which Clarke saw no reason to evict, although the arrangement became the subject of much ribald humour.

Hill encountered the prim Corporal Lewis after interviewing some of the upstairs women, and offered her the job as soon as he heard her proper English voice. 'Sounds like spiffing fun,' she said, and agreed to audition.

Kathy Lewis was not the type of woman who usually attracted Hill. Her hair was good-enough blonde, but clipped too short. Her figure was trim, but too slender. And her face was pleasant, but not nearly snazzy enough.

Jasper took a good look and a long listen and knew he had his assistant. 'You've a lovely figure,' he said innocently.

She turned prudishly pink.

'I mean,' he stammered, 'you'll fit nicely into the boxes.'

Kathy Lewis turned out to be a real trouper. She put in the same long hours as the crew without complaint, rapidly learned her cues and had no difficulty operating the apparatus. She disappeared rapidly, screamed acceptably terror-stricken, and delivered the correct props to the proper position. In addition, she very much reminded Maskelyne of another earnest young woman with whom he'd worked two decades earlier. He'd married that one and hadn't regretted it a single day. Often, watching Kathy move gracefully across the stage, he thought of Mary and wondered what she was doing at that very moment. Mostly, he imagined her doing the mundane things. Making sure his tuxedo shirt was properly starched. Seeing to the children's homework. Sitting down to a hot meal between performances. Theirs was a marriage of the theatre, and when he pictured her it was not at a formal dinner with a Persian ruler, but rather giving him a quick brush before sending him into the spotlight. They lived for the pleasure of the paying audience, snatching private moments for themselves.

How had they managed to fill all those years so easily? he wondered. They did not go to other theatres very often, rarely to sporting events and only occasionally dined out. What things did they do? He loved the family picnics, the nights at home after the show listening to the old gramophone or the new radio, the birthday parties for the children. The house was always filled with friends. Not much, really, not much for so long. Just the normal bits and pieces that comprise the days and become a lifetime. But together it was more than enough, and not a moment passed when he did not miss her very much.

The paint project had briefly focused attention on Maskelyne's new camouflage unit, but when the Mechanical Section took over actual production of the stuff the Experimental Section was once again without a job. This time, though, they would not have long to wait.

Prime Minister Churchill was publicly pressuring Wavell to resume his abandoned offensive with the newly outfitted Matilda tanks. But Wavell resisted. He knew his men were not ready to fight again, and he was grimly aware that Rommel lay waiting for him in the desert like a wounded cat.

While Afrika Korps controlled the passes onto the escarpment there was little chance for victory. As Maskelyne would soon be told, the outcome of Operation Battleaxe might well be determined by his ability to transform a tank into a truck.

FOUR

The situation facing General Wavell in mid-May was distressingly clear: his army was better supplied than Afrika Korps, but the enemy was entrenched in strategically superior positions and was armed with an unknown quantity of tank-killing 88s. Western Desert Force's only real chance for victory was to achieve tactical surprise, but that seemed impossible. Somehow, a substantial number of Churchill's 'Tiger cubs' had to be deployed without being detected by German observers. Since Rommel's land and air spotters had been alerted that the British might soon move again, and the barren terrain made it relatively easy to spot any movement, this could be accomplished only by making the tanks appear in place out of thin air.

General Wavell's slim hope was that Jasper Maskelyne could perform this feat of military legerdemain. He wanted him.

When Barkas arrived at the section with the assignment Maskelyne was four thousand years away, sitting alone, on the dank floor of the Great Pyramid of Cheops at Giza. His eyes were closed, his legs crossed and his hands at ease as his mind drifted through time in search of the magic of the high priests of ancient Egypt.

Truthfully, he didn't really believe the legends. Nothing he had seen during a lifetime devoted to the conjuring arts had even remotely suggested that the force of true magic actually existed. But still he had come, drawn by the enigmatic pyramids to fulfil a promise he had made to himself many years earlier.

He had crawled through the narrow ascending passage and into the past, arranged himself as comfortably as possible on the hard floor, and waited. He had no expectations, being, after all, a man schooled in the refinements of both stage magic and modern science. But there was some vestigial part of him that stirred, that refused to submit to the realities of science, that yearned for communication with his ancient kin, and that part of him quivered with excitement.

He allowed his mind unfettered freedom. His mind roamed the stone walls, searching for some clue, some thread from which to weave the tapestry of true magic. He didn't know what he was waiting for. Certainly not the voices or knocks associated with bogus spirit communication. A sign of some kind. A feeling. Perhaps a thought. If these ancient priests had the powers they claimed, they would have the means to make themselves known. If time could be transcended, these men, the teachers of Moses, these were the men most able to do it.

Outside, the afternoon sun made the air sizzle, but the temperature inside the King's Chamber remained an eternal sixty-eight degrees. A few bare electric bulbs illuminated the burial room and cast angular shadows that did not move.

Maskelyne had hoped to leap the centuries, but the afternoon passed in long minutes. The floor grew colder and harder. His legs ached. He listened to the soft breeze sweeping through a hidden passage and wondered if it carried a message, but it was only the wind. He searched the shadows and found them hollow. Finally a shiver pinched his spine and twisted his shoulders and a cloak of uneasiness swept over him. He knew it was time to leave. No secrets would be revealed to him. He had been foolish to come here, he realized that now. Who was he to believe he might serve as some sort of historical umbilical cord? He was an interloper in time. A magician? The men who had caused this pyramid to be built were the real magicians. It was recorded that with their spells they could cure and destroy, pluck the sun from the heavens and move the earth itself. Through the force of their magic they had ruled the most advanced civilization of the ancient world. He was an entertainer, a showman, working to delight music-hall patrons. His illusions were invented in a workshop and made possible by stagehands.

Jasper returned to the war through the cramped ascending passage and did not glance back as he drove to Abbassia.

Major Barkas was waiting for him at the camouflage tent. 'I hope your wand is in good repair,' he cheerfully greeted him. 'It seems that General Wavell has some business for you.'

Jasper paused, then eyed him suspiciously. 'Wavell?'

Barkas was sitting at the small round table Hill had rescued from the dump, enjoying a cup of tea and some biscuits. 'Yes, Wavell. Apparently he was quite taken with your magic gang's paint job. Now he's got something else he'd like you to look at.'

Maskelyne joined him at the table.

'Look here, Rommel knows we've got to come at him and he knows we've got to do it soon. What he doesn't know is where or when we'll strike. That's our trump card. Now, we've learned a bit about General Rommel in the last few months,' Barkas continued. 'Rather than dividing his armour into penny packets, small roving groups, as we do, he maintains them in rather large assemblages. His main panzer units are kept on the front line and a few highly mobile reserves are held in check. These front-line units are strong enough to meet our probing attacks, and when we go at him in force he waits until he's sure he knows where our hardest blow is being struck–' he slammed his fist down onto the table, rattling the mess silver '–then he brings forward his reserves to tip the balance.'

Jasper steadied the wobbling table.

'What we've got to do is somehow prevent him from bringing up his reserves until we've been able to smash through to his supply line. Once we've broken through he'll have no choice but to withdraw to protect his supplies. Do you see?'

Jasper nodded.

'It's quite simple, really. He'll jump just as soon as he's determined where our main thrust is taking place, and there's no way to hide major armoured concentrations on the open desert. But if we could disguise our intentions, even for a little while, we'll gain the extra time we need.' Barkas reached into his breast pocket and took out a folded sheet of notebook paper. 'The brigadier thought something like this might work,' he said, handing the slip to Maskelyne.

The page had been torn out of Wavell's ubiquitous field notebook. On it the brigadier had sketched the profile of a tank surmounted by a large flat board. A second sketch showed that an aerial view of a truck had been drawn on the board. Theoretically, at least, an observer flying overhead would look down on this and be fooled into believing it was a common lorry.

Maskelyne frowned. He knew that this scheme would never work. The shadow cast by a tank in no way resembles that of a truck, and the shadow created by a flat board looks like nothing else except a flat board. In addition, unless the spotter aircraft was flying directly overhead the observer would be able to see under the board.

'Well?'

Jasper laid the sketch on the table and tried to press the creases out of it with his palm. Remembering his charge to his men, he replied, with as much confidence as he could muster, 'Certainly. When do you need to see something?'

Barkas shrugged. 'Yesterday. Last week. Sorry to lay this one on you so suddenly, but it's got to be a slam-bang job. The attack goes

off in mid-June. If we don't have these–' his hand searched the air for
a proper description '–these what-have-yous, covers, I suppose, to get
our tanks into position, our boys won't have a monkey's chance at
Epsom Downs. Rommel's 88s'll blast 'em to kingdom come.'

Jasper stared at Wavell's rough sketch. His mind began leafing
through the files of his memory in search of a comparable stage
illusion. Transforming a tank into a truck might not be any more
difficult than turning a flaming woman into a butterfly, he decided. A
collapsible frame would probably do the job. It would require some
tinkering to determine how best to make it work, but he'd done many
similar things before. The long hours he'd spent slaving in the theatre
workshop would pay off handsomely here. 'I can give you something
tomorrow,' he said rashly.

Barkas was taken aback. 'Splendid,' he said, 'splendid. Just as soon
as your sketches have been approved Brass'll want a setup.' He stood
up to leave. 'I'm sure you'll do the job. A great many people are
counting on you.'

A translucent dusk had settled peacefully over Cairo while they were
meeting. They stood at the tent entrance watching as the last rays of
the sun reflected off the fine dust that drifted on the breezes and
bathed the city in a wash of royal gold. 'The Egyptians claim they'll
be wealthy so long as they have their sunsets,' Barkas said as night
pushed in. 'There's a legend about a beggar who tried to capture the
gold dust in his basket. When he had it all he was going to sell it back
to the King. After collecting it for years he finally peeked into his
basket, and when he discovered it had all escaped through the woven
bottom he went insane. Even today it's considered terrible luck to
take a picture of it, to try to capture it.' He shook his head in
amazement. 'It's beautiful, though.'

'Magnificent.'

Barkas stuffed his hands into the large pockets of his summer
weights and strolled toward his jeep. Jasper trailed a step behind.
'You know, Maskelyne, day is just beginning for the Tobrukers.
They can't move around at all during the day – snipers – so the
perimeter guards lay in little depressions and bake. The flies, the
heat, the crawling buggers … it's a terrible thing for a man to
have to endure. Let's help the General get them out of there, shall
we.' It was not a question. The major left a set of tank blueprints
with Maskelyne, cautioning him to guard them carefully, then drove
off to meet the next crisis.

Hill was stuffing a biscuit into his mouth when Jasper returned to the tent. 'The Magic Gang, huh? I like it. Packs a wallop, if you see what I mean.'

Jasper's mind was already designing the tank frame. 'What?'

'The Magic Gang. What the major called us. I was just saying I like the way it sounds. It's got a good ring.'

Maskelyne considered it. The Magic Gang. Jasper Maskelyne's Magic Gang. It resounded like a music-hall billing, and it was accurate. A magic gang was precisely what he had on his hands. 'All right,' he decided, 'that's it, then, the Magic Gang.' The name made him smile. 'Sounds impressive, doesn't it?'

After sending Private Hill into Cairo to try to turn up photographs of various trucks, Maskelyne sat down at the wobbly table and went to work. Both the British and the Germans had put dummy tanks into the field, Western Desert Force using full-sized wooden monsters that required six men and a flatbed truck to move them, while Rommel had dropped bulky wooden shells onto Volkswagen chassis. Supposedly the Americans were experimenting with inflatable rubber dummies. But no army had ever attempted to disguise real tanks with anything but paint patterns and foliage.

Jasper began just as he would if he were creating a stage illusion: he listed his objectives, the obstacles that had to be confronted, and the materials available to work with. This time, rather than making a woman appear to burst into flame and emerge as a butterfly, his objective was to design and construct a lightweight, disposable frame that would enable a tank to pass as a truck under close scrutiny. The problems were numerous: enemy Intelligence would be checking shadows and silhouettes, as well as the obvious details, so the shadows cast by the cover had to precisely replicate those cast by real trucks, its silhouette had to be perfect, and the tank's tread tracks had to be wiped out. For practical purposes the frame had to be so simple that a few men could rapidly raise it, even working under adverse conditions, and shed it just as quickly. Sight lines had to be maintained at all times. Finally, the material from which it would be made – and he hadn't determined what this would be – had to be available in the Basin in abundant quantities.

After reducing the large problem into as many small parts as possible, he attacked each one. What materials were easily obtainable? How would this truck frame open? How would it close? Would hooks or latches serve better? How many pieces should the frame break into: two, three, four, or even more? Should these pieces snap together or be bolted together? Should they be reusable or disposable? As he made each decision he incorporated it into a rough sketch, until the frame began to take shape. Gradually, he eased his way through the thick layers of conscious thought into that place he called 'the factory of ideas,' where imagination reigned, and from which solutions blossomed. Almost mechanically, his knowledge and innate creativity combined to present an acceptable construction to him.

The apparatus for transforming a tank into a truck – the 'sunshield,' as it was dubbed – would be made by stretching the painted canvas over two collapsible wooden frames. Each frame would cover half the tank, from front to back. When erected, a sunshield vaguely resembled three rectangular boxes of different heights and widths pushed together, forming a stairway of three unequal steps. The first, somewhat squarish box represented the truck's front hood, the taller and thinner second box was the driver's cab, and the longest and highest section would pass as the covered truck bed.

The frames would clamp onto handles bolted to the sides of the tank and be hinged at the commander's turret on top. When that latch was disengaged, the two sides of the shell would fall away to either side, like a potato sliced in half lengthwise. Although a few inches of tank tread would be visible beneath the sunshield, they would usually be hidden by the undulating desert terrain. 'On paper,' the exhausted Maskelyne said as he showed his sketches to the men the following morning, 'it appears to work very well.'

'Then why don't we just show Jerry the paper?' quipped Hill.

Each man was assigned a suitable task. Robson converted Maskelyne's rough drawings into blueprints, while Townsend rendered the sunshield locked into position over a tank, in the process of unfolding, and finally shed and lying alongside the tank. Hill and Jack Fuller tried to mould a lump of clay into something approximating the shape of a Matilda tank, while Nails Graham made a working scale model of the apparatus to fit over it. Frank Knox struggled to devise a means to replace the telltale tank treads with truck tyre tracks. The men worked steadily through the day, their spirits raised in the morning by the official announcement that the Nazi superbattleship *Bismarck* had been torpedoed and sunk by the cruiser *Dorsetshire*, then tempered later in the day by confirmation that Afrika Korps had regained complete control of Halfaya Pass. All Brevity gains had been wiped out.

But as Maskelyne had promised, before the Muslim muezzins made the call to evening prayer, Sergeant Fuller was on his way to Barkas with blueprints, sketches and a working model of the sunshield. The concept was quickly approved and Maskelyne was ordered to build a prototype for demonstration to the commander of the 7th Armoured Division, Major General Michael 'Dickie' Creagh.

While the section was waiting for this permission to proceed, Knox solved the tread problem. Working with Colonel Meaker of the nearby Mechanical Experimental Section, he fabricated a tank 'tail' consisting of a length of spiky chain metal that would hook onto a bracket welded to the back of the tank. This heavy, dragging tail obliterated the characteristic tread marks and left a facsimile tyre track in its place.

Obtaining the necessary wood and canvas to build the sunshield prototype was simple; getting a tank on which to fit it was far more difficult. Preparations for Operation Battleaxe had already begun, and Wavell had ordered every armoured vehicle with functioning guns to be sent to the front, 'even if they are holed like sieves, have no tracks, and have to be flown forward.' Repair shops strained round the clock patching damaged hulls and overworked engines. A number of the original wooden dummy tanks were repainted and driven to the front on tenders. Another full day passed before Fuller located a marginally operable Matilda tank in a repair shed, but it was absolutely unavailable to Maskelyne.

The captain in charge of the shop refused to listen to Jasper's pleas. 'I wouldn't give a damn if you was the King's chauffeur himself, you ain't gettin' your hands on this can and that's it. I got my orders.'

Jasper tried gentle persuasion. 'We just need to borrow it for two days—'

'Keep your bloody paws offa my tank!'

Back in Abbassia, he outlined the situation for the Gang. 'There's one Matilda that's shot up pretty badly, but still moves well enough to suit our needs. Trouble is, we can't pry it loose from the repair shop. Even General Creagh's people can't help us on this one, they can't buck Wavell's directive.' As he explained the situation he wandered about the tent, stopping, it seemed casually enough, right behind Michael Hill. 'Without that tank we can't demonstrate the sunshield,' he continued, laying a fatherly hand on Hill's shoulder, 'and if we can't demonstrate the sunshield, we'll be out of business.' He gazed down at Hill and asked softly, 'Does anyone have any idea how we might get hold of that tank for a few days?'

Sergeant Fuller raised his hand. 'May I suggest, sir, that we file the proper emergency requisition forms with the Depot Transportation Company, sir.'

Knox caught Fuller's attention and held an index finger vertically against his puckered lips.

Hill gently lifted Jasper's hand off his shoulder. 'Oh no you don't,' the private protested. 'A jeep I could see. Even a small lorry, maybe. But a tank is another kettle of fish entirely. You know what they do to a fellow what lifts a tank?' He shook his head. 'No, thank you, Aunt Mabel. No indeedee.'

The other men tightened the circle around him.

At twelve-thirty the following night a Military Police jeep pulled up in front of the dimly lit tank repair annexe. This shop had been converted from a wagon garage for the emergency and contained only two damaged Matildas. A bored corporal, his rifle slung on his shoulder, casually paraded back and forth in front of the open garage door.

A private hopped out of the back of the jeep, his helmet pulled down over his eyes and the left side of his pencil-drawn moustache drooping slightly. The corporal did not pay too much attention to the moustache at the time, although he would recall it later under questioning.

'Relief,' the private announced.

The corporal did not recognize him. 'You're new.'

Private Hill nodded. 'This morning, from Crete. I figured they'd give me a few days. They figured different. Haven't even had time to get unpacked.'

'How was it over there? Pretty bad?'

'Pretty bad,' Hill agreed. 'Bloody Nazi paratroops all over the place.'

The corporal checked his watch. 'You're early, you know.'

'Don't know anything about that. Sergeant of the guard says get in the jeep, I get in the jeep. He tells me get out of the jeep, I get out.' Hill glanced at the garage. 'Anything around here to watch out for?'

The corporal snickered. 'Here? We got two smashed cans inside. 'Less somebody's looking for scrap metal, I don't think you got anything to worry about.'

'Where's the mechanics? I thought they was workin' all night.'

'Out for midnight lunch. Wouldn't 'spect 'em back too bloody soon, either. The sergeant likes to drink his meals.'

After a bit more discussion the corporal climbed into the back of the jeep, next to Graham, and Robson drove him away. As soon as the guard was out of sight, the righteous Fuller, frightened and complaining about this incredible breach of military procedure, backed the tank transporter up to the garage door, and the Gang went to work.

Ten minutes passed before the exhausted guard opened his eyes and realized that the jeep was heading in the wrong direction. He leaned forward and tapped Robson on the shoulder. 'I say,' he said, 'you're going in the wrong direction.'

Bill turned around enough for the guard to see he was wearing sunglasses. 'Right,' he said agreeably and continued driving. Graham laid a friendly paw on the guard's shoulder and pulled him back.

By the time a squad of military policemen located the Camouflage Experimental Section two days later, the only vehicle in the area was an ordinary ten-ton truck parked in the distance. Maskelyne flatly denied any knowledge of the heist. 'A tank, eh?' he said in amazement. 'That's out of my league. I can produce a rabbit for you if you'd like, or a canary in a cage, but not a tank. That's a bit much even for me.'

'This one of them?' the MP asked the shaken repair-shop guard, indicating Maskelyne.

The corporal shook his head. 'Chap I saw was much shorter, and sort of funny-looking.'

Frank glanced at Hill, who was fighting the urge to reply.

'Couldn't have been any of my men, then,' Jasper said. 'Why not try the Mechanical Engineers? They're always playing little pranks, and quite a few of them are funny-looking.'

Robson bowed his head so he wouldn't be caught chuckling.

Jack Fuller was safely tucked away in Cairo with Graham during the MP's search for the tank, even though he'd been convinced to participate in the heist, as it was feared his years of rectitude might be too strong to overcome.

The sunshield prototype weighed only thirty pounds. Tests using the 'borrowed' Matilda proved that it could be rapidly snapped into place by two men, and be discarded just as quickly by releasing the hand latch. Folded, the apparatus was only two feet six inches wide, so twenty of them could be transported in a single three-tonner. Only one question remained: would it look enough like a truck to fool the Germans?

First it had to fool the generals.

Monday morning, June 2, 1941, was tenderly warm and bright. A gentle night rain had rinsed the Delta and left it sparkling. General Creagh, Lieutenant Colonel Solly, commander of Middle Eastern Engineers, Maskelyne and most of the Magic Gang, Major Barkas, and a small group of 7th Armoured Division senior officers and aides waited on a broad dune overlooking a sand-rippled plain. Above them, a slow-flying Auster observation craft made lazy, pendulous sweeps in preparation for the presumably easy task of finding a tank hidden among a batch of ordinary ten-ton trucks.

Although Maskelyne knew that the future of his section would probably be determined in the next few minutes, most of the 7th Armoured officers treated the demonstration as a welcome relief after a disastrous weekend. The day before, the cruiser *Calcutta* had been sunk by Junkers 88 bombers, raising the losses in the Battle of Crete to three cruisers and six destroyers sunk, in addition to one carrier, three battleships, six cruisers and seven destroyers damaged. Casualty figures had not yet been released, but at least one thousand men had been killed in the campaign and another ten thousand were captured. So these ranking officers greeted the opportunity to match wits with the famous magician Jasper Maskelyne as an opportunity to escape from the cold mathematics of war.

After a brief wait on the dune, one of the aides pointed into the distance and shouted, 'There they are.' Simultaneously, the bevy of officers raised their field glasses and focused on a growing sand cloud.

Maskelyne stood to the side with all the Gang members except Knox, who had crammed into the tank to operate the sunshield. Through his binoculars Jasper could see the big trucks lumbering closer like a colony of ponderous ants. His mouth was as dry as the desert.

Major Barkas, who had wisely asked no questions about the tank's provenance and had supplied an experienced crew to drive it, stood at Maskelyne's side sighting through his own glasses. 'Looks pretty good so far,' he said critically.

One mile from the observers on the dune, the trucks broke into two parallel lines of five vehicles each. Overhead, the Auster swooped in for a low-level pass. Jasper tried to cover his nervousness with a forced cough. He looked carefully at the sunshield. It was covered with a thin layer of dust, but seemed to be sticking out of the line like a brightly coloured stop sign. He suddenly decided the paint job had been botched. 'It's the wrong colour,' he whispered urgently to Robson. 'How could we have made it the wrong colour?'

'It's fine, Jay,' the cartoonist said reassuringly. 'Just relax.'

The phalanx of trucks rumbled past the three-quarter-mile marker without any of the 7th Armoured officers picking out the tank. The front row of vehicles kicked up a sand spray which partially obscured the rear line. A major from 7th Armoured complained that this was hardly sporting, but Creagh shut him up with a testy glance. 'This is not a game, Major,' he pointed out.

Inside the tank, Frank Knox was sweating profusely. At Jasper's insistence, and over his objections, the disguised Matilda had been slotted in the centre of the front row. 'The best place to hide something is in the most obvious spot,' Maskelyne had explained. 'The audience resists looking where they think you want them to look.' Knox remained unconvinced.

On the dune, Nails Graham was whistling a merry tune under his breath to hide his jitters. Fuller was pacing in tight circles.

'Second from right, back row,' a colonel shouted confidently. Like spectators at Wimbledon, the observers swung their scopes to that truck.

'No, that's not it,' Colonel Solly decided. 'Look at the truck on the left end of the front row. Doesn't it look a bit queer?'

The Auster pilot dived low and rippled the sand. 'I can't spot the tank,' he radioed. 'Deception from here is excellent. I'm taking photos for the air recce boys now.'

The trucks formed a single file a few hundred yards from the observers. The disguised tank led the parade.

When they were within 150 yards of the high dune, in plain sight, the pilot suddenly shouted through a storm of static, 'Okay, I got it. I got it. The fourth one in the column. It's number four.' The officers zeroed their glasses on that truck. Maskelyne focused on it curiously. Except for a strip of torn canvas flapping loosely, the vehicle was virtually indistinguishable from the others. Two colonels immediately agreed with the pilot; the rest of the observers, including General Creagh, disagreed. The General glanced at Maskelyne.

Jasper shook his head.

'Well, then,' grumbled the 7th Armoured major, 'where the bloody hell is it?'

The trucks roared closer. When the Matilda reached the seventy-five-yard marker Knox pushed open the heavy commander's hatch a few inches and grasped the sunshield latch. He turned it as if opening a door. 'Here goes,' he shouted, but couldn't even hear himself over the engine.

As the officers scoured the column the lead truck suddenly split precisely in half, as if it had been sliced down its centre by a mammoth butcher's knife. The two sides collapsed lazily onto the desert. Like some surrealistic monster emerging from a wood-and-canvas cocoon, the Matilda charged forward, its thin, deadly snout aimed directly at the dune.

'Hey, presto,' Jasper whispered.

The hatch flipped open, and Frank popped up like a grinning Jack-in-the-box to deliver a rousing salute.

General Creagh returned it. Then, turning to Jasper, he said exuber-antly, 'By Jove, that's a rabbit out of the hat all right. General Wavell is going to be very pleased.' He pumped Jasper's hand. 'Well done, Maskelyne, well done.'

Hill bristled, feeling slighted. 'I stole the bloody thing, you know,' he said to Robson.

'Yeah, but maybe we shouldn't mention that right now,' the cartoonist replied.

Upon receipt of Creagh's account of the demonstration, and an equally enthusiastic report from Air Reconnaissance, Wavell requested that additional sunshields be delivered to 7th Armoured for field testing. The first half dozen arrived at Creagh's desert headquarters in pieces, having been shaken apart during the rough drive forward. Returning to his drawing board, Jasper substituted three-quarter-inch metal piping for the wood frame, and sailcloth for canvas. Nails supervised production of another six frames, which survived the trip to 7th Armoured and successfully passed a series of rugged tests.

Wavell immediately ordered the Magic Gang sunshield put into mass production. Mechanical Engineers took over actual assembly in an abandoned warehouse but all work was done under Gang super-vision. The sunshield was classified 'most secret,' as the surprise element it provided would be lost if the Germans learned the British were planning to disguise tanks as trucks. To ensure total secrecy, all production work was done by enlisted personnel rather than civilian labour, and everyone participating in the project was confined to the factory area. Egyptian nationals were not permitted in the vicinity, and anyone caught nearby was interned. As Maskelyne's sunshields and Frank Knox's track erasers came off the assembly line, they were packed onto trucks and driven forward.

Out on the Blue, preparations for the Battleaxe offensive were already in progress. Each night tank groups gathered at prearranged points, or laagers, and lined up to be fitted with sunshields. Steel handles were welded to both sides and above both tracks, and an apparatus was tailored to each tank. Crews were taught how to manipulate the disguise and were required to practise discarding it until they could do so in less than forty-five seconds.

Once the fitting and training were completed, the sunshield was folded and attached to the rear of the tank. Strict orders were given that it was not to be mentioned, not even in casual conversation. Wireless and teletype operators were forbidden to refer to it.

While the crews were busy learning how to operate the disguises, and stocking their tanks with sufficient food and water and a full store of ammunition, the rest of Western Desert Force was getting ready for the battle.

The Royal Air Force increased the number of reconnaissance flights over enemy-held territory, trying to piece together a picture of Rommel's disposition.

Military policemen made camp on the fringe of the desert and practised setting up thin corridors, marked by flags, through which they would direct armour and infantry at prescribed intervals.

Supply and transport vehicle drivers tuned their engines and changed sand filters. Spare tyres were checked. Summer celestial maps were packed for night navigation on the desert. Unnecessary trips were curtailed to conserve fuel supplies. A brisk market in salvaged German water tins sprang up, as the well-constructed jerrycans were much more desirable than the leaky British models.

During the second week of June infantry companies began moving out of rear camps into forward areas. Most of the troopers wrote long letters to relatives and left them with chaplains – to be delivered in the event of their capture or death. Rifles were broken down and oiled daily, and cloth plugs were kept in the barrels in a futile effort to keep out sand. Bandages were distributed, more to prevent insect bites from becoming infected than to serve in case of battle wounds. Three days' hardtack and salt tablets were issued. Ammunition belts were filled. Betting pools on the day and hour the attack would be launched were established.

Medics prepared their medical kits. Hospital vans and ambulances quietly moved into position, being careful to remain out of sight of the troops. Hospital stations in the rear stocked a full blood supply and prepared their operating rooms.

In the Egyptian cities normal life continued, although merchants stocked up and every car owner filled his fuel tank and reserve cans. Rumours about the impending attack increased, and Dudley Clarke's A-Force agents planted additional stories to confuse their enemy counterparts. Among the mass of intelligence passed along to Axis agents was the actual date and objectives of Battleaxe, in expectation it would be dismissed along with other false information.

The enemy was also active. In the desert, Afrika Korps feverishly salvaged long-abandoned Italian weapons and stockpiled supplies. Meanwhile, in an attempt to prevent the British from completing resupply operations, the full might of the Luftwaffe was brought against Alexandria harbour. Throughout the night of Wednesday, June

4, bomber squadrons blasted the harbour and surrounding area. One hundred and seventy people were killed and two hundred wounded in this raid. Two nights later the bombers returned, killing another 230 people and seriously damaging the harbour. The following day a mass evacuation of the area began and more than forty thousand people were moved to safer districts.

The men of the Camouflage Section watched enviously as other units prepared to take an active part in Operation Battleaxe. Their own role in the offensive had been reduced to checking finished sunshields for defects, a task that required little time or effort and occasional trips into the desert to supervise repairs of damaged frames or help instruct tank crews in their use. Jasper tried to keep his men busy while he lobbied at Gray Pillars for another assignment, but all of his contacts at headquarters were busy doing the vast amount of paperwork needed to start a battle. His only release from the frustration of being surrounded by the war without feeling part of it was his magic. He immersed himself in the show and, for at least a few hours each night, was almost able to forget about the situation. The Gang worked with him, designing, building and painting props and sets. Dates for the variety show had not been announced, although it was to run at least a week.

Saturday nights were the most difficult for him. At home, the Saturday-night performance had always been the most exciting of the week. Audiences came in a weekend party mood. The other acts on the bill seemed sharper. Occasionally, there was a party to attend, but most often he and Mary would take a leisurely stroll alone, perhaps stopping for something light to eat or drink, but mostly just enjoying each other.

On Saturday night, June 14, he was alone in the Cairo flat he'd rented but rarely slept in since setting up in Abbassia. His old stickered prop trunk had arrived by American steamer in late May, but had lain unopened as he worked on the sunshield. The trunk was stuffed with the props for a hundred illusions. His black cape with its handy secret pockets was neatly folded and ready for use. The Linking Rings were there. Linked. He found sets of wooden balls and steel balls and hollow balls, decks of cards, and strings, and magic slates upon which 'spirit' writing would mystically appear, and hand exercisers, two coin boxes for small sleights with money, sets of dice of different colours and sizes, more rope, scissors, straight magnets and curved magnets and thick and thin magnets, two specially altered opera hats, handcuffs, dozens of handkerchiefs, a rolled-up copy of the *Observer* dated

January 14, 1940 (although he could not remember why that had been packed), and a stack of magic wands taped together.

He pulled one of the wands loose and held it in his right hand. And then tapped it lightly on the side of the trunk. And then waved it through the air, waved it more, faster, in sweeping circles. And he closed his eyes and felt terribly lonely.

That same night Mike Hill was sitting in the centre of a loud drinking group bunched into a safe corner of the Sweet Melody Club, Cairo's most raucous bar, telling his favourite joke: 'These three Jerries were out on the Blue in a Volks when their engine goes *kaput*. First one says, "Listen up, lads, I'll unhook the radiator and carry it along, then if it gets too hot we can drink the water." Then the second one says, "I'll take the hubcaps. That way if it gets too hot we can hold them over our heads to make shade." . . .'

Bill Robson tipped back his chair against the barbed-wire fencing that had been erected to protect the band from carelessly thrown bottles and soldiers and sipped his beer. With Hill in good form, it would be a while before anyone else could speak. Nails Graham leaned forward to hear the rest of the joke. This was the Army as he expected it to be, good fellows sharing drink and a story after a day's hard work, and he vowed to remember the feeling of the night. Even Jack Fuller had tagged along. Although he would never admit it, the army veteran was beginning to enjoy being part of Maskelyne's crazy group. At the least, the experience would provide him with a wealth of stories to warm winter nights around the regimental fireplace.

They'd been joined by some cocky Desert Rats, some wounded sappers, and a bunch of the less priggish men and women from NAAFI, the soldiers' canteen organization.

'. . . so the third one thinks a bit and says, "Okay, I'll unbolt the doors and carry them." The other chaps look at him like he's daft, and the first one asks him why he would do that. So he tells him, "That way, if it gets too hot, I can roll down the windows!" '

Everyone laughed hard, though most of them had heard the joke before. But that was the mood of the early night.

In the background, a lusty row was coming to a furious finish, almost drowning out the band's rackety version of 'Over the Rainbow.' Neither brawler was throwing anything but fists, so they were left to fight themselves into exhaustion.

One of the NAAFI men told some ribald stories about Egyptian King Farouk and the claque of young British officers surrounding him. Then the whole club joined in boisterous rounds of 'Bless Them All,' and numerous toasts were raised to the crews of *Ark Royal*, *King George V*, *Rodney* and *Dorsetshire*, who had tracked and sunk the fearsome *Bismarck*. More sombre toasts were proposed for the heroic defenders of Crete, who had finally been overwhelmed by German paratroopers.

Much later, the spirit of the night turned on them. Rather than their voices growing louder and their promises bolder, as usually happened, an uncomfortable hush took over. Large groups splintered into fragments, and whispers of serious thoughts filled the bar. Many people drifted away by themselves. The band finished and packed up and no one noticed. It was one thing to battle Rommel; it was quite another to face one's own fears.

The scent of battle was thick in the air. It took over the night so completely that the more men drank, the more sober they became. No official word had been given, but everyone knew Battleaxe had finally begun.

Jasper found the telescoping fishing pole buried under a sack of black velvet cloth. He'd first used it to 'catch' a fish in the audience during his triumphant African tour of 1930. One night in South Africa, he remembered, his performance of Western magic had been halted by a deluge of huge hailstones, and a Zulu witch doctor appeared in his dressing room to accuse him of stealing the storm. The man demanded payment and, when rejected, cast a killing curse. Jasper had been forced to live with it. He laid the fishing pole next to the magnets.

As he picked up the collapsible birdcage frame he realized someone was watching him from the doorway. He didn't hear anyone, or see anyone, but he absolutely knew someone was there.

Frank Knox cleared his throat. As Jasper stood up, the professor apologized, 'I haven't been here long. I was just...'

'It's all right. I was just going through some old things. Come in.'

Knox remained motionless in the doorway, as if held in place by some great weight. 'They moved out earlier this evening,' he said. 'It's started.'

This was usually the way news of the war came to those people in the middle of it.

FIVE

A crescent moon hooked into the desert sky provided just enough light to silhouette dark shapes moving about the infantry staging area. A total blackout was in effect as Wavell's troops awaited orders to move out. Occasionally, pieces of equipment banged together, or someone slapped at an insect, or out in the darkness a pye-dog yelped, but otherwise the desert seemed unnaturally quiet. No one slept. Soldiers sat in small groups checking their weapons or blackening their pale skin with damp charcoal so they might better fade into the night. They spoke in whispers and mostly about the battle. The men who had been under fire reassured those going into action for the first time, 'If you make it through the first fifteen minutes your chances of making it all the way go up fifty per cent.'

Sergeants walked among their squads inspecting packs and canteens and offering salt pills and encouragement. 'See you in Tripoli,' was the good-luck wish.

By nature, the tankers were more fatalistic. The sunshields had been in place over the hulls for two days as Western Desert Force moved into position to attack. The tanks would lead the offensive at dawn, by which time the disguises would have been discarded.

Although no one could have known it at the time, the weeks of top-secret preparation were all for naught. Throughout the day, German wireless operators in communications vans on the desert had been intercepting uncoded transmissions between British headquarters and forward units indicating that the attack was to be launched that night. Initially, the incredulous operators refused to believe that the British would so carelessly signal their plans, but as the day progressed it became increasingly clear that Western Desert Force was preparing to go into action. Rommel ordered Afrika Korps put on full alert.

General Wavell had postponed the attack as long as possible, but finally submitted to Churchill's blistering demands. Earlier that evening he had signalled the War Office in London, 'I think it is right to inform you that the measure of success that will attend this operation

is in my opinion doubtful,' then reluctantly ordered his field officers
to commence operations.

The objectives of Battleaxe were similar to those of Brevity. Wavell
hoped to dislodge Afrika Korps from the vital access passes to the
desert plateau, but then he planned to move forward and relieve the
Tobruk garrison. On paper his army enjoyed numerical superiority
over the enemy, but he knew this was misleading. Western Desert
Force had not been given enough time to properly outfit the newly
arrived tank force for desert conditions or to instruct their crews in
the rudiments of this special kind of warfare.

At precisely 1:45 A.M., June 15, the silence of the desert night was
shattered by a series of high-pitched whistles. Orders to 'mount up'
echoed down the line. Thousands of soldiers stood up and shook the
dampness out of their bodies, then climbed into the back of ten-ton
transports for the drive to the battlefield.

Eleventh Indian Infantry, reinforced with a squadron of 4th
Armoured tanks, was to sweep up the coast and break through at
Halfaya Pass, then proceed toward the small port of Sollum. Fourth
Armoured's remaining tanks were to join 4th Indian's artillery and
22nd Guards (Motorized) to take Fort Capuzzo, then turn right and
join 11th Indian for the attack on Sollum. Seventh Armoured was to
protect the left flank by engaging enemy tanks in the Hafid Ridge
area.

In the rugged cliffs overlooking Halfaya Pass, at Fort Capuzzo, and
in outposts surrounding Hafid Ridge, firmly emplanted German and
Italian gunners waited patiently.

The British advance progressed smoothly through the night. Occasional contact was made with enemy patrols, but headquarters still
believed surprise was possible.

Just after dawn, Rommel's 88mm antiaircraft crews hidden in the
stony ridges at Halfaya Pass watched a long column of British tanks
materialize out of an early-morning haze. Captain Wilhelm Bach,
commanding these gun positions, sternly cautioned his troops not to
open fire until all the enemy tanks were caught in the trap. 'Lots of
time yet,' the potbellied former Lutheran pastor reminded them.

The tank column paused cautiously at the mouth of the pass, then
rumbled forward. The sunshield disguises had been removed before
sunrise and secured to the hulls. The drivers carefully maintained a
safe distance between tanks, and it was nearly 9 A.M. when the last
Matilda entered Halfaya Pass. At 9:15, Squadron Leader Major C. G.
Miles in the lead tank radioed to headquarters the code phrase 'Pink

spots,' meaning the advance was proceeding without opposition. After finishing that transmission Miles put down his microphone and said balefully to his driver, 'Looks like we've got Rommel right where we want him. Anywhere else but here.' A few seconds later he was dead.

Pastor Bach's 88s opened fire at nearly point-blank range, turning the pass into a bloody shooting gallery.

Within minutes eleven of Miles's dozen tanks were burning. A second squad rushed to their aid and got hung up between a minefield and the deadly accurate antiaircraft cannons. Indian Infantry tried to fight their way to the gun positions, but took heavy casualties, and many soldiers were forced to take cover behind the sunbaked rocks at the foot of the cliffs. They lay there throughout the day in 120-degree heat, watching the horror. A third attack was mounted and arrogantly ripped apart. The fourth attempt to storm the German batteries failed. The fifth was ruthlessly shattered by Bach's murderous guns. By nightfall the pass was a giant cake bedecked with flaming candles. A thick cloud of acrid smoke hung over the battlefield, burning the eyes of the survivors as they walked or crawled out of the pass. On that sunny day in June, the legend of Hellfire Pass was born.

At Hafid Ridge, another battery of German 88s stopped Creagh's 7th Armoured, but 4th Armoured successfully smashed into Fort Capuzzo, then beat off a furious counterattack while 22nd Guards dug into the hillocks.

Maskelyne's Camouflage Section spent the day lolling around the main tent, as if it were their connection to the battle. Working was impossible. The men released their nervous energy walking briskly about the area, arguing nonsense, chain-smoking and raising hopeful soft-drink toasts.

'Nothing yet,' Fuller announced late in the afternoon after sweeping through Cairo to collect the latest batch of rumours.

'You think being in battle makes you a better man?' Hill asked wondering if he was missing something important by sitting safely in the Basin.

Graham was carving a block of wood into a model aircraft. 'If you survive, I suppose it does,' he decided.

Knox wasn't sure. 'Perhaps it gives you a surge of self-confidence, but as for anything lasting ...' He shook his head.

Robson wondered about the question. 'Think you'd prefer to be out there getting shot at?'

Hill shrugged. 'Maybe.'

Townsend looked at him dubiously, and laughed. 'C'mon, Hill...'

'I don't know. I'm just feeling sort of funny, you know. I mean, here I am, sipping pop and watching the sun set, safe as the King at a fancy-dress ball, and just a few miles away ten thousand Rats are eating sand for dinner. Those that are still alive, that is.' He stared into the ground. 'Doesn't seem right, that's all.'

Maskelyne was tamping some Egyptian tobacco into his pipe. 'We've all got our roles to play,' he said, but inside he knew exactly what Private Hill was feeling.

By the morning of June 16 Rommel had learned from intercepted wireless transmissions that Wavell had thrown everything he had into the first day's fighting, and that nearly half of Western Desert Force's two hundred tanks had been destroyed or had broken down. He was therefore free to play his own hand, and he ordered his reserves into the battle. At Fort Capuzzo, the dug-in British knocked out fifty of 4th Panzer's eighty tanks in less than six hours, but 5th Light broke through at Hafid Ridge and threatened to encircle the entire attacking army. Wavell flew to the front.

Battleaxe was in disarray. Seventh Armoured had been reduced to twenty-five tanks. Almost all communications systems were down, and those few messages that got through were read with delight by Rommel. Early on the seventeenth, 4th Indian commander Major General F. W. Messervy, unable to contact headquarters and believing his own position at Fort Capuzzo untenable, decided to withdraw. This action enabled most of Western Desert Force to escape Rommel's rapidly closing pincers. Wavell later congratulated him on this decision, but suggested he should have waited for official permission.

The Battleaxe disaster cost the British ninety-nine tanks, thirty-three aircraft and over one thousand casualties. It also dealt a severe blow to morale. The shattered Matildas were no match for the emplanted 88s, and careless communications had robbed Western Desert Force of any chance for surprise. As battle-weary troops piled into rear camps, and later into the Delta cities, they spoke only of the genius Rommel. Once again, stories of his *Fingerspitzengefühl*, his sixth sense, spread throughout Egypt. A corporal who had taken a bullet in the shoulder during the battle for the Capuzzo military cemetery told Townsend, 'He just knew every bloody move we made before we made it. We couldn't even go to the loo without finding him there to flush it.' The General Staff, fearing the consequences of sending already demoralized troops back into battle believing the enemy was led by

an invincible commander possessing superhuman powers, launched an
intensive campaign designed to halt the deification of Erwin Rommel.
Planted stories attempted to destroy the myth of the Desert Fox by
publicizing his human frailties. Some were complete fabrications, while
others were based loosely on facts. General Rommel did suffer from
rheumatism, for example, but the extent of this malady was grossly
exaggerated to create the desired effect.

'It is impossible to describe the awe in which the men here hold
that Rommel,' Jasper wrote in his nightly letter to Mary.

They firmly believe he is some sort of superman, capable of
incredible feats of magic. If anyone tries to dispute this, that man
is risking a fight. When I hear such talk I cannot help but think
how my grandfather would have laughed at them. 'Magic,' that old
man would say to them, 'I'll give you magic. I'll give you the birth
of a child or the smell of a rose or the setting of the sun, that's
magic. But a soldier in the field? Skill and preparation, skill and
preparation.' As for myself, I believe he is undoubtedly a tactical
genius, probably superior to our best generals, but the family has
debunked too many self-aggrandizing charlatans for me to believe
any man has real magical powers.

She wrote back to him that the newspapers in England were 'full
of talk about Rommel. The way they write about him, one would
think he was leading our boys rather than the Nazis. Wouldn't a bit
of real magic be wonderful, though? Then you could wave your wand
and it would be all over and we would be together again. Does
Rommel have a wife?'

Maskelyne had no time to argue about Rommel's powers, however,
as he and his men were too busy trying to make an entire harbour
disappear. Major Barkas arrived at the Camouflage Section on June
18, even before the full extent of the Battleaxe defeat was known. He
was unshaven and his eyes were swollen, making it obvious that he
hadn't had much sleep in some time. As head of Middle Eastern
camouflage, the major was responsible for keeping a widespread,
loosely structured organization productive, and was managing to do it
by personality and pluck. But the job was taking its toll.

Hot coffee was served, real stuff Hill had appropriated rather than
the usual ersatz mud, and Barkas stared into his mug for a long time
without speaking. Then, pushing out of his mind the memories of the
past few days with a deep sigh, he squared his shoulders and went to

work. 'It's bad,' he said forthrightly. 'We took a real pasting out there. Those 88s ...' He paused and began slipping back into Battleaxe, but caught hold of the moment. 'Well, our boys got chewed up badly. We don't have a thing that can stand up against those guns. And Rommel...'

Jasper nodded. He knew.

'Your shields worked fine, much as they were used. It wasn't them, it was Rommel. He seemed to know everything we were going to do. Every move. It was quite an incredible show, actually.'

'*Fingerspitzengefühl?*'

The major managed a feeble smile. 'More likely damned good intelligence people, and sloppy work on our part.' He paused to sip some coffee. 'Don't worry about your shields, they'll be useful later on, mark my words. This isn't the end, you know.'

'Of course it isn't.'

'The problem is right now. That's why I'm here.' In a corner of the tent Maskelyne had erected a sand-table map, intending to use it as a miniature desert on which he could test camouflage ideas. Barkas set down his mug and walked over to the table. 'Look here.'

Jasper joined him.

'We know it'll be some time before Rommel is strong enough to move again. He's got his own wounds to lick, you know. If we can replenish our people before he can get his vitals across the desert, we've got him. But if he can organize a big push first, he'll be dining at Shepheards. It's simply become a race for supply. The key to it all is right here,' Barkas continued, sliding his finger through the sand to a tiny red-white-and-blue Union Jack flying on a toothpick near the edge of the table. 'Here. Alexandria harbour.' He jabbed his finger deep into the sand. 'They know how desperately we need to keep it open. They've been bombing it pretty regularly; but with the entire campaign in the balance, who knows what they'll drop on us. Air Defence is moving as many ack-ack guns as can be spared up there, and the RAF'll provide whatever additional cover they can, but we've got to give it our best effort.'

'You want us to try to camouflage it.'

Barkas looked at him grimly. 'I want your people to hide that place so well that even Farouk in a bloody rowboat couldn't find it.'

Jasper playfully swirled his index finger through the sand. Alexandria harbour was by far the largest stage on which any magician had ever performed. During his career he'd vanished motorcycles and women and boxes and even the occasional elephant, but an entire harbour was quite a different matter. And he would have no false walls, trapdoors or black velvet curtains to make it possible. The challenge thrilled him. 'I think we can give it a go.'

Barkas smiled for the first time all morning at this show of confidence. 'Good show. Harbour Command wants you people up there straight away. I've arranged transport.'

'You knew I'd agree?'

'I knew you couldn't resist.'

Early the next day Jasper and the Magic Gang stood on a bluff overlooking the sprawling harbour. Crammed into an area about the size of a small country village were freighters and transports and patrol boats and barges, tugs, tenders and huge cranes, flatbed trucks and container trucks, cargo-hauling equipment and mountains of crates, storehouses, low-slung office buildings, garages, even temporary housing for thousands of labourers. And guarding the entrance to this bustling harbour was the giant lighthouse on Pharos Island, the direct descendant of one of the Seven Wonders of the Ancient World.

Concealing an area this large and this active from the Luftwaffe seemed like an impossible task, even given the fact that the enemy bombers had thus far restricted their attacks to night-time.

After a tour of the harbour, the Gang set up operations in a Nissen hut and spent the day trading fanciful concepts. Ted Graham suggested that large sheets of canvas be stretched over many of the ships and buildings so they would fade into the harbour waters, as had been done with some success in England. 'We'll change the visual pattern of the place.'

Jasper turned him down. 'Our job isn't to camouflage parts of it. Somehow we're supposed to hide the whole thing.'

Cartoonist Bill Robson, who thoroughly enjoyed meandering through the realm of the impossible and absurd, wondered if giant mirrors could be used to confuse enemy bombardiers.

'They might,' Maskelyne agreed, 'until they were shattered by the concussion of the first bomb.'

'Then we'd really be in for a streak of poor luck,' Hill pointed out.

Although usable concepts often originated in this type of bull session, nothing practical came out of the meeting. Dinner was served in the hut so that the work need not be interrupted, but at 10 P.M., just as Radio Belgrade began its popular nightly broadcast of Lale Andersen singing the German version of 'Lili Marlene,' enemy Junkers 88s and Savoia S-79 bombers roared low out of the desert. Air raid sirens screamed into the night. Within seconds thousands of men were dashing to their posts, or into shelters, many of them pulling on their clothes and helmets as they scrambled to safety. Every light in the harbour was extinguished. Some of the ships at anchor got up steam in case they had to flee the harbour. A squadron of RAF Hurricanes, bolstered by American P-40 Tomahawks, flew up to meet the Luftwaffe. Batteries of Bofors guns began pocking the sky with antiaircraft fire even before the bombers were visible.

The door to the Gang's Nissen hut swung open and a corporal leaned in. 'This way, please, gentlemen,' he said sternly, and led them to a deep slit trench. They could not see the harbour from this safe position, but it didn't matter. The planes scrapped directly over their heads, in a sky coldly lit by a barrage of pale-yellow flares, and searchlights that etched highways of silver light into the night. One of the Italian Savoias was hit by ack-ack, but escaped into high covering clouds.

Much of the thunder of the enemy bombs was smothered by the harbour waters, but enough of them struck solid targets to make the earth shudder thousands of yards from their point of impact.

'Some show,' Robson yelled above the din. In the excitement his glasses kept sliding down his nose.

Hill shouted right back, 'If you like this one, you should've been in London.'

Seen from a bomber cockpit, Alexandria harbour was an easily distinguishable target. A pathfinder group homed in on the lighthouse beacon, which was visible from deep in the desert, then followed the familiar Egyptian coastline and lit the harbour with incendiary bombs. Succeeding waves dropped their deadly loads into the brightly burning fires. Except for the pesky British fighters and persistent AA gunners, it was a relatively simple hit-and-run job.

The raid lasted only twenty minutes. Two warehouses, six trucks and a crane were destroyed. An unoccupied office building took a direct hit. Two small boats were capsized by near-misses. A pier was badly damaged by fire. A pile of coffins waiting to be loaded on a transport for the voyage home was blown to bits. The fires were quickly brought under control but would not be extinguished for many hours.

Within the Nissen hut a coal fire had been stoked into life inside a potbellied stove. The Gang huddled around it like a group of Newcastle fishermen on a winter's eve and continued trying to find a way to camouflage the harbour. Jasper sat apart, at the only table in the room, examining topographical survey maps supplied by Royal Engineers. It was near midnight when he leaned back in his chair and announced, 'All right, I've got it.'

'Well,' Knox said huffily, 'it's about time.'

The men gathered around the table.

'To begin with,' Maskelyne said, 'the harbour is simply too big for us to do anything with it. We can't cover it up. We can't disguise it. And we can't hide it. There's only one solution left to us, isn't there?'

No one responded.

'We've got to move it.'

Hill smacked his forehead with his palm. 'Of course,' he quipped. 'Now, why didn't I think of that?'

Jasper expertly squeezed every drop of curiosity out of the Gang. While they waited for him to explain his incredible solution, he patted the large pockets of his uniform jersey in search of a match and, when he failed to find one, simply snapped his fingers into flame and lit his pipe. Knox had noticed that Maskelyne played his small tricks only when feeling quite confident.

Once the pipe was lit he settled back into his chair, crossed his legs comfortably, and began his explanation. 'Around the turn of the century my grandfather introduced an extremely effective levitation at the Egyptian Theatre. In a burst of smoke, he'd appear to fly off the stage right up to the crystal chandelier, where he'd perch and answer questions from the audience.' He paused to savour the aromatic tobacco. 'Can anyone guess how it was done?'

'Fairy dust?' Robson ventured.

Frank Knox had been doing some reading on magic. 'Transposition?'

'Substitution. Under the smoke cover a wire-frame dummy was sprung from a trapdoor and travelled up a very thin guide wire to the chandelier. Questions were answered through a rudimentary speaker system. Because the dummy was dressed in exactly the same suit as my grandfather, and rose from the same place he was standing, the audience believed it was him. I think we can adapt that principle to this situation.'

He leaned over the survey map and tapped Alexandria harbour with his pipe stem. 'Here's the harbour. And over here,' he continued, moving the pipe a few inches across the map, 'about a mile down the coast, is Maryūt Bay. Look how the shoreline curves. Not all that different from Alex, is it?'

Fuller peered over his shoulder. 'From eight thousand feet it might be hard to tell them apart.'

Graham nodded in agreement. 'Particularly at night.'

'And especially if the RAF is on their tails and the AA guns are popping away at them,' Jasper added.

'What about the lighthouse?' Knox asked. 'That's one bloody big can to move.'

'We don't have to move anything, that's the beauty of this plan. All we've got to do is lay down a network of ground lights and structures at Maryūt resembling those at Alex. When we know Jerry's on the way, we just turn out the harbour lights, turn them on at Maryūt Bay, and blow off some explosives we've planted. The fires'll draw them like bees to honey.' Similar decoy targets, called Q sites, had been created by Sir John Turner of the RAF to lure German bombers away from airfields in England. Turner's crews laid parallel rows of lamps a few thousand yards away from actual airstrips to replicate runway lights. Later in the war Turner developed the much more elaborate K sites to protect factories and larger airfields during daylight raids, but in June 1941 nothing of the magnitude proposed by Maskelyne had ever been considered. Unlike isolated runways, which looked alike when viewed from the air at night, the city of Alexandria and its vast harbour were unmistakable.

Jack Fuller pointed that out. 'And what about the next morning, then,' he asked, 'when the photo-recce people come over for a look-see?'

'That's the pay-off, Jack. When the audience heard my grandfather's voice answering their questions, they were absolutely convinced he was really sitting up there on the chandelier. And as long as Jerry's spotters see some rubble around Alex, they'll be convinced they hit the right target. We'll simply give them rubble. Peter Proud and his boys made it work at Tobruk. We can do it here.'

Philip Townsend was dubious. 'Frank's right. What about the lighthouse?'

'What about it? It's nothing more than a big light at the end of a stick. From the air it's impossible to determine how high it is. It's just a matter of perspective. We can work it all out.'

Graham had been staring at the map for some tine. 'I suppose we could rig up some wooden superstructures,' he said, but without real enthusiasm. 'And maybe throw some moonlight shadows to screw up their perspective. At night, while they're being shot at ...' he glanced at Hill and Robson, and shrugged. 'It's about all we've got.'

Robson chuckled. 'I still think we should try fairy dust.'

By morning, the Gang had sketched a rough set of plans. They were presented to the Harbour Defence commander, who was admittedly disappointed at the lack of magic in the concept, but finally agreed to its implementation. Approximately two hundred Engineer troops and labourers were assigned to the project.

The following day the desolate area surrounding Maryūt Bay was sealed off, and construction of the decoy harbour began. Using night reconnaissance photographs as their blueprint, the Engineers replicated the ground-light pattern of Alexandria harbour by staking hundreds of electric lanterns into the sand and mud, then wiring them as if solving an elaborate connect-the-dots puzzle. Plywood sheds of varying sizes and shapes were raised under carpenter Graham's direction, some of them packed with explosive charges that would emit flash and smoke similar to that of German aerial bombs when detonated.

Hill worked with Royal Navy personnel, supervising the erection of a small fleet of canvas ship superstructures. Nautical signal lamps were hung on these dummies, and lighted wooden stakes were planted in the bay, to create the impression that numerous craft were lying at anchor.

Robson and Fuller created a working 'lighthouse' by mounting vehicle searchlights on a plywood slab supported by six stilt legs. An ingenious Engineer electrician rigged these lights to a timer that switched them on and off in order, thus making the platform appear to be rotating. Like the real Pharos Lighthouse, 'Robson's Pole,' as it was called, would be shut down when enemy bombers approached, but not until their pilots had ample time to take bearings on it.

As producer of this show, Maskelyne was involved in all aspects. He seemed to pop up everywhere, supervising, solving problems, redesigning props, pushing slow workers. 'It's not much different than staging a full production at the Royale,' he said to Knox as they drove back to the real harbour one morning. 'The show's all planned, now what we've got to do is get the scenery made and raised and the performers rehearsed.'

Knox stayed right with him, occasionally offering a bit of advice. Maskelyne was never happier than when totally enveloped in work, the professor realized, and wondered if it was because the magician enjoyed the work so much or because it kept him too busy to think.

All of the lights and detonators were connected to a master console that Maskelyne and Knox would operate from atop Pharos Lighthouse. Although the decoy layout was in fact much smaller than the actual harbour, great care had been taken to maintain the same size ratios between identifiable landmarks as existed at Alex. As long as these ratios were consistent, it would be almost impossible for enemy pilots to notice the size difference.

Townsend was in charge of 'wrecking' the real harbour. Actual rubble was piled up in numerous places and covered with tarpaulins, to be unveiled for German photo intelligence. In addition, work crews manufactured new 'wreckage' to impress enemy observers. Stage-scenery bomb craters with deep charcoal sides were painted on canvas, and similar canvas drops were prepared to be hung from buildings to simulate damage. Truck and jeep hulks were dragged from the scrap pile and positioned near the dummy craters, and papier-mâché bricks and rocks were strewn on streets and rooftops. In the harbour, splintered beams were put aboard real ships, and three realistic wooden masts rose out of the murky waters, artificial gravestones for nonexistent vessels.

To complete the illusion, Jasper wanted the searchlights and anti-aircraft batteries protecting Alexandria harbour moved up to his decoy. Colonel O. P. Rutledge, of Harbour Defence, grudgingly surrendered most of the lights, but refused to hand over his few Bofors guns. 'There's nothing up there except sand and muck,' he protested. 'You can't really expect me to withdraw my gunners from Alex to protect a swamp!'

The guns were absolutely necessary, Maskelyne insisted. 'If Jerry doesn't receive his usual welcome, he'll know something's up. In the theatre we say, give the audience what they expect and they'll go home satisfied. That's what we've got to do here.'

'I understand all that,' Rutledge said, 'but my hands are tied.' A rather large gap between his front teeth caused him to sizzle his sibilants, making some words sound like incoming bombs. 'This is the most important harbour in the entire Middle East and it's my job to protect it. If something goes wrong with your plan ... and it can happen, you know, a thousand things can go wrong. Suppose some Egyptian caught wind of it and knew a chap with a transmitter? Well, then, I'd be the bloody fool, wouldn't I? I'd be known forever as that silly clod who protected an empty beach while the harbour was destroyed.'

'On the other hand,' Jasper countered in a voice so soft with promise that Rutledge had to strain to hear him, 'you could be known as the hero of Alexandria.'

The colonel frowned. His experience and his nature railed against this sort of risk-taking. Go by the book, he had been taught at Sandhurst, that's why it had been written. Follow procedure. Cover your tracks. But his other self, his hidden adventurous self, the spunky desert rat he felt sure would emerge if given the proper chance – that part of him found this opportunity for derring-do hard to resist. If he let it slip by, he knew he'd face a coward in the mirror each morning for the rest of his life. 'You understand the consequences, don't you? If this fails, they'll swarm all over the bloody harbour and we won't be able to do anything but wave fly swats at them. And if they close up this harbour for any length of time we might just as well invite Rommel for 'downers at Shepheards.'

Maskelyne was fully aware of the consequences. If the German bombers did not take his bait Alexandria harbour would be devastated and the British supply line would be shattered. The Suez Canal and billions of gallons of Persian oil would be within Rommel's grasp. The decoy was much like a pebble tossed into a still pond, for if it failed the ripples it created would be felt around the world. 'It won't fail,' he said.

Reluctantly, Rutledge agreed to move half his antiaircraft equipment and personnel to Maryūt Bay, and to order those crews remaining at Alex not to fire unless directly attacked. The ack-ack guns would remain in place around Alex until the decoy was ready to be put into service; then after dark, they would be moved up the coast.

That business finished, the setting of the stage continued. The Gang worked through every night, pausing only to watch enemy bombers make the 10 P.M. run, and napped during the day as long as the heat and the flies permitted. By Sunday, June 22, most of the scenery was in place. The ground lights had been laid down. Graham's sheds were built and loaded. Hill's 'navy' of canvas superstructures floated sluggishly but remained above water. Townsend's damage looked believably smashed. Robson's pole swayed precariously almost thirty feet above water level. In daylight, Maryūt looked like a shantytown, but Jasper was certain it would pass as one of the world's busiest harbours under the velvet cover of night.

Although the Gang was safely isolated in the guarded Maryūt Bay compound, they could not escape the devastating Battleaxe reports. The offensive had been a bloody failure. Hospitals and aid stations were overwhelmed by casualties. Rumours were spreading that Rommel was preparing for the final drive to Cairo, and once again shopkeepers dusted off their German signs.

To further complicate the situation, the resounding defeat suffered by Western Desert Force, coupled with the temporarily successful military-backed *coup d'état* in nearby Iraq, had aroused the hopes of

Egyptian nationalists. The Delta was shaken by anti-British demonstrations and minor bombings, and the possibility of a full-scale revolt against King Farouk and the battered Commonwealth army was very real.

Prime Minister Churchill, furious at Wavell's repeated failures against Rommel, sacked him. 'I have come to the conclusion,' he wired the fallen hero, 'that public interest will best be served by the appointment of General Auchinleck to relieve you in command of armies of Middle East.'

'The Prime Minister's quite right,' Wavell replied stoically when he received this message. 'This job needs a new eye and a new hand.' Believing his moment in history to be finished, he dutifully accepted reassignment to Auchinleck's relatively quiet Indian Army command.

Jack Fuller was one of the few men working at Maryūt Bay who had been with Wavell from the beginning of the North African campaign. He was one of Wavell's Thirty Thousand and damned proud of it. 'He got a rum deal,' he complained bitterly. 'First they take all his men and equipment and ship it to Greece, then they expect him to fight the whole bloody German Army with tanks that don't work and fuzzy-cheeked platoons.' This was the only time Maskelyne ever heard the sergeant raise his voice against the service.

But Fuller's anger was not given time to come to full boil. Later that same afternoon the BBC interrupted its programming to announce that 120 German divisions, equipped with 3,200 tanks and 1,945 aircraft, had invaded Russia. The second front had been opened. Incredibly, Hitler had abandoned his non-aggression pact with Stalin less than two years after it had been sealed. 'The man's insane,' Hill insisted.

'No foolin', Mr. Holmes,' Townsend replied sarcastically, 'and whatever gave you that idea?'

Suddenly, the immediate future seemed brighter. The demands of the Russian front would undoubtedly force the Nazis to relieve some of the pressure in the Middle East. The confusing situation might even draw the reluctant Americans into the war. Everyone at Maryūt Bay had an opinion and wanted to voice it loudly, and their loud discussions gradually eased into work. By dark, the ground-light network at Maryūt Bay was ready to be tested. Maskelyne and Knox lugged the last of their heavy control equipment up the winding stairs of the old lighthouse to their command post. Although the lighthouse provided a sweeping view of both Alex harbour and Maryūt, it offered no protection from German bombers. 'Try to see the bright side of

it,' Jasper suggested to Knox. 'If our plan doesn't work, we won't
have to answer for it.'

Frank looked at him crossly. '*Our* plan?'

Soon after sundown an Auster was sent up to observe. Townsend
flew as spotter on the flight.

In the cramped lighthouse tower, Jasper stood in front of the
electric console like a maestro tuning up his orchestra. 'Ready?' he
asked Knox.

The professor looked at the complex array of buttons and levers
and shook his head in bewilderment. 'Ready as I'll ever be,' he said
reluctantly. 'I hope you know what everything's connected to. I'd hate
to saw off the limb I'm sitting on, if you know what I mean.'

'Oh, it's much simpler than it looks,' Jasper replied, then added, 'I
think.' With that, he took a deep breath to calm his nerves, then
pushed down a long steel handle. As if a huge black blanket had
suddenly been swirled over Alexandria harbour, it disappeared into
the night. A few isolated lights twinkled aboard ships lying at anchor,
but most of these were quickly extinguished for this 'blackout drill.'

'Well, that's all right, isn't it?' Knox said with great relief.

The city of Alexandria sparkled gaily in the distance, but the harbour
had ceased to exist.

'Lights,' Jasper commanded.

Frank worked his console. A few seconds later, just as if the entire
harbour had been picked up intact and deposited a mile down the
coast, the lights of the Maryūt Bay decoy burst into the night.

Jasper critically examined the display. 'What do you think?' he asked.

Knox paused. It looked far more realistic than he had believed
possible. 'An engraved invitation,' he replied, obviously impressed.

Townsend reported that the aerial view of the dummy was excellent.

Satisfied with the results, they shut down their equipment and
hurried down the lighthouse stairs to safety before the arrival of the
Luftwaffe Bomb Delivery Service. Without the antiaircraft guns and
searchlights in place the decoy could not be used.

Preparations were completed the next day. Townsend moved the
remainder of his new wreckage into place and showed the Engineer
labourers how he wanted it displayed. 'While they're bloody bombin'?'
one of them asked.

'While they're bombing.'

After dark, Rutledge's Bofors were transported to Maryūt Bay.
Maskelyne and Knox once again climbed to the top of Pharos
Lighthouse. Townsend and Fuller waited near the docks with the work

crew. Hill was safely ensconced in a slit trench at Maryūt, lord of the dummy navy. Nails Graham played nursemaid to tons of carefully planted high explosives. Robson sat next to a wireless operator at Alex harbour, ready to fill in wherever he was needed. The Gang spent the early part of the night cursing and shivering as the temperature dropped.

At 9:45 P.M. Jasper began scanning the dark skies. Ten o'clock came, and passed. The enemy bombers had not been sighted. 'They're late tonight,' he said nervously. 'That's a bit cheeky of them.'

'They'll be here,' Frank said reassuringly. 'They wouldn't want to miss the big show.'

By 10:30 Maskelyne was pacing in tight circles around the tiny observation tower, trying to guess why the nightly attack was late.

Knox tried to calm him. 'Just relax, Jay,' he said as he cleaned his spotless eyeglasses for the eighth time in the last forty-five minutes, 'There's nothing to worry about.'

Maskelyne was biting his fingernails at eleven o'clock. 'Look at me,' he snapped. 'It's a good thing Mary can't see me biting away at my hands. She'd give me what for.'

The bombers did not come that night. Maskelyne stared into the skies till long after midnight with a mixture of disappointment and pleasure. The performer inside him wanted the show to go on; the soldier was pleased at the reprieve. But the unexpected break in an established pattern made him anxious. Could the Germans have learned that some sort of trick awaited them? If they had...

'Maybe they think they've finished the job,' Frank suggested as they climbed down the long winding staircase.

'That'd be fine,' Jasper replied.

They took their places again at twilight on the twenty-fourth. But this time, just as Lale Andersen began her mournful love song, the enemy bomber flight was spotted by a Rat patrol on the desert. The planes were behind schedule, and approaching on a slightly altered course, but they were coming. The report was relayed to Maskelyne in the lighthouse tower. 'They're on the way,' he told Frank, and his body tingled with the excitement of an opening night. He slammed down the power lever. The harbour went dark almost instantly. 'Lights!' he shouted into the wireless.

Robson's decoy lighthouse came ablaze. Seconds later, the rest of the dummy harbour twinkled into life. Five antiaircraft searchlights began sweeping the sky.

Maskelyne and Knox waited in the darkness, barely breathing. A light breeze whipped up some whitecaps, but the real harbour was otherwise invisible. At that moment, Jasper couldn't help thinking about the lifetime of illusions that had gone wrong: he remembered the assistant who fell asleep inside the apparatus, the locks that jammed, strings that broke, the night he had appeared on Huey Green's radio show, *Magic on the Air*, when the box in which he had been locked failed to open and he was forced to bang and scream for help while Green covered for him by singing made-up verses of 'Fiddle My Diddle.'

His reverie was broken by the murderous drone of the enemy bombers. They came in a little lower than usual, sighting on the cloud-dimmed stars. They flew directly toward the real harbour, ignoring completely the brightly lit dummy. As soon as they were in sight Maskelyne and Knox began shutting down the lights at Maryūt Bay, just as if Alexandria harbour were blacking out for the raid. But the bombers remained on a true course, toward Alex.

In the cockpit of the point bomber, the flight leader was confused. The rapidly dying lights of Alexandria harbour beckoned to him, but according to his instruments they were not precisely where they were supposed to be. If he was to believe his compass, the entire harbour had been moved.

Jasper held his breath as the enemy bombers remained on course to the real harbour. 'They're confused,' he shouted to Knox, more hopefully than certain. Then, under his breath, he pleaded, 'Come on, you bloody sots, come on, take it, take it.'

'The ack-ack, Jay,' Frank yelled. 'Get 'em shooting.'

'Fire now,' Jasper screamed into his radio. 'Now. Now. Go ahead.' Almost immediately, the antiaircraft batteries surrounding Maryūt Bay began pounding away. Still, the bombers remained on course.

On the ground at the decoy Mike Hill was out of his slit trench waving his cap at the bombers. 'Over here, you dummies,' he was screaming. 'We're over here!'

The first salvo of antiaircraft fire further confused the flight leader. And seconds later a British fighter group was spotted coming in for a scrap. He had no more time to make a decision. Choosing to believe his eyes and ears rather than his instruments, he grabbed hold of his control stick and made a hard turn to starboard.

'He's taking it,' Frank said hesitantly. Then, louder, and with certainty, 'By gum, he's taking it!'

The rest of the enemy flight gracefully followed the leader into the turn. As they did, the RAF squadron jumped them. Instantly, machine-gun tracers began scratching the night. The bomber pilots bravely maintained their tight formation to the target, their gunners swatting at the pesky fighters. Suddenly a Junkers rose out of formation and peeled off, its engine smoking, and made for the safety of the Mediterranean. The other planes quickly filled the hole it left.

They began dropping their loads even before they were directly over the 'harbour.' As the first bombs blasted deep, harmless craters into the sand, Maskelyne and Knox took over. 'Now, Frank,' Jasper screamed, 'now!' The professor slammed down his levers so hard he shook off his glasses. For a long second, absolutely nothing happened. Then a series of staccato blasts jolted Maryūt Bay. Flames clawed into the air. Secondary eruptions thundered above the battle roar.

'Hey presto!' Jasper shouted as he gleefully played his console, but he was drowned out by the noise.

The second wave of Junkers and Savoias sighted on the flames. Hundreds of real bombs peppered Maskelyne's sandy 'stage.' Another enemy plane was hit, and this one twirled fatally into the bay.

Townsend's damage crews went to work as soon as the flight leader turned right. They raced through the narrow alleys at Alexandria harbour, pulling tarps off their rubble, spreading papier-mâché wreckage, scarring buildings with painted dropcloths, uncovering canvas craters.

At Maryūt Bay, bonfires ignited by Graham's explosive charges and fed by a pyre of dry timber made an enticing target for the succeeding waves of bombers. The raid lasted exactly thirty-three minutes.

The dummy harbour was nearly obliterated. Almost all of the lamps were shattered. Many of the sheds were completely destroyed, and those left standing were damaged. One of Hill's 'battleships' fell apart, but the remainder of his fleet survived the attack. Robson's lighthouse escaped unscathed.

The moment the last wave fled into the desert, the Engineers repair crews went to work. By morning the fires had been extinguished, sand had been thrown over the charred wreckage, and crews were at work replacing the destroyed scenery. Jerry would be returning that night, and the 'harbour' had to be ready for the next performance.

Townsend's crews had set the stage at Alex by dawn. Enemy reconnaissance planes arrived over the real harbour as expected and took high-altitude photographs. During this inspection, camouflage nets covered the decoy at Maryūt just in case an enemy observer glanced down the beach and noticed unusual activity.

The Gang piled into their Nissen hut at Alex in midmorning,

exhausted but exuberant. They began reliving the night in loud voices, but Jasper shut them up. 'So far we've done all right. But in the next few hours their photo experts are going to be examining the pictures they took this morning. If they're not perfect...'

The verdict would be delivered that night. A repeat attack on the decoy would prove that the deception was successful. But if German Intelligence detected a single false shadow in Townsend's damage display, they would be selecting their target much more carefully.

The Gang tried to sleep during the day.

The bombers were late that night, bursting out of a thin cloud cover just after Lord Haw Haw, the supercilious traitor, had finished twitting Western Desert Force about Operation Battleaxe, 'that silly affront to the genius of Rommel.'

Jerry didn't hesitate this time. The planes pounced on the decoy. They came in lower than usual, at dangerously slow speeds to increase their accuracy, and plastered the beach with tons of high explosives. It was the most ferocious attack yet. Jasper and Frank added to the pyrotechnics by blowing off Graham's packages.

By the time the bombers climbed back into the sheltering clouds, Maryūt Bay was a flaming wasteland pocked with massive craters. Ribbons of oil smoke swirled thousands of feet into the sky and blacked out the moon and the stars. Seen from the cockpit of a bomber thousands of feet into the air, it looked very much like hell.

Two Savoias went down.

It took all night and most of the following day to replace the damage.

The attackers came eight successive nights. The Engineers slaved through the days turning out brand new damage. To Hill's chagrin, his final 'destroyer' was sunk in the eighth raid.

That proved to be the last attack. Unexpectedly, the enemy seemed to lose interest in Alexandria harbour. For the next week Jasper and the Gang scanned the night skies, but the bombers never returned. British Intelligence did not know it at the time, but, as the rumours had predicted, Hitler had ordered Luftwaffe groups transferred from the desert to Europe and the Russian front.

Alexandria harbour was saved. Although Italian submarines would make a desperate attack a few months later, and enemy sabotage would continue throughout the war, this was the last massive effort to shut it down. Rommel had lost the battle of supply that week in June 1941. Eventually millions of tons of supplies would be safely landed at

Alexandria, enough to overwhelm the Desert Fox and his Afrika Korps.

The success of Maskelyne's transposition concept at Alexandria harbour proved that such decoy installations could be used on a far greater scale than ever imagined. The principles of light, shadow and dummy structures perfected by the Magic Gang would be used around the world to protect strategically important targets. Using these techniques, entire dummy army and navy bases as well as airfields were constructed in most battle theatres and major cities, causing the Luftwaffe to waste countless tons of bombs on beaches, meadows, lakes and pastures.

The Maryūt Bay illusion firmly established Jasper Maskelyne and his Magic Gang as an important, and quite unique, military entity. No one could figure precisely where the unit belonged in the table of organization; they were more than camoufleurs but less than engineers, they had nothing to do with supply or transportation and knew little about combat, but no longer did anyone question the value of a magician at war. Instead, brass hats whispered top secrets about the deeds of 'Maskelyne and his queer little group,' and took comfort that someone had finally outwitted the Fox.

SIX

The war in the desert slipped peacefully into the fiery summer. Out on the Blue the brutal sun baked the men and their fighting machines and made daytime combat almost impossible. A few minor clashes occurred, and were unimportant, because the fate of North Africa was being decided on the oceans. Massive supply convoys were battling submarine wolf packs in a desperate attempt to resupply the armies. It had become clear the army first able to sustain a major offensive would win the desert war. Ironically, in this topsy-turvy theatre, the Battleaxe defeat gave the British an advantage.

Rommel's victorious army had been reorganized as Panzer Group Africa and was stretched in a thin line across the desert, curling around the Tobruk blister like some venomous serpent, devouring supplies in Benghazi and digesting them fifteen hundred miles away, almost in Cairo.

Because the British had been beaten back to their Basin stronghold, their supply line was short and *matériel* was easily distributed. Prime Minister Churchill was determined to profit from Hitler's Russian obsession and ordered the newly designated Eighth Army trebled in size. The make-do days of Wavell's feisty Western Desert Force were over. Auchinleck demanded strict adherence to established military procedure and instituted rigorous desert training programmes. General Sir Alan Gordon Cunningham, who had made his reputation by driving the Italian Army out of East Africa in eight weeks, was made his subordinate.

The Magic Gang's performance at Alex harbour had helped establish the role of camoufleurs in the western desert, and Major Richard Buckley's people were busy on all fronts creating illusions, to hoodwink the enemy. Trapped inside Tobruk, Peter Proud had organized a three-hundred-man unit and managed to convince the Luftwaffe that the besieged city's vital water-purification plant had been destroyed. Wreckage was painted on the roof of the building and cracks were painted down the sides, cinder block debris was scattered over the entire area, and phoney bomb craters were dug. When the Junkers 88s came over the city Proud exploded smoke bombs to simulate direct hits, and when the smoke cleared a wrecked building was visible and reconnaissance pilots reported the plant damaged beyond repair.

South of Cairo, painter Stephen Sykes was constructing an entire railroad spur, complete with dummy campsites, cookhouses, shelter trenches and a dummy fifty-two-car train. His intention was to convince Rommel's Intelligence that a major British attack would be launched from this area. Metal tracks were fashioned from squashed jerrycans, and wooden railroad ties were made of plywood. Sykes had ingeniously compensated for a lack of materials by constructing the entire railroad at one-third normal size. Since there were no landmarks of known height in the area, German Intelligence had nothing with which to make a comparison; so as long as all the elements were in proper scale everything would look accurate when seen from the air.

Sykes's locomotive was made of rush matting set on a timber frame. A camp stove had been put inside to actually belch black smoke. One afternoon, a fierce windstorm picked up the locomotive and sent it skittering across the desert. His people chased it fifty miles before catching up to it, knowing that if Rommel saw a twenty-ton locomotive bouncing about the desert he would know something was afoot.

Other camoufleurs were performing less glamorous tasks. One group was painting giant murals showing an aerial view of houses, streets, even alleys, complete with proper shadows, that were to be stretched on poles eight feet above the ground to serve, literally, as cover for various strategic points. Many men were assigned to units in the field and were helping protect tanks and troops.

Now that Maskelyne's Camouflage Section had proven its capabilities under fire, they were deluged by requests for assistance. Every branch seemed to have an oddball problem that required Maskelyne's attention. Most of these requests were temporarily put aside, however, while the Magic Gang supervised construction of a giant magic factory.

Magic Valley was actually Major Barkas's idea. The Alexandria scam had made it obvious to him that Maskelyne's operation would have to be expanded. So, soon after the Gang had returned to Abbassia he took Jasper to a bluff overlooking a long, narrow valley ringed with a garland of thick foliage, and announced, 'It's all yours.'

Maskelyne looked at the barren sandscape. Its length and width made it look as if God had trowelled a single scoop out of the earth, then abandoned the place. 'What is?' he asked.

'This valley.' The major scuffed at a small stone and watched it bound down the steep slope, then continued. 'I know it's pretty dismal now, but it can be turned into something quite grand if you use your imagination. This is going to be a long campaign and there'll be a tremendous call for your services before we've won it. You'll need first-rate facilities, and I want you to build them here. It's been cleared with Gray Pillars. Put in everything...'

Jasper was stunned. Finally, a real place to work. A giant workshop. As he gazed into the valley it began to blossom with possibilities. Factories and warehouses and living quarters and a spate of offices sprouted in his mind. Within a few months the desolate valley would be transformed into a garden of illusions, in which would grow all manner of military delights.

'... Engineers'll do the actual construction. They're ready to get on with it.'

Barkas's words drifted out of Jasper's mind as he stared into the valley. This barren valley was perhaps the greatest ovation he had ever received. Finally, after the months spent pleading for a military commission, finally, after all those nights of frustration, finally, after being deposited in the desert and shunned like a diseased man, finally, finally, he was being accepted. He took a calming breath. 'It's something, isn't it,' he said lightly, but continued looking straight ahead so the major would not see the tears of relief welling in his eyes.

His letter to Mary that night was long and happy.

It's named Long Valley on the maps, [he wrote] but it will be my magic valley. There's nothing there at all right now, just sand and scrub, but when we've finished it'll be the greatest magic workshop ever built. They've provided me with a generous budget, although Barkas asked that I use salvaged materials whenever possible. When I asked him what we would be building here, he clapped me on the shoulder and said 'Why, Maskelyne, use your imagination.' You know how that sparks me. Oh, I so wish you were here with me right now.

This will give me the opportunity to make the props they need to help bring this horrid fighting to an end. I can make the decoy guns and soldiers here, I can build the largest apparatus ever constructed before...

Although parts of the letter were censored, a surprising number of pertinent details were left untouched. 'Just what you need,' Mary wrote back to him, 'another theatre to manage. I should have thought that one such experience had been enough!' Then she pasted his letter in the scrapbook she was keeping for him and tried to imagine what the place looked like.

If possible, the Gang was even more excited about this recognition of their efforts than Jasper. ' 'Bout bloody time they realized we can win this war for them if they give us the chance,' Hill said, then requested private quarters with a view.

'Listen to him, will you,' Graham complained, shaking his head. 'Private quarters yet. Next thing you know he'll want a brass headboard.'

'Oh, I don't know about that,' Robson said. 'He's already got all the brass he'll ever need.'

Hill rubbed his chin as he reconsidered his request. 'Maybe I should have them build me a room on the second level,' he decided.

Fuller listened to the conversation, and later went off and found some of his old mates. Together they toasted the news. Sergeant Fuller was being taken back into the bosom of the Army.

Frank Knox found Maskelyne working on plans in his tent. 'When do we start?'

'Soon as we can get some plans to the Engineers. I'll get them going on two large shells for work space, an office and some quarters straight away. Once that's under way we can work on the other things we'll need.'

Knox looked at the rough schematic of the area Maskelyne had mapped. It consisted of almost twenty buildings of various sizes. 'It's going to be some project.'

'We'll need all the space we can get. If we're going to be effective, we're going to have hundreds of people working there. We need living quarters and mess facilities, we need supply warehouses, testing grounds ...' Maskelyne paused, and grinned broadly. 'We've done it Frank! We've done it!'

Knox's smile was a bit more conservative. 'Let's just say we've taken a rather large step in the right direction.'

From the very beginning there were countless problems, but maintaining security around the valley was perhaps the most difficult one to solve. A magician's first priority is to protect his secrets, and the long, exposed sides of Magic Valley would make it almost impossible to keep spying eyes away from the shops.

To combat this, Maskelyne designed an elaborate security system that was installed soon after the main buildings went up.

Raised sentry boxes were built at intervals along the crest of the valley, and the open stretches between these posts were guarded by a combination of modern antipersonnel weapons and the genies and spirits of ancient fairy tales.

Warning signs in both English and Arabic were posted at all approaches to the area. A hundred yards beyond these signs, rows of bright-red flags reinforced their meaning. After the signs and the flags, Magic Valley got deadly.

Small minefields dotted the area. Electrified wire ran between these fields and the sentry boxes. Those areas that could not be effectively patrolled because of heavy brush were protected by Maskelyne's magical devices. A trespasser might suddenly find himself caught in a maze of mirrors, or be confronted by a frightful image gushing out of the ground. He might stumble over a trip wire and activate a gramophone that broadcast bloodcurdling threats, or doors that opened and closed untouched by human hands. Under different circumstances Maskelyne would have enjoyed inventing this whimsical security system, but this was a serious matter. The secrets of the Valley had to be protected at all costs.

If, somehow, these illusions did not scare the trespasser away, lethal devices awaited. Pressure-triggered rifles and trip-wire swords and camouflaged pits were placed throughout the area. A few Egyptian spies were known to have reached these obstacles; none managed to survive them.

The remains of those who died trying to uncover the secrets of Magic Valley were collected by Graves Registration and delivered to anyone claiming kinship with the victim. Since a burial payment the equivalent of ten shillings was paid in local piastres, there was never a shortage of available relatives. And, as collaborating with spies was a crime punishable by death, none of these protested the brutality too strongly.

Frank Knox despised the barbarous security system and tried to dissuade Jasper from implementing it. 'If you can kill them so easily,' he complained, 'surely you can find some way to capture them.'

Jasper disagreed. 'The work we're going to do here will save thousands of lives. It's classified most secret because that's what it's got to be. We just can't allow anyone to find out what we're doing, no matter how callous that might sound. If it takes a few dead spies to convince the rest of them that we're serious, that's what the price will be.'

Among superstitious Egyptian peasants the place became known as 'Valley of the Djinn,' the genie who shakes the earth, and no one dared approach it without good reason.

By mid-July the first structure was completed, a low-ceilinged wooden office building partitioned into six small enclosed squares off a central corridor – three on either side – and two double-sized spaces, one to serve as a workroom and the other as a dayroom–meeting room. The Gang worked out of these offices while Magic Valley was built around them.

Once actual construction had begun, Maskelyne resumed working on his variety show. It had originally been slated to open in mid-June, but that date had been cancelled because of Battleaxe. Now, as Gray Pillars attempted to present an appearance of normality while Auchinleck and Cunningham supplied and trained Eighth Army, he was asked to mount his show as soon as possible.

The first performance of the variety was scheduled for the final weekend in July. Receipts would be donated to the war charities after expenses were deducted. Although a four-thousand-seat amphitheatre would eventually be built in Cairo to house Maskelyne's varieties, this run was booked into the Empire Theatre on Sharia Ibrahim Pasha. A number of other entertainers, many of them service people, completed the bill. Large orange-and-white cardboard posters picturing Jasper in Oriental garb, smoking a pipe, waving a large fan and looking particularly inscrutable proclaimed: 'Jasper Maskelyne, The Royal Command Magician, Presents: A Magical Melange. Eastern and Western Magic.' No advance booking was permitted.

Jasper intended to do his first act in dapper evening clothes, then make a quick change to the brightly coloured, flowing Chinese robe. Elaborate costumes had been worn by performing magicians from King Arthur's time to the present, not just to delight the audience but because it was possible to conceal all sorts of props beneath the great robes. In addition, makeup and costume made substitutions much simpler; performers can easily pass for each other when they wear identical disguises.

He had experimented with various characterizations early in his career before settling on the Oriental. At home, it had been a favourite of his patrons, particularly when accompanied by properly mystical 'Eastern' magic. Although he never mentioned it to anyone except Mary, when he donned the makeup and the costume he enjoyed the childlike thrill of play-acting. Under that expressionless mask, with the Manchu moustache, he was no longer the very British Jasper Maskelyne. It was a small escape, but he thoroughly enjoyed it.

As opening night neared, Maskelyne and his men, and his woman, tuned the illusions and sweated to prepare the Empire Theatre stage for magic. Overall, Jasper was pleased with the makeshift show. It could not be nearly as elaborate as some of the command performances he had staged, but under the circumstances it would be quite acceptable. A local club band was hired to provide background music for the mysteries.

Many nights after rehearsals, Jasper and Kathy Lewis and backstage manager Frank Knox took late tea together. In this situation it was natural that the two men would cast themselves into protective roles and, to her delight, so they did. Kathy was only twenty years old and had already been in the services two years. Her job in Clarke's covert operations office permitted her no mistakes; her evenings with Jasper and the Gang let her be a vivacious young woman.

Like a fussy parent, Jasper eventually became concerned she was spending too much time working and not enough time playing. 'A pretty young girl like that should be out having fun,' he told Knox. 'With all the men in Cairo you'd think she'd at least have an occasional date.'

'There's time for that, Frank said. 'Besides, I think she's carrying a torch.'

'For who?'

'Our boy Hill.'

Jasper didn't believe it. 'The way she talks about him?'

'You silly fool,' Frank said, chuckling, and speaking as the father of two teenaged daughters. 'Obviously you don't understand girls at all.'

'Now, see here,' Jasper protested, 'I've got a thirteen-year-old myself, you know.'

'Unfortunately, Jay, she doesn't seem to have taught you very much. The thing about girls is that you don't listen to what they say. It'll make no sense at all to a rational man. She talks about him, that's what counts.'

Jasper found that difficult to accept. His daughter, Jasmine, seemed to make perfect sense when speaking about her school chums. Of course, she was only a child, a baby really, but still she was a girl. And Kathy Lewis was a girl ... well, perhaps she was a woman. He frowned. 'You really think Kathy has eyes for Hill?'

'I'm sure of it.'

'Well, that's a problem, then. He doesn't seem too fond of her.'

Knox removed his eyeglasses and yanked his shirttail out of his khaki shorts to clean them. 'Don't be too sure of that either. He's a street boy. Doesn't know how to deal with someone like her. So he's nasty.' He put his glasses on and pushed them up the bridge of his nose. 'You watch those two, Jay. I think they've got their quivers out, all right.'

Maskelyne was not at all convinced. 'And I think you've seen too many Clark Gable pictures, Frank.'

The variety show came as a welcome diversion to Cairo's military establishment, and all tickets were snapped up as soon as they went on sale. On opening night, the Empire Theatre was packed with ranking officers in medal-bedecked uniforms, fashionably dressed ladies in a pleasing array of pastel summer gowns, important Egyptians, some in traditional garb but most in business suits, and, in the back seats, enlisted men and women in regular summer weights. Almost everyone carried a colourful fan.

Jasper was surprisingly nervous as he waited backstage while Joan Wertheim, an accordionist, finished her number. He hummed a toneless ditty and checked his apparatus again, making sure all the holders inside his waistcoat were loaded, all the pulls securely fastened, all of the props in the correct pockets.

The audience had picked up the rhythm of the accordion and were clapping in time. An enthusiastic audience, he thought happily, in a ready mood.

He stared down at his black shoes and placed the heel of his right foot directly in front of the toe of his left foot, spreadeagled his arms and moved precariously forward. Then, swinging his left heel in front of his right toe, he began walking an imaginary tightrope. Once, he nearly lost his balance. It was not falling that frightened him, but failing.

Wertheim concluded her recital and received a warm send-off, and Jasper moved into the wing, listening to his introduction. The master of ceremonies, an ENSA (Entertainments National Service Association) comedian, was laying it on a bit thick. '... Theatre is proud to present an original and unique entertainment, embracing mirthful and inexplicable wonders, amazing feats of prestidigitation and dexterity...'

Jasper glanced across the stage at Frank Knox, who was standing with Kathy Lewis next to the prop trunk. The professor gave him a cocky thumbs up, which he returned, then moved into the darkest stage shadows.

The first thing he did, from habit, was count the house. At St. George's Hall each head had made a difference. He'd learned to tote a gate long before he was allowed to perform. Here, it was a useless exercise. But he was cheered by the full house.

Suddenly the spotlight was on him, handsomely got up in white shirt and noble tails. He kept his head down and his frown in place as he walked slowly to centre stage. The spotlight was big and warm and fit him perfectly. For a few seconds he did not hear the welcoming applause; the spotlight was a comfortable cloak isolating him from the rest of the world.

Then the cheers broke into his consciousness and brought him back to reality. He walked directly to his mark, and stopped. He inhaled deeply, a suggestion of nervousness to gain the audience's sympathy, lifted his head and smiled his most broad and dazzling smile.

He was at home again.

The pit band gave him soft background music as he moved adroitly through the opening bits. He produced endless cigarettes and snapped his fingers into flame to light them. He drank a glass of blades and did some of the popular handkerchief sleights, milking each trick until he felt he'd got as much from it as the audience was willing to give.

Kathy was visibly nervous when she first came on stage to set down a prop table, but he settled her with a private smile and she grew more confident as the performance continued.

Maskelyne's amusing sleights blossomed into small illusions. After turning a red handkerchief white, he changed it into an egg and tossed it into the air above the audience. At his command, 'Hey presto,' it burst into flame, startling everyone, and from the smoke emerged a white dove. The bird gracefully circled the theatre, and finally swooped down to perch on the magician's outstretched arm.

While the dove was in flight Jasper glanced at the people in the front wicker seats. Each one was craning to see the bird, and he knew he had complete control. He never played to the whim of the audience; instead he established his own rhythm and made them heed that. He had planned this act carefully and paced it well, and his audience had picked up the beat and gone with it.

Kathy put the dove into a sack and hung it in front of a marksman's target. Across the stage Jasper loaded a rifle and took aim. The music climbed to a crescendo.

Jasper looked out at the audience and smiled devilishly. Some patrons shouted no; others urged him on. A few giggled nervously.

He took aim once again, then fired. The acrid smell of gunpowder filled the hall. A puff of smoke wisped from the rifle barrel. A large hole was ripped in the target, but the paper bag was untouched. 'Oh,' he said sadly, lowering the rifle, 'I seem to have missed. I guess I'll have to try again.'

He raised the rifle. Again the music climbed the heights of tension.

Again the audience pleaded and prodded. Finally he fired. The paper bag burst into flame, instantly disintegrating into flame-tipped floating ashes. But this time, when the smoke cleared, the target had disappeared – and in its place hung a wooden bird cage with the white dove safely inside. It chirped.

The audience roared its delight. The women shook their heads from side to side in admiration, the men nodded firmly; yes, by George, he'd fooled them on that one.

The night grew better. Jasper danced across the stage with confident grace, playing, in turn, with each emotion of the audience. Early in the evening they had given themselves to him, willingly suspending their disbelief. What they knew to be impossible by virtue of everything they had ever learned, they believed in. And savoured that experience just as they would have if a sorcerer could really turn a red handkerchief into a live dove. It was not possible and they knew it. But in the sense of the theatre, it was real. That was the magic in Maskelyne's performance.

As he worked, Jasper was acutely attuned to everything taking place around him. He listened for the minute clicks that indicated the apparatus was prepared. He stole glances at Knox to make sure the next illusion was ready. He steadied Kathy Lewis when her nervousness threatened to reveal itself.

He borrowed three gold rings from officers in the audience, including one from Brigadier Chrystall, Cairo Area Commander, and dropped them into a frying pan. After cracking three eggs over them, he fried them over a burner. From the pan he produced three whole eggs, and from these eggs three more doves, and attached to each bird was a slip of ribbon, each ribbon securing one gold ring.

Knox watched with delight from the wings. The performer was not at all the man he knew so well. On stage, Maskelyne was every bit the West End star. Dressed in his formal clothes, bathed in the spotlight, he seemed so much more imposing than in daily life. He was perfectly handsome and perfectly debonair; his voice was deep and melodious, lulling even. Frank had difficulty believing this was the same man who had nervously paced the lighthouse tower at Alexandria harbour.

The professor peeked out at the audience from behind the curtain. A few people were fanning themselves, but as Maskelyne moved gracefully across the stage everyone's eyes moved with him; when he directed their attention elsewhere, they dutifully followed his direction. He appeared to be working effortlessly, but Knox knew that each movement had been painstakingly choreographed. Each foot position, hand gesture, dart of his eyes, even the concerned furrowing of his brow, had been planned to lead, then mislead, the audience, and had been rehearsed to perfection.

The first act culminated with a stylized version of the popular illusion invented by his grandfather, Eye of the Needle. Kathy was sealed inside a miniature pyramid, its only visible opening a tiny hole at the apex, just slightly larger than the circumference of a thin rope. 'This allows her to breathe,' Jasper explained to the absolutely silent audience. 'Otherwise ...' He shook his head grimly. Then he climbed on top of the wooden pyramid, apparently struggling to maintain his balance on its sloping sides. But as soon as he heard the minute click from inside the box indicating Kathy was ready, he steadied himself and nodded to assistants Hill and Graham. They raised an Oriental foulard over the pyramid and, seconds later, lowered it. Kathy was standing on top of the box, arms outstretched in triumph. And when the door was opened Jasper was snuggled inside, incongruously dressed in his flowing Chinese robe.

Frank lowered the curtain.

Sound mimic Tony Francis opened the second half of the variety with an imitation of a Nazi fighter being shot out of the sky by battleship gunners. Auburn-haired soprano Hede Shack followed with a selection of songs from *Madama Butterfly*. Tommy Thomas, a Welsh baritone, sang a medley of spirituals, but finished with a gripping rendition of the newly popular 'White Cliffs of Dover.' Then Jasper reappeared, dressed in the Chinese robe adorned with cabalistic symbols. A finely carved stone sarcophagus was hauled onto the stage with some difficulty to provide authentic atmosphere for the next round of illusion.

He opened with the Linking Rings. After allowing various high rankers in the front to inspect the seven rings, and having them judged completely whole, he did a lovely turn with them, putting them together and pulling them apart, linking two, then three, finally all of them. Lieutenant General Scott Fyfe-Whitney served as his foil. The General turned crimson at his own inability to bang the rings together or, after Jasper had somehow linked them, pull them apart.

Following the rings, Kathy came on stage costumed in the full-length, slit-thigh gown of an ancient Egyptian princess. She lay down on a Mamluk carpet, and Jasper slowly levitated her. The audience chatted while she floated in midair.

Slowly, he lowered her. She awakened from her 'trance' at the snap of his fingers. The band blared victoriously.

He moved right into the Mummy's Case, a trick of torture. A realistic mummy case seven feet high was opened to reveal rows of sharpened spikes protruding from its cover. The good-natured General Whitney returned to the stage to inspect this box. Fooled once, he searched it thoroughly, then pronounced the spikes sharp and securely fastened, and the case itself free of trapdoors or escape devices.

Kathy was trembling as she stepped inside. As Jasper closed the lid she looked at the audience with fearful, pleading eyes. Then he shut it slowly, but firmly.

She shrieked, but her voice died at the height of her scream. A thin red liquid oozed from the bottom of the case.

The diabolic smile dried on Maskelyne's face, replaced by genuine concern. He tore at the seals, practically ripping the case open. Hill and Graham rushed on stage to help him. Quickly they smashed the seal and swung open the case. A blood-red liquid dripped from the spike tips, but the case itself was empty.

A heartbeat later the grating sound of stone rubbing against stone called attention to the sarcophagus. The men hurried over to it and struggled with the massive lid. As they pushed it partially clear a delicate hand appeared, and, seconds later, Kathy emerged safe and sound.

Other wondrous illusions followed. As he worked, Jasper became charged with the most special sense of happiness. It was the joy of the performer on stage, a feeling he'd somehow lost as one show had eased into another and then another through the years, and the years themselves had been measured by the number of performances. It was a feeling of exhilaration so unique that he had never been able to explain it, even to Mary. Only others who had lived in the spotlight, who had heard the applause, who had been loved by an audience, could understand it.

More than a year had passed since he'd worked in front of a full house and, though he was that much older, the audience made him ageless. He fought the urge to smile, to laugh with happiness, as his act required control of every emotion. But he was having a wonderful time.

After a simple substitution, during which he did a quick change back into his formal attire, he stepped to centre stage. 'I've saved this for last because it is the most dangerous,' he explained matter-of-factly. 'There is sufficient air inside a sealed sarcophagus for a man to survive approximately three minutes. I can hold my breath for perhaps an additional two minutes. If I haven't emerged from the box in six minutes or less, I ask my assistants to break me out to save my life.'

The dubious General Whitney inspected the coffin for trapdoors and air holes, and found none. Jasper lay down inside and it was closed. Whitney checked the lid to ensure that it was airtight. On occasion, Maskelyne had had real problems with this type of box trick. Besides the Huey Green fiasco, doors had jammed or assistants had forgotten to open locks on a number of occasions. The danger was small, but real.

Two minutes passed. A faint banging was heard, but soon faded.

The third and fourth minutes ticked by loudly. Some people in the audience began murmuring. It was a trick, certainly, but tricks had been known to go awry. And it was well known that Egyptian stone coffins were airtight to ensure preservation.

The fifth minute passed with no indication of life coming from the coffin. The band played haphazardly, some of the musicians peeking above the rim of the stage to peer at the box.

Six minutes. Graham rushed to the sarcophagus. 'Help me,' he pleaded, waving to a group of assistants in the wings. They rushed on stage. General Whitney strained with them, but the lid wouldn't budge. Kathy stood by helplessly, covering her mouth with a clenched fist. Another thirty seconds passed and still the lid wouldn't budge. One of the stagehands took a step back to wipe his brow. Just before plunging back into the group struggling to lift the lid, he glanced over his shoulder at the audience. And winked. It was Maskelyne.

Then he dived back to work. Those people who recognized him in the grey jumpsuit were laughing hysterically; those who did not were trying to figure out what could possibly be so funny at this desperate time. Finally, the workers managed to push back the lid. Inside the coffin, in Jasper's place, was a child's doll wrapped in mummy cloth.

Maskelyne was sent off with a standing ovation and soon reappeared to thank them all for their attendance. They cheered loudly and he bowed from the waist.

Then, abruptly, the applause fell off. A buzz rose from the audience and grew into a loud roar. Seemingly growing from Jasper's body was – Adolf Hitler! Maskelyne glanced down at his side. Then did an admirable double take. 'I say, I certainly didn't expect to see *you* here tonight!'

The figure reached full growth and stepped away from him. Almost everyone in the audience booed.

'Tell me, Mr Hitler,' Jasper said after quieting them down, 'why did you start this terrible war?'

'Hitler' answered in a voice sounding suspiciously like Bill Robson, 'I need da vork. Iffen I coulda gotten mine work as a painter I vould've been happy.' He lowered his voice and admitted, 'But I ain't such a good painter neither.'

The audience roared its delight. More questions followed, then 'Hitler' began dissolving. Maskelyne shook his fist angrily at the fading apparition, warning, 'And don't come back,' until it disappeared.

Then he took the rousing cheers of the audience, and Knox brought down the curtain.

Everyone departed properly mystified. They gathered in groups as they exited, remembering the illusions that most pleased them and attempting to figure out how they had been accomplished. Jasper relaxed in his small dressing room. In a few hours he would put on his uniform and go back to his military work, but this was a time to be savoured. It had been a good show. Considering that none of his assistants had ever before set foot on a magic stage, it had been a remarkably good show. There were some rough edges that could easily be smoothed over, but he knew his performance had been appreciated and was aware the show would be the main talk of Cairo the following day.

Several people squeezed into his dressing room to offer congratulations, among them Kathy Lewis's boss, Brigadier Dudley Clarke. Jasper had met the popular A-Force commander during the investigation of the mysterious chocolates, but had not seen him since. After the crowd of well-wishers had thinned, Clarke stepped forward and said he'd been delighted by the show, then asked if the magician had ever considered adapting his skills to the world of espionage.

Maskelyne had been thinking about precisely that since the day he'd first heard his father's tale of T. E. Lawrence and the 'magicians.' 'A bit,' he admitted.

'You know, there's not really much difference between what I do and what you do,' Clarke said cheerfully. 'I'll bet if you put your mind to it there's all sorts of wonderful contraptions you can develop to help my people. They can use it, you know; gathering information can be a tricky business.'

Maskelyne found it interesting that Brigadier Clarke avoided the word 'spy.' He agreed to consider the offer, and the two men made plans to meet again.

Cairo loved the magic show. The English-language daily newspaper, the *Egyptian Gazette*, called it 'one of the most delightful entertainments ever seen' in the city. The reception forced him to extend its run. Three performances a weekend were scheduled through the end of the summer, and sold out as soon as the tickets went on sale. Although Maskelyne grumbled about the extra work that would be required, in fact he was quite pleased at the visibility it gave him. Not only did the publicity open doors at GHQ for him, it enabled him to jump the long waiting lines at Shepheards. He enjoyed being treated as a celebrity again.

By August, Magic Valley had begun to resemble a real factory complex. 'In another few weeks,' Maskelyne told Major Barkas as he showed him the facilities, 'this place'll be just like home.'

'If you live in an army camp,' Knox interjected.

Barkas was pleased at the progress of the construction programme, but that was not the reason for his visit. 'As I'm sure you've noticed, things have changed quite a lot since Auchinleck came over. He's much more old school than Wavell, forms in triplicate, everything through channels, training courses in the desert. I must say, we had a time trying to explain your section to him. 'Maskelyne the magician?' he kept repeating, 'What is a magician doing in the Engineers?' The concept seemed to baffle him. And Cunningham's very much from the same mould. Anyway, Maskelyne, we have a problem...'

As Barkas continued, Jasper looked hard at him. He had weathered well. The desert had browned him, and trimmed him, and his eyes were clear, showing no trace of the smoky glaze so common in London. The transformation from peacetime film producer to British Army officer had been complete. The man radiated the strength of purpose necessary in a commander and, had Maskelyne not known better, could have easily passed as a longtime regular.

It made Jasper wonder how much he himself had changed. Was he still a civilian at war or, like Barkas, had he become a soldier? He knew his body was trimmer than in recent memory, and military slang was now a natural part of his language, but what about his mind, the way he thought? Had he begun thinking as a soldier? It was not a question he could easily answer.

'... so, in just a few months, this is going to be a handsome army. Problem is, we may not have a few months. We assumed Rommel would get a bit weary sitting out there waiting, but ...' The war had simmered through most of the summer of 1941, but in early August Panzer Group Africa had begun shifting about the desert. British Intelligence plotted the moves, but could not seem to make any sense out of them.

'Maybe Rommel's just trying to confuse our intelligence branch,' Knox suggested.

'Aren't we ready for him?' Jasper asked.

Barkas shrugged. 'Certainly not as ready as we'll be in two months. We'd give him a good go, no question about that, but as far as the outcome ...' His voice drifted into the unknown.

The three men had settled down in the new dayroom. Two windows were yet to be installed, and a patch of sky was visible through an uncovered portion of the roof, but otherwise it was finished. Knox brewed up.

'How much time before he comes at us?' Jasper asked.

'Might as well ask the fortunetellers in the bazaar. Rommel knows we're bulking up and he must realize we're capable of doing it faster than he is. He might be willing to gamble he's better prepared right now than we are and come at us. That's why I'm here. We've got to prevent him from moving just yet.'

Maskelyne and Frank asked simultaneously, 'How?' – then glanced at each other in surprise.

'I wish I knew. Cunningham is open to suggestions.'

Jasper considered the problem. 'Assuming we could get anything we needed right now, how would we keep him from moving?'

'Fill in the gaps in the front line,' Barkas responded instantly. 'Thicken it up with tanks and guns and perhaps an infantry battalion if you've got a spare one lying about.'

'That's it, then, isn't it? That's our answer.'

Barkas didn't understand. 'Certainly it's an answer, but hardly *the* answer. Needing them isn't having them, is it?'

Jasper smiled smugly. The Magic Gang was about to manufacture an army.

Mike Hill did not like the job of making bodies. 'Strikes me as sort of odd, you know. The kind of thing that brings bad luck.'

Robson patiently explained they weren't bodies. 'They're just dummies, that's all. Like scarecrows, or like the fashion dummies in department store windows.'

'And there's quite a few in the sappers, too,' Graham shouted from a prone position on the hard dayroom floor. He had knocked his back out of whack lifting timbers at Maryūt Bay and was trying to stretch it back into form. 'You wouldn't find me out there digging for land mines. Besides, we're almost finished with that part of the job.'

'Turning 'em out faster than God, I'll bet,' Hill grumbled.

'Here, now, Private,' scolded Fuller, carefully stepping over Graham en route to the kettle, 'let's watch our language, now.'

'But I'm not saying nothing.'

'You can say that again,' Graham said, drawing a mild chuckle.

Robson looked up from the yellowing copy of *Parade*, the soldiers' magazine he was reading. 'Hey, Mike,' he teased, 'what would you know about God, anyway?'

Hill faced him squarely. 'Lots. I've heard all sorts of rumours.'

Robson heaved the old magazine at him.

Hill sidestepped it deftly, then waited for the chorus of hoots and laughter to subside before continuing, 'C'mon, I'm serious. Seeing that line of bodies coming out of the shops gives me the willies, that's all. It's just strange.'

These 'bodies' were the foundation of an entire dummy army that soon appeared on the desert. To help convince Rommel that Eighth Army was prepared to fight, the Gang had begun turning out dummy soldiers, artillery pieces and tanks in large quantities. These props were placed among actual concentrations in the field whenever possible. The plan was to secretly replace this canvas-and-cardboard army with real soldiers as they completed training and with equipment as soon as it arrived.

Actually, Maskelyne had been manufacturing 'men' in his workshop for two decades. Lifelike figures were often substituted for human assistants in difficult sword-passes, locked-cabinet and levitation illusions. With dimmed lighting, black velvet backing and hidden microphones, these stage dummies easily passed as magician's assistants. But Jasper was well aware that his audience in the desert would be much less easily deceived.

Ordinary cardboard flats had been used in great numbers during the post-Dunkirk panic in England, but they cast distorted shadows and would not serve in the desert. To fool sophisticated Nazi photo interpreters, these artificial or 'Chinese' men had to cast lifelike shadows and even appear to be moving.

Maskelyne finally decided to make his soldiers out of cardboard, canvas and tubing. Tubular arms and legs were twisted into various shapes to give the impression of movement. Some of the dummies were in perpetual midstep, others were in sitting positions, many were running, and a few, dubbed 'Hill's boys,' were lying down with their 'hands' clasped behind their neck, as if stealing forty winks. Discarded uniforms were used when available, and the dummies wore the usual wide variety of desert headgear. Townsend, who was becoming an exceptional colour camoufleur, dressed them with paint, cloth and plaster. Robson added a humorous touch by stuffing the bellies of some of them with balled-up cloth and calling them sergeants.

Seen at close range, Maskelyne's soldiers wouldn't fool anyone. They looked like bundles of costumed cloth and cardboard twisted into natural positions. But when these figures were added to dense troop concentrations and observed from thousands of feet in the air, they came alive. Thus, forward platoons became phantom companies, and were outfitted with the appropriate number of tents, dummy wooden rifles and rows of tin hats that were piled up outside the tents. In many camps night fires were lit to keep the 'men' warm, although careful attention had to be paid lest they be set on fire.

From the very beginning of the project, Jasper intended to make lightweight, folding artillery pieces and tanks just as he would make stage tables or prop automobiles, by stretching painted canvas over tubular frames.

Prior to this point, cumbersome wooden dummy tanks had been used by Wavell to dupe the Italians. These 'tanks' were made by tacking painted sackcloth over full-sized wooden frames. The resulting 'tanks' were so unwieldy six men and a truck were needed to move them. Four of these dummies could be squeezed onto the bed of a five-tonner if the truck sides were lowered. Often, because of the difficulty in moving them, after being used once these monsters were abandoned to rot in the desert.

From a distance beyond one thousand yards, the wooden dummy might have passed as a real Matilda, except when it got soaked by the cold morning dew. Then the damp sackcloth sagged and the 'tank' appeared to be melting.

'It's a dummy tank, all right,' Robson said derisively as the Gang inspected one of these hulks, 'named after the dummy who designed it.' He rubbed his hand against the coarse sacking, and bits of paint flaked off. 'Look at this. Just who the devil did they expect to fool with this bonfire?'

Jasper pried loose a rotting board from the hull. 'I'm told it was actually quite effective against the Italians.'

Robson looked at him dubiously. 'Come on.'

'It's true,' Maskelyne insisted. 'They were afraid Wavell was going to make them carry it.'

While Jasper designed a totally new dummy tank, Townsend experimented with tank camouflage patterns, carefully painting in the shadows needed to provide a sense of depth, while Hill supervised the collection of materials from the salvage dump. For the first time, Jack Fuller was given an important assignment. Maskelyne knew that Rommel had mounted his dummy tanks on Volkswagen chassis so that they could scoot about the desert under their own power, and he wanted the Gang's tanks to be able to do the same. Fuller was detailed to obtain as many motorized chassis as he could through the motor pool and, if he couldn't get enough there, to make arrangements to buy them on the thriving black market.

Sergeant Fuller was the perfect man for the task. Having served in the Basin for so long, he knew how to work through military channels and how to bargain with the locals. Indeed, his proper bearing made him an excellent negotiator, for he never gave away his position by showing too much emotion.

Maskelyne's dummy tank was simply an elaborate stage prop. He handmade the prototype with Graham, and they carried it out of the workshop in five separate pieces. Each part was made of white sailcloth stretched tautly over three-eighth-inch rods and three-quarter-inch gas piping, and could be folded flat or snapped rigidly into shape. The massive tank hull, the lower tread section, looked like two four-foot-high pontoons connected by thin wire rods. A rectangular platform approximately one foot tall was laid on top of these pontoons to serve as the turret foundation. Maskelyne designed this platform so that it would protrude over the sides of the hull and cast accurate shadows. An octagonal three-foot turret, resembling a large hatbox with round gun ports scissored into it, was mounted on this foundation, and a smaller, round turret topped the dummy. Five wooden gun barrels, including a three-incher and a swivelling machine gun, completed the replication.

The Magic Gang 'tank' could be hinged together in minutes and carried by two men. Compared to Wavell's wooden dummies that fitted four to a five-tonner, eighteen of these 'tanks' could be folded and transported in the bed of a standard three-tonner.

Standing unpainted in the middle of the main yard, Maskelyne's white sailcloth dummy looked as if it had been sculpted out of a block of snow. But after Townsend's paint crew had finished its detailed work, it was almost impossible to tell the bogus tank from a real Matilda. Even the shadows cast by the prop accurately duplicated those of a genuine tank.

Fuller managed to scrounge twenty-six jeep and automobile hulks and a dummy tank shell was individually fitted onto each of them. Most of these chassis came from the motor pool, but six of them had been purchased on the black market. 'There were these two brothers and they thought they had me over a barrel,' the sergeant said gleefully as he related his adventures in the marketplace to the Gang, 'but when I actually turned around and walked away from them they met my price. Well, I guess we compromised. Hardest part of all was getting them to sign the receipts.'

Robson winced.

'I just told them that I couldn't make a government purchase unless I received an authorized receipt, but I'm not sure they understood.' Fuller laughed at the memory. 'I'll be truthful, I don't believe they signed their real names on the slips.'

'The man's having us on, isn't he,' Robson pleaded. 'Someone tell me he's not serious.'

Hill shook his head. 'Sorry, mate, I'm afraid I've got some bad news for you. He's got the receipts.'

The cartoonist clamped both hands over his heart and collapsed onto the floor.

Townsend came into the dayroom just in time to catch Robson's dramatic reaction. 'What's with him?' he asked coolly, 'Nails's cooking again?' On occasion Graham had made breakfast for the Gang, usually with distasteful results.

'Nothing so simple,' Hill explained. 'It seems Fuller went into the market and asked for receipts.'

'Did I do something wrong?' the Sergeant asked. 'There is a right way to do these things and a wrong way, isn't there? After all, we should remember that we are the King's representatives here.'

Robson was laughing so hard he couldn't get off the floor.

Townsend looked at Fuller and said softly, 'Sergeant Jack, I'll wager His bloody Majesty doesn't even know we're bloody here.'

'Now, that's not the point, is it?' In reality, Fuller never did produce these receipts, and no one ever found out if he was, indeed, having them on.

In addition to the motorized chassis, some 'tanks' were mounted on rubber tyres and attached to the self-propelled dummies by a thin towline. Although these mobile dummies could be used only in areas of 'hard going,' or firm ground, stationary frames could be set up in soft sand for German inspection, then folded up and carried to another location.

The artillery pieces of Maskelyne's cardboard army, like the 'tanks,' were made of canvas, cardboard, rods, hinges and painted sailcloth, and could be folded almost flat for easy transport. Their long 'gun barrels' came out of the salvage dump, where Hill had discovered a field of abandoned piping. These pipes – gas pipes, drainpipes, tubing, rubber-hose sections, thin oil lines, even sewage pipes large enough for a grown man to squeeze through – were cut to required size and painted the correct colour. Under one jumble of twisted and rusted metal hosing the Gang discovered countless cardboard tubes used once to transport Bofors antiaircraft ammunition – all neatly piled, as if just waiting for the proper suitor to come along and claim them. Hill took one look at these long cylinders and envisioned a glorious fireworks display on Guy Fawkes Day. 'Squibs,' he shouted, meaning larger bangers, or firecrackers, and descended on the pile.

'Shell casings,' Maskelyne corrected officiously.

General Cunningham was extremely pleased with the Gang's artillery, and the guns were added to desert batteries as quickly as they could be pasted, stapled and glued together. But Maskelyne was not satisfied. After observing the guns in position in the field he decided they had to fire.

'They can't fire,' Frank pointed out. 'They're made of cardboard.'

If canvas tanks could move, Jasper insisted, cardboard guns could fire. 'As long as our real artillery is quiet,' he explained, 'the dummies are just fine. But once the shooting starts, Jerry's going to realize that entire batteries aren't firing. If we could somehow rig them to produce accurate muzzle flashes and smoke trails, Rommel would never be able to tell they're just flimsies.'

'And if you could make a picture of a diamond sparkle we'd all be rich,' Nails Graham tossed in.

'The guns have got to fire,' Jasper repeated, then set to work figuring out how to make that possible.

The solution came from his childhood. 'The guns are going to fire,' he announced a few days later as he walked into the dayroom. 'They won't do any damage, but they will fire.' Then he joined Knox and Graham at the round table and told them the story of his father and the rocket.

Nevil Maskelyne's great passion was rockets and fire balloons. He combined this love with his knowledge of photography and became the first man to successfully photograph an artillery shell in flight. On the second Sunday of every month he would go into the Kentish fields to launch a rocket or fire balloon. Labels were attached to each balloon offering a reward to the person who found it, and in this way flights were tracked as far away as Germany and Denmark. At about the same time American scientist Robert Goddard was publishing his landmark paper 'A Method of Reaching Extreme Altitudes,' Nevil Maskelyne was launching rockets four feet long and one and a half feet wide miles into the sky.

'My job was to pack the ground firmly at the base of the rocket,' Jasper told the Gang. 'Normally it would rise straight into the morning sky with a furious roar and fiery tail, then curve gracefully back to earth.'

Hill walked in bleary-eyed and poured himself a cuppa as Maskelyne finished his story.

'One time, though, I must not have done my job too well, because instead of rising, the rocket whirled madly in its pit, then tore loose and, instead of going up, sailed like a burning comet a few feet off the ground. It finally slammed into the door of a small cottage and stuck there like a giant flaming arrow. The owner heard this tremendous thump and opened his door. He reeled backward, screaming to his wife, 'Run, Love, the Devil's called,' and fainted dead away.'

Hill stood behind Knox sipping his coffee. When the friendly laughter had died, he asked, 'Is our magician telling stories again?'

Frank glanced over his shoulder. 'Well, well, look who's here. Nice of you to join us this morning, Private Hill. I trust you had a pleasant evening.'

Hill answered with a salacious wink.

'Well, then I'm surprised you're back so early. If I was your age...'

'You would've been here since last night,' Hill finished, meanwhile leaning over to lift a sausage from Frank's plate with his fingers. 'There are—'

'Hey, wait a sec,' Nails interrupted. 'I'd like to know what the connection is between Jay's father's rockets and our guns.'

Maskelyne explained. 'The rockets blasted off in a great explosion of smoke and flame. The higher we wanted them to fly, the more fuel we'd put in the tank; the more fuel in the tank, the greater the blast-off would be. All we've got to do is mix up a batch of rocket fuel and we've got our artillery burst. We'll have to do some experimenting, but we should be able to duplicate any type of cannon flash.'

After testing various mixtures, Jasper finally decided to load the dummy shells for his cardboard guns with aluminium powder, which produced the flash, black gunpowder for smoke and iron filings to add the necessary red tint to the flash. The cardboard packing tubes originally used to transport real Bofors shells were used as casings for this dummy ammunition.

Even with the expert assistance of the ordnance section, it took days of testing and tinkering to match accurately the muzzle flashes and smoke trails of each of the various large guns being used on the desert, but eventually a set of specifications was produced. Unfortunately, each dummy shell had to be hand-packed and there was not enough measuring equipment available in the Delta to ensure the necessary uniformity. Since enemy intelligence would immediately detect firing irregularities, some means had to be found to guarantee the charges would be evenly loaded. 'The wife would do it with spoons,' Fuller said, and was ignored.

Nails Graham improvised a measuring siphon, but it proved too unwieldy to be useful.

'Why don't you try the spoons?' Fuller suggested, and was again brushed off.

Maskelyne's experiment with punctured mess cups failed.

'Spoons.'

After Robson's counterbalance scale fell apart, the Engineers tried the Mrs Fuller method and discovered it was simple and reliable, and that's the way the shells were loaded. A dummy Bofors shell consisted of four dessert spoons of aluminium powder, two teaspoons of black powder and a pinch of iron filings. A twenty-five-pounder required six dessert spoons of aluminium powder, three mess-kit spoons of black powder and, again, a pinch of iron filings. The men loading the cardboard charges wore gloves and aprons to keep the burning powder out of their desert sores and insect bites, and goggles to keep specks out of their eyes. Naturally, the Magic Valley hut in which they worked became known as the Kitchen, while they were 'cooks' and the specifications their 'recipes.'

At dusk one night in late August a demonstration was held on a field at one of General Auchinleck's new desert training sites. Two cardboard guns had been placed at random in a battery of six real artillery pieces. Lengths of metal pipe had been buried in the sand directly below the wooden barrels of the dummy guns and loaded with Magic Gang dummy ammunition. Jasper stood with the invited officers about two thousand yards from the firing line, trying to look as inconspicuous among them as his folding guns looked among real five-inchers and howitzers. At seven-thirty a spotter aircraft circled overhead, and the battery fired its first salvo.

Eight balls of flame ripped into the twilight, and coils of smoke twisted lazily from each barrel as the crews rapidly reloaded. Care had been taken to make sure the location of the dummy guns was not given away during reloading.

Maskelyne silently mouthed his magic words 'Hey presto!' just as the second volley exploded. The illusion was so complete none of the assembled officers even attempted to pick out the cardboard guns.

The third round had the brass agreeing that the dummies could not be detected in the field. 'They're absolutely amazing,' gushed an Armoured colonel. 'Why, except for the fact that they don't do anything, your guns are just as good as real guns.'

Jasper was quite relieved Hill was not there to make the same comment about ranking officers.

After the demonstration, the effusive colonel took him aside and reminded him that something would have to be done about flash burns. 'You can't fire the big guns without scorching the earth in front of them, you know,' he said.

Black cloth would be laid in front of the dummies to simulate scorched earth, Maskelyne replied. When the guns were folded up the pieces of cloth would be picked up and all traces of the battery would disappear, 'just as if someone had waved them away with a magic wand.'

The folding guns and the dummy ammunition were put into production and quickly joined the 'men' and 'tanks' of the Magic Gang army 'filling the gaps' in the front line. Although Panzer Group Africa continued shifting about, no offensive in force was attempted.

Major Barkas was elated by Maskelyne's bogus army, and he frequently stopped by Magic Valley to watch the cloth men, canvas tanks and cardboard guns be carted off to the front. 'It's amazing, Maskelyne,' he said one day. 'It takes you two years to get into the army, and less than a year later you're making your own.'

SEVEN

Maskelyne was stalking a beefy fly in his office one morning a few
weeks later, armed only with a bloodied swatter, when Major Barkas
knocked politely on the doorframe. The long-promised office doors
had not yet arrived. Jasper ended his hunt with a powerful but
ineffective slap, and watched unhappily as the desert fly disappeared
into the whirling blades of the overhead fan. 'What do you think,' he
asked in greeting, 'more flies or sand in the desert?'

'Sand,' Barkas said emphatically. 'The real question is, are there
more dotty officers out here than flies?'

'Well, now,' Jasper teased as he hung up his weapon, 'aren't you
the cheerful one this morning.'

The major settled into the easy chair. 'On your behalf,' he pointed
out. 'It seems you've finally succeeded in convincing Gray Pillars
you're some kind of Merlin.'

'Oh?'

'They'd like you to have a go at hiding the Suez Canal.'

Maskelyne assumed Barkas was kidding. 'Hide it? Is that all? I was
hoping for something more difficult.'

'Hide it. Disguise it. Turn it into a dance palace for all they care,
but they want something done to protect it from German bombers.
It's absurd, of course, it can't be done.' He paused, then grinned
mischievously. Maskelyne had already proved he could accomplish the
seemingly impossible. 'Can it?'

The Suez Canal was the most important link in the British supply
chain. It connected the Mediterranean and the Red Sea, cutting the
maritime distance between London and Far Eastern ports almost in
half. As Barkas pointed out – using a series of topographic maps to
illustrate the problem – its size made it extremely vulnerable. The
canal was one hundred and seven miles long, but less than seventy
yards wide and only forty-two feet deep at most points. If the Germans
were able to close it, or even block it temporarily by sinking a single
ship, British convoys would be forced to make the longer, hazardous

voyage around the Cape of Good Hope, and every Commonwealth army would suffer.

Intelligence Branch did not believe that the Luftwaffe would saturation-bomb the area, as had been done at Alexandria harbour, because Rommel would desperately need the canal once Eighth Army had been defeated. But GHQ did fear that the Germans might attempt to shut it temporarily by sinking a ship in the narrow channel or, failing that, mining it. To prevent this, anti-torpedo nets had been stretched just below the surface of the water to catch anything dropped from an aircraft, and minesweepers continually patrolled it, but the Canal Defence Force wanted to do more to ensure its security. Having learned through the 'old-boy network' of Maskelyne's success at Alexandria, they wanted him to make the entire canal disappear.

Jasper and Frank Knox flew to Suez to inspect the canal defence system which was nothing more than a thin line of antiaircraft batteries placed at the most vulnerable points. Looking down on the majestic waterway from one of these raised gun positions, Maskelyne was taken by its simple beauty. 'It's really quite lovely,' he said admiringly. 'You know, Frank, the first canal was built in this area almost twenty thousand years ago. It was blessed by Egypt's high priests. If you close your eyes, and let your imagination go...'

Knox was not impressed by this history lesson. He thought the request was ridiculous, and suggested the Gang could better spend its time on more practical assignments. 'Do you know how an African elephant hides from its enemies?' he responded.

Maskelyne did not.

'It doesn't. It's too bloody big. And that's what you've got here, Jay, a big, bloody elephant.'

After finishing their inspection they sat in a Suez café drinking warm Stella beer. It seemed as if years had passed rather than months since their indecorous landing there in the midst of Wavell's retreat, and the clamouring, overcrowded city had settled back into its normal chaos. While Maskelyne sketched in his notebook Knox remained silent through two full drafts, then, perhaps emboldened by the heady brew, declared flatly, 'We can't do it, Jay. You'll have to tell them it's a no-go.'

Jasper disagreed. The Gang, he reminded Frank, had managed to 'move' an entire harbour. And Barkas had told him that the Germans were camouflaging rivers near power plants by sprinkling their surface with coal dust, thus making them all but impossible to distinguish from nearby macadam roads.

'Might that work here?' the professor wondered.

'No, 'fraid not. They know precisely where the canal is. I daresay if a motorway suddenly appeared in its place they'd be pretty certain not to drive over it.' Even the officially neutral Americans were working on methods to protect large targets, he continued, telling Knox about a scheme to protect the George Washington Bridge in New York. An aerial view of the bridge had been painted on a canvas which was to be suspended across the Hudson River downstream, and lighted when enemy aircraft approached. High winds had ruined the first attempt by tearing the canvas to shreds before it could be hung. 'We can do something with the canal,' he concluded. 'It's just a matter of applying the proper principle to the situation.'

In the street directly in front of them an exhausted gharry horse had collapsed onto its haunches. Its driver was kicking the animal while loudly beseeching his favourite gods to make it get back to work. A small crowd had gathered to shout advice. Maskelyne understood enough of the local dialect to realize that they were mostly critical of the man's kicking technique. A lively debate was in progress concerning the proper method of booting a lazy horse.

Jasper's examples had not convinced Knox. 'I still think there are better ways to spend your time,' he said. 'The blasted thing is over a hundred miles long. Just one small mine planted anywhere, and all our efforts would be wasted. He set his mug down thoughtfully. 'Look here, I don't like being the voice of doom, but there are some projects we simply will not be able to do. Just because some colonel wants us to make a camel fly doesn't mean we can do it. You've got to realize that, Jay, because it does us no good at all to waste our time running fool's errands.' The shouting in the street was getting louder, so he had to raise his voice to hold Maskelyne's attention. 'It's no bloody disgrace admitting someone's idea isn't possible. We've come here and looked the place over, and it just isn't possible.'

Jasper was not yet ready to admit that. 'Be optimistic, Frank. There's a way to do almost anything. Once, you know, I actually did manage to hide an elephant at centre stage.'

Frank looked at him dubiously. 'No. How'd you manage that?'

'Put a horned helmet on its head and taught it to sing soprano.'

On the pavement behind them, two Egyptians in the crowd began hurling terrible curses at each other. One of them, in a rage, knocked the tarboosh from the other's head. The second man retaliated by ripping the first man's jellaba, and they started banging away at each other. They locked arms and fell heavily into the street. Meanwhile, the gharry horse, having rested sufficiently, stood up and pulled the carriage away, being careful to step over the street fighters.

While Maskelyne and Knox were touring the canal fortifications, work continued at Magic Valley. Graham was nominally in charge during their absence, but had little to do. The factories were busy turning out soldiers, tanks, guns and ammunition for the ghost army, and construction of the Valley was almost complete. The men of the Magic Gang had taken full advantage of this summer lull to explore the Nile Basin. Because the enemy concentrated their efforts on strategic targets rather than population centres, Cairo was considered a safe city.

The great city was an oasis of pleasures. There existed something to fulfil any man's desires, be it watching Errol Flynn and Bette Davis cavort in *The Private Lives of Elizabeth and Essex* or Roland Drew and Steffi Duna in *Hitler, Beast of Berlin*, taking in a cricket match or a football game, betting on the horses on Gezira Island, attending a symphony concert, dining and dancing on a moonlit rooftop, touring historic Cairo and the biblical desert, playing ping-pong, polo or golf, shooting skeet or game, going for a camel ride, shopping in luxurious department stores or in the alley bazaars, participating in discussion groups, studying languages or drinking and socializing with women.

Private Hill, in particular, was enamoured of the city. It had not taken him long to discover that Cairo was a vineyard ripe with women: hundreds of women, thousands of women, women of substance and breeding and street women, beautiful women and ugly women, women of all sizes and shapes and ages and colours and nationalities, women to bring pleasure and women to pick pockets, women to predict the future, women to satisfy every conceivable desire. The city was redolent with their perfumes. And, although Hill cut a path into their numbers, and some of them made him temporarily cheerful, none of them made him content. For the first time in his life, Michael Hill felt terribly unfulfilled.

Something was most certainly wrong. The fun that had once lasted through the night now bored him early in the evening. The women seemed less desirable, the cheap alcohol tasted cheap, and, worse, he found himself placidly moving to the sidelines when a brawl threatened to erupt in the clubs. There were still great moments to be savoured, memories that would warm distant years, like the night he nearly married the *danseuse du ventre* from the Kit Kat Cabaret, but these came less frequently.

He wondered if it had to do with the presence of fluky death. In his old days in London, there had been a few close brushes with the cold hand. At eleven, he had watched a playmate disappear under a collapsing brick wall and that had hurt, but briefly, and differently. And once he'd seen a local character stabbed to death on a back street. But there seemed to be an explanation for these deaths. His friend had gone into a condemned building to prove his bravery; the street chap was being repaid for an earlier slight. Here, in the desert, death was capricious. Men he drank with at the Melody Club at night were corpses baking in the desert the next morning. There was no sense of order to it, no means of increasing the odds. One sergeant who survived the massacre at Hellfire Pass took a local girl into the desert and died when they lay down on a German mine. A Desert Rat in after a two-month trek through Jerrytown died in a traffic accident. Death happened too often and too randomly. Survival had become a game of chance.

At first, Hill tried to ignore this uneasy feeling, hoping it would disappear like one of Maskelyne's handkerchiefs. But it persisted, and none of the old balms, the women, the alcohol, the fists or the games, made him feel any better. Sometimes he thought he must be losing his nerve, but he steadfastly refused to believe that was really possible. Not him. It had to be something else.

Whatever its cause, it plagued him through the summer. Only when he was totally absorbed in some Magic Gang project or, surprisingly, with Kathy Lewis, did he feel like his good old self. And at those times, he roared.

The proper sergeant Jack Fuller had no such troubles. He was a soldier and his army was at war. He was content. His assignment was a difficult one for him, but still better than spending the war in the supply room to which he had been attached. The Magic Gang was not part of the army he had been trained to serve. The troops arrived at work and left on their private schedules, formations were nonexistent, the commander, Maskelyne, was on a first-name basis with his enlisted men and wouldn't have known how to conduct an inspection if one had become necessary, uniforms consisted of whatever rig-out was available and the basic military courtesy, the salute, was an odd relic.

Occasionally a new unit would arrive in the area and come marching jauntily into a bivouac site, and he would stand to the side and watch proudly as the lines paraded into camp, heads bobbing as one on each upstep, singing cadence as they marched. He longed for just one proper formation, just one hot day hike to test his fitness, just one good round of standard marching tunes.

He fought the disorder as best he could, standing tall among the Gang like a gentleman in a Cockney whorehouse. His uniform was always in order, even if no one cared, and he always saluted – or, if he dared not risk the indignity of having his salute ignored or mocked, he saluted mentally at the correct moment, imagining his right hand arching to his brow, meanwhile fighting that inveterate urge and holding his arm tightly to his side. He was determined to set an example, even if no one followed.

But, to his amazement, Union Jack, as he had become known within the Gang, found himself taking real pride in his membership in this strange little outfit. There was an innocence about Maskelyne and his chaps that made them endearing, even to one so firmly schooled in tradition as himself, and made him want to protect them from the regular establishment he knew so well. The Magic Gang was a bunch of outcasts, even in an army filled with rogues, and there was some thrill in being an irregular. Fuller believed that the jungle boys in the Italian campaign must have experienced that same feeling, that surge of pride in being dismissed by right-thinking officers and fighting past them to an important slot in the Army.

Just to prove to Jasper Maskelyne and the understanding Frank Knox and the rest of them that he could be one of the boys if he so desired, he allowed his moustache to sprout far beyond regulation length and took to wearing a bright-red bandanna around his neck. It was all terribly non-uniform, and uncomfortable, but it was necessary. He did remove the scarf when he had to go into the city, however. There was such a thing as propriety.

Squeezed between the opposites Hill and Fuller, the other men experienced similar emotions. They fitted nowhere else, but they fitted together tightly. Each man had carved out his own area of responsibility. Graham with his blacksmith's arms took charge of anything to do with wood. Robson would push his eyeglasses high up on the bridge of his nose and make things appear on paper as well as the head magician would on stage. Union Jack was their connection with the Regular Army. At times the others thought his behaviour was a bit off the mark, particularly his adherence to archaic military regulations, but he was always good for a beer, a fiver and advice on how to buck the system. That last, though, was always tempered with the phrase 'Not that I would do it myself, or suggest anyone else do it, but ...' And Hill ... Private Michael Hill was the troublesome itch that they made a great show of tolerating but in fact really enjoyed.

He did whatever had to be done, always with loud complaint, but somehow got his assignment accomplished.

Without talking about it, or consciously deciding, they found themselves spending their free time as well as their workday together. The pride they took in their accomplishments bound them together. They called themselves the Gang, and enjoyed thinking of themselves as a bunch of unruly artists fighting the rigid military establishment. In fact they had become a well-organized unit.

Only the brooding painter Philip Townsend remained aloof. No matter how they tried to draw him into their tightening circle, he resisted, preferring to go his own way without explanation. He was usually polite, unless pressed, and did his work well, but seemed weighted with secrets and dark possibilities. The others finally left him alone.

He had painted furiously throughout the summer, attacking his canvas with violent colours and hideous figures. He painted his surrealistic view of war: soldiers without arms playing ball sports in the desert, bloody skeletons in full dress on parade, corpses melting into the sands. Once Frank Knox, trying to be friendly, asked him why he painted death. 'I don't,' he replied, 'I paint life the way it is.'

Maskelyne shared the painter's secret, but could not tell anyone else. As unit commander it was his responsibility to read and censor all mail. It was a job that made him feel like an intruder bumbling into other men's lives, but it was necessary. And while doing this job he had learned that Philip Townsend's wife had fallen in love with an American Army Air Force pilot stationed in England.

'Just now,' she had written in June, 'I am afraid I am in the process of falling in love rather badly. I feel awful about it and hesitated a lot about telling you. It is an American pilot and he tells me he loves me. At the moment I don't know what to do about it. Oh, Philip, I feel so awful about it – a bitch, in fact – and I just wouldn't have let it happen. I'm fighting against it, but it's going to be rather difficult...'

And later in the summer: 'I have tried so hard to fight against these feelings, but I must tell you I have not been able to. Perhaps if we had been happier together it never would have happened...'

Townsend's letters to her rambled, sometimes forgiving, other times vitriolic. His emotions shifted as aimlessly as the desert. In some letters he pleaded with her to return to him, pouring out his love and offering understanding. But just as often he wrote hateful things, things that would hurt her.

Invariably, as Jasper read these letters, he thought of Mary. Theirs was an almost perfect relationship. His mind was full of warming memories. The Sunday afternoon they rented a punt and floated the afternoon away on the Thames. 'Have you ever been happier in your whole life?' she had asked him.

'No, never,' he had replied, and meant it.

He remembered their last night together. 'Will you love me forever?' she had asked.

'More,' he'd answered. 'More than forever, and even that isn't long enough.'

She had smiled shyly, her cheeks had turned pink, and she told him, 'I'm so pleased.'

Those were the thoughts a man at war should have about his wife, Jasper knew, not the bitterness of Townsend. He avoided looking directly at the painter when the man handed over letters to be censored, as much to hide his own embarrassment as to protect Townsend. He made a few dutiful attempts to discuss the situation, but was rebuffed each time. Eventually, he asked a major in the Mechanical Section to censor the letters for him but by that time Townsend had already engaged a solicitor to begin divorce proceedings.

While the desert armies sweated through the summer busily arming for the next massive thrust, the German Wehrmacht smashed deeper into Russia. Kiev and Leningrad were under attack, and Stalin's armies were retreating deeper into the Soviet heartland.

In London, Churchill was grateful for the temporary reprieve. The American Lend-Lease programme had finally begun, but President Roosevelt was still having difficulty in Washington with isolationists who wanted to keep the United States out of a European war, and with militarists who believed that even with the additional ships and guns England could not survive, and that any arms sent there would eventually be turned against America. The Prime Minister knew that if his dream of a grand alliance of Britain, America and Russia was ever to be realized he needed a major victory to convince the Americans Britain would endure. Victory over the great General Rommel in North Africa would serve as proof that the Commonwealth could carry its share of the burden.

Churchill continually pressured Auchinleck to begin the promised offensive, but the new Middle Eastern Command Commander-in-Chief refused to attack until he was satisfied his army was properly armed and trained. Asked by the Prime Minister when that might be, the 'Auk' promised an offensive in late autumn.

In Egypt, Auchinleck and Eighth Army Commander Cunningham

were carefully shaping the army to their own specifications. Although Cunningham maintained a confident appearance, in fact he was having a difficult time. In addition to the tremendous logistical and planning problems he had to deal with every day, his doctors had forced him to quit smoking, and the effects of tobacco withdrawal were making him miserable.

As Auchinleck had told Churchill, Operation Crusader was scheduled to begin in November. Crusader was the most ambitious offensive yet mounted in the desert. Eighth Army was to break out of its staging areas and draw Rommel's outnumbered armour into a decisive battle, then lift the siege around Tobruk, reconquer Cyrenaica and, finally, proceed toward the enemy's headquarters in Tripoli.

If Rommel did not attack first.

Maskelyne had returned to Magic Valley confident he could make the Suez Canal disappear. There was really no reason it couldn't be done. The same optical principles that applied to stagecraft would work here – it was just a question of providing the proper apparatus.

The magician attacked the problem logically. What method might he use to make a large object disappear from the stage? If possible, a trapdoor. Traps were efficient and easily concealed from the audience. But that would not be possible, not unless the legendary Ali Baba and his Forty Thieves showed him the magical means to do so.

Second, he might drop a black curtain over the object to be concealed, and that curtain would blend into the black background. But, as Knox pointed out, there was no curtain large enough to drop over the canal.

He considered an arrangement of mirrors. There was a juicy story spreading through the Delta that a Polish officer had the ability to remove his head and cradle it in his arms. Jasper recognized this as an old and rarely produced illusion made possible by carefully positioned reflectors. In fact, sections of the canal could be made invisible from the air by mirrors, but whether the entire waterway could be hidden that way was doubtful. He worked with the concept for a few days, standing over his sand table and moving small mirrors around, until he became convinced that the number of mirrors needed to accomplish the feat made it impractical and, at least under existing conditions, impossible.

He decided he could distort the location of the canal by throwing shadows across the ground, thus making it an extremely difficult target to hit, but that too would require vast amounts of specialized equipment.

At times he felt close to the answer, but as days and nights passed without a practical solution emerging he grew discouraged. He began working on other small projects for General Dudley Clarke to take his mind off it, knowing that his subconscious would be churning away and might simply present the answer to him.

But it was his perseverance that finally paid off. With a wave of his magic wand, in a puff of smoke and flame, he figured out how to make the Suez Canal disappear.

He tested his solution on Frank Knox. Seating the professor in the easy chair rescued from the dump, he stepped behind a table and began his demonstration. 'I was looking for something overly sophisticated,' he explained as he placed three black wooden balls and two army flashlights on the table, 'and that's why I overlooked the obvious solution. Frank, you know why magicians use flame and smoke on stage?'

'Part of the show, I assume. To hide whatever they're doing.'

'Right. Generally those devices are used to obscure a disappearance or an exchange taking place on the stage. But sometimes they're used to draw the audience's attention to a specific area of the stage. No one can resist turning to look at an unexpected burst of flame or a sudden puff of smoke. And while their attention is there, you can be quite certain something else is taking place on another part of the stage.' He held up the three balls, two in his left hand, the third in his right hand. 'I am holding three small wooden balls,' he announced somewhat dramatically. 'However, I want only one. Watch carefully, please.' With a sudden, sweeping movement, Jasper smacked his hands together and, so quickly that Knox almost missed it, dropped two of the balls under the table. 'Hey presto!' he sang, extending two closed fists toward Knox. 'Okay, Frank, in which hand are the little balls?'

Knox was slightly embarrassed at having seen the gimmick. It was not in his nature to unmask anyone. 'I'm afraid I got you this time, Jay,' he said almost apologetically. 'I saw you drop them under the table.'

'Of course you did,' Maskelyne said triumphantly. 'In order to make a simple trick like this work I need something to divert your attention. And that's what I've been overlooking. I needed some sort of cover.' Reaching down into the sack suspended from his belt, he retrieved the two balls. 'Now I want you to watch carefully. But first...'

The two flashlights on the table were aimed directly at the professor. Jasper flicked them on, forcing Knox to squint to see. 'Watch carefully, now,' he cautioned.

Knox couldn't see anything at all. The lights burned into his eyes, causing his pupils to contract. He turned his head and tried to look from the corners of his eyes. He shaded his brows. Nothing helped. A wall of bright light separated him from Maskelyne.

'Hey presto!' Jasper claimed, then asked Knox in which hand he was holding the balls.

'You know bloody well I can't see anything,' Knox replied a bit huffily. 'Just turn those lamps off, please.'

Maskelyne snapped them off. 'Now tell me. Which hand?'

The room was only barely visible to Knox. Chips of light danced gaily in front of his eyes, and there was nothing he could do to stop them. 'All right,' he said, pushing his fingers under his glasses and trying to rub the popping specks out of them, 'you've obviously made your point. Now what is it?' A full minute passed before he could make out the grin on the magician's face.

'The answer was right there when we toured the canal.' Jasper picked up one of the flashlights and snapped it on and off. 'The antiaircraft lights. Listen,' he said, striding gracefully around the table and standing over Knox, 'if we could get enough searchlights around the canal we could create a curtain of light. If the lights were bright enough, trying to see through that curtain to pick out the canal would be like trying to see the filament in a lighted bulb. It just couldn't be done.'

As Frank's eyes gradually readjusted to the normal light, the room and the concept became clear. 'Can we get enough lights?'

Jasper laughed. 'Of course not, we can't get enough of anything. But we can increase the luminosity of those that we've got.'

Knox twisted the tip of his moustache as he considered the proposal. 'And it would work in daylight?'

'It's pretty bright in here right now, isn't it? And you still couldn't see.'

The concept was so simple it was difficult for Knox to believe it would work. But Maskelyne's demonstration had been convincing. In theory at least, the one-hundred-mile-long Suez Canal could be made to disappear in an ocean of light.

There existed in the autumn of 1941 a tremendous shortage of high-intensity antiaircraft searchlights in North Africa. The few working beacons that were available were constantly being shifted in anticipation of bombing raids. A wrong guess or misinterpreted intelligence allowed the German bombers to ride the night skies with impunity. Maskelyne knew that only a few searchlights were available, even for the protection of the canal, so somehow the power of each one would have to be magnified.

The properties of light and their manipulation was a subject on which Maskelyne was an expert. Many of the most popular tricks done at the Egyptian Theatre and, later, at St. George's Hall were simply sophisticated optical illusions. Maskelyne's thorough knowledge of light physics had enabled him to make countless 'ghosts' materialize and to dissolve and 'behead' numerous assistants, and would now make it possible for him to hide the Suez Canal.

Theoretically, for a man who had often made disembodied heads float across a stage, creating a super-searchlight should have been a relatively easy task. Tin reflectors properly arranged around the beacon would magnify its projection, but determining the most effective reflector shape and the precise angle at which light would bounce farthest required a great deal of testing. It was not difficult work, just time-consuming. 'I thought I'd escaped this trial-and-error stuff when I left university,' Frank complained after days of twisting square, rectangular, triangular, obtuse, round, oval, diamond and various other shapes of tin around the 'searchlight' Graham had fashioned from a rubbish bin and army flashlights.

There seemed to be an infinite number of possibilities, and over a two-week period in September the Magic Gang came close to trying them all. The arrangement that they finally settled upon consisted of twenty-four fan-shaped reflectors welded to a steel band which fit snugly around the lens.

Eventually the Gang progressed from workshop miniatures to experiments with a borrowed searchlight. Maskelyne's 'dazzle-light,' as it became known, divided a single searchlight into twenty-four individual beams, each capable of covering approximately the same area of sky as the original, and projected each of those beams nine miles into the heavens. During tests Jasper frequently flew with the Auster pilots to observe the effect of the dazzle-light. Although generally pleased with the result, he realized that the relatively static device could be greatly improved by making the twenty-four reflectors spin rapidly, thus creating a cartwheel of light whirling through the sky.

He worked with an Engineer electrician to design the modification. Each tin reflector, or 'flickover,' was bolted to a rotating metal ring powered by a small gasoline engine. Its rotating speed could easily be regulated. A working model was fashioned and shot a whirling spray of light spokes into the sky at dizzying speeds. Once Jasper was satisfied with the scale model, he scheduled a formal demonstration of the actual device for Air Defence and Air Staff. As before, he would fly in an aircraft to view the effect of the dazzle-light from the pilot's vantage point, while Knox would be in charge on the ground.

To determine the practical value of the 'Spray' against aircraft capable of flying higher and faster than the Auster, Staff provided an American-built C-47 Dakota and a speedy Spitfire for the test. Jasper invited Professor M. W. Sawyer of Cairo University, a well-known expert on light physics, to come along on the flight.

On the night of September 21, 1941, the two aircraft flew at wing tips twelve thousand feet above the North African desert. Maskelyne was in the Dakota with Sawyer, peering down at the ground through light cloud cover. Above them the heavens sparkled, while far below a ribbon of small craft showing navigation lights formed a constellation along the twisting path of the Nile. But as the Dakota flew deeper into the desert the lights of civilization began to recede.

When Cairo was little more than a gem sparkling on the horizon, Maskelyne asked the pilot to signal the searchlight crew to begin the test.

Knox received the request and flicked the light on. 'Put your goggles on, chaps,' he reminded his crew. Huddled near a truck a few yards away, the observers also followed his command.

The light illuminated slowly, a speck of light on the black velvet desert. The beam was aimed quite a bit to the left of the aircraft and was, at first, a dull brown. But as it gained power the brown grew into orange, then yellow, then a clear river silver, and finally white. Pure white. Twenty-four white spikes of light cutting into the night. A few thin clouds were jabbed and glowed a dull grey, but most of the beams stretched into the heavens beyond the senses.

The two pilots adjusted their course and flew toward the lights. Maskelyne pressed against a cabin window and watched with satisfaction as the beams climbed into the sky.

On the ground, Frank Knox had everything running smoothly. He checked to see that everyone on the site was wearing dark goggles and again warned them not to look directly at the swirling beams. 'Please remember to keep your eyes down,' he directed.

When the beams reached full illumination the spikes began rotating. They moved sluggishly at first, casually floating in an eight-mile-wide circle. Gradually, though, like a carnival ride gaining momentum, they picked up speed. They began spinning rapidly. Snapping through the sky. Whirling. They twisted into a deadly tornado of light, ripping open the sky directly in front of the two planes.

Maskelyne tried to watch the spinning beams as they accelerated, but he quickly became dizzy, then nauseated. 'Oh, damn!' he shouted angrily, realizing what a terrible mistake he had made. Then the Dakota flew into the maelstrom, and the whirling spray turned the world inside out.

The light poured through the windows and ripped into Maskelyne's soul. He tried to squeeze his eyes shut, but the glare sliced through his eyelids. He covered his eyes with his hands, but that didn't help. The light pried his mind open, overwhelmed his senses, made rational thought impossible. He felt as if his brain were being torn from his skull.

The Spitfire went down seconds after the light hit. The Dakota began sideslipping through the sky, desperately trying to escape the strobe-light trap. Suddenly, its nose glided up smoothly, toward eternity. For a moment it balanced playfully on its tail. Then it fell backward and began somersaulting toward destruction.

Even then it could not escape the madly whirling beams.

Sawyer, the professor of light, was thrown into a steel bulkhead and sliced open his arm. Maskelyne was yanked from his seat and hurled against the fuselage.

The flying lights of the planes had briefly been visible as they made their approach, but had disappeared into the dazzle-lights. No one on the ground realized what was happening.

The Dakota was dying, twisting toward the desert. Its pilot fought for every inch, but the plane was out of control.

Maskelyne couldn't stabilize reality. The whirling beams hit the plane again—again—again. The ground was suddenly above him. Then to his right. Then below. He clawed for the wireless, knowing it had to be within his grasp, but the world had become nothing except light. It had no feel; no sound. Just light. There was no wireless in this world.

Knox yawned. He checked his watch and wondered what they were doing up there. He tried to estimate the speed of the planes against the amplitude of the beacon. Were they out of range? He wasn't sure. It was impossible to hear the drone of the engines above the searchlight's cooling-system motor. He finally decided that enough time had passed. No need to risk attracting any stray Jerries who might be on patrol. Cupping his hands around his mouth, he shouted, 'Let's shut it down.'

The spinning beams slowed. The light began browning out. The Dakota pilot fought the flashes exploding his eyes and somehow managed to read his altimeter. The plane was six hundred feet off the floor and dropping. He reacted instinctively, diving onto the elevators, then began praying his plane up into safe sky. It continued plummeting for a few seconds more, then paused, its engines complaining, then it reluctantly began to ascend. Maskelyne breathed.

The Spitfire was in an even more precarious position when the searchlight was dimmed. It was flying upside down, less than four hundred feet off the ground. Its pilot read his altitude correctly, but did not immediately realize he was inverted. So he started climbing, down, into the desert. At the final moment, for a reason he would never be able to understand, nor explain, he knew he was going to die. He punched the stick forward, raising the nose of the inverted plane, and it began climbing to safety. Later he would joke that his Spit had an itchy back and he was just scratching it on the sand.

Both planes landed safely.

Maskelyne was stunned and nauseated, his hands wouldn't stop trembling and his head pounded, but he suffered no serious injury. Professor Sawyer's wounds required some stitchwork. Air Staff Command insisted the passengers and both pilots be checked into Number 8 General Hospital for complete examination and observation. Jasper protested mildly, as he felt was proper, but was actually glad for the medical attention. He felt a bit dopey.

As he was assisted into the van for the short drive to the hospital he smiled wanly and said to Frank Knox, who had raced to the airfield, 'It works quite well, doesn't it?'

More than anything else, Knox couldn't help being aware that Maskelyne's always perfectly combed hair was finally a mess. Long strands of black hair stuck to his sweaty face and resisted his efforts to brush them into place. For some reason, that made Frank feel good. He smiled. 'Yes, Jay, it does seem that way.'

'We had a rough time of it in the air testing out something I'd invented,' Jasper wrote to Mary from his hospital bed two days later. 'Perhaps you were right after all about this flying business being dangerous.'

'It seems that these planes are perfectly safe,' she wrote back. 'I don't know what you're doing to them, but I must believe it's your own fault. Please desist instantly. I would like you back home in one piece.'

Eventually, a chain of twenty-one searchlights covered the Suez Canal for its entire length. When illuminated, they created a curtain of swirling light over more than a hundred miles of Egyptian sky. In the following months enemy aircraft made a number of attempts to penetrate the curtain, and failed, and the canal remained open to Allied shipping throughout the war.

After the 'Whirling Spray' had proven its value in the desert, similar devices were manufactured in England for use on the home front. Maskelyne's magic mirrors eventually became an important weapon in Britain's air raid defence system. Although the precise number of enemy pilots who became disoriented when 'hit' by the beam and lost control of their aircraft has never been totalled, the Spray received credit for assisting in numerous Heinkel and Messerschmitt kills as well as preventing countless others from reaching their targets.

But the incorporation of the Spray into the Canal Defence Force was only the beginning of its service in North Africa. Toward the end of 1941, enemy bombers began making regular attacks on the oil storage tanks holding Eighth Army's precious fuel reserves. The Desert Air Force made a valiant effort to fight off the raiders, but had neither the manpower nor the equipment to ensure complete protection. Various camouflage schemes were tried but none of them seemed likely to fool Rommel's air reconnaissance experts for very long.

Brigadier Selby, charged with protecting the oil tanks, asked the Magic Gang to install a dazzle-light system around the depot. Maskelyne pointed out that, unlike the ribbon-thin canal, the tanks were concentrated in a relatively small area. One lucky bomb dropped through the curtain of light would still be enough to wipe out much of the reserve. The only sure way to protect the tanks, he wrote in a long memo to Selby, was to convince the Germans they had already been destroyed.

A variation of the Alexandria harbour deception was proposed. Using papier-mâché, rubble, painted canvas dropcloths and oil fires, it would be relatively simple to make the tanks look as if they had been bombed out of service. But drawing the bombers away from them in the first place would be considerably more complicated. Like the harbour, the tanks had to be 'moved,' but, unlike Alex, there was no open area nearby large enough to substitute as the tank farm.

After various experiments convinced him he couldn't 'move' them or adequately camouflage them, Maskelyne decided to create the world's largest optical illusion. While still very young he had learned in his father's magic workshop that he could make an object look bigger or smaller, or even 'move' it to a different place, simply by changing the relationship between it and objects of known size. This principle would enable him to 'move' the tanks by destroying the aerial perspective.

Among other devices, air photo interpreters and bombardiers used the shadow cast by an object to help determine its size and location. By comparing the length of a shadow at a specific time with shadows cast by nearby objects of known size at the same time, all sorts of vital information about the original object could be gleaned. On the desert, where there were few fixed objects on which to make such a comparison, small objects could easily pass as larger things as long as each part was in scale. This is what made Stephen Sykes's bogus railway possible. But in populated areas buildings, streets, minarets, even donkey carts could be used as a basis of comparison. Maskelyne knew that by changing the relationship between the oil tanks and the surrounding area he could make it extremely difficult for pilots to even find the field, much less bomb it with any accuracy at all.

Working with Knox and Townsend, Jasper redesigned the flickovers. New, curved tin reflectors were made to flatten searchlight beams rather than magnify them. These lights were situated behind the tanks and aimed at them instead of into the sky. Just as a man standing in an open doorway with the sun directly behind him would cast an elongated shadow out of all proportion to his size, the lights drastically altered the size and shape of the tank shadows, thus giving aerial observers a completely false impression of their location.

To test these new flickovers, Maskelyne directed a dummy air raid on the depot. Pilots tried to drop flares as close to the tanks as possible from three different altitudes. The nearest flare landed almost half a mile away.

The low-light flickovers and Whirling Spray, in addition to anti-aircraft gunners and the Desert Air Force, provided a powerful defence for Brigadier Selby's oil tanks. The persistent Luftwaffe attacked the depot for several months. They tried various methods to break through the light camouflage, including dropping flares of their own to eliminate misleading shadows at the beginning of a raid. Nothing worked. Their bombs fell harmlessly in areas surrounding the depot. After each raid, papier-mâché, rubble and painted dropcloths were put in position and smoky oil fires were lit. By the beginning of 1942 the Germans either were convinced they had successfully destroyed the tank farm or could no longer absorb the losses they were taking, because the attacks ceased. The storage tanks were left alone for the remainder of the North African campaign, and eventually provided the millions of gallons of fuel that powered the final desert offensive.

EIGHT

On a golden afternoon in late September, Maskelyne and Knox were enjoying a refreshing sundowner on Shepheard's crowded deck when a paunchy Egyptian business type shyly approached their table. The man was wearing a neatly tailored white tropical suit and clutching a panama hat in his hands. He was obviously a member of the upper rank, and Knox guessed he was an exporter.

'I beg all your pardons,' he said in halting English, 'but you are not the famous magician Maskelyne?'

Jasper acknowledged that he was the magician. 'And this is my good friend Lieutenant Knox.'

The man dipped his head politely to Frank. He asked if he might join them for a moment and was offered a chair, but once seated he bowed his head and was silent. Knox glanced at Jasper, who shrugged, then leaned loser to the man and asked, 'Can we help you?'

The Egyptian stared into his lap as he spoke. 'Not for me that I come to see you. It is for my son. He is a boy very sick.'

Maskelyne gazed into his cool drink and took a deep breath. He knew what the man wanted.

'I'm sorry,' Knox said compassionately.

'I am wealthy man,' the Egyptian explained, 'many business. I have many animals too, you see.' He finally raised his head. Long strips of tears wet his dry brown skin. 'But without my son I very poor man.'

'Of course,' Knox said, averting his eyes. It embarrassed him to see the other man's pain.

The Egyptian looked directly at Maskelyne. 'I pay you anything to come to my home and fix my boy up.'

Jasper could not bear to meet his eyes. 'I'm sorry,' he began, 'but I can't—'

'I have heard stories of big miracles. Many friends tell me what is happening there behind the walls of your camp.'

'I don't think you understand. I would help you if I could, but—'

'I pay you with big money. In pounds, too. I give you everything I have,' the man begged, his voice growing louder. 'Just come. This is my son, you see.'

Maskelyne found it difficult to breathe. 'I'm sorry, but I can't help your son. My magic isn't big enough.'

Knox attempted to help. 'Have you seen the English doctors?'

The man waved away the question. 'Doctors can no help. You must come with me. Please. He is in much pain. The stories I have heard are true. I know them to be true.' As his pleas grew louder and more urgent he attracted the attention of people sitting nearby. The deck manager and a tarbooshed waiter came to the table and asked the man to leave, but he ignored them and continued beseeching Maskelyne.

Knox stood and grasped Jasper's arm. 'Come on,' he ordered.

Maskelyne's legs were weak. 'I'm so sorry,' he said as Knox pulled him away. The man followed them out of the hotel, begging Maskelyne to reconsider, offering riches. He stood in the middle of the street crying as his last hope disappeared in a taxi.

'It's terribly sad,' Knox said after a few moments. 'These poor people really believe in our magic. If you stay on here after the war you can make a tidy fortune, you know.'

The Egyptian was screaming in Maskelyne's mind. His cries drowned out Knox. Jasper wanted to turn the cab around, to go back and put his arms around the man and convince him that he was a charlatan. But he knew it would be useless. The man's pleas were based on thousands of years of history. He believed, beyond reason, in the powers of magic. Maskelyne felt utterly helpless.

'That fakir business is bloody profitable,' Knox continued, aware that he was probably talking to himself. 'A good magic man in this region can open up a small temple and salt away quite a sum. Not too much overhead, either.' He hesitated briefly, and was struck by a horrifying thought. 'Oh dear, I hope young Hill doesn't get that idea under his cap.'

It had been spread throughout the entire Nile basin that the wizard in the British Army could cure the desperately ill and heal the hideously deformed. Stories of such miracles being performed inside Magic Valley and on the theatre stage had passed easily from rumour to legend. Each morning scores of Egyptians would gather at the Valley's front gate in hopes of being touched by the wizard who lived inside. Among them were old and young, men and women, nomadic tribesmen and educated people, Egyptians wounded by war or by nature, and always many, many children. In high shrill voices they begged anyone going into the camp to pass slips of paper bearing their names and addresses and ills to the wizard. As gently as possible the military police would move them away from the gate, pushing them off to the side, where they would spend the day. Many of them made camp there, determined to wait until the magician came to heal them. The long wait, they believed, was a test of their faith in his powers, and they would not be moved.

Understanding that it was useless trying to convince these desperate people that his magic was less powerful than they believed, Maskelyne began slipping in and out of the Valley through a small gate on the northern perimeter. British Medical Corps personnel visited the Egyptian campsite twice weekly to offer their services. Most of the faithful refused their help, however, believing much more in magic than medicine.

Knox cursed the whole situation as a damn shame.

By this time Eighth Army was in the midst of a businesslike calm before the eruption of battle. Every trooper knew his specific job and was busy doing it, or training to do it, in preparation for Auchinleck's Crusader offensive. At Magic Valley, the factories were turning out sunshields, elements of the dummy army, and dazzle-light components, while the individual members of the Gang worked on local camouflage jobs. As Graham wryly remarked, 'Except for the food and the killing, the Army isn't actually such a bad place.'

Maskelyne had started working for Brigadier Dudley Clarke's A-Force organization on a regular basis in August. Clarke had called him into his office beneath the brothel one morning to report that the mystery of the chocolates had been unravelled. The long trail had led his agents from a newspaper in Ankara, Turkey, to a steamy café right in Cairo. One of the young dancing girls working there had taken up with a low-ranking officer in Personnel, and had managed to squeeze all sorts of seemingly unimportant information out of him. The officer had been demoted and shipped back to England to await further disciplinary action. The girl had been shot for spying, and the ring for which she worked was smashed.

As the brigadier coldly related this story, Jasper imagined a blindfolded young girl being tied to a wooden post.

'Brutal,' Clarke admitted, 'but necessary.'

Maskelyne could hear the echo of his own words.

When the brigadier had finished relating details of the spy ring to Jasper, he closed the folder on his desk and tossed it on top of a pile labelled 'To Be Filed,' then again suggested the magician join his group. 'I now it would be a drag on your time, but we really could use you.' A-Force, he explained, had been asked to conduct a series of escape and evasion lectures for soldiers and airmen. 'The material is a bit dull, I'm afraid, but it's vital. Too few of our boys are getting back after they've been captured. We've got to try to change that. I thought you might be able to spice up the lectures with a few tricks or something. It'd just be one evening a week, that's all.'

Maskelyne, who had lately found himself squandering too much of his free time thinking about Mary and the children and missing them to distraction, accepted.

One or two evenings each week through the autumn, normally accompanied by Knox and one other Gang member, he would be flown to a training site or a desert laager, a night tank encampment similar to those made by America's Old West pioneers, and lecture from the tail of a Fordson or Bedford lightweight truck. 'I'm merely here to tell you what you might expect if you become a prisoner of war,' he would solemnly begin. 'Under the agreements of the Geneva Convention the only information you are required to give your captors is your name, rank and serial number. Nothing more. However, Jerry is a clever fellow and will try many different methods to trick additional information out of you. If you're wounded, for example, you may well be visited by a darling little old lady who will speak English, who will be very sympathetic, and who will ask you seemingly innocent questions about your hometown. Anything you tell her will go directly to German Intelligence and may provide important information for some Luftwaffe bomber pilot attacking your home. Also, you must assume all of your mail will be opened and read...'

Maskelyne's reputation kept his audience wide awake at the beginning of his lecture, but after a few minutes their attention would begin to drift. Most of them had been working in the heat all day and were exhausted, and Maskelyne, looking all pressed in a short-sleeve uniform shirt, long desert shorts and dusty black shoes, hardly appeared capable of amusing them out of their lethargy. So when he saw their heads begin to nod, he would reach into his knapsack of tricks and turn an ordinary lecture into a splendid show. 'When you are put in the bag,' he yelled, holding high a rucksack and turning it inside out to show that it was empty, 'the first thing you want to do is begin making plans to escape, or give aid to anyone else who means to escape. Depending on your specific situation, there are any number of methods you might try. For example,' he said, reaching into the sack, 'you might try to fly out of the camp.' With that, he withdrew a white dove and released it to fly into the dusk. 'Or you might try tunnelling.' Again he dug into the bag, this time pulling out a rabbit. 'Best of all, you might simply become invisible,' he added, turning his back and making the entire bag disappear. For the next ninety minutes he held everyone's attention, illustrating each point in his speech with a suitable sleight. The Linking Rings became a cooperating escape team. A deck of cards was a conspiratorial barracks. Objects small and large appeared and vanished to the absolute delight of the tired troops. As Brigadier Clarke had figured, Maskelyne's magic reinforced the important aspects of the lecture, pounding home the message in an unforgettable manner. Jasper Maskelyne's escape and evasion lectures became famous throughout the Middle East and later the Far East, and large crowds of soldiers pushed in to see him work. Before the war was over he had given variations of the basic lecture to more than two hundred thousand officers and men in twelve countries, travelling 135,000 miles to do so. The show proved as effective as it was entertaining. Innumerable Tommies who got out of 'the bag' to return and fight again credited something remembered from Maskelyne's lecture as having played an important role in their escape. Jasper eventually received an official commendation, and his work in this area figured prominently in his eventual promotion to war substantive major.

Clarke used the lecture as a means to ease Jasper into his growing spy organization. Eventually, Maskelyne became an important member of MI9, the section of A-Force dealing specifically with escape and evasion. From a badly scratched wooden desk at the headquarters beneath the brothel, Maskelyne produced some of the most ingenious spy devices ever used in warfare.

The techniques of the conjurer adapted particularly well to escape devices. One of the most important lessons Jasper had learned from his grandfather was how to make maximum use of limited space. On stage, it was vital to be able to conceal equipment in a space so small that the audience would never suspect that anything was there, or create 'invisible' compartments inside apparatus so that an assistant might hide there undetected. John Nevil Maskelyne had been a master of this art. In 1875 he had introduced the automaton Psycho to European audiences. This mechanical marvel resembled the upper half of a human body seated on a transparent pedestal. Psycho was not connected to any outside power source, yet it was able to nod, give the Masonic handshake, solve difficult equations, accomplish small sleights, spell, smoke cigarettes and play an extraordinarily good game of whist. Two years later he was joined by the lovely Zoe, an automaton capable of sketching profiles in an accomplished hand, and Fanfair and Labial, mechanical musicians who, upon request, would play any popular tune on the cornet and the euphonium. Thousands of people carefully inspected the clockwork mechanism of these rudimentary robots, and no one ever suspected that small men could be fitted inside the workings in such a way as to be completely hidden.

Jasper Maskelyne put the family secrets to work in the development of escape kits for airmen and foot soldiers. Unlike the great escape artist Houdini, who among his other skills was able to swallow a key and regurgitate it when it was needed, soldiers had to be able to hide their escape tools on their persons or inside equipment that would be carefully inspected by the enemy.

Faced with that problem, Jasper designed tools that could be hidden in the most obvious places, or that didn't have to be hidden at all. The aglets, or, shoelace tags, of a seemingly ordinary commando boot, for example, were actually tiny compass needles, while a map was concealed in the boot tongue, and a file and a hacksaw were hidden beneath the side flaps. A compass needle, two paper maps, a hacksaw blade nine inches long and a small file could be squeezed inside a regulation sock made of loofah sponge and lined with oil silk. The handle of a nail brush or a shoe-polishing brush held an escape kit consisting of nail puller, file, hacksaw, screwdriver, wire cutters, spanner, compass and two maps. Maskelyne's safety razor was easily turned into a capable wire cutter, and his toothbrush cleaned teeth while concealing a map, compass and hacksaw. Even standard sock suspenders held cutters, maps and a compass.

The most utilitarian device he invented for MI9 was a tooled-steel chainsaw blade with teeth measuring three-sixteenths of an inch. Manufactured with a chromium-plated finish, the saw could be made to look like an ordinary identity-disc chain, a watchband, a key ring, a good-luck charm or any other small trinket. It could be carried openly by a soldier or an undercover agent and would cut wood or iron as efficiently as a large hacksaw.

Tens of thousands of British troopers were issued Maskelyne escape tools, but there is no accurate way of measuring their importance in escape attempts. Complete kits or individual components were used everywhere in the world British soldiers, airmen or agents were in contact with the enemy, and they aided in countless escapes. The chainsaw, for example, saved the life of Sergeant Nussbacher of the famed Buffs, as well as a carriage full of his fellow prisoners. Nussbacher was captured in occupied Hungary wearing civilian clothes and was squeezed into an overcrowded railway car destined for a Nazi extermination camp. But before the death train reached the camp he was able to cut out a side panel with his chainsaw, enabling everyone in the car to leap to freedom.

Once a man escaped his captors, his chances of making it back to his own lines usually depended on his courage and his compass. A compass was a most essential escape tool, hence the most difficult to obtain. Maskelyne solved this problem in various ways. Most Desert Air Force crewmen carried a miniature compass screwed into the back of a brass uniform button, while foot soldiers wore a battle-dress belt buckle that could be broken down and converted into a compass. Magnetized needles were concealed inside pipe stems and celluloid collar stays. Jasper's compass needles became so sophisticated they could pass as bamboo slivers and be carried in a pocket without fear of detection, yet when they were dropped into a water puddle they always pointed north–south. MI9 eventually put more than two million miniature compasses into service, including ninety-one thousand collar stays.

For each spy tool Maskelyne received the usual five-pound bonus from the War Ministry.

MI9 also put into good service some of Jasper's more esoteric spy devices. What appeared to be a common cigarette holder was in fact a very powerful miniature telescope, focused by sliding the mouthpiece back and forth. His leakproof fountain pen allowed an agent to write in a bold hand, but also fired a single high-density tear-gas shell. His rice-paper maps were sprayed with salad oil for protection against rain and sweat, as well as to make them more palatable if they had to be eaten. Invisible inks had long been employed by stage magicians and phoney spirituals to present messages from the 'departed'; with some slight chemical alterations they were used by undercover agents all over the world.

John Nevil Maskelyne had publicly exposed many 'mental telepathists' who communicated with their assistants by subtle, intricate codes. Jasper put his knowledge of their methods to work to enable spy masters in Cairo to get messages to their 'puppets.' His simplest device proved to be the most practical. Before leaving for undercover assignments in occupied territory, agents were issued common leather belts approximately three-quarters of an inch wide. When headquarters had to send them an important message, a length of shop-bought string would be wrapped lengthwise around a belt of exactly the same three-quarter-inch diameter. The message would be plainly written on the string in dark ink. The string would then be unravelled and used to wrap a gift box. The string appeared to be covered with ink spots, but no one ever suspected that these spots formed a message.

Inevitably, the package would be searched, but as it contained no contraband, it would be delivered to the agent. Upon receiving it, the agent would wrap the string lengthwise around his three-quarter-inch belt and simply read his instructions.

Maskelyne loved working at MI9. For the first time the Army was actually encouraging him to commit his wildest schemes to paper, then giving them serious consideration. The work at Magic Valley was difficult, and important, and required creative solutions to military problems – but in each case he was given the problem to solve. MI9 wanted the produce of his imagination, and he delighted in delivering it to them.

Not all of his inventions were put into service, although he was convinced each of them was practical. Among these was a submarine with a detachable conning tower that would safely carry the crew of a downed sub to the surface, an aircraft with a tow-hook device capable of clearing razor-sharp piano wire from the invasion beaches, and a method of communicating between ground and air by transforming ultraviolet rays into sounds.

Maskelyne worked at MI9 on a part-time basis for almost three years, and during that period contributed to the success of one of the most elaborate spy operations of the war. But only once did Clarke allow him to work as a spy, an incident that took place just prior to Operation Crusader. Jasper put on a grand magic show for Clarke, and it almost cost him his life.

October 1941 was the most profitable month yet for the spies of Cairo. The armies were in the field preparing for a showdown battle, and the information vendors were feverishly concocting rumours to be sold to the highest bidder. It was possible to buy guaranteed information on any topic. At times the deck at Shepheards resembled a busy auction house, with spies outnumbering waiters. The most desirable secret was the exact time and place the British offensive would begin, and every spy had an 'impeccable source' who could supply that information. Among the other stories that were sold on the deck, and quickly became good gossip throughout Cairo, were that Prime Minister Winston Churchill was coming to the desert to personally launch the attack, that Russia was beaten and secretly negotiating a separate peace, that the United States was finally coming in, and that a dust devil had overturned Rommel's armoured car and he had been critically injured. According to these 'reliable' sources, the garrison at Tobruk was about to surrender – or break out; the Germans were testing aircraft that flew without propellers, and Hitler was rounding up every Jew in Europe for deportation.

'Ah, they're just flying their kites,' Fuller scoffed when Hill told him one of the latest bits of gossip. 'It's all a bunch of tommyrot. None of that's going to happen. And if it does, it does. Just do your job, you'll be all right.'

'That's it for you, then,' Hill said, a bit miffed. 'That's the last bloody time I'll give you the news. Rommel could be eating at the Kit Kat and you won't hear it from me.' Then he went off to share the latest gossip with Robson.

MI6, Clarke's intelligence section, actually created many of the rumours just to keep their German counterparts thoroughly confused. The identities of most of the spies in the city were well known to them, and the quality of their work was generally poor, but there was one unknown source that did concern them. A powerful transmitter broadcasting from Cairo had been sending remarkably accurate information to Afrika Korps. The transmitter had finally been located, but there was little A-Force could do to silence it.

'The rub is that it seems to be hidden somewhere in Farouk's palace,' an exasperated Brigadier Clarke told Maskelyne. They were sitting in his Kasr-el-Nil office, and the hollow music of a wooden finger pipe drilled through the thin floor from the establishment above. 'We can't take any decisive action until we're positive it's actually there, and the King isn't going to let us go mucking about the place searching for it. So you see, it's rather a sticky problem.'

For the past few weeks Maskelyne had been opening Farouk's mail for A-Force, then reconstructing the royal seal after the contents had been copied by intelligence agents. The letters had verified the existence of a large Swiss bank account, but offered no real proof that the young King was cooperating with the enemy. The existence of a transmitter in his palace seemed to remove any doubts. 'Then he is collaborating?'

Clarke frowned. 'We're not sure actually. Abdin Palace is a large place and the King is often ...' he groped for the polite words, '... otherwise occupied. There's much that goes on inside that he doesn't know dickens about.'

The corpulent twenty-one-year-old Farouk I had ascended the Egyptian throne in 1936 and enjoyed a large and loyal following. Because Egypt remained officially neutral in the war despite the massive British presence in the country, both sides attempted to win his support. The Berlin-Rome Axis believed that he might lead an anti-British uprising, while the British simply wanted to keep him out of their way. He had fallen in with a claque of playboy British officers who provided him with unending delights and thus kept him happy and busy. His collection of ties, American comic books and pornography materials supposedly rivalled the largest of their kind anywhere in the world.

Because he still held the loyalty of the Egyptian people, the political implications of accusing him of collaboration were chillingly clear.

Egyptian nationalists were known to be well armed and waiting for the suitable time to rise against the British. Although most of these patriotic groups despised the monarch, they would rally to his defence. The provocation might be enough to spark an uprising in which all Egypt would join.

But the transmitter had to be silenced before Operation Crusader began. 'Can't one of your people touch on it with him?' Jasper asked, meaning one of the young British officers who provided the King's pleasures.

'We could try that, but it would certainly tip our hand. It would be much better if we knew precisely where the radio was before anything was said. He could hardly deny it then, could he?'

A series of sharp jolts shook the ceiling. Jasper tensed and glanced upward, but almost instantly relaxed. 'How do you stand it?'

'What's that?'

'The noise from upstairs.'

'Oh, I hardly hear it anymore. One can get used to almost anything, you know. Anyway,' Clarke continued, returning to the subject, 'we need to get our people inside Abdin Palace so they can have a proper look around. That's where you can help.'

'I get people out of cabinets, Brigadier, not into heavily guarded palaces.'

Clarke laughed politely, but there was little humour in his voice. 'I want you to put on a magic show inside the palace. Big as you can mount. Costumes, big boxes, everything. The longer the better. You'll take some of my people in to assist you. Once they get inside, they'll know what to do. You and your people will be perfectly safe.'

Jasper did not respond immediately. One night King Farouk had shown up unexpectedly at an Empire Theatre performance, and seemed to thoroughly enjoy the show, but this was something else entirely. 'What makes you think he'll want a show there?'

'His ego. His Majesty would welcome the opportunity to host a command performance. Proceeds to charity and all that. It's not exactly a secret that he enjoys the spotlight. Well, you can refuse, you know. I can't order you to do it. But you told me once you wanted to see how the spy business works. Here's your opportunity.'

Maskelyne grabbed it. As Clarke said, neither he nor any of his crew would be in danger. The magic show was simply a cover to get A-Force professionals into the palace. Besides, after spending so many months in a rear support role, he didn't dare pass up this chance to be close to the action. 'It'll take some preparations, of course.'

'And some rehearsals, I imagine,' the brigadier added. 'We'll need as much time in there as we can manage. Now tell me, how many assistants do you use?'

'It varies, depending on the programme. I suppose we could use some of the larger boxes for the escapes. We'd need additional men to carry them in and shift them about backstage.' Jasper made a quick estimate. 'I could probably justify about a dozen. Five or six of them will have to be my own people.'

Clarke beamed like a proud father. 'That's the spirit. I've always suspected you'd make a dandy spy. I'll begin making the necessary arrangements.'

His Majesty King Farouk was delighted to host an evening of Maskelyne magic and illusion at Abdin Palace. The show was scheduled for the second week in November. A lavish banquet was to follow the performance.

Frank Knox was the only member of the Gang to whom Maskelyne revealed the reason behind this command performance. Everyone else was told it was being done at the request of the Egyptian monarch.

As soon as the royal bash was announced Cairo society began manoeuvring for invitations. The chosen two hundred included the requisite British and Egyptian military officers and government officials, the favoured members of Farouk's court, a few random sheikhs and tribal leaders, some lovely city women to garnish the affair, the royal family, various businessmen and those social lions with the sharpest claws. Maskelyne was allotted ten invitations, six of which went to Clarke, and was permitted a company of twenty-one performers and crew. Each member of his troupe was issued a green identity card that provided access to the palace, but they were thoroughly searched every time they entered or departed. Only Maskelyne was allowed to pass without inspection.

Like the fabled royal estates of Europe, seventy-year-old Abdin Palace was actually a small community. Its operation required a permanent staff of more than two hundred and fifty, many of them Italian immigrants who had attempted to farm the fringes of the desert and had moved into the city after repeated crop failures. Besides the luxurious royal quarters, the palace contained numerous guest rooms and reception halls, fully supplied workshops, dining halls, modern kitchens, and wings of servants' rooms. The royal command performance was to be presented in the Byzantine Hall, a spacious room just off the Belgium Wing.

The specially built stage was much too large for the production Maskelyne planned, so curtains were hung to frame the centre portion of it. Farouk assigned a short, chain-smoking palace clerk named Ben-Morsi to serve as a liaison between his staff and the show people. Each time Maskelyne requested a structural change Ben-Morsi would wipe his brow and explain that it was impossible but that he would try to get permission, which he always managed to do. Thus trapdoors were cut into the stage, scrims were added, scenery was painted and seats were moved. In addition to working with the show, Ben-Morsi was an Egyptian spy. 'A very bad one,' Clarke explained, 'but in the employ of the Egyptian Special Service. He's ambitious, so be a bit careful what you let slip around him.'

Once the Gang was made aware of his real profession they took every opportunity to torment him. His foul-smelling Egyptian cigarettes gave his presence away long before he actually appeared, and the Gang invented an entire vocabulary of spy talk to use when he was around. 'The operation begins at oh-four-hundred tonight pass the hammer,' Nails Graham would yell to Robson, who might reply, 'And when will the camel fly?' There is no record that any of these conversations were reported to Libya by the hidden transmitter.

The magic show provided perfect cover for Clarke's undercover agents. Magicians have traditionally taken elaborate precautions to protect their secrets. The Great Lafayette, for example, died in a theatre fire when he went backstage to make sure no one was taking advantage of the bedlam to steal his illusions. Maskelyne played the role of the temperamental artist well, announcing loudly the first day of rehearsals that absolutely no one would be permitted near the stage without his authorization. Then he locked the doors from inside, allowing A-Force personnel to move about the palace without worrying that someone would notice they were missing from the company.

During the weeks preceding the performance Maskelyne was at the palace almost every day, even when a run-through was not scheduled. Some of Brigadier Clarke's men were with him each time. The Gang quickly realized that something queer was going on, but asked no questions.

The agents took every opportunity to search the palace, but Farouk's guards were well trained and these excursions were most often curtailed.

The transmitter was not found. 'Is it possible it's not there?' Maskelyne asked Brigadier Clarke.

'It's there,' Clarke stated flatly.

Maskelyne carefully planned his show. He decided to do a basic first act featuring sleights and small illusions, during which he would always be on stage, then don his Oriental costume for a second act packed with cabinet and box productions and disappearances. Thus the final act could be drawn out to allow A-Force additional time to explore the warren of rooms. Much depended on Kathy Lewis's ability to prolong suspense while he was inside the cabinets, but he was confident she could do the stage work.

Meanwhile, out on the Blue, Auchinleck's training schools began closing their gates. The training phase was finished. Eighth Army was finally prepared to fight the prolonged battle that the Auk and Cunningham anticipated. Fuel, ammunition and rations were being shipped into staging areas. High-ranking officers were receiving their assignments. The usual betting pools were established. Still, Auchinleck waited. He was well aware his soldiers could not be kept on the cutting edge too long without going stale, but he refused to move until he was sure Eighth Army was provisioned to drive Rommel back into Libya.

Clarke's men still could not find the transmitter inside the palace. 'Thought I had the bugger picked off,' one of them, a chubby spy named Michael Reese, said during the daily afternoon debriefing in the brigadier's office. 'Traced a wire through a wall, under the carpet, around a hall bend and into a storage closet. Turned out to be a hidden radio set tuned to the BBC.' He chuckled, and shook his head in disbelief. 'I must say, I'm not crackers about the programming myself, but I hardly think it deserves that sort of treatment.'

'Maybe he's listening to the Parliament reports,' a second agent suggested facetiously.

'Or our comedians,' shouted another.

'Same thing, isn't it?' deadpanned the first one.

Clarke's spies laughed easily and often during these meetings. Maskelyne took a spot in a corner and enjoyed a pipe of sweet tobacco and the spy talk. He'd got to know and admire these men. Although their work was deadly serious, they treated it as some sort of country game. Stakes were never mentioned, as if playing for keeps was in dreadfully bad form. Their behaviour might easily have been dismissed as adolescent bravado, but there was no sense of lurking fear in the group. These men were clearly enjoying themselves. They had been plucked out of normal existence and set down in the middle of a grand adventure. They were having the best time of their lives and were lucky enough to be aware of it. Maskelyne, who had spent much of his life chasing family reputations and gazing into the future for fulfillment, envied these men this time.

None of these spies fit the romantic description created by adventure writers. None of them was particularly dashing, there was no hint of mystery in their eyes, they did not reek of intrigue. As a group they were perhaps slightly older than the hotshots rummaging after Rommel in the desert, but were otherwise very normal. Just an average group of spies.

'Well, we're certain it's there,' Clarke said. A cardboard floor plan of the palace was propped up on his desk, and each room that had been searched was crossed off. 'How about this pantry?' he asked. 'Jack, it's yours, isn't it?'

Agent Jack Smyth was distinguished by the reddish beard and whiskers that overwhelmed his thin face. 'There's nothing there. Had maybe five minutes, just me and some cook. Told 'im I had to find some eats for the poor starving actors. It's just a pantry. Food's bloody awful, too.' He glanced over his shoulder at Maskelyne. 'You owe me a spot of thanks for eatin' it.'

Jasper responded with an appreciative salute.

Clarke crossed the pantry off his board. 'How about this ... this whatever. Looks like a little dressing room. Who's got it?'

Ike Simon, a muscular, round-faced agent, answered, 'Me.' He shook his head firmly. 'Nothing.'

It was crossed off. 'And this loo?'

Jack Smyth boomed heartily, 'Spent a bloody half hour in there!' Then he lowered his voice and confessed, 'Had to, after eatin' all them cakes.' The transmitter was not in the loo.

After two weeks of work half the palace still remained to be searched. 'We might as well cross off Farouk's private wing,' Clarke decided. 'There's no way he'd stash a radio there, and we can't get in anyway.' Looking over his spotted chart, the brigadier said realistically, 'There's quite a bit to be done, and it's going to be rough getting at it all. We're going to have to take full advantage of the show.' Turning to Maskelyne, he asked, 'How much time can you give us, tops?'

Maskelyne shrugged. 'How much do you need?'

Ike Simon answered sarcastically, 'November,' but then the spies began discussing the question.

Maskelyne did not believe they could complete the search. The numbers were against them: too many rooms divided by too few agents, over not enough time. He continued staring at the floor plan. A block of rooms across a corridor from the Byzantine Hall, labelled 'Shops?' had not yet been crossed off. The entrance to this area was almost directly opposite the backstage door. He'd passed it numerous times on his way to rehearsal. It was usually guarded by a single man who walked the entire hall. If his attention could be diverted for a few seconds someone could easily slip across the corridor...

'I suppose two hours would be the minimum,' Clarke said, breaking into his thoughts, 'but any additional time would be a great help.'

'I can give you that,' Jasper said, 'perhaps a bit more.' He paused, then blurted out, 'But I have another idea. I think I can handle the rooms behind the stage, the shop area.'

Clarke was taken by surprise. He glanced at the floor plan, then at Maskelyne. 'Are you serious?'

'Absolutely.'

The brigadier looked at the floor plan again, considering the offer. Then, abruptly, he rejected it. 'Sorry, no, we can't have you running around like that.'

'But I'm in the best position to get the job done. I know more about hiding things than anyone else in the room. And there's a box illusion I'm doing in the second act – I could be gone six or seven minutes without anyone suspecting a thing. And it would free up someone else to cover another area.'

'C'mon, Jay,' Michael Reese said, trying to make light of the notion, 'you haven't even been to His Majesty's School for Spies.'

'If the transmitter's there I can find it.'

'It's too much of a risk,' Clarke said, 'If you were caught...'

Maskelyne pressed harder. 'I won't get caught and it's really no risk at all. Everyone in the palace will be positive I'm inside one of the boxes.'

The brigadier knew that the magician's suggestion made good sense. Crusader was scheduled to begin on November 17, and GHQ wanted that radio silenced before that date. Looking at the chunks of white space remaining on his chart, he knew it was unlikely his men would complete the search. Maskelyne could help. But if he slipped up and was discovered at the job the entire ploy would be exposed. Farouk would look like a fool, and the nationalists would have their cause around which to rally the people.

But the transmitter had to be found. Lives depended on it. 'I'm quite reluctant to permit this,' Clarke finally said, preparing himself to be convinced otherwise. 'What do you fellows think?'

'Ah,' Jack Smyth said, 'let the man go. He can't botch up the job any worse than the lot of us.'

Reese agreed with him. 'We'll give him the secret password. He'll be all right.'

Reluctantly, Clarke agreed. 'You've got six minutes,' he warned. 'If you don't find it straight away, get out of there. The transmitter has a rather long range, so it would be difficult to disguise. Now, I suppose you can pick a lock?'

Maskelyne smiled broadly. Finally, he was going to get in on the action. He was going to play the game. 'Call me Houdini,' he answered.

He was not the only one aching to get a player's role. Most of the Gang felt the same way. Like all soldiers, from the moment each of them arrived in Egypt they had talked about getting a cushy job in Cairo, something that would allow them to live in safety and work in relative comfort. But as time passed, and they worked at their 'cush' jobs in Maskelyne's Camouflage Section, they began to realize they were living on the periphery of a most important experience. For them, the palace magic show wasn't the answer. It kept them occupied for a while, but as Eighth Army roused for the offensive they felt more and more left out. Union Jack Fuller knew that this would be his last campaign and wanted a piece of it before it ended. Hill wondered if getting involved in the thick of it might fill the void in his life. Townsend saw it as an escape into adventure, and perhaps a means of proving himself. Robson, a pacifist, and Knox, a realist, accepted their situation. Nails Graham, the carpenter, simply couldn't resist – the desert had got into him.

Once, when Graham was freshly arrived in Egypt, he had taken the desert for granted. It was a big open space with a lot of sand. After serving in Cairo for a brief period, it began to interest him. Then, as he heard the stories, it intrigued him. And finally, inevitably, it obsessed him.

He had seen its skirts teasing the edges of the city. He had driven its long, flat highways and seen the mirages dancing in the distant heat waves. He sat listening in the town bars to tales of survival. He'd even gone so far as to read a book about it. The more he learned, the clearer it became that he knew nothing about it.

It was not so much its physical presence. Like everyone else, Graham had become accustomed to coping with the fine dust that sprinkled every aspect of life in Cairo, and the intense heat which sucked the afternoon air. It was what the western desert did to the men who served on it that so fascinated him. A corporal in the King's Royal Horse Artillery summed it up best: 'The man that comes out of there is different from the fellow what went in.'

It was pulling at him.

'What's it like out there, eh?' The man speaking was a Hussar sergeant. Graham was drinking with him at the Bloomsfield Bar a few evenings before Maskelyne's palace show. He and Hill and this sergeant, a burly man from Lancaster, were two bottles into the night when he asked the question. The sergeant repeated, then sneered, then boomed it loudly a third time. Some of the men drinking nearby stopped their own conversations to listen to his speech, but most ignored him. They'd been out there and had their own answer. 'I'll tell you what it's like. It's like sitting in the middle of a frying pan with the lighter on underneath, surrounded by nothing but sand. Now, the sand is burning hot and there's always a spray of it blowing in your eyes and your ears and up your nose and you can't never get away from it. Every part of your body aches, specially your feet 'cause they've swelled up from the heat, but you can't do anything about it 'cause if you take off your boots you can't get 'em on again and you can't walk on the sand without 'em 'cause it's burning.

'Now, during the day you can't touch any part of your tank hull 'cause it's so hot you burn your skin, and at night it gets so cold you get the shivers. The flies are at you day and night, buzzin' in your ears, nippin' at you, and you got to be careful when they bite you 'cause then the sand gets under your skin and it gets infected and blisters and there isn't too much you can do about it except suffer.

'Now, then, taking all that in your stride, plus the fact that there's never enough food and you've got to husband your water, the thing you want to be wary of is the Nazi. Rommel's always out there gunning for you. You can't never relax. You sail over a dune and there he is waiting for you. They've got the best equipment out there.' The sergeant's eyes had been clear and his voice bold when he began, but as he continued he saw the hell he was describing and his voice became low and respectful and when he was finished he turned his back to Graham and threw down a long shot of whisky and didn't say very much more for a long time.

None of the other veterans in the bar bothered him. They knew.

Graham was beginning to understand what it was that made Maskelyne give up his position in England and fight to get into the war. The carpenter couldn't properly define it, but he could feel it in his gut. Once survival would have been sufficient, but that was no longer true. Something was driving him to test himself against that vast measuring stick. 'It's crazy,' Graham muttered, almost to himself.

The Hussar sergeant looked over and chuckled maniacally.

NINE

His Majesty King Farouk waited until all his guests were seated and restless, and the court photographers were in position, before making his entrance thirty-five minutes after the performance was scheduled to begin. As he walked casually down the centre aisle to his hand-carved wooden chair in the front, dressed in a finely tailored Egyptian Army officer's uniform, the photographers snapped away and the entire audience stood and applauded politely.

'Why don't you get yourself a bloody watch,' Hill snapped contemptuously as he watched the pageant from backstage.

Maskelyne was pleased that the King was tardy. Every extra minute that could be squeezed out of the night was vital. Clarke's men had rummaged through a spate of rooms during the afternoon dress rehearsal but had not found the radio. Now, as Farouk made his grand entrance, MI6 agents were swarming over the palace like bees in a flower garden.

As had become his custom, Jasper went over to Kathy Lewis, who was sitting on a prop trunk, and whispered to her, 'Remember, no tricks!' And, as always, she looked up at him and grinned. It was his means of helping her relax, but also served to remind her not to change a single step that had been rehearsed. Ad-libbing was not permitted in a Maskelyne magic show. 'Ready?'

She nodded.

'Nervous?'

'A bit.'

'Me too.' He wasn't, really, he was too exhilarated to feel the jitters, but he knew that his false confession buoyed his young assistant. 'Try to draw out the boxes as long as possible tonight, will you?'

She had learned not to question his instructions. He always had a strong reason for wanting something done a particular way. 'Perhaps we can bring someone up to inspect them,' she suggested. They hadn't rehearsed it that way, but had done it often in the Empire Theatre shows.

Maskelyne thought it was a fine idea. 'Let's.' Then he was struck with an amusing thought. His eyes twinkled in delight. 'Perhaps the King would help us.'

'No,' she said, drawing out the word. She knew when he was teasing her.

'I'm serious. He'd love it. Anything to be in the spotlight.'

Knox came up to them. 'King's seated. Two minutes.' Frank was doing his best to hide his nervousness in good cheer. 'Good show.'

Maskelyne gave Kathy a peck on the cheek for luck and began moving to his position in the shadows, but paused after a few steps and returned to her side. Crouching down so he could catch her eyes, he warned, 'Don't be alarmed if anything seems amiss during the boxes. Just keep playing. Understand?'

The humour was gone from his eyes. She looked at him questioningly, but said she understood.

'That's my pretty lady,' he said, forcing a quick smile, then brushing her cheek again and hurrying to his opening spot. While awaiting his musical introduction he checked to make sure his props were in place and his crew was ready. He was fortunate, he knew, to have the Gang with him. They had asked no questions when the new men slipped away during rehearsals, and never complained about picking up their work.

Farouk had taken his time getting settled. When he was finally ready, he nodded to an army officer standing against a side wall. The officer, in turn, signalled two trumpeters, who blared a royal introduction to the evening.

The lights dimmed and Maskelyne's regular musicians began a brief overture.

Kathy took her place in the left wing, next to a prop table laden with pop-up flowers, empty wells and hidden compartments. She was to carry it out to Maskelyne as soon as he finished his opening sleights. Wetting her fingers, she patted down a new curl against her forehead and demurely pressed the sides of her short-skirt costume. When she looked up, she saw Michael Hill staring at her from the opposite wing.

Caught, he grinned.

She firmed her chin and turned away. Idiot, she thought.

Maskelyne walked out of the shadows to appreciative applause and locked his stage smile in place. Reaching into his pocket, he pulled out a package of V cigarettes, the popular Indian brand, and removed one. After snapping his fingers into flame and lighting it, he puffed out a few smoke rings to convince the audience it was real, then pushed it into his palm, and as he did another cigarette popped out of his ear.

Meanwhile, in another wing of the palace, Jack Smyth slipped into a bedroom. If the room was not quite fitted for a king, it would certainly please a prince, and it greatly impressed the British agent. He searched it professionally, starting behind the full-length brocade curtains, crawling under the bed and picking through a closet. He checked for false walls and stepped carefully over the carpet, feeling for a trapdoor latch. The agents were convinced there were secret passages and hidden chambers in the palace, but only one tunnel had been discovered and that led into a wine cellar. Smyth completed his search in four minutes. Satisfied that the transmitter was not in the room, he opened the door an inch and listened for footsteps. Hearing none, he moved quickly into the corridor and to the door of the adjoining room.

Maskelyne's show was moving along efficiently. After Kathy had set the black-velvet-covered production table in position, he poured a goblet full of ink and wrote a short, sweet poem for one of the overdressed women in the front row. He then covered the goblet of ink with a handkerchief and – hey presto! – turned it into a fishbowl of sparkling water complete with a shimmering goldfish. Then, 'because none of us should be alone,' he cast a fishing line into the audience and 'caught' a second goldfish.

He did the silks and followed them with a variety of paper bits. After cutting a double page from the *Egyptian Gazette* into long strips, he dropped the pieces into an ordinary glass bowl and, magically, restored the pages. He twisted these pages into a cylinder and poured into it the contents of the goldfish bowl, including the two fish, then unrolled the paper: it was absolutely dry, and goldfish and bowl had vanished.

Almost everyone in the hall had seen variations of his first act done by other magicians, but that in no way diminished their enjoyment. Maskelyne had been taught that it is not the conjuror's tricks that delight his audience, but rather the presentation of them. His strong suit was his ability to act the role of the magician, to convince his audience that he was not merely performing simple tricks, but rather sharing strange and mystical secrets with them, and he did this with his famed broad smile and warm, omniscient eyes. It seemed obvious he was having a splendid time. Other magicians may have done the tricks with better technique, but few ever dominated a stage as he did.

'I have in my hand a length of rope which is much too long,' he announced, thus beginning a series of rope moves.

On the second floor, Ike Simon was jimmying a door lock when a palace guard turned the corner, perhaps fifteen yards away, and came directly toward him. There was nothing the agent could do but try to bluff his way out of the predicament. So, as the guard approached, he continued picking at the lock. The guard marched up to him, and past him. As he walked by, Simon inhaled the unmistakable aroma of hashish. The man had obviously been smoking the drug on duty and was probably more afraid of being caught than worrying about a stranger in an upstairs corridor. Simon popped the door open and found it was a closet stocked with boxes of British rations. He closed it up and moved along.

King Farouk delighted in the show, reacting as would any other young lad watching Maskelyne's performance of wonders. Throughout the first act he was whispering over his shoulder to one of the young British officers in his private group, a sure indication of his interest.

To prepare the King for his participation in the second-act boxes, Jasper went into the audience with the Linking Rings and used him as his foil. The King could neither separate the linked metal rings nor, after Jasper easily did so, chain them back together. Maskelyne urged the King to try harder, which he did, clanking them hard and, of course, unsuccessfully. Farouk basked in the friendly laughter of his guests, continually twisting around to show them that he too was amused by this ancient puzzle.

Maskelyne concluded the first act with a new production that he had named 'The Djinn,' or 'The Genie.' After 'discovering' a rusting lantern in a previously empty wooden crate, he rubbed its side and it began smoking. He placed it down on stage, and Kathy Lewis seemed to materialize, dressed as a legendary genie, from its smoking spout.

She offered to grant him three wishes.

He faced the audience and frowned. 'Only three?' he complained. When their laughter had subsided he asked for their advice. A wide range of suggestions were shouted at the stage, some of them evoking more laughter, and finally he raised his hand to quiet them. 'Riches,' he demanded of the djinn.

'Oh, that's an easy one,' she replied in a perky voice, then reached into the empty box from which Maskelyne had pulled the lamp. From it she withdrew a seemingly endless silk stocking, a veritable treasure in Cairo at that time.

Now thoroughly disappointed, Maskelyne requested beauty.

Again reaching into the apparently bottomless wooden crate, she produced a mirror which could not possibly have been hidden there, and held it up in front of him. Maskelyne admired his own reflection from a number of different angles, dabbed at his hair, plucked a bit at his moustache and finally agreed, 'Now she's on the right track.' For his last wish, he requested love.

Lewis pulled two adorable rabbits from the crate. As Maskelyne cuddled them, she checked her wristwatch and told him she had to go home. 'My parents don't allow me out of the lamp in Cairo after ten o'clock,' she explained, and appeared to dissolve back into the smoking lantern.

Maskelyne exited to a thunderous ovation.

Refreshments were served to the audience during intermission. The crowd of young British officers gathered around the King and merrily replayed his failure with the rings.

Clarke came into Maskelyne's dressing alcove as Jasper was changing into his Oriental costume. The brigadier had been officially invited by Kathy Lewis, to allay any suspicion. 'Nothing yet,' he said, 'but the boys are still at it. You still want to take a crack?'

Maskelyne pulled a flesh-coloured skullcap over his head and carefully tucked long strands of his own dark hair under it. 'Certainly.' He dabbed some rouge on his cheeks, created shadows around his eyes with a cosmetic pencil, and added long upraised greasepaint eyebrows. 'I'll just have a quick look-see, that's all.'

'Just remember, six minutes and out.'

'Believe me, I will.' He examined his makeup critically in the mirror, turning, raising and lowering his head to inspect all angles. Finally satisfied, he affixed a flowing white beard to his chin and glued a squarish Manchu moustache under his nose, completing the transformation from debonair entertainer to ancient Chinese scholar.

The brigadier helped him on with his robe. 'It's a bit heavy, isn't it?'

'It's necessary, unfortunately,' Maskelyne replied as he checked himself in the standing mirror. 'The magic is in my pockets.'

They shook hands. 'Good luck, then,' Clarke said.

The second act proceeded quite well. Kathy Lewis had some difficulty with a latch inside a cabinet during a disappearance, but Maskelyne stalled until she fixed it, and the audience never knew there had been a problem. Following some minor feats, he did an effective Sword Cabinet, and his Sarcophagus was well received. Building toward the final box production, he levitated Kathy four feet above the stage and kept her suspended four minutes while twirling metal rings around her to show that wireworks were not in use. Although no one in the audience knew it, this popular illusion had been created by Maskelyne's grandfather just before the turn of the century. King Farouk led the rousing cheers after Kathy had been lowered and 'awakened.'

The audience was in splendid humour for the final boxes. Stepping to the front of the stage, Maskelyne held his palms in a prayerful position and bowed gracefully, then announced in the high, croaking voice of an aged wise man, 'It has been a pleasure performing my humble illusions for you this evening, but there is yet one final mystery to be presented for your approval. The perambulations of the spirit have long fascinated my people,' he began, and spoke briefly of thousands of years' investigation into the nature of the human soul. Behind him, the Gang was placing eight boxes of varying sizes and construction in a semicircle. These boxes ranged from a large rattan trunk to a tiny ivory-inlaid music box. 'In recent months I have made an amazing discovery,' Jasper continued, 'and this allows me to transport my human body from one place to another, which I shall do for you tonight. But to accomplish this, I require the assistance of a truly honest man.' Extending an inviting arm out to Farouk, he said, 'I hope the King will assist me.'

The King could hardly resist. The audience cheered him onto the stage.

While attention was focused on Farouk, Maskelyne glanced at Clarke. The brigadier gave him the thumbs-up, the signal to proceed with his search.

By the time the King had taken his bows the stage was set. Farouk was asked to examine every box for trapdoors, false sides or fake locks. He inspected each one, banging and pulling at several, and stated he could find nothing irregular. After each box was searched, chains were drawn around it and it was padlocked. The keys were attached to a metal ring held by Farouk.

When the inspection was finished, Kathy produced two pairs of handcuffs, which the King examined and judged normal. Maskelyne's hands were cuffed with one pair and his feet with the other. Farouk then unlocked a medium-sized steamer trunk, having to try five keys before finding the correct one, and Hill and Graham lifted Maskelyne and placed him inside the trunk. From inside he could hear the chains being resecured and the padlock snapped closed. By the time that was finished he was ready to make his exit.

Kathy asked the King if he was confident the box was sealed.

Farouk agreed he was.

In a much louder voice she asked Maskelyne if he was all right.

He replied by banging three times against the side of the trunk.

He was free in seconds. Although his hands were bound, his arms were loose, so he had no difficulty reaching up and grasping the duplicate handcuff key taped inside his beard. Holding it firmly in his teeth, he popped open the wrist cuffs, then reached down and opened the second pair. As he worked to free himself, he could hear Kathy's muffled voice explaining the difficulty in effecting human transference.

'... spirit moves in unpredictable direction and the body has no choice but to follow,' she said, 'so it is not possible for us to know into which box he will wish to enter...'

Upon receiving the three-knock signal from Maskelyne, Frank Knox opened a trapdoor in the stage directly below the trunk. Although Farouk did not detect it, half of the trunk bottom was on camouflaged hinges and could be opened outward by pressing a spring bolt hidden inside. Once Knox had tapped twice on the bottom of the trunk to indicate that the trap was open, Maskelyne pressed the bolt. Sliding out of the trunk, being careful to snap it closed behind him, he climbed down a three-rung ladder to a small, dimly lit space below the stage.

Knox fastened the trapdoor after him. 'You've got a touch over six minutes.'

'Right.' Maskelyne quickly removed his robe and, dressed in Engineer shorts and t-shirt, crossed to the door. Knox could barely resist laughing, as Jasper was quite a sight in his Engineer gear and Oriental getup, but there was neither time nor reason to do anything about it.

The hallway guard was peeking into the theatre through a fire door at the far end of the corridor. Maskelyne had no trouble slipping into the workshop area without being seen.

On stage, Kathy concluded her long-winded explanation and asked, loudly, if the spirit had settled. Knox was standing under a chalk spot marked '1' and, in response to her question, banged the stage floor three times with a broomstick. From the audience, even from the stage, the banging seemed to emanate from a small trunk. Farouk and Lewis went across the stage to it, and the King began fiddling with the keys.

He unlocked the trunk, pushing the chains aside, and lifted its lid. It was empty. Kathy's shoulders sagged in disappointment, and she again asked the spirit to reveal its location. Knox, having moved across the small room to chalk mark number 2, banged the stage floor three more times.

'Oh dear,' Kathy exclaimed, her distress almost believable, 'I'm afraid the spirit is unruly today. This will be more difficult than I imagined.' She followed the King to the second box.

Maskelyne eased his way into the shop area. The first room contained woodworking tools. Lathes, presses and hand tools were lying on long work tables, and scraps of wood littered the floor, but there was no indication of a transmitter.

Farouk did not find the spirit in the second box and followed Knox's banging to the third, an oversized leather suitcase.

A second shop was obviously not in use, and Maskelyne quickly moved on to the third room in the area. As soon as he opened the door he saw a radio and, for a moment, thought he had found the transmitter. But then he saw a second radio, and a stack of three radio cabinets, and realized he was in the electronics shop. Numerous sets in various states of disrepair were scattered on tables, on metal shelves and on the floor. He knew he would have to examine each one. What better place to hide a transmitter than a radio shop?

Farouk did not find Maskelyne in the leather suitcase. The audience was beginning to titter at the antics of the playful 'spirit,' and the King managed to keep a smile on his face. He trailed Kathy back across the stage to the ivory box.

Knox nervously checked his watch. It would be just like Maskelyne to get back late, he thought. The man was irritatingly convinced nothing bad could befall him. Three minutes were gone. Frank moved the ladder to spot number 8, directly beneath the standard prop trunk in which Maskelyne was to reappear.

It had taken Maskelyne about a minute to conclude that the transmitter was not among the small forest of radios. He figured he had two minutes left, and three rooms to search.

Farouk opened the tiny ivory chest; and it began playing tinkly music. The King shut it off in midtune by closing it hard. Kathy noticed he was beginning to perspire. 'You're doing brilliantly,' she whispered to him, but she was starting to worry.

Maskelyne went into the sewing room. Multicoloured stacks of material and garments were piled on tables, and he poked into each one, hoping to find the transmitter hidden beneath one of them. He did not. He estimated he had a minute left.

Farouk's face was turning a light pink as he continued opening the boxes. The audience was laughing out loud while he traipsed back and forth across the stage. Only two boxes remained to be opened, and they were set on opposite sides of the stage. The King whispered something to Kathy, but she did not understand him. He began opening the seventh box.

Maskelyne found the transmitter in the printing shop. It was hidden behind stacked boxes of paper, and he did not spot it immediately. But he found a wire pushed against the floor moulding and traced it. There was nothing extraordinary about the transmitter, a microphone was plugged into it and a pair of headsets rested on top, and he felt no great sense of relief in locating it. As Clarke had requested, he briefly scoured around for a code book, but did not find one. Time was running out and he left the room to complete his illusion.

When Farouk found the seventh box empty he marched rapidly across the stage to the last box. He was not enjoying his role and wanted it to end.

Maskelyne peeked into the hallway. The guard was busy watching the stage, and in an instant Jasper was across the corridor. Knox was holding his coat for him and he quickly put it on and held out his hands for the metal cuffs. The professor fumbled with the first pair but managed to snap them closed. Maskelyne grabbed the second pair and started to climb up the ladder to box number 8.

'Not there,' Knox whispered, grabbing him by the shoulder. 'It's too late for that one.' He looked up at the chalk numbers, trying to remember which stage traps were under large boxes. 'That one,' he decided, pointing to number 5.

King Farouk opened the eighth box, expecting to find the magician haunched and chained inside. It was empty. He whirled around and glared at Kathy, his look demanding an answer.

She kept her cool magnificently. Rising on her tip toes, she looked into the box and frowned. 'Dear me,' she pondered aloud, 'now what's happened to him?'

The audience accepted this as part of the illusion, but Farouk did not. His face was taut. Just as he opened his mouth to shout orders to the palace guard, a muffled cry came from inside one of the previously inspected boxes. 'Hey,' Maskelyne was yelling, 'help me out of here, help me out of here!'

The audience roared. Farouk, unsure, opened the box again. The magician was curled up inside, handcuffed as he had been when placed inside the steamer trunk. Hill, Robson, and a grinning Graham came on stage to lift him out. The King unlocked the wrist cuffs. Although he may have suspected foul play, he said nothing, and he took his bows alongside Maskelyne and Kathy Lewis.

During the King's banquet following the performance Jasper

Jasper's grandfather, John Nevil Maskelyne, was considered to be the father of modern magic. Conjuror and inventor, here he is photographed with two of his famous 'automated' musicians, circa 1890. © *Hulton-Deutsch Collection/CORBIS*

TOP An early dummy motor transport vehicle of the 4th Armoured Division in the western desert, November 1940. *Imperial War Museum E1005*

ABOVE Despite wanting to use his magic to fight rather than entertain the troops, Jasper Maskelyne was often persuaded to perform. Here he demonstrates his conjuring skills during an 'At Home' given by the Hon Lt. Col. C. G. Prior, Representative of India on the Middle Eastern War Council, in honour of the Indian Army officers at Mena House, Cairo, April 10, 1942. *IWM E1081.3*

TOP A British dummy tank seen on the road to the forward areas after Rommel reaches Gazala, February 1942. *IWM E8360*

ABOVE A dummy tank is manoeuvred into place in the desert after being transported on the back of a lorry, April 1942. *IWM E10147*

The various kinds of tank deception employed in the desert: a dummy Sherman being set up (*IWM NA14415*); a tank camouflaged with netting and foliage (*IWM E12289*) and a tank disguised as a lorry on the back of a transporter (*IWM E12293*).

OPPOSITE PAGE TOP The crowded Alexandria harbour which Maskelyne relieved from repeated German bombings by 'moving' it a mile along the coast, encouraging the Luftwaffe to hit the deserted Maryūt Bay instead. © *Scheufler Collection/CORBIS*

OPPOSITE PAGE BELOW A dummy fighter aircraft under construction, February 1942. *IWM 8344*

ABOVE A decoy Bofors ack-ack gun complete with dummy crew in the western desert during the battle for the Gazala Line. These dummy guns were invaluable to the Allies. *IWM E13758*

BELOW Maskelyne's Magic Gang was heavily involved in the Battle of El Alamein, helping give Monty's men the vital element of surprise against Rommel. Here, 25-pounders hurl their shells at the enemy hour after hour as they try to break through the line in the early stages of the battle, October 1942. *IWM E18467*

OPPOSITE PAGE TOP Tanks were disguised to look like lorries so that the enemy would not be able to properly gauge the Allies' armoured strength leading up to the Battle of El Alamein. *IWM E18461*

OPPOSITE PAGE BELOW Looking back at the British guns from an observation post during the El Alamein battle: the flashes of the hundreds of 25-pounders illuminate ambulances and infantry carriers. *IWM E18466*

After the night-time bombardment of the enemy positions, British infantry advanced through minefields to take up positions close to those held by the Germans and Italians. Here trucks carrying infantry come under heavy shellfire. *IWM E18542*

After the war, Jasper Maskelyne returned to his conjuring in England. Captain A. G. Forbes, manager of the Kingscourt Hotel in Bayswater, challenged Maskelyne to escaping from a sealed coffin in his bar after seeing him perform the trick on stage. Here he is photographed having a celebratory drink after winning the wager in twenty seconds. *Getty Images*

reported his discovery to Dudley Clarke. Soon thereafter, the brigadier made polite excuses and departed.

The dinner was impressive. After rounds of cocktails, freshly caught Red Sea shrimp was served on a hand-painted platter four feet long and two feet wide, depicting an ancient fishing fleet sailing into Alexandria harbour at sunset. This was followed by steaming lamb kebabs and vegetable dishes, and each course was accompanied by an ample quantity of the proper libation.

The night proved less than a complete triumph for the magician. Because Farouk was in military uniform, Maskelyne addressed him as 'sir.' A sticky British colonel took him aside and suggested he refer to the King as 'Your Majesty,' a suggestion to which Jasper took exception. 'Look,' he said, feeling a bit giddy about the evening, 'he's a soldier and I'm a soldier and I'll call him sir. The next day the colonel placed him on report, and an official letter of reprimand was added to his personnel file.

Kathy Lewis had more to drink that night than ever before in her life. This gave her the courage to tell Michael Hill that he was often a royal pain, but that he was also charming. Hill agreed, then replied that for someone who walked around like she was trying to scratch her nose on the sky, she too had some appealing qualities. They taxied to her flat together and he kissed her sweetly before leaving.

So ended the night of illusion.

The following morning GHQ took action on Maskelyne's discovery. At dawn Abdin Palace was surrounded by Commonwealth troops in combat gear. The portly British ambassador, Sir Miles Lampston, marched to the main gate and demanded an audience with the palace chief of staff.

Once inside, Lampston told the startled aide, 'We have irrefutable evidence that a radio transmitter operating on these premises is communicating vital military information to the enemy. You have exactly one hour to hand over this transmitter. If this is not done, I'm afraid we shall have to take steps to silence that transmitter. Now, what are you going to do?'

All sorts of threats and counterthreats were swatted back and forth throughout the morning, and a number of deadlines were set and extended, but eventually the transmitter was produced. A contingent of New Zealanders then entered the palace and confiscated the communications equipment in the shops. Unquestionably, the Axis spy would soon relocate and be transmitting again, but the radio had been silenced for the critical period just prior to the attack.

While the loss of this source of reliable information was a severe blow to Rommel's intelligence operation, it was only one of many problems facing the newly promoted Tank General. Though victorious in battle, Panzer Group Africa had been ensnared in the great irony of desert warfare: the army had to resume the attack to protect its extended supply line, but lacked sufficient supplies to sustain such an attack. Unlike the British, who had been beaten back to their supply depots, Rommel had to have his stores shipped across the Mediterranean to Tripoli, then driven one thousand miles to the front. Royal Navy destroyers had won control of the sea and turned it into a 'German swimming pool,' while RAF bombers and hellbent Long Range Desert Group commandos harassed truck convoys. In September, Hitler ordered twenty-seven U-boats to the area to protect supply convoys, and this helped relieve the immediate pressure, but the Royal Navy was still sending thousands of tons of rations, equipment and ammunition to the bottom of the Mediterranean.

Tobruk remained the key to victory for Rommel. Like a glass of icy water just beyond the reach of a sun-baked man, it tormented him. If he captured the city his supplies could be landed at its deep-water port, and the threat of a British breakout severing his lines would be eliminated. But he could not attack the fortress until sufficiently provisioned, and he couldn't get those supplies until he attacked.

The desert was forcing his hand. The sucking heat, the deprivations, the flies and bugs and constant enemy pressure had taken a toll on his army. Morale was low. Thousands of soldiers had been sent to the rear suffering from dysentery and infectious jaundice. And there had been another disastrous setback: temporary hospitals had been set up in coastal wadis, natural desert trenches, and covered with camouflaged canvas to protect the sick and injured from the sun and RAF bombers; the first major rainstorm in five years sent flash floods cascading through the wadis to the sea, drowning and injuring scores of troops and destroying thousands of tons of equipment and rations.

Even the fresh reinforcements who had arrived in the last few months were becoming mentally and physically exhausted. Rommel had no choice. At whatever cost, Tobruk had to be captured. The attack was set for November 21.

Meanwhile, the exasperated Winston Churchill was imploring General Auchinleck to attack Rommel. The Prime Minister's enemies in government were denouncing his plodding conduct of the war, and his military advisers were warning that Russia would soon be defeated, leaving Hitler free to concentrate on the prized oil fields of the Middle

East. The Germans had taken a million prisoners. Martial law had
been declared in Moscow, and women and children were evacuating
the city. On October 3 the Führer boasted to his nation, 'The enemy
is broken and will never rise again.' For strategic as well as political
reasons, Prime Minister Churchill needed a decisive victory in the
western desert, and he needed it immediately.

The Auk refused to be cowed. He was a professional soldier sure
of his business. Operation Crusader had been carefully planned for
mid-November, and he saw no reason to alter that schedule. At that
time Eighth Army would be fully prepared to destroy Rommel's Panzer
Group Africa.

Jasper Maskelyne's Camouflage Experimental Section, the Magic
Gang, had already played its part. An army of canvas and cardboard
was in the field, and the spy network in Cairo had been temporarily
silenced. Maskelyne had never told the Gang the real purpose of the
show, but they guessed correctly that it had much to do with the
dramatic confrontation outside Abdin Palace. Once that job was
finished, however, they returned to their regular tasks, and had to
stand by wistfully as the rest of the army prepared for battle. A
depression thick as a London fog settled over the men.

Finally they could take it no longer. Hill and Graham marched into
Maskelyne's Magic Valley office and stood directly in front of his desk.
Jasper was busy trying to sort out some of the paperwork that had
accumulated over the past few months. When he failed to look up at
the duo, perhaps knowing the purpose of their visit, Hill said loudly,
'Knock, knock.'

Maskelyne got the point. Putting down his pencil, he leaned back
in his chair and sighed. 'Sometimes I really do wish I had a door.'

Hill collapsed into the easy chair and took off his field cap. Graham
remained standing, shifting uncomfortably from foot to foot. 'The
chaps wanted us to talk to you,' the carpenter said.

'Right,' Hill interrupted. 'See, what it is, see ... it's like ...' He
looked at Graham for help. 'Nails's got something to say.'

Graham glanced at Hill and shook his head despairingly. Then,
returning to Maskelyne, he said, 'It's a bit difficult, Jay. It's not like
the guys aren't happy here, they are that, and ... but ... what it is, is
that the push is about to begin and I was thinking—'

'We were thinking,' corrected Hill.

'You want a part in it,' Maskelyne said evenly.

Hill smacked his hands together. 'That's it, you've got it. We just ...'

Jasper prodded him, 'All the sitting around.'

'Yeah, right.'

'It's got to us all,' Graham said. 'You know, it's difficult ...' He shrugged. 'You know.'

Maskelyne inhaled deeply, then slowly released a long stream of breath, as if he might escape the moment on a puff of air. 'I do. Believe me, Nails, I do.' He heard the song of the desert, too, but knew there was nothing he could do about it. He would have liked to run off with them into the great adventure and dash about gallantly and experience the exhilaration of putting himself on the front line. But it wasn't possible. He was an officer in His Majesty's Service, charged with specific responsibilities. He didn't like it, but he accepted it. His time in Egypt had taught him the importance of military structure. Suddenly, he realized that this acceptance was the difference between the soldier and the civilian at war. His transformation, then, was complete.

'Jay?' Graham asked.

Maskelyne frowned. An instant later his defences crumbled, and he admitted to himself he wanted to be out there as much as any other man. Maybe more than most. Neither his famous grandfather nor his famous father had ever served under fire, and he'd lived under the protection of their guns far too long. He wasn't going to miss this battle. It was a right he had earned. 'Okay, I'll see what I can do. Do me a favour, find Fuller and have him bring the jeep around.'

Hill snapped to like a trained soldier.

Jasper watched them leave. Some transformations, he thought to himself, were less permanent than others.

Getting an assignment was much easier than Maskelyne had anticipated. The Gang's accomplishments gave him access to the top brass. By calling in some chits, applying a bit of pressure, and pledging future wonders, the Camouflage Experimental Section was temporarily attached to the 24th Armoured Brigade, a Royal Engineer decoy unit composed entirely of Bedford trucks and cardboard tanks and guns. It would be their job to attract the attention of the enemy, and perhaps even draw his fire.

Maskelyne offered each Magic Gang member the opportunity to come along or bow out. Not surprisingly, everyone wanted to go. Frank Knox leaped at the offer and immediately began hurling outlandish threats at the Afrika Korps. Fuller was grateful for the chance to do a soldier's job. Hill was delighted, Graham, as usual, stolid. Robson was grateful that the mission did not require anyone to carry arms. Jasper expected some hesitation from Townsend, but the painter said, 'I'm in,' and allowed no further conversation.

The Magic Gang was ordered to forward status on November 14. They trucked to the rim of the desert to join the gathering army. Twenty-fourth Armoured was already in position when they arrived, equipped with thirty-five Magic Valley folding tanks (ten self-propelled), twenty-four dummy field guns and sufficient dummy ammunition, and twelve Bedford trucks. Its assigned strength was forty-two men, all Royal Engineer volunteers, plus Maskelyne's group. Twenty-fourth Armoured's only real weapons were some infantry rifles and officers' sidearms, which, according to the complaining Private Hill, 'might prove handy if we get attacked by a squad of ducks.' The unit's mission was to proceed south along a carefully mapped desert route, 'until observed or engaged by enemy forces. When attacked withdraw rapidly.'

'Rapidly's not fast enough,' Robson said, drawing a laugh.

Most of the Bedfords were radio-equipped, and their drivers were encouraged to chatter away in an effort to convince the enemy that a brigade was manoeuvring in the area. An entire mock designation code had been issued to 24th Armoured for this ploy.

In addition Maskelyne equipped the Magic Gang's truck to blare 78-rpm records into the desert. Impressed by Rommel, who was known to have mounted aircraft engines on flatbed trucks and sent them meandering about the desert mimicking the thunder of an approaching tank force, he bolted four loudspeakers to his Bedford and connected them to a wind-up gramophone sitting on the front seat. A recording of tanks at full attack was to be blasted through the speakers, thus giving the puny force the growl of a tank brigade.

The objective of Operation Crusader was to push Rommel clear back to Libya. Specifically, Eighth Army was to drive directly toward Tobruk, destroying enemy targets as they appeared. At the moment of opportunity, the garrison inside the fortress was to smash out, squashing Panzer Group Africa between General Cunningham's well-equipped attackers and Tobruk's defenders. Once Tobruk was relieved, Eighth Army was to pursue the enemy into Cyrenaica.

To lock Rommel's widely scattered divisions in their present positions as long as possible, a series of feints was to be made at their supply lines in the south. Twenty-fourth Armoured was assigned to make one of these dummy attacks.

By the evening of November 14 the Magic Gang was camped at the assembly area. Within days the desert would be littered with busted tanks and trucks and blackening, bloated corpses, but on this night, as the largest tank force in history gathered for the historic attack, it was washed spotless by a high silver moon. It was, in fact, starkly beautiful.

The majority of Cunningham's troops had never been under fire, and the waiting was difficult. The men gathered in small groups around jerrycan petrol fires for the security of comradeship, as men had always done in the night, and passed the time with lies and dreams. Some veterans reminisced about earlier battles, but there was little boasting, as if death might be lurking within range and become angered. During the nights in the desert it was difficult not to look around the fire and wonder which men might buy a Nazi bullet in the next few days.

The Magic Gang integrated easily into 24th Armoured, and temporary friendships were struck. Like many first-timers, Hill spent part of the evening sewing a makeshift green-and-red Desert Rat patch onto his jersey. And, naturally, he quickly became an expert on the forthcoming attack. 'Tomorrow it is,' he announced, 'we go tomorrow.'

'Righto, mate,' Engineer Corporal Leslie Ferguson chided, '*bukra!*' – invoking the Arabic term for a tomorrow that never arrived.

The fifteenth passed quietly. The men spent it tuning up equipment or exercising or drilling in squads, visiting other units, eating, playing cards, or writing long and emotional letters. Those men with entertainment skills employed them. Maskelyne and Knox, assisted by various Gang members, went down the line giving the trick-filled escape lecture. A sergeant from XXX Corps set up shop in a tent and read palms, decently guaranteeing each customer a long and prosperous life.

As the launching hour approached, a torrent of men and machines flowed onto the desert. Many of Eighth Army's tanks were wearing sunshield disguises. A small city had been founded and settled in a few days. Signposts had been erected, military policemen directed traffic at busy intersections, long lines formed at the canteen wagons, and word spread where the high-stakes poker could be played or black-market goods purchased. It was rumoured that a team of prostitutes was working out of a rented van, but this bint-mobile always seemed to be one more unit away from the soldiers searching for it.

Jack Fuller had provisioned the Gang's truck with tinned sausages, milk, fruit, tea and other treats, so dinners were pleasant. Afterward, Maskelyne strummed familiar songs on his ukulele and many troops joined in with enthusiasm.

As the fires died on the night of the fifteenth, Hill confided to anyone who would listen, 'Tomorrow for certain. I got the word from a South African who's got his cousin working on the inside. It's tomorrow.'

The force was intact on the sixteenth. At muster parade Prime Minister Churchill's charge to the troops was read aloud:

I have it in command from the King to express to all ranks of the army and RAF in the western desert, and to the Mediterranean Fleet, His Majesty's confidence that they will do their duty with exemplary devotion to the supremely important battle which lies before them. For the first time British and Empire troops will meet the Germans with an ample equipment in modern weapons of all kinds. The battle itself will affect the whole course of the war. Now is the time to strike the hardest blow yet struck for final victory, home and freedom. The Desert Army may add a page to history which will rank with Blenheim and Waterloo. The eyes of all nations are upon you. All our hearts are with you. May God uphold the right!

Standing there listening to the Prime Minister's stirring words, as the sun's sweetest rays threw the shadows of one hundred thousand soldiers onto the desert plain, it was indeed possible to feel part of history. Even in the morning heat, Maskelyne felt the chill of destiny straighten his spine. During the next few days he would be writing his own part; it was a role that neither his grandfather nor his father had played before him. It was only a bit player's role, but it would be his alone. Finally, in the midst of war, he had found a certain peace.

After the parade had been dismissed, Hill reminded everyone, 'I told you it was kick-off today, didn't I tell you that?'

In the afternoon a single German spotter flew nearby and the men scurried to their trucks, but otherwise the day passed slowly and without incident.

Crusader had to begin soon. The tanks and trucks were fuelled and their ammunition racks stuffed. The troops were near bursting with nervous energy, but they were sweaty and dirty and sleep was impossible and they could not maintain their edge much longer. Small incidents that would have been overlooked a day earlier now provoked loud arguments and fistfights. Rumours about a further delay whipped through the desert and added to the anxiety. Even the usually placid Knox was sitting on thorns. 'When?' he demanded of Maskelyne. 'What the dickens are the fools waiting for?'

'Divine inspiration,' Jasper ventured.

Knox shook his head in disbelief. 'Bloody Churchill.'

Hill took a long stroll at dusk and returned with a preposterous tale about a commando raid on Rommel's villa at German headquarters in Beda Littoria. The details were sketchy, but apparently the Desert Fox had escaped without injury. Weeks later the rumour would be confirmed. The raiders' commander, Lieutenant Colonel Keyes, was killed in the first burst of fire, and twenty-seven of his twenty-nine men were captured. Although they were wearing civilian clothes, Rommel ordered them treated as regular prisoners of war and awarded Keyes a military funeral with full honours. No one was surprised at this behaviour.

Hill also returned with the definitive word: 'Tomorrow. The orders are cut. One of the boys in the Twenty-second saw 'em. This time it's for real.'

But Eighth Army sweated in the desert all day the seventeenth of November. The officers were becoming concerned that their baking troops had already lost their enthusiasm for the fight, and pressed HQ to give them the go. The Army of the Nile was wilting on the desert.

At 2000 hours that night, orders were issued to prepare to advance. 'I told you so,' Hill boasted once more. Desert kits were rolled up and tied onto tank hulls or suspended from the sides of armoured cars and trucks for added protection from bullets, and the men climbed aboard. In a violent thunderstorm the army sloshed forward to the start line.

Finally, at 0600 hours November 18, the overcast sky was tinted by a rosy red flare, then a green one, then a second red. A solitary military policeman stood in front of the army and, like a racetrack starter, blew his whistle and dropped his right arm. Other MPs down the line picked up the signal and echoed it, but their whistles were drowned out by a swelling cheer that arose from the troops, a cheer that got so loud it could be heard above the rumble of the thousand engines. The British Eighth Army was coming to life. Seventh Armoured began moving out to fight. Operation Crusader was under way.

TEN

Like a legion of serpents awakening from a long sleep, Eighth Army emerged from beneath camouflage netting and uncoiled gracefully into the desert. Operation Crusader was launched by sections. Twenty-fourth Armoured was not scheduled to pull out until 0830 hours, so the men sat by their vehicles watching the wave of tanks and trucks and Bren-gun carriers and armoured cars sweep across the morning plain. It was an awesome sight. Maskelyne glowed with pride and tried to see everything and store it in his memory. The Empire was on the move.

Graham counted thirty-two new American Stuart tanks -- nicknamed 'Honeys' by their British crews -- before the line was broken by a yellow Rolls-Royce armoured car, one of a handful of relics from the Great War still active in the desert. 'How many tanks do you think there are in all?' he asked Knox.

The desert seemed spotted with them. The professor shook his head. 'Enough, I should hope.'

The 24th got under way as scheduled. They followed the desert track for ten miles, then broke off and turned south. Within minutes all that was visible of the main force was a giant dust cloud rising into the grey sky, and even that settled onto the horizon after a while. The cardboard brigade was alone. After spending months in the crowds and clamour of Cairo, and days camped with the Army, everyone in the Gang found the sudden isolation unnerving.

In the afternoon a dust cloud raced toward them, and the column paused until its source could be determined, but it was simply a dust devil, and it swirled past in the distance as if late for an important engagement.

The men tried to hide their nervousness with small talk. 'You know what Churchill said when they told him that Italy was in on Germany's side?' Graham asked no one in particular. 'He said, "Why, it's only fair. We had them the last time."' Everyone laughed a bit too hard.

The 24th maintained radio silence throughout the day, waiting for confirmation that the enemy had been engaged. The code word did not come. Crusader's initial phase was a complete success. The camouflage effort, particularly the sunshields, and improved communications security had paid off. Panzer Group Africa had been caught by surprise. Eighth Army moved unimpeded toward Tobruk.

At 1500 hours, as scheduled, 24th Armoured stopped for the night and made its first camp. The Magic Gang's cardboard tanks were snapped together and set up in laager position surrounding the trucks. Bedrolls were spread out for the two hundred mythical crewmen of the canvas tank force, and at dusk dozens of fires were lit to keep those nonexistent men warm. As Robson rubbed his hands by one of the fires he pointed out that they made the 24th sleeping targets. Knox reminded him that that was their job.

'Like the decoys in a duck hunt,' Graham explained.

The professor chuckled. 'More like the ducks, I should think. They'll be shooting at us.'

After the cooking fires had been extinguished and the night watch posted, Maskelyne strolled through the bivouac checking his men. Fuller was just turning in, stiff from the bumpy ride across the camel scrub, but terribly excited. He had waited a career to make it into the field and was savouring every moment. Knox and Graham were sitting against a Bedford bumper, staring at the million stars of the night, speculating on the first day's progress. The professor's knee was cranky, and Nails's right eye had been scratched by sand dust, but neither man complained. Maskelyne chewed on the tip of his unlit pipe and spoke softly of mundane matters, then moved along.

As he walked among the men he heard whispers drifting on the night breezes, and a pye-dog was crooning in the dark, but otherwise the only sound was the crunch of his boots against the hard sand.

Hill wasn't ready to sleep and wanted to talk, and asked Maskelyne numerous questions about his stage career. He listened in childlike silence as Jasper described the night of his first appearance on stage, at a command performance in the Palace Theatre decorated with one million roses, then told him the story of the titled Russian who offered him a fortune to make his wife really disappear. Hill belly-laughed with innocent pleasure. These two men had nothing in common but this time and place, the war had made them friends and they would remain friends as long as they served together. Eventually, the young soldier asked Maskelyne his honest opinion of Kathy Lewis, and Jasper replied, 'I think she's splendid.'

'You think she's a looker?'

'If I didn't I'd be about the only man in Cairo who thought that. That interested Hill. 'Really?'

'Absolutely. Why? What do you think about her?'

'I like her all right, I guess. Nothing big.' Hill paused and thought about that, then repeated, 'Nothing big.'

Before Hill could ask any more questions about Kathy, Maskelyne patted him on the shoulder and moved away, leaving him the gift of a pretty young girl to dream about.

Townsend was sitting alone by a smouldering fire, nonchalantly flipping pebbles into the ashes, lost in a memory.

'Okay if I sit?'

Townsend didn't look up. 'Pull up some sand.'

Maskelyne settled down, drawing his legs into his chest and wrapping his long muscular arms around them. The sand was still radiating the heat of the day, and the night biters hadn't yet appeared in any numbers. The two men sat in uneasy silence for a few moments, staring into the embers, then Maskelyne blurted out, 'I'm terrified of fire, you know.'

The painter did not realize the enormity of that admission. 'Didn't your mum ever tell you it keeps the heart beating?'

'No,' Jasper said softly, 'never heard that one.' He scooped up a fistful of warm pebbles and began flicking them off his forefinger into the darkness. Why had he made that sudden confession to Townsend, a man he barely knew? he wondered. Perhaps, Jasper thought, by opening himself up to Townsend the painter might, in turn, reveal himself. But more likely, he simply needed to get it out and believed Townsend was a guardian of dark secrets.

Townsend was paying almost no attention to him. He was staring into the past, trying to remember how his wife had looked on their wedding day. He could visualize her dress, white with a lace neck and ruffled belt line, he could even hear her laughing, but, hard as he tried, he could not picture her face.

Maskelyne slapped a fly off his arm. The bugs were coming out of their sand burrows. 'You all right?' he asked.

'Oh, just chipper,' Townsend said bitterly, then corrected himself, 'Yeah, I'm fine.'

Maskelyne made an attempt at light conversation, but the painter did not pick up his end, making Jasper feel like an intruder. 'Well,' he said finally, standing and stretching, 'try to get some sleep. It may be a long trek tomorrow.'

Townsend looked up at him. The corners of his mouth began

curling into a half-smile, but he caught himself. 'Thanks for trying,' he said. 'You're a good sort.'

Maskelyne returned to his bedroll with a sprightly step.

Twenty-fourth Armoured broke camp before dawn. The trucks continued south, leaving a trail of litter in hopes it would be discovered by the enemy, stopping every few hours as scheduled to set up a tank display. Surveillance aircraft in the sector reported no sign of Jerry. The lack of contact was making everyone testy. 'Okay, Jay,' Knox teased the magician, trying to relieve the tension, 'what'd you do with them?'

Late in the morning news was passed down from the lead truck: Eighth Army was proceeding toward Tobruk without encountering serious opposition. It was as if the desert had opened up and swallowed Rommel's army. The men of 24th Armoured scoured the horizon as they would watch a dangling butcher's knife. The absence of Rommel was somehow more frightening than his presence. Innocent landscapes became fearsome forms. Natural shadows veiled all sorts of threats. The silence grew louder and louder.

In fact, Panzer Group Africa was not hiding at all. The enemy had simply been taken by complete surprise. Rommel was so confident Auchinleck would not make his break until early December that he had flown to Rome to celebrate his fiftieth birthday with his wife, then dallied in Athens before returning.

His usually efficient intelligence section informed him the desert was quiet. The scraps of news received from Cairo were confusing and contradictory. Raging thunderstorms had turned Luftwaffe airfields into swamps and kept most planes grounded, and those few spotters who managed to get off the ground reported no unusual enemy activity.

Rommel was greeted with sketchy reports of British movement upon his return to Libya on the morning of November 18. Some armoured cars had been reported moving toward Tobruk, and scattered radio transmissions had been intercepted in the south, but he dismissed this as nothing more than a reconnaissance in force. He took no action to counter this threat, instead concentrating his efforts on his own forthcoming offensive against Tobruk.

The fighting finally began on November 19. Twenty-second Armoured Brigade ran smack into the Italian Ariete Division and began slugging it out. Southeast of this battle, General Alec Gatehouse's 4th Armoured Brigade was attacked by 21st Panzer and took a beating. But Seventh Armoured met only light opposition and got to within ten miles of Tobruk before camping for the night. And 6th Royal Tank overran the important airfield at Sidi Rezegh, destroying nineteen planes on the ground by running over their tails.

The isolated 24th Armoured (cardboard) got news of the actions late in the day. 'It's on,' Maskelyne reported to the Gang. 'The Twenty-second's been hit.' But around them the desert remained empty and threatening.

Crusader's initial encounters were inconclusive. Twenty-second lost forty tanks, some of them dropping out with mechanical problems, while the Italians lost twenty-four. Fourth Armoured had been battered, losing sixty tanks in the fighting.

That night Rommel finally realized this was the beginning of Auchinleck's major push, perhaps convinced by the 9 P.M. BBC Home News which reported, 'Eighth Army with a force of seventy-five thousand men excellently armed and equipped have started a general offensive in the western desert with the aim of destroying the German–Italian forces in Africa.' Rommel began drawing his panzers into a cohesive force. He was still hampered by incomplete intelligence, however, and was not able to determine precisely where the heart of the attacking force lay.

Auchinleck was also confused by the disposition of forces, signalling Churchill, 'It seems the enemy was surprised and unaware of the imminence and weight of our blow. Indications ... are that he is not trying to withdraw from the area Bardia/Sollum. Until we know the area reached by our armoured troops today it is not possible to read battle further at the moment. I myself am happy about the situation.'

The 24th spent the day chugging around the desert with loudspeakers blaring and mobilized dummy tanks in attack formation, but did not make contact with the enemy. After the initial wave of excitement over the battle news had subsided, Maskelyne found himself watching the canvas tanks bouncing over the desert and feeling terribly depressed. The whole ploy suddenly seemed ridiculous. The greatest armies in history were smashing armour only a few hundred miles away, and he was stuck in the middle of a military sideshow. He felt the aching despair of the performer working in front of an empty house.

He set his jaw and stared straight ahead, and said nothing for a long time.

Once it became obvious that Rommel appreciated the magnitude of the offensive, everyone expected that the unarmed decoy units in the south would be quickly recalled. But HQ, hoping to confuse Jerry a bit longer, ordered them to 'proceed to your objective,' meaning they should continue raising dust in the area.

The 24th set out its dummy bedrolls for the second night without making contact. Fuller cooked for the Gang. After cutting an empty German gasoline can in half, he filled the bottom half with sand, sprinkled gasoline on it and ignited it. Then he filled the upper half with water and placed it over the fire. This scalding removed the gasoline taste so that the top could be used as a pot. Dinner consisted of desert stew, a mixture of bully beef (Argentine corned beef), onions, potatoes, a can of soup, some vegetables and a topping of Worcester sauce. Hill made a bucket of drink: gin, lime juice and water.

Maskelyne shared a ration-crate table with Knox. The desert was getting blowy, so they hunched over their cans as they ate, unsuccessfully trying to keep the sand out of their meals. After eating in silence for a bit, Knox suggested pleasantly that the stew wasn't unusually dreadful.

After biting down on a piece of sandy meat, Maskelyne gave up chewing and gulped down tiny tasteless portions. 'It's decent,' he said.

The professor looked at him over the rim of his glasses. 'You're not the only one feeling it, you know.'

Maskelyne feigned ignorance. 'What's that?'

'You know exactly what I mean. This whole outing. Canvas tanks. Cardboard guns. It's an impressive collection of nothing, isn't it? The real fighting's so close we can feel the bloody desert rumbling and we're here playing with toys.'

Jasper forced a feeble smile. 'Depressing, isn't it?'

'Damn right it is.' Knox sighed. 'I'm the chap who's supposed to appreciate the value of a decoy better than anyone else. Perhaps I do. But, crikey, it certainly isn't much fun playing the part.'

An evening peace had settled over the camp. Groups of soldiers had gathered around small fires. A corporal was vainly attempting to tune a crackling wireless, but otherwise it was a quiet time. 'You think they feel it, too?' Jasper wondered.

'Every one of them. What makes you think you're so special? They feel just as forgotten, just as left out. Hill wasn't the only one wanting a taste of it, remember.'

'That's true.' Maskelyne lifted his canteen to the professor. 'Better days.'

Knox bumped it with his own. 'Better days.'

By the morning of November 20 Rommel realized that the most immediate threat to his position was the possibility that Tobruk would be relieved, enabling the British to resupply on the march. To counter this, he began massing his army in the area.

The feints made at his supply lines in the south had been marginally effective. Panzer Group Africa seemed briefly confused by the simulated army, but recovered rapidly and prepared for the battle at Tobruk.

Twenty-fourth Armoured knew none of these strategic details, however, and spent the twentieth roaming the desert searching for the enemy. 'Just like Jerry,' Graham grumbled, 'only showin' up when he's not invited.'

'Maybe he's got his own magician,' Robson suggested, 'and he's made the whole army invisible.'

First contact was made during morning tea break. The column had paused to refuel and brew up when an Arab was spotted watching them from the crest of a dune about ninety yards away. The Arab held the reins of a restless camel and appeared to be alone. He did nothing except stand firm and watch the camp.

Hill stared back at him for a while, then decided to take some action. Cautioning Graham and Fuller to 'watch this one,' he planted one of the Gang's dummy shell charges in the sand, then he lit the fuse. Aside from his two companions, no one was aware of his joke.

The shell blasted a spout of sand six feet into the air.

The camp exploded into action. Mess tins went flying, tea was splashed over everything, helmets were slapped on as the men scattered like Scotsmen at the scent of a bill. They dived under trucks and buried their heads in the sand as they waited for more incoming artillery fire.

The Arab fought to hold the stampeding camel, somehow managing to swing onto its back, and fled at a gallop.

Nothing happened. At first Hill thought the pandemonium was hysterically funny, but his laughter stopped when he realized he was responsible for it. After the frenzy had settled, he mustered enough courage to shout into the sticky morning heat, 'Sorry about that one, lads, I'm afraid it was a mistake.'

No one budged.

Hill walked into the centre of the camp. 'I just blew off a dummy,' he yelled, turning around so everyone could hear him. 'I was just trying to scare that Arab.'

The men crawled slowly out of their hiding spots. One Engineer private, wearing a layer of white sand on his face, screamed, 'You bloody crackpot!' and charged at him, but he was restrained by two others. Once the shock had worn off, and the moment of anger had passed, some of the soldiers began laughing at the absurdity of the situation, and eventually everyone joined in.

They attacked Private Hill. They grabbed him, turned him upside down and stripped off his uniform, then gave him a good sand bath. By the time they set him free he was so chock-a-block with sand a week of showers wouldn't wash it all away. Even Maskelyne and Knox joined in, throwing handfuls of sand as Hill received his due. To Mike Hill's credit, he played his part well, fighting hard enough, but not overdoing it, and laughing good-naturedly at his punishment. By the time 24th Armoured struck camp the tension had evaporated.

At 1430 hours they were ordered to return to Cairo. They folded up their tanks and began the long drive home. Only upon their return did they learn that the Crusader offensive was in trouble.

General Auchinleck's gamble that his drive on Tobruk would lure Rommel's armour piecemeal into the fray had failed. Instead, the panzer units maintained their integrity and forced Eighth Army to abandon its timetable. Both sides lost communications vans in the early fighting and were out of direct contact with rear headquarters. Officers in the field were forced to improvise without adequate knowledge of enemy deployment. Victory would depend on leadership, fortitude and good fortune.

The breakout from Tobruk began at dawn on the twenty-first, earlier than originally scheduled. Lieutenant General Scobie's 70th Division, expecting to find the panzer divisions encircling them destroyed or badly damaged, met unexpectedly heavy opposition. After fierce fighting, the 70th forged a four-thousand-square-yard salient.

While the heavy fighting was going on around Tobruk, the major armoured battle of the offensive developed near the airfield at Sidi Rezegh. As troops from both armies blindly manoeuvred for position, an incredible five-layer military sandwich, thirty miles thick, was being formed. The Tobruk garrison, backed against the Mediterranean, was the bottom layer. A joint German–Italian force, the second layer, was spread the length of the perimeter. In the middle of this disposition, 7th Armoured was simultaneously attacking the German–Italian force to its north while attempting to beat back General Crüwell's panzers in the south. Crüwell, in turn, was being attacked from his rear by 4th Armoured and 22nd Armoured.

The fighting raged through November 22 and was at times so bitter that the desert battlefield was completely obscured by smoke from cannon and burning tanks. During the afternoon 4th Armoured rushed to support the 22nd, but was forced to stand by helplessly because it could not distinguish the combatants.

That night, 15th Panzer, searching for elements of 21st Panzer, accidentally ran smack into 4th Armoured preparing to laager. 15th Panzer turned on its headlights and charged into the camp, inflicting such extensive damage that the 4th was incapable of returning to the battle the following day.

An unusually heavy morning mist hung over the desert the next day. Sunday, November 23, was the German remembrance day, *Totensonntag*, the Day of the Dead. As the mist lifted, 15th Panzer pounced upon the lightly defended transport and supply of 5th South African Infantry. 5th Panzer raced to join the slaughter, and by dusk 5th South African had ceased to exist. Three thousand four hundred of its 5,700 troops had been killed, wounded or captured, and all of its equipment was lost.

Reports of this disaster shattered General Cunningham's already weakened resolve, and he began considering a full-scale retreat to save Eighth Army. Auchinleck flew to the front for an emergency meeting.

The Auk remained confident. Although his army had taken severe losses, he knew that Rommel had also received a nasty beating in the prolonged battle. And while fresh British tanks were already en route to the front, he was certain Rommel could not be resupplied. Responding to Cunningham's request for direction, he ordered boldly, 'You will continue to attack the enemy relentlessly, using all your resources even to the last tank.'

Twenty-fourth Armoured (cardboard) reached Cairo in mid-afternoon. Some of the Engineers had infected insect bites and open pus sores, one corporal was painfully sunburned and another had wrenched his back digging a truck out of soft sand, but otherwise the unit was unscathed. The column drove out of the desert into the normal afternoon traffic jam and had to inch its way through the city. Knox decided this was a stroke of luck. 'It'll be dark before we get back to the Valley,' he explained, 'and no one will be there to see us sneak in.'

The Gang actually arrived at Magic Valley just before sundown. A mob of poor and sick Egyptians crowded around the front gate and wailed for help, but the usually sympathetic Fuller gunned the engine and roared past them at an unsafe speed.

A bedsheet had been hung over the entrance to the dayroom, and on it someone had painted in bright red letters, 'Welcome Home,

Fighting 24th!' The Gang piled off the truck silently and walked under it. Hill, fifth in line, reached up and ripped it down.

Some of the civilian factory workers watched the dispirited group unload. As the welcoming message fluttered to the ground, one of them said, 'Poor chaps. Must have seen a rough time out there.'

Maskelyne told the men to report back after they had rested. 'We've got things to get done around here,' he said as vigorously as he could manage, but even he couldn't figure out exactly what work there was to be done. The men drifted off to their quarters for a good sleep.

They awoke the next day to terrible news. With his usual flair for the unexpected, Rommel was leading his last ninety tanks on a wild dash for the wire, the Egyptian border. Once he'd got behind Auchinleck's armour, he meant to wreck British communications and supply lines, then attack the unprotected infantry. This brazen charge through British lines had caused panic among support units. Rear-echelon supply and administration companies abandoned their positions without waiting for orders, creating total chaos. Communications broke down and headquarters had lost control of the army. Units were fleeing in every direction. Stories were spreading that German troops wearing British uniforms had infiltrated Eighth Army's ranks. By the end of the day the situation was so hopelessly confused that XIII Corps briefly battled its own friendly forces. A British military policeman at a desert crossroads found himself directing German traffic. Late in the afternoon 7th Armoured was drawing supplies at the south end of a depot while enemy troops were replenishing at the northern end.

The commanders were just as mixed up as their troops. General Cunningham was almost captured while visiting 30th Corps, and his plane was shelled as it took off. Rommel's staff car broke down and he hitched a ride with General Crüwell in a captured British armoured car. The driver got lost and drove into a British camp, where the generals quietly spent the night.

In Cairo, British command tried to maintain a calm front. Maskelyne was invited to golf at Gezira, but refused. The polo matches took place as scheduled.

By the twenty-fifth, Rommel's powerful force had blitzed fifteen miles into Egypt. The despondent Cunningham was ready to abandon Crusader and prepare to defend the Nile Basin.

The Auk remained steadfast, refusing to be bullied by this audacious rush at his rear lines. Rommel, he told his staff, 'is trying to lash out in all directions to distract us from our object, which is to destroy him utterly. We will not be distracted and he will be destroyed ... He is making a desperate effort, but he will not get very far. That column of tanks simply cannot get supplies. I am sure of this.'

Auchinleck was absolutely right. On November 26 the panzers had to retire to Bardia for refuelling and supply. Moreover, Rommel's absence from his rear headquarters while leading this heroic charge had caused severe command problems, and the rest of his army was bogged down on the desert.

Auk resolved his own leadership problems the moment Rommel began withdrawing, replacing Cunningham with his little-known deputy chief of staff, Major General Neil M. Ritchie. Cunningham entered a Cairo hospital suffering from mental and physical exhaustion. At forty-four, Ritchie was the youngest general in the British Army, but he had not commanded troops in more than twenty years. In fact Auchinleck was personally taking charge of Crusader. But even before these staff changes had been made the German counterattack had stalled, and the availability of supply was beginning to tip the battle in favour of Eighth Army.

During the night of November 26, while Rommel's armour was refuelling, the New Zealand Division of XIII Corps burst out of Tobruk and linked up with Eighth Army elements on the El-Duda heights. Thirteenth Corps commander General Godwin-Austen signalled news of the successful breakout to Auchinleck: 'Corridor to Tobruk free and secured. Tobruk not half as relieved as I am.'

But control of the western desert remained in doubt into December. Although outnumbered almost four to one in tanks, Rommel invested his limited resources brilliantly and was able to combat the much larger force on even terms. 'What difference does it make if you have two tanks to my one,' he lectured a captured British officer, 'when you spread them out and let me smash them in detail.'

On December 1 his battered army was able to reimpose its siege lines around Tobruk.

Gray Pillars finally had an old-fashioned war to fight. Until Crusader, the war in the desert had been an irksome series of titanic battles followed by long periods of reinforcement and resupply. Top brass had had a difficult time finding the pulse of the campaign. But now Jerry was standing tough and appeared ready to fight to a conclusion. Here, at last, was a battle with which an officer conversant in history could be comfortable.

The residents of Cairo got used to the idea that Crusader would continue for a while and began weaving it into their daily lives. It became habit to listen to the overnight war news each morning before going to the office, and to pause regularly during the day to catch the hourly reports. The stock exchange stabilized. Restaurant prices rose slightly, but there was no shortage of prime beef or alcohol, and the run on the food markets halted. The autumn social season was resumed.

Most Europeans kept their suitcases packed, but took them away from the front door and stored them in closets.

Maskelyne once again found himself seeking a project for the Gang, but those ranking officers in the city were occupied with Crusader, and thus not available to him. The Valley workshops continued producing dummy equipment, but most of it was left to weather in the yard. With the pipeline from Britain flowing with freshly trained soldiers, new guns and tanks, the dummies would no longer be needed. The day of the ghost army seemed to have passed.

'We did a good job,' Knox declared. 'They didn't even know we were coming.'

Hill, chuckled bitterly. 'Hell Professor, they didn't even know we were there.'

'I meant the sunshields, Michael,' Frank corrected softly. In fact the Magic Gang had contributed substantially to the success of Crusader. Their sunshields had helped hide the existence of a massive armoured force from Rommel's observers, allowing Eighth Army to achieve total surprise, while decoy artillery pieces and soldiers had swelled British lines. Somehow, though, none of this made the men of Maskelyne's Magic Gang feel any more a part of the action.

Adding to the Gang's difficulty in readjusting to normal city life was the lack of a routine to which they could return. As Knox had promised when recruiting them, the Camouflage Experimental Section had always been without formal structure. They had worked long days and nights when there was work to be done and rested and played when it was finished. But with two great armoured forces slugging it out around Tobruk, there were no projects that required their unique abilities. No generals or admirals stopped by just to see what they were cooking up. Time hung over Magic Valley like a midsummer heat wave, and allowed the men to wallow in their depression.

The next few weeks were the most difficult Maskelyne spent in the desert. In his own mind, he had achieved his original goal: he had proved that the techniques of stage magic could be adapted to warfare. But he felt he had really accomplished nothing. He had failed in his desperate effort to step out of the family shadows. Rather than making his own name important, he felt doomed to be remembered as a bizarre footnote to history: a magician playing at war. In the end, only the guns made a difference.

To boost his own spirits, and those of his men, he organized Sunday-afternoon drinks at the Valley. Among the invited guests were the best-liked Engineers, Kathy Lewis, Geoffrey Barkas, Dudley Clarke, a few men from the Mechanical Section who had stayed behind when that unit moved forward, and some lady friends of the Gang. Camoufleurs Jack Keefer and Donald Kingsley, graduates of Buckley's school at Farnham, came down from Alex, and Tony Ayerton, just back from constructing an entire dummy airfield in the desert, showed up with a number of his people. There were, in all, about thirty-five people at the party. Only Phil Townsend did not show, which surprised no one, and he was not missed.

Although it had been planned as a spirit-lifter, it turned into a celebration. Before dawn that morning, Rommel, unable to properly support his troops at Tobruk, had begun a staged withdrawal to El Gazala. The eight-month siege was finally over. A prime objective of Crusader had been achieved.

The gramophone music was loud, the ladies were lovely, the alcohol was plentiful. For this afternoon, at least, everyone was carefree. Fuller, it was discovered, could hold his brew, and engaged in a memorable chugging match with one of Ayerton's boys. Knox revealed a heretofore unsuspected talent for wild-bird calls. Even cartoonist Bill Robson, properly loosened up, told some risqué stories when his turn came round. Everyone danced madly.

Townsend arrived when the party was nearly over. When he did appear, ashen-faced, he quickly downed two shots and stood in a corner watching the dancers with glassy eyes. Knox spotted him standing alone and brought a mug of stout to him.

The artist did not take the brew. 'Yanks are in,' he said in a stunned voice.

'What?' Frank shouted. It was impossible to hear him above the noise.

In precisely the same soft tone, Townsend repeated, 'Yanks are in.'

'Who's that?'

'America,' Townsend said a bit louder, but evenly. 'They're in the war.'

A group standing nearby overheard him and immediately gave him their full attention. 'What's that?' one of them asked.

'The Japs bombed the American fleet in Hawaii this morning.

They're going to invade. Roosevelt's making it official tomorrow, but they're in.'

The news jolted the room like a Joe Louis punch. The gramophone plug was pulled and Jo Stafford groaned to a halt. Everyone gathered around Townsend and pumped him for details, but he had nothing to tell them beyond those few facts. Someone switched on a radio in time to catch the end of the brief bulletin that would be repeated throughout the night. Heavy damage was mentioned.

The room was momentarily silent as the startling news was digested, then a growing buzz burst into bedlam. With the United States in the war, the Germans would really be up against it. The men shook hands and pounded each other on the back, as if they had personally delivered America into the war. Toasts were raised to Roosevelt and Churchill and even Stalin, whose Russian armies had taken advantage of savage winter weather to halt the German blitzkrieg. There was speculation about a European front being opened within a few months. The Nazis would fall to the combined armies of the US and the Commonwealth, just as the Kaiser had. The Yanks were coming back!

The celebration roared into the night, and later, as the revellers slept it off, visions of soldiers and tanks marched in their dreams. Only days later was the severity of the Japanese attack completely understood. The America entering the war was a lion without claws. Its Navy had been shattered at Pearl Harbor. Its Army was shockingly unprepared. Its Army Air Forces were nearly obsolete. But the Empire was no longer going it alone, and that was enough to inspire renewed confidence.

Reams of paper were frantically pushed during the following week as officers rushed around at top sweat, and Cairo seemed even more chaotic than usual as everyone waited expectantly for some demonstration of mighty America's entrance into the war, but aside from a protest march organized by the Muslim Brotherhood, nothing out of the ordinary occurred. The beginning of the week had been hectic for the precious few Americans in the city, as there weren't enough of them to satisfy all the locals who wanted to show their gratitude by entertaining a Yank. They were feted and toasted and able to savour all of Cairo's delights without forking over a red cent. But by Friday the excitement over the United States's entry into the war gave way to widespread resentment. Where had America been when the going was really tough? Wasn't it typical of them to join in after the battle was nearly won! By the end of the week the Americans in town were paying top price for a drink, dinner or a woman, and everyone was again focusing on the desert war. The Yanks might be coming, but it wasn't worth holding up the battle for them.

Eighth Army resumed the Crusader offensive on December 15. Ritchie sent his main force directly into Rommel's strong defensive line, at the same time dispatching an armoured brigade to circle his southern flank and cut off Panzer Group Africa's escape route. Grudgingly, the Germans retreated, extracting a bloody price from the British for every foot of worthless desert sand.

Auchinleck's persistence had resulted in victory. Three hundred enemy tanks had been destroyed, 33,000 prisoners were taken, Tobruk was relieved, and Rommel had been driven back to the place from which he'd begun the fight nearly a year earlier. Eighth Army had suffered substantial losses, but replacements for men and equipment were readily available. For the first time since Rommel's arrival in North Africa, the British controlled the desert. The next stage of Crusader would be the final destruction of the enemy.

But for Maskelyne and the Magic Gang the battle, perhaps the war, was over. Like supply clerks and WAAFs and over-age officers, they were forced to follow the battle in newspapers and on the radio.

'It was a grand show, wasn't it?' Knox said as he sat with Maskelyne in Jasper's office, trying to pull him out of the doldrums. Their conversation eased into the recent past, and they recalled with great delight the good times they had shared: the look of astonishment on Lord Gort's face when he discovered Maskelyne's broomstick aimed at his belly, Mike Hill's adolescent exuberance when the Luftwaffe bombers veered toward the Maryūt Bay decoy, Barkas's embarrassment during the legendary Dung Patrol collections. Knox reminded Maskelyne of the day Townsend got lost in the salvage-dump maze, and Jasper remembered that glorious rainy afternoon when Fuller and Graham, demonstrating for the brass that the dummy tank could easily be hefted by two men, lifted it and uncovered a naked warrant officer entwined with an equally bare WAAF.

Eventually, they came round to the future, and their laughter faded. 'If we can just hold it together a while longer something'll come up for us,' Maskelyne said fervently. 'I know it.'

Knox didn't agree at all, feeling that the Army, just like the African elephant, now had too much firepower to bother with deception. But he indulged Maskelyne, because he believed that was the job of a friend, and they huddled together as they had long ago in Farnham and tried to cook up a plan.

As events soon proved, Professor Knox was wrong. The Magic

Gang's show was about to begin a long encore. In November, German submarines had sunk the aircraft carrier *Ark Royal* and the battleship *Barham*. On December 10, Japanese planes sank the battleship *Prince of Wales* and the cruiser *Repulse*. Admiral Andrew Cunningham's Mediterranean Fleet was still reeling from these losses on December 19 when Force K from Malta ran into a minefield while pursuing an Italian convoy. The cruiser *Neptune* and the destroyer *Kandahar* went to the bottom, and the cruisers *Aurora* and *Penelope* were heavily damaged. That same night three Italian chariots, midget submarines, slipped through the boom defences of Alexandria harbour behind a destroyer. Once inside, six frogmen attached timed explosives to the hull of the battleship *Queen Elizabeth* and the tanker *Sagona* and planted another time bomb in the seabed beneath the battleship *Valiant*. Three hours later the harbour erupted. *Sagona* was destroyed. *Queen Elizabeth* and *Valiant* settled on the shallow bottom, although most of their decks remained above sea level. Both battleships would be out of service for months.

Only eight weeks earlier the Royal Navy had controlled the Mediterranean, attacking German and Italian convoys with impunity, depriving Rommel of desperately needed supplies. Suddenly, the situation was reversed. The battered British fleet was no longer capable of maintaining its stranglehold or providing security for convoys. Desperately needed supplies for Panzer Group Africa began getting through to Libya. The Luftwaffe renewed its attacks on Malta, Britain's most important naval base in the Mediterranean and a keystone of Auchinleck's defence.

Admiral Cunningham needed a new navy. The Magic Gang was back in business.

ELEVEN

Christmas 1941 was a depressing day. The sun shone as brightly as a queen's diamond, and Cairo smelled sweetly of blossoming flowers; all the fine hotels served scrumptious holiday dinners and there were endless parties. The celebrating Europeans smiled their teeth and laughed till their stomachs ached and shared sincere toasts and, most of all, yearned to be back home in the winter cold, stoking a crackling fire, hanging balls on sappy trees, slaving over a sinkful of dirty dishes, and warmed by familiar voices.

The Gang shared a special dinner at the Valley consisting of 'Grapefruit à la Volturno' and 'Dindon roti au Salerno,' with 'Spuds au Termoil,' 'Petits pois au Shepheards,' 'Saucissons au Foggia' and 'Sauce sans origin.' This was accompanied by 'Christmas pudding à la workhouse.' Hill decided it was 'the best Christmas dinner I've had this year.'

After the meal Maskelyne and Knox led a Christmas singalong. Holiday cigars were lit, a solemn prayer for deliverance of the men in battle was offered, and, quickly, the room emptied.

Maskelyne went over to Communications and tried to put through a patch-call to Mary, but it proved impossible. Earlier in the day he'd written her a long letter, a letter full of memories of past Christmases, and told her how much he loved her and missed her.

This is a difficult day for all of us here [he wrote], and I hope it ends quickly. If I could spin the earth on its axis to speed up the hours, I would do so. I miss you always, but today the pain is more severe.

Shepheards has put a large tree on the deck and hung crepe on it, and Christmas music is piped outside into the sun. The gyppies seem to enjoy it, but most Englishmen are depressed by it all.

This is not much like other Xmases we've shared, is it? Well, I trust good St. Nicholas was generous with everyone. Please tell the children I miss them and love them.

He'd mailed out a lovely silk robe and various toys in late November, but had little hope his package had arrived.

Jasper knew she would make the day as busy and noisy as possible. If he closed his eyes and inhaled deeply, he could smell the roasting turkey. He also knew that much of her day would be spent thinking of him.

The new assignment was the best present anyone in the Gang received that Christmas. There was revived spirit in Maskelyne's voice as he laid it out the next day. 'Both *Queen Elizabeth* and *Valiant* were flooded, but they remained on even keel and much of the damage has been concealed. Jerry knows they're wounded, but not how badly. Soon as he realizes they're going to be out of commission for a bit he's going to scrape up every supply ship he can find and shoot it down the pipe to Rommel. Before that happens, Admiral Cunningham wants us to give Rommel something to think about. What he had in mind, actually–' he paused, and held the silence long enough to promote suspense '–was a fleet of submarines.'

Graham sighed aloud. 'Had me worried there for a sec. I really thought he was going to ask for something difficult.'

With most of the warships of Britain's Mediterranean Fleet damaged or needed elsewhere, Admiral Andrew Browne Cunningham was forced to rely on his submarines to close the German supply route to Libya. Luftwaffe reconnaissance made this difficult by counting the subs in their pens every two hours, thus enabling Rommel's Intelligence to track every arrival or departure. This information substantially decreased the efficiency of the submarine fleet. Cunningham intended to counter this by substituting dummy submarines for real ships when they sailed, thus enabling his subs to slip away from port undetected. Impressed by the Magic Gang's dummy tanks, he requested full-size, buoyant cardboard submarines that could be folded up, loaded onto five-tonners and set up somewhere else within hours.

The Gang began the assignment with a significant handicap: none of them had ever seen a real submarine. 'Actually I did see one once,' Fuller confessed, 'in Southampton about ten years ago. But it was at night.'

Cunningham's staff provided them with top-secret blueprints – and armed guards to protect the plans. According to these layouts, each dummy submarine would have to be 258 feet from bow to stern and rise twenty-seven feet from the waterline to the tip of the conning tower. It would have to be equipped with a deck gun, anchors, chains, railings and all proper markings.

'Plus the periscope,' Hill loudly reminded everyone. 'I've never seen a submarine without a periscope.'

'You've never seen a submarine,' Knox reminded him.

While Auchinleck's Eighth Army relentlessly pursued Rommel across the desert, once again dangerously extending its own supply line, the Magic Gang went to work on the seemingly impossible task. 'Dummy subs aren't all that different from dummy tanks,' Maskelyne insisted, 'just bigger. The construction techniques are basically the same. We'll get some wooden rods, make a frame, stretch some canvas – all we need to begin is something large enough to serve as a foundation for the upper works.'

'How about a real submarine?' Robson suggested.

The Gang began searching the Nile Basin for something large, useless and available. By this time, each of them had become accustomed to delving into unusual places in search of obscure objects. They were used to asking ridiculous questions without being able to provide sensible answers for people who wondered what they were up to. And they were used to seeing Arabs pointing at their foreheads and making small circles, the universal expression of insanity. 'Remember,' Maskelyne said after the first day ended without results, 'it doesn't have to float. We can rig some barrels under it.'

Later, Knox reminded him that they had no barrels. Barrels were added to the shopping list.

On the third day Graham was offered a hundred pounds of camel dung by an Egyptian entrepreneur who remembered the Gang's earlier quest. But nothing that would serve as a foundation for the submarine deck and conning tower was found.

Two more days passed. Those objects that were available to the Gang weren't large enough, and those few things large enough weren't available. Scraps of metal were in demand in real tank and aircraft repair shops. Auto hulks were already being used for dummy tank chassis. Even the twisted frames of smashed aircraft were being cannibalized by the miracle-working mechanics of the Desert Air Force. Burned-out tank hulls were available, but they weighed tons. 'It would be like putting a lump of lead in your tea,' Graham pointed out. 'All our dummy submarines would do is sink.'

Fuller finally discovered the solution rotting in a scrapyard. 'I was on the tram trying to think about the problem,' he explained with as much enthusiasm as anyone had ever seen him show, 'but the bloody train was making such a racket it was impossible to think about anything at all. Then we went screeching around that dreadful corner at Bab el Luq and the wheels sounded as if they were screaming at me. Railway cars would do nicely.'

Maskelyne agreed railway cars would serve, but reminded the painter that every tram in Cairo was already being overused. 'The Egyptians never replace them and we can't simply lift a few of them.' He hesitated, and turned to look at Mike Hill. 'Can we?' Before the private could reply Jasper shook his mind clear of such thoughts and answered his own question, 'No, of course we can't.'

'Actually, that's not a problem,' Fuller said, smiling broadly. 'There's a whole bloody yard of rusting sleeper cars near the station. Seems they were built for the Trans-Arabian Railway, and by the time they got here Lawrence had blown the railway to bits. They're of absolutely no use at all to anyone but us.'

There were eighteen sleeping cars in all. As Fuller said, they had been ordered from England at the turn of the century to run on the 883 miles of track that linked the Ottoman Empire of Sultan Abdul-Hamid II. The line had been completed in 1908 and served primarily to carry Muslems to the holy city of Mecca. After ten years of successful operation, the Great War began. T. E. Lawrence and his Arab bands regularly attacked the single-track line and blasted it out of business. The sleepers had been manufactured to fit its narrow-gauge tracks and could not be used elsewhere. Although homeless Arabs occasionally camped inside, the cars sat forgotten in a railway graveyard between wars. Fuller was absolutely right. They were unserviceable as railway cars, but they would make fine submarines. So the rusting remains of a sultan's dream became the foundation of the Magic Gang's fleet.

Admiral Cunningham's office purchased the lot of them, supposedly for scrap metal, and had one of them carted to Magic Valley by a tank recovery unit. The rusting sleeper sat ludicrously on the baked sand in a corner of the yard while the Gang planned its transformation. Once, two decades and a war earlier, the car had been sleek and lovely, a symbol of the new technology that promised to tame the desert. Instead, its expensive sliding windows and marvellous ceiling fans, its metal doors and covered seats had been brutally ripped out, and it was left a giant shell to be cracked open by that desert. The last remnants of its past, the serifs of some skilfully painted Arabic letters, remained barely visible under layers of decay.

'It looks so forlorn sitting there,' Knox said sadly.

Robson tried to imagine the car in its original splendour. 'Just think what it must have looked like to some superstitious tribesman out on the Blue, coming out of nowhere, belching black smoke. Must have been somethin'.'

Hill placed it nicely in perspective. 'About the same as seeing a three-humped camel loping through Trafalgar Square, I s'pose.'

After discussing various concepts with Graham and some of the men from the Mechanical Section, Maskelyne decided to build a wooden frame around the railroad car and anchor the necessary hinged beams to this frame. The frame was designed to be lifted off the floating sleeper, folded flat and shipped to the next harbour, there to be unfolded and slipped over an identical car. Beams and tubing would be nailed and welded to the frame and painted sailcloth stretched over it. 'The entire contraption could be folded up in a few minutes,' Maskelyne claimed as he showed the Gang his rough sketches and estimated specs for the submarine dummy. 'The sides extend out like the wings of a moth and can be pulled out into position or pushed back against the frame for easy transport. The conning tower is nothing more than sailcloth stretched over an arrangement of flexible rods and seven wooden rings of decreasing circumference. It's raised into position by pulleys and locked in place with pegs. The rings'll make a framework for the canvas, but they can also be compressed inside each other and lie almost flat. We can use painted sailcloth for the deck gun and ropes for the chains. A cardboard anchor ought to be enough to impress Jerry. Now, who's got questions?'

Fuller asked the only one that mattered. 'Will it float?'

Maskelyne shrugged. 'I haven't the foggiest.'

Graham made a scale model from the plans and a few days later the Gang crowded around a water tank that had been set up in the dayroom as he prepared to launch it. The railway-car model had been fashioned out of a shell casing. 'Remember,' the carpenter cautioned, 'it doesn't have to move at all. It just has to stay afloat.' He placed it delicately on the water and it rode high for a few seconds, then began quivering. Suddenly, it turned turtle. It floated upside down for a few more seconds, then slipped gracefully to the bottom of the tank.

'Seems a bit top-heavy,' Knox observed.

Maskelyne returned to his drawing table. Admiral Cunningham, meanwhile, was pressing the Gang for the dummy submarines. German Intelligence was successfully tracking his small submarine fleet, making it extremely dangerous for them to leave port. The Axis Mediterranean supply line to Tripoli had been reestablished, and Rommel was again receiving war *matériel*. On January 5, a large Italian convoy carrying fifty-four tanks and tons of gasoline got through. Once more, the balance of power in the desert had shifted. Panzer Group Africa had been pushed within range of its supply depots, while Eighth Army's lines now stretched across Cyrenaica. Auchinleck's troops had not been able to deliver the knockout blow he had envisioned, and the wounded Desert Fox, with his new tanks, was more dangerous than ever.

By January 16 the Gang had solved the flotation problems, at least in the tank, and built a prototype for inspection and testing. As Admiral Cunningham and his staff stood in the Valley yard watching, the contraption was placed over the railroad car. When it was firmly in position, Fuller and Graham pulled out the side wings. Then Hill and Knox began yanking on the pulley ropes, and, like a flag being run up a staff, the conning tower rose into place. Maskelyne clasped his hands behind his back and crossed his fingers as the bulky sticks and painted canvas were transformed into a full-size replica of a British submarine in a matter of minutes. 'Hey presto,' he whispered.

Cunningham turned to him. 'That's quite a show, Maskelyne,' he said coolly, but quite obviously pleased. 'I assume it will float?'

Maskelyne avoided a direct answer. 'I hope so as much as you do, sir.'

The dummy was transported to a heavily guarded beach on the Red Sea south of Suez for launching. The Gang travelled to the site under strict orders to maintain absolute secrecy about the canvas boat. 'No one must know about it,' Cunningham personally told them, 'and I mean no one.'

The launch was scheduled for January 19. It turned out to be a propitious day. That afternoon Eighth Army finally captured Halfaya Pass.

At twilight, the Gang set up the dummy. From the waterline to the tip of its wooden periscope, the sailcloth, tape, rope and rod submarine looked quite realistic, observed from a respectable distance, of course. But below its waterline it appeared to be suffering from a case of monstrous barnacles. Black oil drums, filled with sand to provide buoyancy, had been roped together and secured to the front and back of the sleeping car, while large rocks had been hung from the keel to add stability.

Hill had brought along a bottle of respectable Italian wine for the launching ceremony. The dummy had been named H.M.S. *Hopeful*, primarily because the Gang hoped it would stay afloat. As custodian of the wine, Hill nominated himself to christen the ship. In a loud, and proud, voice, he said, 'I dub this ...' He hesitated, unable to find an accurate description.

'Boat,' Robson urged.

Hill shrugged. 'Okay. I dub this boat His Majesty's ship, sort of, *Hopeful*, and all of us are really hopeful that it serves us very well.' Not daring to strike the dummy with the bottle, he instead pulled out the cork with his teeth and splashed a bit on the canvas, then took a long swig before passing it down the line.

Aided by a Royal Navy motorboat, the *Hopeful* was pulled and pushed and cursed down a greased slipway into the calm sea. The Gang stood watching on the beach as it glided into the shallows, a team of nervous fathers sending their virginal daughter into the world. The *Hopeful* pitched forward and threatened to plough straight under, but righted itself. Then, as everyone held his breath, it began tottering sideways and leaned heavily to starboard, but again righted itself and rode somewhat precariously on the Red Sea.

'Look at that, will you,' Graham said, 'the son of a bint actually floats.'

'Easy,' cautioned Knox. 'Give the lady some time to get settled.'

A slight breeze rippled the canvas deck and it shivered slightly, but held. 'We'll have to tack it down,' Maskelyne said critically, as if debating the length of her skirt hem. The wake created by the motorboat rolled toward the dummy, and under it, before crawling up the beach and fading into the sand. The *Hopeful* rocked gently and complained in woody squeaks, but steadied.

Maskelyne radioed the launch to move a bit farther from the shore, and the dummy was tugged into deeper water. Its silhouette against the pastel sky nicely matched that of a real ship of the line. 'She's grand,' Fuller decided. Maskelyne had already satisfied himself the dummy would pass German inspection. Townsend's paint crews had done a splendid job.

Reluctantly, the Gang abandoned her to the night. 'She'll be just fine,' Knox assured everyone as they boarded their three-tonner, but the men recognized this as Frank's usual optimistic chatter.

They were back on the beach at first light. The *Hopeful* was riding a few feet lower in the water and the oil barrel rafts, which were barely breaking the surface the night before, could no longer be seen. The sailcloth submarine appeared to be playing confidently on the light swells, rising and falling with them, pulling at her sea anchor.

'I told you,' a greatly relieved Frank Knox exclaimed. 'I told you she'd be fine.'

The Gang took off their shirts and boots and spent the morning sunning on the beach, awaiting the arrival of an inspection team from

Admiral Cunningham's office. 'This is the life,' Graham said, 'the Mediterranean sun beating down on us, the beach...'

'And not a bloody girl within a hundred miles worth lookin' at,' Hill sighed.

Shortly after ten a dispatch rider from the Ismailia area commander came roaring up to the security barricades well off the beach with most-urgent orders for Maskelyne to report to local headquarters immediately. 'I guess the commander wants to see her for himself,' he guessed as he buttoned his shirt and quickly brushed his gleaming black hair into place.

He did not. He wanted to know exactly what it was that Maskelyne had in the water.

Jasper stood before him with a carefully rehearsed look of astonishment on his face. Cunningham had made it expressly clear that the existence of the *Hopeful* was not to be disclosed to anyone. The entire submarine-warfare programme depended on secrecy. 'I've got nothing in the water,' he lied.

'You have,' the General retorted. 'I must know what it is.'

'No, sir. Nothing at all.'

'We're on the same side, you know. You can tell me.'

'I know that, sir, but believe me, I've got nothing there.'

The commander frowned. Then, in a firm voice, he warned, 'Don't stand there lying to me, Maskelyne. This is not one of your Piccadilly magic shows. I assure you, if you are not telling me the truth, I will take full punitive measures. Now I will ask you once again, have you got a submarine in the water?'

'I have no submarine.'

The General nodded, and told Maskelyne to sit down. 'Look here,' he continued in a conciliatory tone, 'I'm sorry to be so tough, but I've been getting reports from the RAF that an unidentified submarine has been spotted off the beach south of Suez. The Navy says they have no ships in the area. So I thought your presence here might have something to do with it. I had to make sure it didn't before I took any action.' He reached across the desk and picked up the telephone. As he cranked it, he added, 'Wouldn't want to go blasting one of our ships, you see.'

Maskelyne sat tight-lipped. Orders from an admiral, he knew, were serious orders.

The General spoke into the phone. 'Signal Air Command, please. That's a good fellow.' While waiting, he covered the mouthpiece with his hand and said to Maskelyne, 'Must be an intruder, then, although

I can't figure out what he's doing in these waters. Battery trouble, perhaps. We'll take care of him quick enough. I've got a squadron bombing up and two destroyers racing down to cut off its escape.'

If the General was bluffing, Maskelyne thought, he was a fine player. Suddenly he found himself facing the dilemma he created for his theatrical audiences: he didn't really believe the General, but his disbelief was not strong enough to offset his fear of the consequences if he was wrong.

'Archie? Malcolm here. So sorry, but I can't get a reading on that submarine. It's not one of ours, it seems, so you'd best go ahead–'

'It is mine, General,' Maskelyne said clearly.

The commander looked at him. 'Hold on a bit, Archie, would you?' He laid the phone on the desk. 'Why didn't you tell me?'

'I think we'd better contact Admiral Cunningham's office.'

The mess was quickly straightened out and the bombing mission scrubbed. Later that afternoon the area commander received a note from Cunningham reading: 'REGRET MISUNDERSTANDING BUT MASKELYNE IN YOUR AREA AND OTHER TRANSFORMATIONS WILL BE TAKING PLACE.'

Although the maiden voyage of the *Hopeful* was an unqualified success, Knox discovered a serious flaw before it was put into service. 'She doesn't leave any tracks,' he said after comparing a set of aerial photographs of the dummy with recce photos of real submarines in their slips.

'It's a boat,' Nails replied. 'Boats don't leave tracks.'

'Evidently they do when they're docked.' While lying at anchor, Knox explained, a submarine creates a mild wake in the form of two thin white trails which flow around its hull and beyond the stern. The *Hopeful* left no such signature. The professor solved the problem after a day's experimentation by suspending four forty-four-gallon drums of whitewash from the bow. A thumbnail hole was punched into each of them, and the seeping whitewash duplicated the wake. Its flow was controlled by the tide.

After the *Hopeful* had passed Cunningham's inspection, Magic Valley workshops went to work producing the rest of the canvas fleet. The 258-foot-long dummies were first used at the naval base in Beirut, Lebanon, and later in other ports throughout the war, to substitute for real submarines when they sailed, or to convince the enemy that Allied subs were operating in an area where in fact there were none. There is no record that the enemy ever caught on to the ploy, and the dummies were repeatedly attacked in their slips. The original sailcloth sub, the *Hopeful*, was blown into splinters seven months after launching.

But long before Maskelyne's submarine had passed inspection, Rommel was ready to turn on his pursuers. To bait his trap, he torched dozens of buildings in the city of Mersa Brega and scuttled numerous supply ships in the harbour. Allied Intelligence duly reported that Panzer Group Africa was destroying its strongholds and supplies, presumably in preparation for a withdrawal from Libya.

This was precisely what Rommel wanted them to believe. The 'strongholds' burned for the benefit of British agents in the city were actually abandoned houses, the ships useless hulks. Rather than retreating, Panzer Group Africa was going to attack. The Germans advanced in the night and spent the days sweltering beneath camouflage netting. On Wednesday, January 21, Rommel launched his counter-attack.

Eighth Army was stunned. The cities of Agedabia and Beda Fomm fell on the twenty-second. Benghazi was captured on the twenty-ninth, complete with stores including thirteen hundred trucks and tons of petrol. Within another week the British had been thrown back into the western desert, and were running short of supplies. Once again, Rommel had outwitted his opponent.

Auchinleck considered sacking Ritchie, but finally decided against it. By February 6, Rommel had progressed as far as his supply lines could safely be extended. Having finally learned the reality of desert warfare, he dug in until his army could be properly replenished. This last stroke of Crusader left the enemy armies facing each other across the Gazala Line, Eighth Army's sixty-mile-long chain of strongholds linked by dense minefields. These strongholds, called 'boxes' or 'keeps,' were each roughly two square miles in area, and were provisioned to withstand a week-long siege without requiring assistance. Approximately five hundred British tanks patrolled the sections between the six boxes, ready to blunt any attempt to manoeuvre through the minefields, or to race to support any box under attack. Each of these 'islands of resistance' was ringed by minefields, barbed wire, slit trenches and machine-gun pillboxes. Auchinleck was depending on the supposedly impregnable Gazala Line to stop Rommel, for if he broke through, the Nile Basin and the oil of the Middle East would be within his grasp.

General Rommel was content to let his battle wounds heal. He intended to summer on the Nile.

Maskelyne and Knox, meanwhile, were on their way to Malta. Air

Officer Commander-in-Chief, Middle East, Air Marshal Arthur Tedder, knew of the marvels the Magic Gang had produced for the Army and the Navy, and wanted them to reach into their bag of tricks to aid the Royal Air Force. He was hoping they might hide an entire island.

From the beginning of the desert war Malta's three airfields and deep natural harbour had serviced the aircraft, ships and submarines that had devastated Rommel's supply convoys. In November 1941, for example, Malta-based attackers sank nearly three of every four ships bound for Libya. German command realized that the survival of its African army depended upon the destruction of this blockade. To accomplish this, Malta would have to be obliterated.

Late in 1941, as Axis wolf packs hunted British warships on the high seas, the Luftwaffe and Regia Aeronautica began one of the most intensive bombing campaigns in history. Tens of thousands of tons of bombs rained on the tiny island weekly. Valletta, the capital city, was attacked eight times a day. The airfields and harbours were blasted into pitted ruins. The Maltese people were forced to live in caves and bomb shelters. Casualties mounted. Food and ammunition were scarce, and every British attempt to resupply the island was crushed. Malta resisted heroically, but the bombers came in waves, day after day, week after week.

The few underequipped and undermanned RAF fighter squadrons on the island were somehow managing to stay in business, but Tedder hoped Maskelyne and the Gang might figure some means of relieving the incredible pressure on them. He suggested that the appearance of new fighter aircraft on the island might at least cause the enemy to waste their bombs on useless targets, and perhaps make them wary about daylight raids. 'It's not much,' he admitted, 'but we haven't got much. Anything you can do would be most appreciated.'

The RAF Wellington ferrying Maskelyne and Knox to Malta touched down softly and bounced to a halt, its pilot deftly managing to avoid the worst of the bomb craters that pocked the dirt runway. Three-man shovel crews were swarming all over the field, trying to fill in the deepest holes with rock and dirt. The Wellington taxied to a spot next to a shattered tree trunk, and a ground crew was pulling camouflage nets over the plane even before its props stopped spinning. Two trucks and a jeep pulled up alongside and soldiers began rapidly unloading the precious supplies from the fuselage. Maskelyne and Knox were raced off the field in the jeep. 'No time to dally now,' their driver, a cheerful Irish corporal, said pleasantly. 'Never know when they'll decide to visit, eh what.'

After the months Maskelyne and Knox had spent in the tidy white cities of Egypt, the brief drive through Valletta staggered their senses. The full might of the enemy's air power had been brought against it. Entire districts had been bombed into barren fields of broken rock, glass and masonry. Rows of buildings were crushed as completely as eggs bludgeoned with a sledgehammer. Everywhere in the city civilian crews were building mounds of rubble, mounds identical to those Maskelyne had left behind in London when he sailed into the war.

The western desert was particularly well suited for warfare – there were no structures to be fought over, no civilians to be hurt. Just acres of brush and sand and the equipment of two sophisticated armies. Soldiers died and weapons were destroyed. There was a certain justice to that. But here, in Malta, the innocent suffered most.

A perpetual grey haze hung over the city, fed by wispy funnels of smoke rising from charred houses. Dying fires could be tasted in the air.

Children were playing in the rubble while adults picked through the remains of their homes or stores, occasionally emerging with some bright-coloured article of clothing or an unbroken piece of furniture. The Irish driver pointed out the remains of the Royal Opera House, now more of a quarry, the miraculously untouched Phoenician temple ruins, and the tunnels and bomb shelters that had been cut into the soft limestone.

The Royal Air Force had gone underground, setting up operations in a deep shelter. Maskelyne and Knox were greeted warmly, served tea and crumpets, briefed, and dispatched on a tour of the island. Pilot Officer Robert Simon accompanied them.

Simon was one of the brassy young fighter pilots the RAF was finally beginning to turn out in decent numbers. In peacetime, he might have been just finishing at university or beginning a trade; instead he had become a high-flying gunfighter. 'Missed the big one,' he said casually as they drove down a rutted street, meaning the Battle of Britain, 'but since I've been here I've got me four kills and a prob. The prob was a Stuka. We all saw it go into a spin, but it was night.'

Maskelyne studied him as he rattled on. He was small and slender, cockpit-sized, and his face was pleasant enough, although traces of an adolescent complexion problem were visible beneath a mild tan and the peach-fuzz beginnings of a beard.

Simon kept up a continuous line of chatter, changing subjects at no apparent crossroads. 'In Holland,' he told his older charges, 'the Dutch go round giving the Nazi salute and saying, "Heil, Rembrandt. Heil,

Rembrandt." And when a Jerry asks what they're doing, they say, "We've got a great painter, too!" '

The few planes Jasper spotted on or near runways were covered with canvas, or camouflage netting, or parked beneath wooden boards painted to resemble farm equipment when seen from the air. 'Gotta keep some of 'em clear,' the young pilot volunteered, 'so that we can get 'em up quick when Jerry comes visiting.'

The remainder of the Maltese air wing was carefully hidden. Aircraft were concealed in barns, tunnels, under piles of potatoes, onions and tomatoes or phoney mounds of rubble. Some were even hidden on small meadows, covered with grass carpets. 'Dirty, but effective,' Simon explained.

'How many in all?' Knox asked.

'Usually between seventy and a hundred serviceable. Mainly Hurricanes, but we've got some Spits and a batch of the Navy's Swordfish. Supposedly there's a flight of Spits coming in this month, but there's always a flight supposedly comin' in.'

'And what's Jerry got?' Jasper wondered.

Simon laughed. 'A whole bloody circus, that's all. Junkers, Heinkels, more Stukas than Stalin's got Commies, Messerschmitt nines and tens, probably even some wind-up bombers we don't even know about yet.'

While they were bouncing about the island the air raid sirens began whining and a flight of enemy bombers and fighters attacked Grand Harbour. Even from their safe position miles away, Maskelyne and Knox could hear the hideous, screeching wail that ripped through the bomb thunder. 'That's the Stukas, the dive-bombers,' Simon screamed over the din. 'They've put sirens on the engines to frighten people on the ground.'

Knox watched them dive behind the hilly horizon. 'It works,' he yelled back.

That raid lasted twenty minutes, but less than an hour later the sirens cried again and another flight of bombers appeared. This time their target was the city of Sliema. Both Maskelyne and Knox watched in awe as the planes flew overhead in tight formation, but Simon barely noted their presence. When the professor remarked about this, Simon said impassively, 'Oh, you get quite used to them. It's almost like they've taken a flat here.'

After completing the inspection tour, Jasper and Frank went to their underground quarters and began drawing up a camouflage plan. From the outset it was obvious that few options were available to them. Unlike Alexandria harbour or the Suez Canal, Malta could not be moved or hidden or made invisible. It was a ninety-square-mile target in the middle of an ocean. Nothing short of real magic would serve in this case, and Maskelyne did not have the skills to produce such wonders.

They devised a practical two-part plan using camouflage techniques perfected during the war. Their plan wouldn't prevent the Germans from attacking and would not protect the Maltese from their bombs, but it might make the raids less effective, and that was the purpose of this mission.

As they sat in their shelter discussing the situation, both of them stripped to their waists and khaki shorts, sweat pouring down their chests, Maskelyne never felt farther away from the world of magic. This was a standard camouflage job.

Early the following morning they met with a group of air officers and civilian defence leaders in the command shelter. Like the board of directors of a shabby corporation, they sat around a wobbly table made by lying a plywood sheet over three wooden horses.

'There's nothing we can do to keep the bombers away,' Maskelyne began, 'so our objective should be to make them expend their ammunition in the least effective way. Lieutenant Knox and I can help you do that. We can show you how to provide worthless targets and we can help you protect your runways. That's not much, I know—'

An RAF officer interrupted, and drew a good laugh, by suggesting, 'Throw in a few squares of chocolate and you've got a deal.'

The two parts of the camouflage plan presented by Maskelyne and Knox were as different as night and day: deception would be used at night, decoys during the day.

The deception plan was based on the Maryūt Bay ploy. Dummy airstrips would be lighted at night to draw enemy bombers away from the real fields. 'They've added an interesting twist back home,' Knox said after outlining the basic procedure. 'Aircraft landing lights are mounted on jeeps and run up and down between the dummy runway lights to simulate air traffic. Evidently it's quite effective, though I shouldn't want to be driving that jeep!'

An air raid warden objected to the plan. 'We're only sixty miles from Sicily. When we sneeze, they catch our germs. They'd know about dummy airfields in an hour.'

'Turn the information about on them,' Maskelyne replied. 'Once they know for certain you're using dummy fields, set your lights and bomb fires next to your real runways. That'll send 'em to the dummies straight away.'

'Look here,' Knox emphasized, 'we're not magicians. We're just–' The men in the bunker burst into laughter at that gaffe, causing the professor's fleshy cheeks to turn red with embarrassment. 'At least *I'm* not a magician,' he corrected. When the laughter had faded he continued. 'Point is, you've got to keep Jerry confused. Let him see whatever it is he expects to see. That's the game.'

Making the deception pay off by providing damage for German inspection during daylight hours would be burdensome, but not difficult. The only thing Malta had in abundance was rubble. In England, Maskelyne told the group, camouflage expert Colonel John F. Turner had protected RAF runways by hauling tons of debris to the site the enemy believed it had bombed. Shattered rock and masonry were scattered all over the landing strips, and the skeletons of wrecked airplanes were put on display for German cameras. In addition, lightweight plaster-of-Paris 'bomb craters' were constructed ('The world's first portable holes,' Knox called them), and Turner's artists painted craters on pieces of canvas that were pegged to the tarmac. 'Two versions. One for sunny days and the other for overcast days.'

The props and scenery had to be shifted throughout the day to correspond with the movement of the sun, Maskelyne reminded them, so that the painted shadows would be accurate.

An enemy bomber squadron attacked the waterfront during the meeting, but Maskelyne and Knox took their lead from the defence committee and pretended to ignore the raiders. Only once, when a large device exploded nearby and made the oil lamps shiver, did they exchange nervous glances.

Professor Knox shifted easily into a discussion of the various decoy aircraft that could be employed during daylight hours. Canvas flats were the easiest to construct and would pass high-altitude visual inspection as long as they cast accurate shadows, he began, then told them about Peter Proud's celebrated scam at Tobruk. Finding himself with few guns but numerous gun-pit camouflage nets, Proud had suspended canvas guns beneath the nets. German artillery spotters, as well as the Luftwaffe, saw the shadows beneath the nets and assumed they shielded real guns, and wasted a tremendous amount of precious ammunition blasting them. 'There's no reason a similar ploy wouldn't work here,' Knox concluded.

Then Maskelyne took over. 'The aircraft flats will not pass camera inspection,' he pointed out, 'but you've still got to give as much care to camouflaging them as you would to hiding real fighters. Remember, we're simply trying to confuse Jerry as to what is real and what is illusion.'

'And once he picks out the dummies, and he will,' Knox chimed in, 'that's the time to turn it about on him. Intersperse canvas flats among your real planes. You *must* keep them confused.'

During the initial inspection tour Maskelyne had realized it would require dummies far more sophisticated than were currently being built on Malta to convince German Intelligence that the island's RAF wing had been reinforced. To fool the enemy's cameras the dummies would not only have to cast accurate shadows, their 'wings' and 'fuselage' would have to reflect sunlight and their cockpit instrumentation would have to be visible beneath the camouflage netting. 'In other words,' the RAF officer joked after listening to the magician's pessimistic report, 'what we need are some real planes we can use as dummies.'

The only possible alternative, Jasper replied, was to utilize damaged or destroyed metal equipment. 'So long as the nets are stretched as they would be if concealing an aircraft, any reflective metal or glass could be placed beneath them. We can use parts of planes, motorcars, even trams – almost anything will serve.' Later, in private, he admitted to Knox he had no real expectations suitable decoys could be built on the island.

Construction of the individual pieces for the master plan began immediately. During the next few days the two camoufleurs helped design equipment and supervised construction of the prototypes. Everyone on Malta, foot soldiers, cooks, pilots, civilians, contributed to the work. The plaster-of-Paris 'holes' looked as deep as any stage props Maskelyne had ever worked with. Work on the canvas runway craters progressed at a steady pace. The aircraft flats were quite passable, although their canvas wings had to be propped up with sticks. A few metal decoys were thrown together, looking more like something made by a madman with a Meccano set than an aircraft, but it was the best that could be done under existing conditions.

It was a hectic few days, during which work was constantly being interrupted by enemy bombers, but Maskelyne and Knox learned to accept these raids as bothersome intrusions rather than inhuman violations. By the end of the fifth day the props were in place. There was nothing more for them to do on Malta.

The C-47 Dakota that would ferry them back to Heliopolis sneaked in at dusk overloaded with tons of supplies. A flock of soldiers swarmed over it, and managed to unload the plane and juice it up in less than two hours. Maskelyne spent this time glancing from his watch to the pasty sky. Oddly, it was the absence of German bombers that made him nervous.

Most of Malta's defence committee was on hand to see them off. 'Now that you've provided us with an air force incapable of flight,' the air raid warden said cheerfully, 'perhaps you might find some way of getting a few thousand tons of supplies through the blockade.' Everyone chuckled at this friendly tease.

Minutes later the Dakota bounced and rattled into the air. The long flight back to Cairo gave Maskelyne time to reflect on the past few days. Everything possible had been done, but it amounted to little more than a bucket of sand in the desert. Three hundred thousand people were packed onto the small island without enough food or medicine, without even adequate means to protect themselves. Jasper snuggled into his seat and drew a blanket up to his neck. It was cold enough in the back of the plane for him to see each breath. He closed his eyes and tried to sleep, but specks of thought raced through his mind, each of them just beyond the grasp of his consciousness. Some magician, he thought bitterly. People were being blown to bits under an endless shower of bombs, and he showed them how to make artificial holes. He remembered the children who had watched him with deepset sad eyes, and knew more than ever that there was no such force as magic, only tricks, and fools to play them on.

Jasper had always prided himself on being a compassionate man, and at home he had always been careful to contribute the proper amount of time and money to the charities, but as he flew away from the horrors of Malta he found himself examining his motives. He admitted to himself that he made those contributions because he was expected to do so; it was the right thing to do and he always tried to do the right thing. Somehow, though, he had managed to keep a safe distance from the pain of the maimed and the needy. Even in Cairo, at Shepheards when he had been beseeched by that wealthy Arab businessman, he had felt as much embarrassment as empathy.

Malta had shocked and humbled him. It had opened him up in a way that nothing before had ever touched him. The visit had changed him forever, he realized that even before the Dakota set down at Heliopolis. He just didn't quite know how.

Life in Cairo became difficult for him. The city was too lush; its grand hotels and elegant restaurants made a mockery of the struggle of the Maltese people. Numerous times each day he'd pause, wherever he was, whatever he was doing, and try to imagine what was taking place on Malta at the exact moment. Inevitably, he concluded that the Luftwaffe was blasting it.

The day after Jasper's return to the Valley, Hill had charged into the mess hall waving two buff envelopes. 'Some chaps really must've been tight,' he said, ''cause they've went and made you and Frank captains.'

Maskelyne didn't react. He took the orders from Hill and read them. He had been appointed temporary captain and promoted officially to war substantive lieutenant. Carefully folding his promotion papers into precise thirds, he slipped them back into the buff envelope and walked out of the mess.

'What's chewin' at him?' Hill asked Knox.

The professor watched him leave. 'The usual, I suppose. Man's inhumanity to man. The bombings. The war.'

Private Hill sat down to finish Jasper's meal. 'He'll get over it,' he said confidently.

Maskelyne missed Mary desperately. She shared his deepest feelings, and by so doing relieved him of some of the burden. Frank Knox was a reliable sounding board and a good friend, but Jasper realized there was a vast distance between male bonding and the intimacy of a man and woman in love, and the measure of that distance was his loneliness. At night he'd lie in bed with his eyes open and conjure images of her; he would bring her, smiling shyly at some small compliment, into his room, and he would hear her voice, and the room would be full of her presence. And he would be calm, with her in his mind, until some sharp sound thrust him into the reality of Cairo, and then the emptiness would return.

Numerous requests for Magic Gang assistance had piled up on his desk during work on the submarine fleet and his mission to Malta. With Crusader done, commanders were already preparing for the next round. An infantry brigadier wondered if the Camouflage Section could suggest a way to disguise the slit trenches that stood out on the desert like inkblots on white paper. A transport major requested suggestions for hiding tons of gasoline in the desert. Air Marshal Tedder wanted to drop supplies from an aircraft without using a parachute. NAAFI asked him to perform at a charity gala. The armoured corps needed a mobile mine-clearing device. Admiral Cunningham was so delighted with his dummy submarine fleet that he wanted a 720-foot-long battleship to replace those in dry dock.

Maskelyne turned over many of the requests to newly constituted camouflage units in the Nile Delta. In the year since his unruly arrival at Suez, camouflage had become an important branch of the service. High-ranking officers had seen tons of bombs falling onto empty beaches at Alexandria, and Luftwaffe planes blindly groping for the canal, they saw his dummy army in the field and knew that he had secured a safe escape route to the east. Because of Maskelyne's work, as well as Peter Proud at Tobruk and Tony Ayerton and the rest of Buckley's boys, camouflage was now taken seriously. The problem now was that there was too much work for too few people.

Jasper had no choice but to concentrate on the most pressing requests. He decided that the Gang would build Cunningham's battle-ship.

'A battleship?' Hill repeated incredulously after Maskelyne had revealed the Gang's next job. He turned to Graham, sitting at his shoulder, and laughed. 'You hear that? Now they want us to build a bloody battleship.'

Nails smirked. 'So?'

Hill rolled his eyes back in his head. 'If I'm the only sane one here, we're all in big trouble.'

British Intelligence was reporting that the dummy submarines were forcing enemy shipping to operate with unusual caution, particularly Mussolini's Mediterranean war fleet. Now Admiral Cunningham's office wanted to compound the ploy by adding a new battleship to the area. 'Any questions?' Maskelyne asked as he passed out photographs of the 720-foot-long, 34,000-ton Royal Navy battleship H.M.S. *Nelson*.

'Me,' Robson said, staring intently at the picture he held in two hands. 'They only want one of these, right?'

TWELVE

After the requisite griping was finished, the Magic Gang set about building a 720-foot-long battleship. The days of wondering if such an incredible request could be fulfilled had ended long ago. They had become
professionals in the world of military make-believe, and derived great
satisfaction from the knowledge that their small group could create war
machines that no other army in military history had even imagined.

They were confident that all that stood between them and the
battleship were many long days and nights, innumerable cusses and
bitter jokes, blisters and aches, a touch of luck, and something on
which to pin the entire bloody superstructure. And, in fact, at the
beginning it did seem that would be true – it was only toward the end
that this became the Magic Gang's most unusual experience.

Jasper welcomed the arduous assignment. By focusing his complete
attention on this project he was able to temporarily put aside the
depression he had carried back from Malta. He began by dividing up
the work. Phil Townsend would help him with the rough sketches
and blueprints. Bill Robson was to secure some battleship-grey paint.
Nails Graham and Union Jack Fuller were to gather construction
materials, primarily lumber and metal. Mike Hill was responsible for
finding big guns. 'We'll need nine sixteen-inchers, a dozen six-inchers
and some ack-ack,' Maskelyne explained, sounding as if he were
equipping an actual dreadnought. But he shattered that impression by
concluding, 'Start by checking the dump for drainpipes. There should
be something there.'

Frank Knox served as liaison to Admiral Cunningham's office. At
Maskelyne's request, the Navy agreed to help the Gang find something
afloat that would be large enough and stable enough to serve as a
platform on which to build the superstructure. The battleship dummy
would be almost four times the length of the submarines, and would
ride considerably higher out of the water, so Jasper decided the best
thing to do was disguise a real ship. Finding that craft was the difficult
part.

While the rest of the Gang were making their own preparations, Frank was shown just about every scrap of junk floating in North African waters. Out of a wretched lot, he finally selected an aged cruiser that was decaying on a salt lake in the Suez. The rusting hulk, its painted name long since flaked into history, had been launched before the turn of the century and refurbished for coastal patrol duty during the Great War. After being decommissioned, it had been retired to a Scottish loch until Dunkirk, when the desperate situation forced the Royal Navy to return such relics to service. Unable to sail under its own steam, it was towed to the Suez Canal and used as a flak ship. The efficient Royal Navy captain escorting Knox tried to make this boat seem more impressive than it actually was, pointing out, 'It's still floating, you'll notice. It certainly was well made.'

Compared to the other wrecks and shells Knox had been shown, this vessel did have distinct advantages. 'It's about the only thing large enough to support a sizeable platform,' the professor told Jasper, 'and as many as a dozen men might be able to stand on deck at the same time without its turning turtle, assuming of course that they're properly positioned.'

Even before Jasper saw the hulk, he was dubious. 'It's forty years old, Frank,' he complained.

'So are we, nearly,' Knox reminded him.

First sight did nothing to alleviate Jasper's fears. The cruiser was over five hundred feet long, but barely seventy-five feet wide. It had three outdated smokestacks and two masts, the rear mast sporting a crow's nest. Its naval guns had been removed decades earlier, and the wooden planking that had been bolted over the resulting holes in the deck had rotted through, leaving gaping cavities both fore and aft. Previous renovations had made the ship so top-heavy it wobbled in a slight breeze.

The Gang stepped aboard as gingerly as a *corps de ballet* cavorting on a bed of nails. 'Everybody stay calm,' Hill implored nervously. 'Nobody make no fast moves.'

'Fast moves, hell,' Graham responded. 'Nobody best breathe too deeply.'

'It's not all that bad,' Knox declared in his most professional voice. 'If we're just a bit careful not to overload one side, if we avoid the holes in the deck, if we don't put any heavy machinery on board, and if each of us stops eating and loses two stone I shouldn't think we'd have too much difficulty.'

Jasper did his best to reassure everyone, reminding them, 'We can all swim.'

The conversion of the dilapidated cruiser into a modern ship of the line began with a tape-measure assault. The Gang recorded the length and width of every nook and cranny above deck. Good sense prevented anyone from going below.

Maskelyne and Graham then built a scale model of the ship. All the modifications were first fitted to the model, and tested in the dayroom water tank. The masts of this model were removed, and scaffolding, represented by sticks, was added to the top. Everything put above the waterline was counterbalanced by submerged oil-drum floats and pontoons. Every outrigging, or boom, attached to the port side was matched by a similar boom starboard. Additional extensions were fitted over the bow and stern, lengthening the scale model two feet, and thus the real dummy two hundred feet. The battleship would have to carry four 'catapult-launched aircraft,' which Jasper figured could be faked with the same type of painted canvas flats used on Malta. 'Jerry'll be looking down at them,' he told his artists Townsend and Robson, 'so as long as they cast the correct shadows we don't have to be concerned with depth.' Hill's salvage-pipe gun muzzles would be balanced on board during their installation.

The finished model had all sorts of sticks and gizmos rising high off its deck and protruding out over the gunwales at various angles. It looked more like the skeleton of a wooden building designed by a deranged architect than the foundation of a ship, but Jasper was confident that once painted canvas had been stretched over the frame it would be able to pass as a battleship. The model had outgrown the water tank and had to be tested in the Suez lake in which the actual transformation would take place. Although minor adjustments had to be made, it managed to stay afloat.

Then crews trucked in from Magic Valley began converting the aging cruiser into a modern warship. A precise schedule was followed to ensure that there would never be too many men on board at one time, and much of the painting, cutting and fabrication was done ashore. The dummy battleship rapidly began to take shape.

The men laboured around the clock in six-hour shifts. By devoting himself to the project, Jasper successfully pushed most thoughts of Malta out of his mind. There was an occasional odd moment, though, when he could not help thinking about the bombers. Whenever it got too bad, and feelings of inadequacy threatened to overwhelm him, he'd sit and write out his frustrations in a long letter to Mary. Sometimes he mailed these letters, sometimes he did not, but simply writing them enabled him to regain control.

Phil Townsend worked closely with him on the sketches. At first, their conversations were brief and professional, but gradually they moved to subjects of common interest. Townsend felt himself beginning to trust Maskelyne. To his own amazement, he began exposing some of the beasts living deep inside his mind. Late one evening as he sketched, while Jasper tried to paste a tiny shaft to the model, he casually said, 'Guess you know the wife and me are splittin' up. From my letters and all. I mean, I know you have to read them.'

Jasper sidestepped the question, explaining that he'd been trading letters to be censored with the head of a mess outfit, 'and now I can tell you twenty or more ways to prepare bully beef.'

Townsend kept his head buried in his drawing as he spoke. 'Well, we are. Seems she's taken up with some Yank flyer.'

Jasper held the thin stick in place while the paste dried. He understood he was being shown a man's soul. 'Sorry,' he said evenly. 'I know it's hard.'

'Very,' the artist agreed, and chuckled morbidly. 'Very.' But suddenly, having finally heard his own voice say the dreadful words, he felt strangely relieved.

As Maskelyne blew gently on the paste to accelerate the drying process, he thought of Mary. In this thought she was dressed in white linen and smiling, and her black hair was flowing in a breeze. She was looking into the distance for something. He smiled to himself. Just thinking about her temporarily filled that gaping hole in his heart.

The sham battleship was completed in mid-February. Maskelyne named it H.M.S. *Houdin*, for the illustrious conjuror Robert-Houdin, but the dummy was a great disappointment to him. It was the requisite length and carried the correct armament, including four aircraft, but its massive flying bridge was decidedly off centre, sheets of canvas bulwarking constantly ripped loose and flapped in light breezes, it rode much too high in the water for a 34,000-ton vessel, and numerous other minor defects betrayed the illusion. Only from a great distance and in poor light or bad weather could it possibly be taken for a real battleship, and even in those conditions that was still doubtful.

'Sorry about this,' Admiral Cunningham said after returning from an aerial inspection of the dummy. 'I'm afraid it was a bit much to ask you to pull a battleship out of that hat of yours.' The Admiral was sitting with Jasper and Frank at a spindly-legged table set up in the square of shade created by propping up the rear canvas flap of a three-ton truck. H.M.S. *Houdin* bobbed at anchor on the calm lake waters a few thousand yards over Maskelyne's shoulder. 'Your boys are to be congratulated for a superior effort, but we can't risk using it. Best take it down before Jerry spots it and gets onto the severity of our situation.'

Knox suggested they have a go at bringing it up to snuff. 'Give us another week or so. There's nothing that can't be corrected. The men've worked dreadfully hard.'

Cunningham was steadfast. 'It's more than a few touch-ups. It just doesn't have the right feel to it, you see.'

Knox didn't. Mistakes can be corrected. He looked at the Admiral blankly.

A naval person would have understood immediately, Cunningham realized, but it was difficult explaining his meaning to a land type. 'It just doesn't have the soul of a fighting ship.'

This the professor understood. Part of that mysticism of men of the sea.

Maskelyne had listened to Cunningham announce his decision and agreed with it, the transformation was not effective, but he was reluctant to allow the Gang's hard work to go for naught. He knew there had to be some way to make a profit from the job. The *Houdin* couldn't pass as a battleship, of course. Jerry would examine it thoroughly and discover the errors and —

In the flash of a thought, he had the answer. The sucker switch. 'Pardon me, Admiral,' he said, 'but perhaps I have a solution.'

'Yes?'

'I think so. Seems we've been trying to convince the Germans that our cruiser is actually a battleship, when in fact we should be trying desperately to convince them that that's precisely what it's not!'

'That it's not a battleship, you mean?' Cunningham asked, perplexed. 'Right.'

'Well,' the Admiral replied, 'that shouldn't be too difficult, eh?' Truthfully he had no idea what Maskelyne was blustering about.

Jasper's entire body became animated as he began explaining his plan to save the *Houdin*. 'You see, the burden's on us to make sure every bloody knot and anchor is a bang-on duplicate for the real thing. Suppose, though, just suppose we had a real battleship. Considering that Jerry just sent two of the best to the bottom, we'd be doing everything possible to protect it, wouldn't we? We'd be hiding it, or camouflaging it or,' he paused here, and suggested softly, 'or disguising it.'

Cunningham furrowed his brow, indicating thought, and confusion. 'I suppose,' he said uncertainly.

'Obviously, we won't be successful. You see?'

'No' the Admiral admitted, 'I don't.'

'Let me explain, then. Magicians often use a stage technique known as the sucker effect, or sucker bait. The object is to allow the audience to reach its own conclusion from evidence it detects by observation. Let your audience believe they've caught you in an error and you've got them right where you want them. If, for example, I told you a box was empty you might not believe me, but if I tipped the box accidentally and gave you a peek inside and you saw it was empty, then you'd believe it. In fact, you'd be certain you knew much more than I intended you to know.'

Cunningham was listening intently, his shoulders hunched slightly forward, his elbows resting firmly on the shaky table, hands clasped in front of him, forming a fortress with his thick arms around a cup of dead-cold coffee.

'My grandfather's partner was the great magician David Devant,' Jasper began. 'Among many other illusions, Devant used to make a livestock vanish. It made no difference what sort of animal was used, it might just as easily have been a pig as a pigeon, but the illusion was most commonly performed with a rabbit.'

Admiral Cunningham tried, but was unable to find the connection between making a pig disappear and turning a floating woodpile into a battleship.

'After producing the rabbit, he'd carefully place it in a plain box sitting on what appeared to be an ordinary table. Then, piece by piece, he would take the box apart. The top, then each of its sides in turn, was handed to an assistant or discarded on the floor behind the table, proving that the box was empty and the rabbit had been successfully vanished. The table was the only piece of apparatus remaining on the stage.

'However,' Jasper continued, 'the audience could still see what appeared to be a tuft of white fur sticking out of the top of this table. Devant used to make a wonderful show of attempting to conceal it with the last box side. Some other magicians doing a similar bit might step in front of it and feign embarrassment. There are any number of techniques used to achieve the same effect, but the object is to appear to be trying to hide the tuft of fur while actually bringing the attention of the audience right to it. By attempting to hide it, the magician is in fact convincing the audience that they've discovered the trickery. Eventually, the audience will call the magician on this mistake, sometimes led by a confederate planted in the rear seats, and after the magician has done everything possible to ignore their cries he will reach down and pluck the object from the table. Devant used to pull out a marshmallow, but a handkerchief or anything similar can easily be used. Finally, after holding up the object for the audience to see, he folded up the table to prove the animal was not hidden inside. See what I'm getting at?'

Cunningham sighed. 'I think so. Yes, I think so.' Waving his index finger through the air to underline his thoughts, he carefully summarized the proposal. 'If we want Jerry to think this ... uh, thing is a battleship, we have to convince him that we actually want him to believe it's something else.'

'There, now you've got it,' Jasper said.

'Where's the rabbit?' Knox demanded.

Jasper glanced at him. 'Why, in the table, of course.'

In the distance, the disguised cruiser drifted in a mild breeze.

Maskelyne continued. 'We've got to let the Germans reach their own conclusions. If we take obvious pains to camouflage our boat, but do a bad job of it, their intelligence people will be quite happy to discover a real battleship beneath all our canvas and papier-mâché. At that size there's really nothing else it could be. All the mistakes we've made will work for us then. They'll assume we made them intentionally to cover up the real ship.'

Cunningham was so delighted in the audacious plan he immediately agreed to implement it. After the beating his Royal Navy had absorbed during the past few months it would be quite satisfying to give the Nazi buggers a cardboard comeuppance. 'What shall we disguise our battleship as?' he asked.

Jasper delivered his punchline smoothly. 'Perhaps a rusted cruiser?'

The Gang went directly to work doing a good job of bad camouflage. Blue-painted canvas 'lids' or 'flats' were stretched between the masts and booms in what would normally be an attempt to make the ship blend into the water, as the chameleon changes colour to fade into its background. In this case, however, the blue was purposefully painted too green and the 'lids' were cut perfectly square, rather than being cut irregularly, which would enable them to fade into water. Observed from the air, these would stand out like pink squares on a chessboard. In addition, the 'bulwarks' were loosened so they would billow in a breeze, a cardboard smokestack was intentionally watered into sog- giness, a dismal effort was made to disguise the dummy prow of the dummy dreadnought, and oil-barrel floats were positioned only inches below the surface. By the time the Gang had finished the sophisticatedly crude job, it was virtually impossible to determine exactly what lay beneath the network of false beams, cardboard stacks and canvas lids. Only its great length and girth, and its barely visible big gun drainpipes, hinted it was a battleship.

'She's a fine tribute to her name,' Jasper proudly pronounced as the Gang stood on the lake bank taking a final look at her before returning to Abbassia.

Hill frowned. 'One thing's for sure. There ain't another one like her anywhere in the world.'

'She'll certainly keep their intelligence people fascinated for some time,' Robson decided.

'Ours too,' Knox added, 'ours too.'

The *Houdin* had to be towed into place after dark, very slowly, and in calm waters, lest it be shaken apart by a small wave. Unlike the dummy harbour or the cardboard weapons, it would take some time, if ever, to determine its success. The Admiralty firmly believed that the Germans and the Italians would take advantage of the lack of a British warship in the area to drastically increase the size and flow of their supply convoys. But there was no hard proof of this. The success of the decoy might be measured by a change in the number of escort vessels shepherding the convoys, or an alteration of route, but it would be difficult to directly credit these modifications to the presence of the *Houdin*.

Admiral Cunningham decided to stick the thing out in the water where it would be seen, and take his chances with it. He was confident it would, at worst, confuse the enemy. 'It certainly has me confused,' he admitted to the Gang.

A German reconnaissance plane spotted it at anchor off Suez. The twin-engine craft made a sweeping turn and dived in low for a closer look. A few hours later two more spotters arrived. Onshore ack-ack batteries popped away at them to keep them some distance from the ship, but the planes got close enough to snap some fascinating photographs. At night, the *Houdin* was towed to a different area.

After returning to Magic Valley, Maskelyne waited patiently for reports on the maiden voyage of the cardboard man-of-war. If the Germans took the sucker bait, as he suspected they would, the Gang could justifiably claim another impossible assignment successfully completed. But if the attempted fraud was discovered ... He smiled confidently at that thought. If it was discovered he still had one more twist up his sleeve. The skilful magician always held the final ace.

Requests for Magic Gang assistance continued to pile up. Dudley Clarke needed some tools for his A-Force operatives. More sunshields were requested. Intelligence expected him to suggest some clever means of safely positioning a forward observer on the desert. The major in transport was still pressing him for some way to hide thousands of gallons of gasoline on the Blue. Admiral Cunningham wanted yet another addition to his growing dummy navy – a disappearing speedboat. Even the courageous Desert Air Force had an assignment for him.

During a high-stakes rummy game, an aide to Admiral Cunningham casually mentioned Maskelyne's 'magic navy' to an air force officer, who discussed it while attending a cricket match at Gezira with a flight officer working for Air Marshal Tedder, who told Tedder, who was intrigued and contacted Cunningham, who was delighted and put him onto Geoffrey Barkas, who casually requested that Maskelyne drop by Royal Air Force Staff in Cairo.

Air Officer Commanding-in-Chief, Middle East, Air Marshal Sir Arthur Tedder simply wanted Jasper to figure out how the Air Force could drop supply containers thousands of feet without a parachute, 'due to the current shortage of same,' so that their contents would not be dashed to pieces upon impact. Although Tedder's aide explained that this would be used to supply ammunition to partisans fighting in occupied countries, Maskelyne realized that the same method could be adapted to get food and medicine to the besieged Maltese people. This became his priority project.

On a pleasantly cool afternoon in late February, Jasper was standing on a chair in his office dropping eggs sheathed in various wrappers onto a canvas sheet when Phil Townsend walked in. About a dozen eggs had been smashed, creating a rather dicey pale-yellow viscous pool in the centre of the canvas.

The painter looked at the mess and grimaced. 'That's just about the sorriest mess I've ever seen.'

'Research,' Maskelyne responded, 'research. I've got to work out a way to keep these eggs from cracking.'

Townsend suggested tentatively, 'Have you thought about not dropping them?'

Jasper snickered. 'It's for Tedder's people. They want to drop supplies without parachutes.' He held an egg wrapped in thick layers of cotton between his thumb and forefinger.

Townsend averted his eyes from the pool. 'Nails said you wanted to see me.'

The egg dropped like a thousand-pounder, plopping onto the canvas. Within seconds a gooey liquid seeped through the cotton. 'That won't do,' Jasper said, frowning, and stepped down. As he wiped his hand, he told Townsend that the infantry had requested bulletproof forward observation posts. 'I was thinking about dummying up sand dunes, or perhaps we can do something with hollowed palm trunks. See what you can come up with, will you? There's no hurry on it, sometime tomorrow would be just fine.' Hands dried, he took another egg from a sack and began crisscrossing strips of cotton around it.

'How about some sort of suspension system?' the artist suggested.

Jasper considered that. 'With a hard outer casing, you mean?'

'That's it. Let the container absorb the shock.'

'Hmmmp. Might work. Let's see.'

As Maskelyne searched the room for a box in which to encase the egg, Townsend poured himself a cuppa. His friendly attitude was new and welcome. For some unexplained reason, the artist had lost his chip. He had even begun hanging around with the Gang. Although his initial efforts at fitting in were as awkward as a circus strongman trying to walk the high wire, the boys overlooked his mistakes. 'Here, what's this?' he asked, holding up a ration box.

'Sure,' Jasper said. While Maskelyne banded the egg with long strips of tape, and stuck the ends of the tape to the inner sides of the box, then began swaddling the outside of the box in layers of cotton, they talked amiably. As always, the war was their primary concern. Even considering Rommel's last foray, Operation Crusader had to be considered a success. Eighth Army had finally regained its fighting spirit. The Fox's Afrika Korps had been soundly thrashed. The war in the desert was not over, the end was not even on the horizon, but no longer was there a question of the Empire's ability to smash the best of the Führer's army. With the United States finally in, and the Soviets having stopped the Nazis in Russia, Hitler was suddenly on the defensive.

When the box was completely covered with cotton, Jasper climbed back onto his chair and dropped it to the canvas. It landed on a corner and flipped over once, like a tossed die. Townsend picked it up and opened it. The egg had cracked, but had not broken. 'Let's try it again,' Jasper said, 'but this time let's crisscross the tape, make them suspension strings, so they'll be a sort of support netting.'

Once they were at work again, their conversation shifted to the second most popular topic. 'I'm telling you, these girls were really smashing,' Townsend boasted, relating the details of a night in Cairo with an Engineer chap. 'One of them, one of them – I've never seen anything like her. I mean she had ... she was ...' Deeming mere words insufficient to describe her, he moved his hands in two softly curved, seductive, flowing lines.

Maskelyne got the idea. He believed the woman actually existed and was perhaps as lovely as the artist remembered, but he also knew Townsend didn't believe it. The boasting protected his ego as surely as the suspenders had saved the egg. Jasper saw nothing wrong with it, either.

But the subject couldn't be ignored. Now that Townsend was capable of talking about it, he needed to talk about it. Jasper prodded him gently, asking if he had received any communication from his wife.

Townsend spat in disgust. 'Her? Naw, not that I'm likely to, either. The solicitors are on the case. When I think back on it, I mean the whole thing, I can't believe what a bloody fool I've been. Even if this hadn't happened, except for the little baby, and I swear I'm not goin' to let that child be hurt by this – but other than our baby there was no reason we should've stayed together. It's not like things were goin' so good with us at the end, I've got to be honest about that. We did have our problems. We were pretty young when we got married and I've changed a lot, I'm not the same man I was then and...'

Jasper listened, nodded when it was appropriate, and offered an agreeable word when it seemed called for. Having devoted his life to the production of illusions, he saw no need to destroy those of another man.

Additional cross straps held another egg loosely in place, as if it were lazing in a tiny hammock, and when the box was dropped on the canvas the egg remained intact. 'Now all we have to do,' Jasper said, 'is substitute a thousand rounds of ammunition for one egg and we've got it made.'

They were just finishing a cleanup when Knox came in with a newspaper folded under his arm. 'There's the hero himself,' he said smartly.

Jasper glanced at Townsend, who was looking right back at him. They both looked at Knox.

'You,' the professor said, indicating Maskelyne. 'Guess you haven't seen this then?' He waved the newspaper. 'Seems like you've received some attention.'

Puzzled by Frank's teasing, Jasper took the paper from him. It was a week-old French-language edition of *Berliner Illustrierte Zeitung*, a German newspaper.

'Page three.'

Jasper turned to that page. It was devoted to news of Rommel's desert campaign and included a large photograph of a smouldering Matilda. Rapidly scanning the article, he was absolutely shocked to find his own name sharing a sentence with Adolf Hitler. 'What's this all about?'

Knox took a slip of paper from his breast pocket. 'One of Clarke's chaps shot the paper down to me. Thought you might be amused. This,' he said, flapping the slip of paper, 'is the official British Army translation.' Pushing his glasses high up onto the bridge of his nose, holding the slip at eye level, he harrumphed for attention, then began reading, pronouncing each word distinctly. ' "The British have realised their situation is desperate and have employed a famous magician, Jasper Maskelyne, to try to scare off the Afrika Korps!" ' He looked up from the translation. 'How 'bout that?'

'What's all this Hitler stuff?' Townsend asked, pointing to the next paragraph in the *Illustrierte*.

'Calm down, I'm coming to that. See, it says that the Führer was complimenting Rommel on his brilliant counterattack. "Indeed, the Führer told Tank General Rommel, the German Army does not need a Maskelyne to make the British Army disappear." ' Frank peered over the translation to Jasper. 'It seems our Mr Hitler has been talking about you behind your back.'

Townsend curtsied in jest. 'And all this time I didn't know I was working with such an important person.'

Jasper did not know whether to be pleased, embarrassed, amused or annoyed. 'Well,' he finally decided, 'I suppose I've been insulted by nicer people.'

Thanks mainly to the boasting Mike Hill, word of Hitler's comment spread quickly throughout the community of British officers in Cairo, and during the next few days Maskelyne received substantial ragging about it. Although most rankers thought it was humorous and made good-natured remarks, a few were actually jealous of this attention and said so bitterly. Maskelyne came to regard the whole thing as a rather awkward joke and accepted the jibes of his mates without rancour. 'It seems some of the chaps feel I must be a friend of his,' he wrote to Mary, enclosing the translation. 'Now, that's certainly a case of guilt without association!'

Mike Hill enjoyed the stir, telling everyone, 'If you think that was an insult, wait till you hear what Maskelyne has to say about Hitler.'

Neither Barkas nor Clarke found the article amusing. 'They obviously know you're not here doing stage tricks,' Barkas grumbled. 'They'll be watching you from now on, and that's going to make your work more difficult.'

Clarke was quite distressed. 'I'm afraid this makes you a prime target. It's impossible to predict what the Brotherhood madmen might do to try to please their Führer. I'd suggest keeping a less visible profile for a bit.'

'We're all targets, aren't we?' Jasper replied. 'That's the job of a soldier.' Besides, he was working too hard to spend time worrying about sinister Arabs plotting devious acts. Magic Valley was as frenetic as the Egyptian Theatre had been in its halcyon days. But instead of actors, managers, agents, press men, female would-be assistants, mechanics and bookkeepers, the camp was practically overrun with camoufleurs, carpenters, painters, electricians, weavers, mechanics, machinists, draftsmen, clerks and assembly-line workers, all rushing about furiously on some mission. Jasper's days swirled with activity as he tried to give parts of it to as many people as possible. The busier he was, the less time he had to be lonely, or to think about the suffering Maltese people. There were old projects to be completed, new projects to be initiated, future projects to be contemplated; in addition, he had to make time in the evenings to exercise his fingers, and Clarke had asked him to give his popular escape-and-evasion field lecture to newly arrived troops. Only at the end of the night did he relax, when he sat alone and wrote his thoughts to Mary.

To his own chagrin, he had not been able to deliver to the Air Force a supply container that could be dropped from an aircraft without a parachute. The first test of the suspension device he had worked up with Townsend took place on March 1, 1942, on the desert.

Maskelyne shaded his eyes as a lone Wellington circled once, then dropped the prototype supply container from an altitude of five hundred feet. The crate, a wooden packing case almost five feet wide and four feet deep, was swathed in a thick layer of cotton waste. Inside, ten sealed plaster trays, each containing fifty rounds of .38, .45, .303 or antitank ammunition, five hundred rounds in all, were loosely suspended by canvas strips and further cushioned by additional cotton.

The crate fell straight down the first hundred feet, then slowly began rolling end over end. It slammed into the ground. An instant later, it exploded.

No one said a word until the fountain of debris had settled, then Bill Robson observed, 'Well, that's not very good.'

'Perhaps a few alterations are necessary,' Jasper admitted, and turned away from the new crater in the desert.

As usual, Hill managed to put the test into perspective. 'Hey,' he suggested, 'we can use it to dig instant foxholes.'

Fortunately, other projects fared better. The Royal Navy reported H.M.S. *Houdin* was doing a yeomanly job in the Mediterranean. The Axis had not increased the frequency of its convoys to Tripoli, and at least two Italian warships had altered course, apparently to avoid making contact with the British 'battleship.' The ship itself was holding together as well as possible, but its permanent two-man crew had encountered some problems figuring out where pieces fit when they popped loose. Graham and Fuller were dispatched twice to supervise repairs.

Phil Townsend, assisted by Bill Robson, had drawn up several clever proposals for concealing forward observation posts. Foremost among these were the dummy sand dune and the metal tree. The dune, based on the stage-magic principle that the most obvious thing is usually overlooked, was actually a sand-coloured humped shell, spacious enough to seat one man, that could be placed in the open and covered with sand so that it was nearly indistinguishable from the normal desert drifts. The tin palm tree was designed for use in the lush oases that served as important landmarks and staging areas. Similar to those used during the Great War, it was lined with bulletproof steel and housed one observer equipped with telescope system and radio transmitter.

The original tin tree was fashioned in the workshop in a few hours and, after some touching up, looked natural enough to make its occupant hope that no one decided to use its branches for a night fire. Unfortunately, its spyholes were visible at close range. After some experimentation, it was discovered that a gauze covering painted the same colour as the rest of the trunk made the holes nearly invisible. Knox, the professor of animal camouflage, reminded workshop labourers to hand-cut each observation hole in an irregular shape, since perfect geometric forms rarely occur naturally.

After a series of tests the observation dunes and trees were put into mass production at the Valley, and by the end of March the Long Range Desert Group, the Desert Rats, were planting them on the Blue.

Soon after the first dunes were put into service, Maskelyne suggested to the transport major that larger artificial sand dunes could be used to hide large caches of fuel and ammunition on the open desert. During the next few months large 'dunes,' in actuality mountains of supplies, appeared overnight at strategic points along the main tracks.

These dumps, hidden in plain view, would prove vital when the final battle for North Africa began.

Throughout the spring of 1942, Axis forces in Europe and Asia pushed sluggishly forward against stubborn Allied resistance. In the Atlantic, U-boats continued to take a heavy toll of merchant marine and warships. In the Pacific, Japanese armies began occupying those islands left isolated after the stunning success of the attack on the American fleet at Pearl Harbor. General Douglas MacArthur left the Philippines by submarine and, upon arriving in Australia, vowed he would return to the islands. For weeks afterward no one in Cairo left a room without first declaring they, too, would return.

The Allied armies were fighting for time, knowing that reinforcements – and supplies – would begin arriving as soon as the great American industrial machine got into full production.

In North Africa the Germans continued blasting Britain's Mediterranean supply line while reinforcing Rommel's Panzer Group Africa. The stalemate at the Gazala Line was broken only by occasional probes into enemy encampments, and by the persistent hit-and-run attacks made by the bearded Desert Rats. Auchinleck was satisfied to let Rommel rust in the desert while he refit his own army for an early-summer offensive.

At Magic Valley work progressed on various projects. The devastating Luftwaffe attacks on Malta spurred Maskelyne to devote much of his time to perfecting the unbreakable supply canisters. After the failure of the prototype, he realized it was necessary to slow the rate of descent, which seemed difficult to do without adding some sort of parachute apparatus. After conferring with a number of engineers, he attached long canvas streamers to the case to act as a drag, thus reducing the falling speed.

The small group reassembled on the desert's edge for a second test. Once again, the Wellington swept in at five hundred feet, circled once and dropped an ammunition crate. The big box wobbled from side to side as it fell, until the streamers caught the wind and held it nearly upright. With its long tails shivering in the airstream, the container very much resembled a dead octopus dropping from the sky.

The crate slammed into the desert, sending up a splash of dirt and sand. Then, as everyone waited tensely, nothing happened. Maskelyne's shoulders sagged in relief. 'So far, so good,' he said tentatively as he climbed into his jeep.

The crate had cracked, but remained intact. When Graham opened it, though, the Gang found that most of the shells had become stuck to the soft plaster trays into which the ammunition had been pressed for protection. Almost every round would have to be cleaned before it could be used. Obviously, this could not be done on any battlefield. 'At least half the problem is solved,' Graham said philosophically after they had returned to the Valley. 'We got 'em down. Now all we have to do is find a way to pack 'em.'

The solution to this problem was quite simple. Jasper decided that the ammunition trays should be moulded out of nonadhesive papier-mâché rather than plaster. The entire Gang spent a gossipy afternoon sitting around the dayroom, like a women's knitting circle, cutting useless requisition forms into scraps, then tossing them into a vat of smelly billposter's paste made from water and condemned flour. The ammunition was pressed into the trays while the papier-mâché was still wet, thus providing adequate protection, while allowing each round to be easily removed once the trays had dried and hardened.

The third test was a complete success, and after Tedder's people conducted additional tests, the RAF requested as many crates as could be produced at Magic Valley. Nails Graham set up an assembly line in a sunshield shop, but had difficulty figuring out how to shred the hundreds of pounds of paper that would be needed for the trays. Cutting it by hand would take much too long. So, after considering several alternatives, and eliminating each of them, he concluded he had to steal a motorbike.

It was an accepted aspect of life in Cairo that nothing, absolutely nothing, could be left unattended without serious risk. Things that could not possibly have value to anyone except their owner disappeared in an instant. Lights were taken from guarded hallways, ratty shoes vanished from closets, half-chewed pencils were lifted from desks, there was even a brisk black market in automobile hubcaps in the bazaar. Therefore, the Hussar corporal-clerk was not at all surprised that his chained bike was stolen from its secure place directly in front of Gray Pillars.

Hill made the actual pinch, although Robson provided the necessary diversion by posing as an American reporter for *Stars and Stripes* and interviewing the guard about life in the Middle East.

Graham converted the Harley-Davidson bike into a factory machine by mounting it upside down on anchored bricks and replacing the rear tyre with a rubber belt that was connected to the chaff-cutter drive-wheel. Outdated maps provided most of the pulp. The improvised system was capable of turning out almost fifteen pounds of scrap per hour.

At Mike Hill's suggestion, different-coloured canvas streamers were used to indicate the contents of the various crates. Red was ammunition, green tools, white meant rations, and so on.

Maskelyne celebrated the successful completion of the project with an expensive lunch with Frank in the city, a full pouch of imported tobacco, and an afternoon passed strumming his ukulele and allowing his mind some play. The free afternoon was the luxury.

His fingers plucked out sad tunes. The following morning, as soon as he could clear the paperwork relating to the crates off his drawing table, he would begin another job. Admiral Cunningham would get his speedboat that could change shape in mid-ocean. After that ... After that ... After that, he knew, there would be another job to do, a dozen more jobs to do, and eventually all of them would get done, and he wasn't sure any of them would really make any difference.

During his performing days he had become accustomed to the period of melancholy that quite often followed hard on success, but he had believed he put those blue times behind him when he packed up his wand. To his dismay, he realized he hadn't. The old, familiar symptoms had returned. His stomach was churning, his shoulders felt terribly weighted, his eyes were exhausted, and he felt all used up. The very appearance of these symptoms, aside from the bothersome physical effects, was greatly disturbing. There was no reason for this attack. He was doing the work he had so wanted to do. He had achieved the celebrity that he admittedly needed. The Gang was firmly established and busier than any unit of its size in the entire Eighth Army. But something was causing this anxiety. Something.

'Perhaps you're just lonely,' Knox suggested during their fine lunch. 'You've been away for some time now and...'

Of course he was lonely. Everyone at war was lonely. He knew that. But he had carried that ache for a long time and recognized it as a familiar enemy. This was something different. 'No,' he mused, 'no...'

The professor wondered if he had become bored by the lack of real action.

He was too busy to be bored, Jasper replied. Besides, each new request presented a unique challenge. The work was vital. It had to be done. 'They're depending on us,' he insisted, but the more he protested the more he began to believe that Frank was right. The work no longer sparked him. But why? he wondered.

The answer came to him that night as he sat in the audience at a touring ENSA Variety. Each of the performers was terribly sincere and energetic, but the show itself was flat. It was failing, Jasper recognized, as he attempted to stifle a yawn, because it had opened and progressed at the same level, leaving the audience with nothing to anticipate.

Anticipation, he had learned in his life backstage, was the secret ingredient in every successful show. It was the elixir that brought the audience into the theatre and kept its interest alive. As he had been told by his grandfather, no one goes to the circus to see the lion tamer live.

Knox was right, he was bored. Bored by the fact that all he had to look forward to was doing variations of what he had already accomplished. He had been stuffing corks into a leaking dam. The dummy men would confuse the Germans. The *Houdin* would slow the Italians. The dummy tanks and planes and trucks, the containers, the harbour, the spy devices – all of them had practical use. But all of these separate pieces, put together, added up to a lot of separate pieces. There was no theme to his performance. His illusions were all good ones in their own right, but, as every magician is taught, the great act builds to a grand finale. His performance, he knew, had no finale.

He knew it had to be something big, something that would make a difference. Something bigger and better than anything ever performed on the stage of war. The excitement created by this realization almost made him leave his theatre seat and rush to his table to begin working, but a young crooner was giving his best on stage and Maskelyne was much too polite to disrupt his performance.

Besides, Frank Knox was fast asleep in the next seat.

On that same evening, while Jasper and Frank watched the show, Michael Hill and Kathy Lewis registered at the Royal Arms on Sharia el Gumhuriya as Private and Mrs Moore. They rode up the pulley-operated lift to the third floor in absolute silence, neither risking a look at the other. Their small room, overlooking Azbakiya Park, was tidy and clean. Besides the brass-frame bed, which was covered with a bright flower-print spread, it contained two high-backed wooden chairs and an imitation-Victorian chiffonier. Two towels were neatly folded on the bed. A framed print of the Mosque of Mohammed Ali was hanging on one of the beige-papered walls. The WC was at the near end of the hallway.

Although it had been less than an hour since the muezzin's final summons to prayer had marked the sunset, and the evening was balmy, Kathy was chilled. She went to the window to close the shutters.

Hill tipped the porter who had followed them up carrying their empty suitcase, then locked the door. 'Well,' he said, turning to face her, 'here we are.'

She stood at the window, her back to him. 'Yes,' she agreed weakly.

Michael went to her and grasped her arms, then gently kissed the back of her neck.

She broke away from him and went to the mirror. 'Look at me,' she wailed, starting to fuss with her hair. 'I look a mess.'

'You look fine.'

'No, I don't,' she insisted. 'My hair looks awful and my makeup is smeared and I ... I ...' She paused in midsentence, her hands fell to her sides, and she gazed down at the floor. Then she said softly, 'I imagine ... you've been with a lot of girls, haven't you?'

'Some,' he admitted.

She looked at him over her shoulder with wide-open, innocent eyes. 'I'm very nervous, you know.'

'Of course you are.' He started to move toward her.

'No,' she said, stopping him with an open hand. 'I mean, just give me a bit, please.' She moved away from the mirror, closer to the bed, but caught herself and abruptly turned again, finally sitting down on one of the high-backed chairs. She crossed her legs and folded her hands in her lap, and found it absolutely impossible to look at him.

'If you'd rather not,' he offered.

'I didn't say that,' she snapped. 'I'm here, aren't I? That's what you wanted.' She stared at her black shoes. Never before had she realized what large, ugly feet she had.

Michael began protesting that he didn't want to force her into anything, that he respected her, that, in fact, he actually thought she had suggested the hotel room.

Kathy didn't hear him. Her mind was running faster than a spring river. Who was this man? Why had she agreed to come with him? Oh, what was she going to do?

He stood on the other side of the bed, afraid to go to her. He was suddenly very aware of his hands. He didn't know what to do with them, so he clasped them behind his back, out of sight. 'Listen to me, Kathy,' he said.

She closed her eyes. Say the right thing, Michael, she prayed, please say the right thing.

'I want you to know that I think you're very, very special. To me, I mean. I just ... I don't want you to do anything you'll regret...'

She opened her eyes and glared at him. 'Look here, Michael Hill.

I'm not a child and don't you dare treat me like one. I know what I'm doing here.'

'No, I didn't mean anything,' he apologized. 'I'm sorry, don't get me wrong. But I mean ... what I mean is, you're special to me, see. You're the most special girl I've ever known. Ever in my whole life. But I don't know what's going to happen when this bloody war's over, about me, about my life, so if it's marriage you're thinking about—'

'Marriage! Who said the first thing about marriage!' She was so angry she had to grab the seat with both hands to keep herself in the chair. 'I never said a word about marriage. Not a word!'

Hill had not the slightest idea what to do. 'Well, I just thought. You know, the kind of girl you are. And this ...' He indicated the bed with his hand. 'You know, I just thought, that's all.'

Marriage? It was all so confusing. 'Marry you?' she sneered. Then she forced a laugh. 'I wouldn't marry you for all the tea in China.' Finally she relaxed her grip and stood up. 'In fact,' she continued, straightening her skirt, 'I don't even know what I'm doing here with you. This is a mistake, a horrible mistake.' Gathering up her purse and light jacket, she walked around the bed, being careful not to actually touch it, and went to the door. 'I'm terribly sorry,' she announced stiffly, 'but this – this isn't right. I don't understand this at all.' Then she left, leaving the door open behind her.

He followed her out of the room. Grasping the doorknob in his hand, he took a final look at the unwrinkled flower-print spread. He was smirking. Quite a lady, this one, he thought with some relief, quite a lady. Then he shut the door.

They rode down in the lift silently, neither daring to look at the other. As they passed the front desk Michael laid down the key. 'I think that'll be all,' he said devilishly, and winked.

The concierge winked back. 'I hope you enjoyed your stay, Mr and Mrs Moore,' he said in broken English, but by the time he reached that surname they were out the door.

THIRTEEN

The Royal Navy urgently needed a bit of legerdemain that would enable small, swift craft to operate safely in the enemy-controlled Mediterranean. 'These boats have got to be so well disguised they'll be able to pass close scrutiny from curious U-boat commanders,' explained Captain D. F. Gregory, an experienced naval camouflage man injured on a night run near Cyprus and sent to assist the Magic Gang while his leg recuperated, 'and they've got to be able to rapidly shed that disguise should a fight break out.' These boats, Gregory continued, would be used primarily to transport undercover agents and vital cargoes across the ocean, 'plus whatever other errands the office chaps might think up.'

Maskelyne knew that this assignment was not the grand illusion that would 'make the difference,' but until that one presented itself, or until he could create it, he would continue to do these little bits. This one was tricky, though. Having suffered through the difficulties of the *Houdin*, he realized from the outset that he could not rely on painted flats to disguise the boats, not if he expected these boats to make speed. All modifications would have to be made to the basic structure, and would have to be made in such a way as not to slow the boat at all. After inspecting the various types of craft available, Jasper and Gregory settled on the RAF's streamlined Miami rescue launch. This sleek, torpedo-shaped boat had a low forward cabin topped by a communications mast, and a long, narrow rear deck. Its overall length was approximately one hundred feet, much of it open deck space.

Photographs of the boat were taken from above by surveillance aircraft and from all angles at sea level, sixty pictures in all, and tacked to the walls of Maskelyne's office. But even after thoroughly studying the photographs Jasper couldn't decide how he would disguise the boat. 'What do we want it to look like?' he asked Gregory.

The tall, lean captain shrugged. 'Anything but what it is, I suppose.'

They began by listing the various craft that might sail the wartime Mediterranean with impunity. Safest among these, they decided, would be a millionaire's yacht flying a neutral flag, preferably that of a rich sheikhdom, and a filthy working caique. Jasper had Townsend do rough sketches of both boats, using proportions similar to the RAF speedboat, and when they were completed he laid those designs over the basic Miami hull.

Gregory pinned the roughs to the wall, then stepped back alongside Townsend, Jasper and Frank, critically examining them. 'What do you think? Which one?'

Jasper bit down on the stem of his cold pipe and looked from one to the other, back and forth. 'Both,' he finally decided. 'We can do both.' Picking up a drawing pencil, he moved forward and began altering Townsend's sketches. 'Some of the additions we've got to make can serve for both a yacht and a scow. This funnel, for example,' he said, using his pipe to point out a stubby funnel on the yacht's rear deck. 'We can easily convert that. And if we add a second mast here...'

Once Jasper started, everyone had an idea or two to add, and by the time they had worn holes in the sketch paper with their erasures and additions they were convinced this multiple conversion was theoretically possible.

'Well, that takes care of the easy part,' Captain Gregory said. 'Now we've got to concentrate on the real problem.'

'What?' Townsend asked, as if he hadn't heard the captain correctly. 'I thought the real problem was making the boat look like something else.'

Gregory shook his head. 'Look at this,' he said, tracing the smudged line of the hull from stern to prow with his index finger. 'Any salt worth his stripes'll recognize this silhouette straight away. Unless we can do something to alter this shape, it really doesn't matter what we do to the superstructure. It would be like lying a flat board on top of a bull and trying to pass it off as a table.'

'We jolly well can't reshape the hull,' Townsend snapped.

Jasper studied the sketches. 'And the thing has to make speed,' he added thoughtfully, 'so we can't attach anything to it.'

'The sea would tear it right off as soon as it got under way,' Gregory agreed.

Knox stared silently at the drawings, combing his memory for a naturally occurring parallel to the problem. Many animals and insects have the ability to change their exterior appearance. Gradually, he began to invest the craft with animate characteristics, transforming it in his mind into a fleet animal bounding over the waves in desperate flight from some unseen predator. He began to see its sharp, gritted teeth and its ears cocked as it raced for survival. Then he said cautiously, 'I believe I may have a solution.'

The three other men turned toward him in unison.

He continued staring at the drawing as he spoke, still visualizing a terrorized animal. 'In nature,' he began, sounding as though he were reciting by rote, 'there are any number of dimorphic animals and insects, meaning they are able to display two quite distinct forms. The peacock butterfly, for example, *Vanessa io*, usually shows the remarkably beautiful wings for which it is named. However, when this butterfly senses danger, it is able to fold its wings so that it resembles an ordinary leaf, and thus fools its enemies. Incidentally, there are also a number of trimorphic animals, but I'm sure you gentlemen understand the principle.'

Like respectful students, they murmured agreement.

'Now,' he continued, lapsing into his droll professorial tone, 'how do these remarkable creatures accomplish this feat?' He did not wait for an answer. 'They do so by taking advantage of the visual limitations of their natural enemies. They change their colours!'

'Watch me,' he commanded, picking out the red, yellow and green crayons from Townsend's sketch box and springing forward to the drawings on the wall. 'I'm sorry I don't have my proper illustrations to show you all of this, but it seems to me it would be possible to alter the lines of the hull through adaptive colouring. Technically, it's a variation of Thayer's Principle. I don't suppose any of you can explain that to me?' He glanced over his shoulder at the three silent figures, then chuckled to himself. 'No, of course you couldn't.'

Maskelyne glanced at Townsend, who shook his head in amazement at the professor's performance, and grinned.

'Thayer states, basically, that graded tints of colour will make it very difficult for the human eye to follow the borders of the lightest shades. So, I should think if we paint the hull in gradually decreasing intensities of one colour, its borders will be extremely difficult to discern. Something like this might work very well, I should think,' he concluded, stepping back to admire his handiwork. The centre section of the hull was a very dark green, which gradually lightened and seemed to fade into a lime which, in turn, washed into an even lighter yellow. The professor's shading was very uneven, but it illustrated his point: even from a few feet away it was difficult to determine the yellow borders. 'I imagine we can do much better in shades of grey or blue, which'll fade into the water, but I'm quite certain we can make the hull appear to be just about any shape we want it to be.'

'From a distance, you mean,' Captain Gregory corrected.

'From a distance,' Knox agreed.

Gregory was intrigued by the concept. He was quite familiar with the normal use of colour for camouflage purposes, but this was something new and exciting. He suggested Frank begin his experiments with omega grey, the bluish grey colour of the Antarctic petrel, a seabird. 'During the last war,' he explained, the American Navy tested every conceivable colour for its value in camouflage. Their researchers found that the petrel became virtually indistinguishable from the ocean when flying above it. By duplicating the optical properties of the bird, they produced the colour omega grey. They've used it since.'

Knox was agreeable.

'Hold on, now,' Townsend protested, 'I'm not collectin' any more camel pats, and I don't think any of the boys...'

Gregory looked at the artist as if he were daft, until Jasper explained. 'Oh, that won't be necessary,' the captain promised. 'We've got thousands of gallons of the stuff. Times have changed, you know. We're here to stay.'

Townsend remained dubious.

By the end of the week Graham had carved a wooden model of the speed launch, without modifications, and Knox had begun testing various shade patterns on it. Although it soon became apparent he was making progress, the job was a difficult one, and, periodically, the model had to be sanded clean so he could make a new start.

Maskelyne worked with Gregory on the superstructure modifications. Many small changes added up to major alterations. An ordinary life preserver affixed to the side of the cabin, for example, could be hung on its bright side to look like the clean, crisp gear normally found on an expensive yacht, but in seconds it could be flipped over onto its dirty, decaying side and look as though it had been hanging there in all weather for many years. A rear mast was raised, and from it the yacht would fly bright signal pennants and the caique would hang seamen's dirty laundry. Even the ship's nameboard would be convertible.

With work on the boat progressing satisfactorily and the rest of the Gang occupied on various other projects, Jasper told Brigadier Clarke he could resume the field-lecture series. Clarke's office had scheduled his first performance for Thursday, April 16.

But on the morning of the fifteenth Barkas phoned up at the Valley to change those plans. He wanted Maskelyne to attend a Gray Pillars conference the following afternoon. 'It's a strategic-planning seminar and I think it would be very valuable for you to sit in.'

Jasper told him that he was scheduled to fly to one of Auchinleck's Gazala Line strongholds at 1130 hours.

'Well, never mind that,' the colonel decided. 'I'll clear it with Clarke's people. We'll stall it till next week, that's all.'

Although Jasper's initial reaction was to agree to this, the many years he had spent making sure the show went on as scheduled made him reluctant to do so. 'I've got a better idea. Frank Knox can handle the lecture well enough. He's done the show with me plenty of times and does a fine job.'

Barkas had no objection. 'The chaps'll be disappointed, of course. They're expecting to see Hitler's favourite magician.'

'Frank'll win them over quick enough.'

Professor Knox thought it was a splendid idea, and immediately began worrying about his performance. 'I'll need to brush up on the sleights,' he said professionally.

'Right,' Jasper said.

'And you'll have to review the patter with me.'

'Right.'

'And then I've got to go through the rings too,' Frank continued, his confidence draining just as rapidly as it had swelled.

'That's right.'

Frank sighed, then suggested, 'Perhaps I'd better have a run-through.'

So, that night, the Magic Gang and a few select guests squeezed into the dayroom to tip a few and cheer Knox through his paces. 'Now, remember,' Jasper cautioned as Frank got ready behind the white-sheet curtain hung for the show, 'this is just a rehearsal. There'll be no heckling from the audience.'

'Don't worry, folks,' Knox shouted happily from behind the sheet, 'you'll all get your money's worth tonight.' Everyone hooted.

Jasper waited until they quieted down, then announced, 'I am pleased to present, for one performance only, the one, the only, never-seen-before-on-this-or-any-other-stage Professor Knox-O the Magnificent!'

Frank stepped out from behind the sheet to a smattering of applause, an ill-fitting black cape draped around his shoulders. 'This lecture is for all of you,' he said sternly, a tremble of nervousness evident in his voice. 'It is important to remember all the things you'll see and hear this evening, because someday very soon this information might come in handy.' Stepping in front of Nails Graham, he asked in an appropriate stage thunder, 'And what is your name, soldier?'

'Fish, sir,' Graham replied, 'Private Cod Fish.'

Knox persevered. Spreading six playing cards in a fan, he asked, 'I wonder if you would assist me by distributing these six playing cards at random.' As Graham passed them out, Knox asked each recipient to write his or her name on the face of the card. 'Don't be shy, ask for spelling help if you need it.'

When everyone had finished, Nails collected the cards and handed them to Knox, who stepped back behind a production table and laid down the six cards in full view of the audience. 'The main thing you want to avoid,' he began again, 'is being put in the bag.' As he said this, he held up a canvas rucksack and turned it inside out to show that it was empty. Then he laid it down on the table next to the cards.

Jasper leaned against the rear wall, enjoying his pipe, basking in Frank's glow.

'... But suppose you and your mates are out on the Blue and you get separated. The first thing you must try to do is find some sort of cover. It can be anywhere,' Knox explained, reaching into his shirt pocket and pulling out a signed card, 'behind a dune or an outcropping, in a dry wadi,' he continued, meanwhile removing cards from both pockets of his shorts and his sock, 'and you must never forget that destroyed vehicles can provide excellent hiding spots.' Finally, he went to Kathy Lewis and appeared to pull the card she had signed from behind her left ear.

The group applauded warmly even though they had seen Jasper do this same trick numerous times.

'Unfortunately,' Frank pointed out as he returned to his spot behind the production table, 'some of you may get taken by Rommel ...' working smoothly, he reached into the rucksack, 'and put in the bag ...' and withdrew the sixth signed playing card, this one with a shameful word Hill had written on it. Again the audience cheered, Maskelyne loudest of all.

The professor dropped the card back into the sack. 'So, you're in the bag. What is your first objective?' He paused to allow the tension to build. It did not. 'Escape,' he whispered, as if it had. 'Escape,' he repeated a bit more loudly. 'It should be your first thought in the morning and your last thought at night. Get out of the bag. Get back to your fellows.'

In a high-pitched, womanly voice, Robson asked mockingly, 'Could that be possible?'

Frank ignored him. 'It can be done, and hundreds of your mates have already done it. All it takes is a little ingenuity.' With that, he turned the bag inside out again. The card had disappeared. Laying the bag on the table again, he pattered on about the soldier's oath, reminding them that it committed each of them to try to escape if captured and, if that was not possible, to aid his fellow soldiers in their efforts. Then he picked up the sack again. 'Sometimes, you have to put aside your own plans for those of your mates,' he said, dipping into the bag and pulling out four aces.

'Blimey–' Hill swooned in jest '–the man's a regular Maskelyne.'

Kathy elbowed him in the ribs and shut him up with a severe look. And Knox continued.

Jasper revelled in the show. Frank was in his greatest glory, hard at work pleasing other people; his face was beaming, his voice strong, his movements sure. Here was Dr Watson finally getting the chance to solve his own mysteries, and having a grand time at it. Jasper noted dozens of mistakes in the performance, but these were errors so small that only a practised eye would catch them, certainly not a desert audience, and he knew he wouldn't risk embarrassing Knox by mentioning them.

'... you've escaped and you're trying to locate the nearest friendly forces,' the professor continued.

The transformation in Frank Knox was the real magic in this act, Maskelyne realized, and savoured it.

The following morning Knox-O the Magnificent arrived at Heliopolis Airport at 1100 hours, and his Dakota lifted off within minutes. Its destination, he knew, was one of the six front-line strongholds, or 'boxes,' into which Eighth Army had gathered its forces. Besides the professor, the passengers included five enlisted men returning from leave, an American lieutenant, two young female nurses, two replacement officers and an RAF pilot with a cast on his ankle. The plane also carried a hold of supplies.

Once it was safely airborne, Knox closed his eyes and fell into a light sleep.

Jasper, meanwhile, reported to Gray Pillars at 0800, but the strategic conference did not begin for another two hours. General Auchinleck chaired the meeting. Over fifty officers of all ranks assembled in a ballroom in which tiered benches had been built to allow full view for everyone. Jasper was seated in a rear section.

'You have been invited here to begin preparations for the greatest offensive in the history of armoured warfare,' the Auk announced to the absolutely still room. Pointing with his baton to a large situation map mounted on the ballroom wall, he promised, 'This time we are going to drive the enemy out of the desert. We will have him outmanned and outgunned, our men will be better supplied than ever before. We will be physically ready and mentally ready...'

The meeting lasted most of the day. It involved a full explanation of the current stalemate at El Gazala, including a breakdown of supplies on hand and supplies expected. Maskelyne had never before been privy to such vital information, and he listened intently as the General, and then his aides, outlined what sounded like a nearly perfect plan.

Eighth Army had remained in position along the Gazala Line, the sixty-mile-long chain of strongholds and minefields stretching south from the Mediterranean through the heart of the desert. The way one general after another described these positions, there seemed to be no way Rommel's Afrika Korps could smash through them to the Nile. But as Jasper listened to them speak with such confidence he could not help thinking of the French Maginot Line. It too had been declared impregnable. And nothing, he had learned from that debacle, was so precarious as a general's certainty.

While Maskelyne was listening to the parade of officers, Knox was starring in his desert show. The silver Linking Rings sparkled in the afternoon sun as he held them high for inspection. 'Sometimes it will seem as though escape is impossible ...' he shouted so everyone sitting in the semicircle around him could hear, then invited one of the most popular officers to come forward and be his foil.

Frank's lecture at the El Adem box was well received, and he enjoyed a staff lunch before boarding the plane for the return trip. Although he would never admit it to Maskelyne, he thoroughly enjoyed his moment of celebrity. Travelling with him back to Cairo was a sergeant who had broken his hip in a football tumble, and three other men on emergency leave. One of these men suggested cards as the trip began, but Knox decided to read instead.

Minutes into the flight the pilots received reports of a major sandstorm brewing in the Sidi Rezegh area, and turned north, toward Tobruk, to avoid it. Unknown to them, German Messerschmitts had recently begun operating in that area.

The conference at Gray Pillars was concluded with the announcement that each officer in attendance would be expected to submit written comments and suggestions 'ASAP,' as soon as possible, but no later than May 1. 'Here's a chance to use the old noodle,' the lecturing staff officer reminded them. 'We're looking for innovative ideas, even daring, I might say, but strictly within reasonable bounds.'

They want the same old stuff, Jasper thought as he collected his notes. That meant dummy tanks and guns, 'Chinese' men and sunshields from his section.

'The PM's put the cooker on,' the staff officer continued. 'He wants everything day before yesterday, so we'd appreciate it if you'd jump to it.'

An Ops major invited Jasper to join a group heading to Shepheards for 'downers, but Maskelyne wanted to put in some time on the speedboat project, so he headed back to Magic Valley.

Frank Knox was laughing his way through the misadventures of Evelyn Waugh's mythical Fleet Street correspondent, William Boot, in *Scoop*, when the German fighters pounced. They came directly out of the sun, and the Dakota pilots did not even realize they were under attack until the first machine-gun bullets ripped into the starboard wing. The co-pilot immediately ordered everyone in the cabin to lie on the floor.

Knox lay down flat, his arm draped over the injured soldier. There was some yelling at first, and some praying, but then everyone was silent. The pilot took evasive action, wrenching his plane straight up, grasping for altitude, then nosing it into a hard dive. The co-pilot radioed for assistance.

One of the Messerschmitts caught the Dakota in its dive and fired a fusillade into its undercarriage, then began swinging around for a third pass. But as he did, he spotted two RAF Spits at high altitude and immediately broke off the attack. The two German raiders fled into the desert at low level.

The Dakota pilot quickly assessed the damage. Some rounds had smashed into the cabin without causing injury. One of the fuel lines had been punctured, and was trailing gasoline, but there was enough reserve in the other engine to make Cairo. The most serious problem seemed to be the shot-up undercarriage. The landing gear would not lower automatically and there was some doubt it could be manually cranked into position. If the wheels wouldn't go down the pilot knew he'd have to pancake in, an unpleasant situation considering that gasoline had been sprayed over the fuselage. 'Any chutes aboard?' he asked the co-pilot.

The co-pilot chuckled bitterly at the question.

The pilot frowned. 'Didn't think so, actually.' He decided to go for Cairo. Heliopolis had the best emergency landing equipment of any airport within range. The long flight would give him time to fool with the gear, perhaps even rig something, and it would exhaust most of the volatile aviation fuel. He knew he could land the plane; he was just scared to death it would blow up on him during the attempt.

Jasper had barely settled down to work on the speedboat when Jack Fuller came roaring hellbent into the Valley. He slammed the jeep to a spinning halt in front of Maskelyne's office and was inside even before its motor sputtered silent. 'Come on, Jay,' he blurted, taking big gulps of breath. 'I was just in town. Some M-Es attacked Frank's plane on the way back.'

Jasper froze. 'No.'

'He's all right, everybody's okay, but their landing gear got shot up and they can't get the buggers down. They're coming in flat.'

Mike Hill and Bill Robson had seen Fuller dash up and were wandering over to investigate. They quickly hopped into the back of the jeep.

'Hold on,' Fuller warned and banged down on the accelerator. He raced through Cairo, ignoring traffic signals and Egyptian policemen. He drove hunched over the steering wheel, his eyes fastened on the road, dodging other vehicles like a racing driver. 'Don't worry,' he yelled, 'we'll get there before they will.'

Jasper sat in the front bucket seat staring straight ahead.

Aboard the Dakota, Knox and one of the other men held the co-pilot's feet as he dangled in the cabin crawl space and tried to manually lower the landing gear. 'The struts are so mangled nothing works,' he reported when he was pulled back in.

The pilot remained composed. 'So we'll belly in, that's all. Get everyone as far away from the wings as possible. And make sure they get out of here one-two when we stop moving.'

Frank took a seat next to the boy with the broken hip. The lad was sweating and shivering. 'You think this is it?' he asked fearfully.

Frank smiled and shook his head. 'Hardly. Actually, I've been in a few tougher scrapes myself.' Then, modestly, he regaled his fellow passengers with the story of 'his' narrow escape from the dazzle-beacon. 'I thought for sure I was a goner that time. This? This,' he said, dismissing the danger with a casual wave of his hand, 'this is nothing.'

The Dakota was on its final approach even before he had finished his tale.

Jasper and his men stood on the apron searching the late-afternoon sky for the Dakota. Fire trucks had watered down the runway and were in position to race alongside the plane when it hit, spraying a carpet of water in an effort to prevent sparks from igniting the gasoline.

'Nothing to worry about,' Hill said aloud. 'Piece of cake, piece of cake.'

All air traffic around Heliopolis was locked into holding patterns. Fuller spotted the Dakota through his binoculars. 'I got 'em!' he shouted, pointing into the overcast sky. 'There they are.' The word quickly spread over the airfield, and everyone stopped work to watch the dramatic landing. Fire sirens began screeching.

Inside the plane, Frank told the injured soldier calmly, 'Soon as we stop moving, I'm going to pick you up. I want you to hold tightly on to me. Got it?'

The boy nodded.

'Good,' Knox said, and patted him fondly on the leg. 'Now, don't worry, we'll be down safe in just a few minutes.' For the first time, he realized his mouth was as parched as the summer desert.

Jasper's shoulders felt as if they were supporting the plane. He prayed.

'Here's at it!' the Dakota pilot screamed as he shut down the remaining engine. The plane glided in as gracefully as a gull on the wind, its speed well below one hundred knots when it touched the runway and began skidding. Knox heard the plane screech in agony as the concrete runway tore open its belly. He pressed his palms against his ears as hard as he could, but he could still hear the wounded soldier's screams.

The Dakota careened down the runway throwing sparks as if it were a giant Roman candle. The pilot had the flaps down, desperately trying to stop the beast.

In a horrified, incredulous whisper, Robson said, 'She's going to blow.'

Flames were shooting out of the starboard engine long before the plane finally came to a halt, and they rapidly enveloped the entire fuselage. The firemen made a heroic effort to get close to the plane, but the intense heat drove them back.

'Oh, good God, no!' Jasper screamed. 'No, please no!' Then he stumbled forward three, four, five steps, and finally started running toward the burning plane.

'Jay! No!' Hill yelled, and took off after him.

The two pilots managed to scramble out of the cockpit windows and dropped safely to the ground. Inside the cabin, Frank was struggling with the injured soldier. One of the men managed to get the rear door open. He turned around to call to the other men.

The plane exploded. The soldier in the doorway was spat out as if he were a bothersome pit. He was hurled about twenty yards, a living ball of fire, and smashed into the runway.

Hill dived at Maskelyne's legs, bringing him down with a flying tackle. Jasper fought to break free, kicking his legs, screaming, 'Do something! Help them, for God's sake...'

'It's too late,' Michael sobbed. 'It's too late, Jay, it's too late.'

The plane became a metal sun, illuminating the dark afternoon and warming the skin of men standing as far as a thousand yards from it.

The fire fighters could do nothing. Slowly, the Dakota's skin was peeled back. For a few horrid seconds it was possible to see two shadows moving grotesquely in the flames, moving as slowly as if they were swimming in a blazing yellow ocean. Soon, mercifully, they fell.

'Frank!' Jasper shrieked; a single bloodcurdling cry that would haunt the nights of everyone who heard it.

But it was to no avail – Frank Knox was dead.

Jasper stayed at the airport most of the night, leaving only after the remains of the passengers had been removed from the charred hulk. Somehow, he managed to get through the next few days. It was a dreadful time. He felt as if God had reached into his chest and ripped out his heart. Just rising in the morning sapped all his strength. He was always tired, no matter how long he slept, and always cold, even in the warmest hours of the day. He barely ate, but was never hungry. He was numb, and the world he saw through his insensible eyes was devoid of bright colours and hope and laughter and excitement and, too, of physical pain and fear; whatever happened simply happened. It was the galaxy of indifference. Life continued.

He managed to drag himself through each day's required motions, but had no desires except to lose himself in long and warm sleep.

It wasn't possible, he told himself, Frank Knox simply could not be dead. Soon, he'd come walking through the office door, maybe stumbling once, as he often did...

The Gang, friends, all offered comfort, but he rejected their efforts and abhorred their pity, because he knew the truth: he was supposed to have been on that plane. It was his seat, his job. Knox had died in his stead. He felt certain that if he had been aboard the Dakota it wouldn't have happened. There would have been no attack, no crash, no fire; he would have prevented it. Somehow, he would have prevented it.

He vaguely remembered speaking at the crowded memorial service, but could never recall exactly what he said.

After the service he had spent a full day trying to write the terrible letter to Frank's daughters. There was so much he wanted to explain, but the thoughts he put down were wrong, or confused, or inadequate. Finally he wrote, 'Your father was my best friend. He was a good man and a brave man. He died as he had lived, trying to help someone. I will miss him greatly. I loved him very much.'

He wrote a longer letter to Mary pouring out his feelings. In this letter he told her that he should have been on that plane.

He tried to bury his grief under a mammoth work load, but found it impossible to concentrate for any length of time. Memories of Frank Knox would strike him, and he would suddenly be back in Farnham heaving water balloons, or aboard the *Sumaria* playing a lively duet, or trailing a camel caravan, or orchestrating the ploy at Maryūt Bay ... He often thought he heard Frank's familiar laugh and turned around fully expecting to see him standing there with his shirt bulging from his trousers or, stranger, felt his presence in a room. Always, with the realization that his mind was playing dreary tricks, came renewed sadness.

Worse than the pangs of loss and loneliness was his overwhelming feeling of inadequacy. He desperately wanted to find some way to give meaning to Frank's death, but as much as he tried he was unable to think of a single thing that would serve some purpose.

Night after night he relived the crash at Heliopolis, trying to determine if anything could have been done that might have made a difference. His life became a barrel of ifs. If he had delayed the trip to the desert. If the Dakota had flown earlier or later. If there had been no sandstorm. If the German machine-gun bullets had been inches off line. If, if, if. If there had been no fire ... The more thought he gave to the tragedy, the more frustrated he became. If there had been no fire ... they would have survived. It was the fire after the crash that had killed them, just as similar fires had killed so many other men in crashes.

Fire. Fire, the devil's breath. Oh, how he hated and feared it. Even during his early years in the Egyptian Theatre he would sweat and his head would ache when a performer worked with fire. It had been excruciating for him to watch from the wings when his grandfather did the Vanishing Moth, an illusion in which a beautiful female assistant vanished in a burst of flame.

Frank Knox had survived the crash landing. He had died in the fire.

It was this irrefutable fact that set him to work on a substance that could have made a difference at Heliopolis, a fire-resistant cream. This 'magic' substance would be the most fitting memorial to Frank Knox; it would save lives.

He knew he could produce it. His father had supplied such a cream, or paste, to the Admiralty back in 1916 to protect ships' gunners of the Grand Fleet from searing flashbacks. This time, he believed, it could be used in aircraft to give crew and passengers a vital few minutes' protection from fire. Too often, those few minutes were the difference between life and death.

He told no one about this paste and asked for no help. He rushed through his routine work in the mornings, then went to work by himself in the afternoons. The Gang tried hard to bring him out of his depression, but did not succeed. Within a few days he had mixed up the first batch of the paste.

Nails Graham strolled into Maskelyne's office with some routine paperwork just as Jasper was lowering his right hand into a sizzling wastebasket fire. It took Graham's senses a moment to register, then – exclaiming 'Jesus!' – he dropped his papers and raced across the room. He grabbed Maskelyne's hand and forcibly pulled it out of the flames, almost knocking Jasper over, and singeing his own hand in the process. 'What the hell's the matter with you?' he screamed as he picked up the hot basket in his bare hands and hustled outside with it. 'Are you nuts? Are you crazy?'

Jasper examined his hand.

Quickly dousing the fire with a few scoops of sand, Graham marched back inside to confront Maskelyne. 'Goddammit, Jay, I've had it. We've all had it. I don't know what the hell to do. We all miss Frank, but you just sit in this office...'

Maskelyne began peeling a hard white crust off his hand.

'Look,' Nails pleaded in a milder tone, 'Jay, please listen to me. There's nothing we can do about it. He's dead. Frank's dead. Don't you understand that? People get killed in wars. I know it hurts–' He paused, suddenly aware of Maskelyne's actions. 'What're you doing?'

Jasper held his hand out to Graham. Bits of white paste still clung to it, and his skin was abnormally pink, but otherwise it was fine.

'I don't understand. How...'

Jasper took a deep breath and told him about the fire-resistant paste.

'And it works?' Graham asked when he had finished.

'You just saw me put my hand in a fire. It works,' Jasper said. Although the first test was finished, he was still sweating and his head was pounding. It had been a difficult moment for him, and he had made a number of false starts before being able to put his hand into the flames. He found the necessary courage to do so in the memory of two shadowy figures falling inside the burning fuselage.

Graham examined Maskelyne's hand. It was unscathed. 'It's amazing. Bloody damn amazing. I got burned just picking up that basket.'

'It's science, that's all,' Jasper said as he searched the first-aid box for some burn ointment for Graham's hand. His intention, he explained, was to test the cream by covering his entire body with it, then walk into a large fire. After he had proved it worked, he would offer it to the services.

When Graham told the rest of the Gang about this plan, they desperately tried to talk him out of it. 'We won't permit it. It's too bloody dangerous,' Hill argued. 'You're much too valuable, with all your big ideas and everything.'

'Just look at you,' Bill Robson chided, 'always looking to be in the spotlight.'

Jasper refused to pay attention to their protests. This was a small repayment for the debt he owed Frank Knox. He would make it and he would test it. By himself. If he failed, he would be the only one to suffer. No one else would die in his place.

The paste itself was similar to that used by carnival fire-eaters. It was a mix of ordinary carbolic soap, asbestos powder or common whitening, water, and a few minor but absolutely essential ingredients. The result was a thick white paste that crusted under intense heat, thus providing complete protection from fire until it vapourized, usually after three or four minutes.

Barkas was flabbergasted when informed that Maskelyne intended to walk into a raging fire in street clothes. 'That bloody idiot!' he roared, and raced to Magic Valley. 'The answer is no,' he snapped at the surprised magician after storming into his office. 'Absolutely not. You do not have permission to experiment with any so-called magic paste.'

Jasper tried to defend himself.

Barkas raged on. 'No matter what you might think, no one can walk into a fire without an asbestos suit and survive. I'm astonished that a man with your background could possibly believe, even for an instant—'

'Do you want to save lives?' Jasper asked calmly.

'Save lives, yes, not waste them on grandstanding tricks.'

'My paste'll save lives,' Maskelyne insisted. 'It would have saved Frank and all the rest of them.'

Barkas finally sat down and tried to discuss the situation rationally. 'Jay, I know how you feel about Frank. He was a fine man and it's a great tragedy. But we can't afford to risk you. You were there at Gray Pillars, you know what's shaping up. This is no time to be playing games.'

'This isn't a game,' Jasper replied in a controlled voice, 'and there's no risk. You've seen the locals walking on burning coals and licking red-hot pokers, haven't you? Don't tell me you believe in magic, Major?'

'One thing has nothing to—'

'Oh, of course it does. Variations of this paste have been used by performers for hundreds of years. I'm just putting it to a new purpose, that's all.'

'I'm sorry, Jay,' Barkas said firmly, 'I just can't permit it.'

'Well, I'm sorry, too,' Jasper retorted, 'but I'm going to test it with or without your permission. Don't you understand? This will save lives.'

Barkas went to the dayroom and appealed to the Gang for support. 'Isn't there anyone who could talk him out of it?'

'Sure,' Mike Hill said smartly, 'Frank Knox.'

Up against it, Barkas finally agreed to schedule a demonstration for the combined forces, but only on the condition that Maskelyne allow a fire-safety officer wearing an asbestos suit to accompany him into the inferno. 'If you refuse,' he threatened, 'you can spend the remainder of your brief time in Cairo playing with fire, but no one will witness your little demonstration.' Reluctantly, Jasper agreed to this demand.

He worked on the paste for a week, trying to prolong its effectiveness by adding and subtracting different elements. He tested each mix by dipping his hand into a bucket of it, then holding his encrusted hand directly above a wastepaper fire.

His great fear of fire was with him always. His nerves got so sensitive he flinched when someone unexpectedly struck a match, but he kept at it. He knew he had no choice. This paste would save lives, he was sure of that. He had to test it.

Barkas had difficulty convincing the brass that this was not simply another exhibition of Maskelyne magic. No one seriously believed Jasper was going to walk into a real fire. It's a trick, they scoffed. But the major, like a carnival pitchman, raised their curiosity by striking a match and holding it up to his cream-protected wrist in front of their very eyes.

A few of them figured the match had to be a prop and burned their fingertips proving it was not.

The demonstration of Maskelyne's fire-resistant paste was scheduled for April 30 at Heliopolis, but Jasper planned to test it before that within the privacy of Magic Valley.

This rehearsal, as he called it, was to take place in a secluded corner of the compound. Those few people in attendance were asked to keep the nature of the test secret. 'If word gets around that someone is walking in fires without being burned,' Jasper explained, 'we'll have every religious fanatic in North Africa banging on the front gate.'

The night before the test he had to take pills to sleep, the first time he had ever done so. Still, he tossed restlessly throughout the night and awoke feeling groggy and slightly disoriented.

The morning was bright and warm. 'Perfect day for a short stroll in an inferno,' Fuller said sarcastically during the drive to the site. Jasper dressed in a pair of bathing trunks, a suit of hooded coveralls Kathy Lewis had tailored from unserviceable army blankets, welder's goggles to protect his eyes from the brightness of the flames, a homemade mask, gloves and boots. Gauze filters would enable him to inhale without searing his throat.

Six wooden crates, each about five feet tall, had been arranged in a circle. All of them were filled with wood chips and rags and doused with gasoline. At Maskelyne's signal, Hill would ignite them and they would become a true ring of fire.

Jasper avoided looking at these crates as he prepared. He tried to think of anything except the fire, but of course could think of nothing else. Never in his life had he been more determined; yet never had he been more frightened.

A large washtub was filled with the paste, and Jasper sat down and bathed in it. The boys swabbed the coveralls, mask and boots with brushes, being careful to cover every inch of his body with a thick coating of white lotion. When he finally stood up, he looked much more like the legendary Abominable Snowman than an officer of His Majesty's Service.

The Gang crowded around him like a boxing team giving their fighter last-minute instructions before the big match. Hill slapped another dash of paste on Jasper's shin and patted it down. Robson cautioned him to get out quick if he felt the slightest pinch of fire. Maskelyne barely heard them; his eyes, his mind were now riveted on his opponent, the six boxes standing in the centre of the vacant field, looking somewhat like a children's-play-ground Stonehenge. Abruptly, he pulled loose from the Gang and started walking toward them, walking into his own special hell.

About fifteen feet from the ring he paused, adjusted his goggles, reached under his mask and scratched his nose, took a steadying breath, and dropped his right hand.

Hill lit his torch, some rags soaked in gasoline and wrapped around a long stick, and approached the ring. Like a man handing a sweet to a gorilla, he reached out as far as he could extend his arm and laid the torch next to one of the boxes. Then he turned around, put his head down and ran.

With a tremendous, air-sucking *whoosh!* the first crate exploded into flames. Then, in quick succession, like matchsticks in a single box, the other five burst into blazing life. Black smoke poured out of the ring, and the heat was so intense the spectators had to back off.

Jasper was staggered by the first gust of fiery wind, but held his position. Then resolutely, he began walking into the circle.

'Cripes almighty,' Fuller murmured reverently as Maskelyne disappeared into the fire.

He stood in the centre of the blaze. Flames washed his body, furiously searching his protection for the slightest chink. Again and again and again the fire attacked him, raging at its failure to devour him. The fire roared fearfully, roared louder than anything Maskelyne had ever heard. He turned slowly round and round. Burning pieces of the crates floated away.

He was tranquil. His fear had been left in some distant world. Now, here, at the absolute heart of his terror, he was at peace. He closed his eyes and imagined he was lying on a summer beach in Jersey. The sun was August hot on his face, and he knew he would turn bright red in the evening. Calmly, he counted seconds, '... ninety-two, ninety-three, ninety...

'... one hunnred nineteen, one hunnred twenty ...' At the two-minute mark Robson looked up from his wristwatch. The fire was beginning to die down, but Maskelyne was not visible. Besides, the cartoonist knew that time really didn't matter. Even if Jasper needed help, there was nothing that could be done to help him.

Jasper had become attuned to the fire and was acutely aware when it lost its spirit. Its rage dissipated. Its thunder was reduced to the rush of bedsheets snapping in a strong wind. He was having some minor difficulties breathing, and was very warm, but was otherwise fine. After he had counted off three minutes he walked briskly out of the fire.

'Son of a bee,' Fuller said admiringly. The others started shouting with joy and ran toward Maskelyne. 'Don't touch him till he cools down,' Union Jack yelled, but no one heard him.

Once he had cooled, and then been hosed off, the Gang practically carried him back to the dayroom on their shoulders.

Barkas was not informed that the paste had been tested and so was understandably nervous and unhappy as representatives of the different branches arrived at Heliopolis Airport the morning of April 30. The major had made a halfhearted effort to convince Maskelyne to abandon the test, but he knew even before he began it that Jasper would not listen to reason.

The night before had been extremely difficult for Jasper. He sat alone in his room strumming on his ukulele until almost eleven o'clock. He was tired, but the moment he closed his eyes he was back in the fire and this time it was biting at him and dragging him down, as if he were trapped in quicksand wearing cement boots. In this nightmare he could not escape. The successful test had done nothing to quell his lifelong fear; instead, the experience enabled his mind to make it more realistic and terrifying.

Just before midnight he took a leisurely stroll around the Valley. A million stars sheltered him. Some night creatures were singing pleasantly. Guards marched the perimeter. He walked for a long time, his hands stuffed into the back of his shorts, nodding to the occasional passerby, thinking mostly about the coming morning. He had no particular destination, but found himself standing outside Frank Knox's office-workroom for the first time since the crash. It seemed right that he should go in.

He snapped on the light and stood holding the door. The room was exactly as it had been the day the professor left it. His half-empty tea mug sat on a file cabinet, papers and pencils were strewn on his desk, the partially painted wooden speedboat model was on his work table, and next to it was a textbook opened to a full-colour drawing of a bird. Jasper stared into the room for a while, then snapped off the light and turned away, letting the door slam behind him.

He thought about Frank Knox as he bathed in the paste at Heliopolis Airport the following morning.

Rather than using crates in this demonstration, Maskelyne had ordered an entire wing and part of the fuselage of a wrecked bomber hauled to an isolated section of the airport. The wing was propped up on heavy timber supports, and its hastily plugged fuel tank was filled with aviation petrol. Piles of flammable material, including straw and broken packing cases soaked in sump oil, were scattered beneath the wing. A detonator, its fuse stretching fully fifty yards to a protected observation post, was set in the centre of the debris.

The RAF rescue man jeeped in shortly after 0900, already zippered into one of the precious few asbestos suits in North Africa. Holding his helmet in his gloved hands, he lumbered out of the jeep and waddled over to Jasper. 'Dick von Glehn,' he announced. 'Understand we're to take a little walk together.'

Jasper looked up from the washtub. For this demonstration he was wearing a standard RAF flight suit as well as his homemade mask, goggles, boots and gloves. 'Shouldn't last too long,' he replied. 'It'll be a mite warm, though.'

Von Glehn tapped his helmet. 'That's why I brought my friend here. Now, is there anything I should know about? I mean, about this paste here, anything I should watch out for?'

Jasper shook his head. 'No, nothing. Three minutes, in and out, that's all. Just follow me.'

The rescue man paused, then grinned. 'You're really gonna do this, aren't you?'

Jasper looked at him evenly. 'It's necessary.'

'Okay, then, I'll be right on your heels. Good luck.'

At 0930, Jasper put the gauze filters into his mouth and walked toward the wreckage. As before, his head ached and he was nauseous. His legs were wobbly. For a moment he thought he might heave, but did not. Twenty feet from the wing he turned around to check von Glehn, now an unrecognizable creature in his protective suit. Von Glehn signalled thumbs up.

Just behind the observation stands an ambulance and fire truck surreptitiously rolled into place.

Seconds later the peaceful morning was ripped apart by an explosion, and the wreckage was turned into a blast furnace. Jasper squared his shoulders against the powerful gust and, as if tramping in a blizzard, trudged into the fire.

Once inside the flames, he turned and found von Glehn only a few feet behind. The rescue man looked at him and gave him the high sign.

The top brass watching this display were speechless. A man had actually walked into an inferno without the protection of an asbestos suit. The first blast of wind had knocked off a few braided caps and they had skittered across the field, pursued by hapless aides, but not a single ranking officer took his eyes off the incredible sight fifty yards in front of the post.

Jasper caught von Glehn's attention and held up his index finger. One minute had passed.

The flames tore at the wreckage. Chunks of fuselage and wing dropped onto the concrete, gradually curling up like dying spiders drawing in their legs. With a *whoop!* a large section fell out of the centre of the wing, exposing a slice of blue sky for an instant before smoke and flames filled the hole. Instinctively, Maskelyne the performer moved over and stuck his head through the burning wing.

'Show-off,' Hill muttered.

After a few seconds he stepped away. Other sections of the wing were dropping and he didn't want to be crowned by the debris. The paste could withstand heat, but it could not protect him from a chunk of falling metal. Looking over at von Glehn, he held up two fingers. Two minutes gone.

Robson snapped photographs. The ambulance and fire-truck attendant had moved away from their vehicles to see better.

The soles of Jasper's feet were getting hotter and hotter, as if he were standing barefoot on sun-baked flagstones. He began lifting one, then the other, in turn, in a sort of slow-motion folk dance. Finally, when his count reached 160 seconds, nearly three minutes, he signalled von Glehn it was time to get out.

He marched out proudly, fully aware his paste had been proved completely effective. They would have to use it in aircraft. As soon as he cleared the burning wing he glanced back to make sure the rescue man was with him. In that instant, his satisfaction turned into white horror. Von Glehn seemed to be having difficulty fighting his way out of the fire. Suddenly, he staggered, and nearly fell into the flames.

Jasper whirled around and started to go to help him, but von Glehn jerked himself upright and held up his hand to indicate he was all right.

The fire roared like a great bear cheated out of its due.

Maskelyne waited until von Glehn was safely away from the fire, then walked on. He wondered if his eyes had tricked him, or if the man had tripped on some debris. Every few steps he looked around to check him. The rescue man's head was lowered and he was moving sluggishly, but he seemed to be in control.

As soon as Jasper reached the safety of the observation stand, he ripped off his mask and goggles, spat out the charred gauze filters and sucked in a long breath of refreshing air. His shoulders relaxed. He took another deep breath, and only then did he hear the shouting.

Von Glehn was down on one knee, like a warrior being knighted. He tried to struggle to his feet, swaying from side to side as he did, and had almost made it when he suddenly collapsed onto the ground. Tiny flames shot out from beneath his helmet. He was on fire inside the asbestos suit; he was being roasted alive.

Jasper got to him first. His gloved hands were still protected by the paste, so he could grab the suit's red-hot metal clips without burning himself. He tore at the clips and zippers, frantically trying to get von Glehn out of the suit.

There was great confusion among the spectators as everyone raced to see what was going on. A well-intentioned fireman, reacting naturally, picked up the uncoiled pumper hose and began spraying Jasper and von Glehn.

'Wait!' Maskelyne screeched in horror, vainly trying to block the stream of cold water with his hands, but his cry was lost in the commotion.

Von Glehn sizzled, white smoke billowing from his suit. He writhed in agony.

The stunned fireman dropped the hose and it snaked along the ground, harmlessly spewing water onto an empty field. A second fireman shut it down.

Jasper grappled with the protective helmet, trying to get it off so von Glehn could breathe, but the water had warped the metal fastenings, making them inoperable.

The crowd of brass that had gathered around the fallen man stood by helplessly. Jasper screamed furiously at them, 'Get him out of this! Do something, dammit, do something!' They moved back a step.

A fireman broke through their ranks carrying a hacksaw and clippers and deftly began cutting von Glehn out of the suit. A gush of steam hissed out of the first cut, as if whistling out of a tea spout. Von Glehn's screams were muffled by his helmet. As soon as Jasper got a finger hold, he began tearing at the suit, but one of the medics stopped him. 'We can take it from here,' he said kindly.

Hill and Graham helped Jasper to his feet and stood by supporting him as the fireman finally managed to free the helmet.

The safety officer was no longer recognizable. Two marble eyes bulged from his hideously swollen face, his blackened tongue protruded from his mouth, his skin was scorched dark brown and covered with pussy blisters. He was still alive, though, and making dreadful sounds.

Graham grimaced. 'Poor bastard,' he said involuntarily.

Von Glehn was rushed to the hospital, although one of the medics indicated with a shake of his head he didn't give him much of a chance of surviving.

Jasper peeled off his encrusted flight suit and gloves, put on a dry uniform and demanded to be taken to the hospital. Hill tried to talk him out of it, suggesting he first return to the Valley to clean up. 'There's nothing you can do for him, Jay. The doctors are doing everything they can.'

Maskelyne insisted. 'I'm going. It's my fault...'

'It's not,' Hill replied. 'It's just an accident, nobody's–'

Jasper exploded. 'Don't patronize me, dammit! And don't tell me my responsibilities. I know what I've done. I know–'

Graham, who had been holding Maskelyne's gloves, angrily threw them onto the tarmac. 'Bloody rot! Mike's right, Jay, it's nobody's fault. I don't know why the hell you feel that everything that happens in this war has something to do with you, but it's getting pretty tiring listening to you whine.'

Jasper glared at him. 'How dare you,' he said, his voice trembling with rage, 'how dare you. Frank is dead and another man is dying because of me, and you have the temerity to stand there–'

'And a lot of men are going to walk out of plane wrecks because of this paste of yours, too. I don't know who the hell you think you are, Jay, or what, but you're no miracle man. You set yourself up like ... like I don't know what.'

Fuller stepped between them. 'Can it, both of you,' he commanded forcefully.

Maskelyne ignored him. Taking a threatening step closer, he warned, 'You listen to me, Graham. I–'

'Shut up!' Fuller shouted at him. 'That's enough.'

Jasper spun around and stalked away. Hill glanced at Graham, and sighed, then chased after him.

FOURTEEN

Geoffrey Barkas's true talent was his ability to relate individually to the highly creative officers of his widespread Middle Eastern camouflage organization and motivate each of them to work to his fullest capacity. In this role he served as friend, instructor, confidant and, when necessary, stern commander. Maskelyne, for example, might have languished in deep depression if given the luxury of doing so. But Barkas refused to allow this, heaping more work on him and the Gang than ever before. 'So sorry,' he apologized, 'but we're gearing up for the big push and there's ever so much to do. My chaps on the Blue already have their hands full, so a lot of it has to be done in your shops.'

Jasper welcomed the work. Never before had he felt so emotionally crippled. Knox was dead. The rescue man, von Glehn, would live but probably be disfigured. Even the news that Air Marshal Tedder was recommending that the fire-resistant paste be made available to all desert airmen did nothing to lift his spirit. During his first year in North Africa the letters he wrote to Mary each day had given him time to think out his problems, just as if he were sitting and talking to her, but now he found himself hiding his feelings even from her, a circumstance he would never have thought possible. So he responded enthusiastically to Barkas's demands, pleased to have the opportunity to lose himself in familiar territory.

It was May 1942. The largest battle yet fought in North Africa was about to begin. It was a battle the British had to win.

All of continental Europe except neutral Switzerland and Sweden were under German dominance. The Nazi army in Russia had weathered the brutal winter and was ready to start its march on Stalingrad. Japan ruled Southeast Asia and appeared to be near victory in China. Added to all of this, the loss of Egypt, the Suez Canal and the oil fields of Persia would be disastrous.

The pressure in the western desert had been building up to a great explosion. Both sides had gorged themselves through the spring on tanks, supplies and fresh troops. Rommel fielded an army of 90,000 men, 560 tanks and almost 500 flight-ready aircraft, and the German Navy controlled the Mediterranean. Auchinleck countered with 100,000 soldiers, 850 tanks and 190 planes, not enough, he believed, to mount the decisive offensive demanded by Churchill. But the Prime Minister insisted he attack soon, fearful of a rumoured invasion of battered Malta, concerned about the ability of Fortress Tobruk to continue holding out, and desperately in need of a morale-building triumph.

Every request received by the Gang bore an 'Urgent' designation. Hundreds more sunshields and dummy tanks and dummy guns were needed. The unbreakable supply crates were in short supply. The Canal Defence Force wanted Whirling Spray devices. The Air Force wanted as much fire-resistant paste as could be supplied. And the Navy was still pressing for its convertible speed launch.

With Graham and Hill capable of supervising workshop production with the assistance of Royal Engineer officers, and Jack Fuller handling the paperwork, Jasper was able to devote himself to all these projects. He darted from one to another like a chess grand master playing simultaneous matches. He filled his days and evenings with work so completely that there was rarely an empty moment when an unpleasant memory might slip through his defences. This hard-work bandage would not heal his deep wounds, but it at least staunched his emotional bleeding.

Some of his nights were very bad, however, and he'd lie awake until sunrise to keep fiery nightmares away.

The first job off his desk was the detailed plan for converting an RAF Miami speedboat into a floating 'stage' that might rapidly be transformed from a military launch to a luxurious cabin cruiser or a native scow.

He had attacked the problem as if he were dressing a bare stage in the Egyptian Theatre. To turn the launch into a pleasure craft, a substantial saloon was placed on the afterdeck, a metal funnel was set up amidships, the deckhouse was altered, and a telescoping radio mast was planted forward. In addition, cabin portholes were affixed to the sides, bright pennants were hoisted, and sparkling nameboards were added to the transom and the bow.

But in a matter of minutes, using drop levers, traps, counterpoise weights and slides, the sleek yacht became a filthy tub. Rubber tyres were draped over the bow. The radio mast disappeared. The portholes disappeared. The nameboards disappeared. The bright pennants disappeared. The sheet-metal funnel was wound tighter and became a rear stack from which smudge pots would belch black oil smoke. The prop saloon, under which bags of potatoes had been hidden, was flattened as if it were a cardboard box, and the potato sacks were piled on top of it. The deckhouse shape was modified. A warped mast was raised on the stern, and a torn sail and seamen's laundry were hung from it. Portions of the deck were oil-stained. A ripped fishing net was strung along the side, and the life preservers were flipped onto their dirty side.

The boat's main armament was a Bofors gun, which was hidden in the dummy saloon of the yacht and beneath the scow's potato pile. In addition, one potato sack was filled with grenades, and handguns were stowed behind a false bulkhead below deck. The boat could not fight an extended battle with a larger craft, but could protect itself long enough to make speed and get away.

Phil Townsend had assumed the task of distorting the shape of the hull through optical shading. Jasper looked in on his work occasionally, but these brief visits set him back for hours, so he left the supervision to Gregory, the navy man.

By the time Maskelyne's plans were forwarded to Admiral Cunningham's office, Captain Gregory had already begun the tedious job of creating documented identities for one dozen of these 'magic' boats and their crews. In some cases the 'yachts' would assume the identity of actual pleasure craft and carry their logbooks. Naval Intelligence registered other fictitious pleasure boats at exclusive boating clubs and provided Maskelyne's crafts with meticulously forged, backdated logs that could be verified against doctored port-of-call records.

The work boats did not need such extensive identification and were given dirty, incomplete logbooks in a number of different languages.

The crews of these ships had to be able to pass as either spiffy yachtsmen or salty fishermen in the occupied ports these boats would be visiting. Royal Navy Intelligence Branch gave each man two carefully authenticated identities and provided necessary documentation, including photographs of his home village, crumpled letters from family and friends, a baptismal certificate and other common papers. By the time their intense training period was completed, these sailors could recite facts, figures and vivid descriptions of two totally different lives in Greek, Turkish, Italian and other Mediterranean languages. All of them were volunteers, some of them veterans of earlier commando actions.

Gregory had the prototype launch in the water by midsummer. Eventually a score of these convertible speedboats, with their equally convertible crews, were put into service. They sailed with impunity between British bases and Axis-controlled ports, delivering and picking up undercover agents and valuable cargoes, including weapons and gold, and conducting spy operations for Allied Intelligence. Although these boats were challenged on occasion, their crews were able to bluff their way out of each encounter, and their disguises were never penetrated.

But even while he was hard at work on the launch, sometime during each day Jasper would contact the hospital for a report on von Glehn's condition. The man was holding his own. On May 10, he was upgraded from the critical to the dangerously ill list.

A few days later a rare, drenching rainstorm inundated Cairo. The city's ancient drainage system quickly backed up, and the streets flooded so badly that two Australian soldiers made the front page of the *Egyptian Gazette* by rowing past Shepheards in a washtub. The unexpected downpour created a holiday atmosphere and made normal work impossible. Jasper put on his Wellington boots and slogged his way to the hospital.

Von Glehn's entire body was swathed in antiseptic white bandages and he was sedated into painless sleep. Jasper stood at his side for a bit, feeling quite helpless, then left without saying a word or leaving a note. He never returned.

His guilt was the engine of hard work and he continued to drive himself at a killing pace, as if some punishment would catch up to him if he slowed down. Every member of the Gang tried, in his own way, to break through his despondency, but failed.

'Just what is it you're trying to prove?' Mike Hill demanded one afternoon.

'It doesn't matter,' Jasper replied, leaving young Hill to wonder if that was an answer or a rejection.

It was during this period he received some additional sorry news. He was working over the speedboat blueprints when Graham walked into his office. '*Houdini*'s kaput,' he said. 'It got caught up in a nasty tide and just fell apart.'

Jasper did not even pause in his work. He was not surprised. Lately, it seemed, everything he had a hand in was falling apart. 'Where is it now?'

'Beached just north of Suez. Evidently it's got Jerry confused. He's overflown it a number of times to take some pictures.'

'Too bad,' Jasper said, almost to himself, 'too bad.'

Graham excused himself and went off to find 'Admiral' Hill to inform him that the pride of his fleet was in tatters.

After he had been left alone, Jasper typed a memo to the Admiralty finally revealing the ace he'd been holding for just this eventuality:

SUBJECT: A METHOD FOR LURING ENEMY SHIPS INTO CLOSE RANGE THROUGH CAMOUFLAGE

After winning the confidence of his audience, the main objective of the performing magician is to gain control of their perceptions – to make them think what he wants them to think. This may be accomplished through demonstration, subterfuge, and the necessary appreciation of human behaviour. Once this is done, the magician is free to manipulate those perceptions in any way desired. For example, if an audience is convinced a pitcher contains some milk, the entire white contents of that vessel will be perceived to be milk.

Enemy intelligence will undoubtedly realise the flotsam on the beach north of Suez is the remains of a dummy ship that has been operating in this area, and has been spotted by aircraft on a number of occasions, and the information that dummy fighting ships are being used in this area will be communicated to all German and Italian naval forces operating in the Mediterranean. This perception can then be manipulated to our advantage.

It is my suggestion that some fighting ships be given crude camouflage similar to that of the dummy battleship, the *Houdin*, to lull the enemy into a false sense of security and thus bring them within range of small guns. Such camouflage as is necessary can be designed and produced by my troops at the Camouflage Experimental Station in Abbassia.

It was dated May 19 and signed 'Captain Jasper Maskelyne, R.E.' It was almost the last trick he ever devised.

The following morning, May 20, Maskelyne and Hill drove into the desert to test a tiny compass Jasper had developed for MI6. Hill knew that this trip had little to do with tests. Maskelyne was having an attack of Cairo fever and hoped he might find a cure in the freedom of the desert.

Hill had picked up Maskelyne at his quarters in the rosy light of dawn, hoping to be back in town before the midday sun broiled them. He was driving the three-quarter-ton Fordson truck that was used at the Valley to haul light equipment about. They drove east through a gaping hole in the Wire, a two-hundred-mile-long barbed-wire fence anchored in concrete that Italian settlers had erected before the war. Jasper hadn't slept very well in the night and dozed off in the truck.

Hill was surprised the man could sleep through the bumpy ride, but it didn't bother him. He had his own problems to think about.

Kathy Lewis had him all mixed up. The very things that pleased her one night angered her the next! No matter how nice he tried to be, she'd find a beef; but no matter how determined he became to stop seeing her, she'd lure him back. He thought he'd finally begun to figure it out, or as much of it as a man is capable of figuring out about a woman. The fact was that she liked him a lot, but didn't like herself for liking him. So she took it out on him for making her like him. That was why she was so snappish when he was nice. She was in love with him; that was why they fought so much.

That conclusion, he knew, made as much sense as was possible to make out of a girl's behaviour. She really cared. It so delighted him that he began whistling, softly, so as not to wake Maskelyne.

Cairo sank into the desert behind them. Hill followed recently made tracks toward the escarpment, the vast, desolate desert plateau. Gradually, as the sun climbed, the day turned from dawn brown to a pale, complacent yellow. By 9 A.M. it would be white, and it would be hot.

There were no paved roads onto the desert, so he continued following the track and charting their course over the baked sand and brush by landmark. They drove past the silly signposts claiming it was a thousand miles to Piccadilly Circus and Charing Cross, past rusting trucks and jeeps too damaged to manage the final forty miles to Cairo and not valuable enough as scrap to be tendered in, past the neatly piled gasoline cans and worn tyres marking the location of an abandoned laager, past three cement grave markers of Italian settlers who died in the desert before the soldiers came, past the skull-and-crossbones minefield markers, and, once, past a team of Desert Rats hightailing it to town in their machine-gun-mounted Bentley.

Maskelyne had been awake after the first hour, but just stared into the open desert and said little. Hill tried some conversation openers but took the hint from Jasper's one-word replies. Actually, he didn't mind the quiet.

He was enjoying the ride. The pricking sand and the flies and the heat were bothersome, but the endless horizon gave a man a real chance to think, and that was welcome. The desert was as still as one of Townsend's canvases and it was difficult to believe that this silent wasteland was the great battlefield while peace and safety existed in glaring and raucous Cairo.

They stopped two hours out to stretch their legs and sip some refreshing lime juice and water. The wind was swirling sand around, so they both tied bandannas over their faces. It would help a bit, but the sand would still penetrate every body cavity. It was generally agreed that it took two days of showers to erase each day in the desert.

'What about here?' Hill asked.

Maskelyne was gazing at the horizon. 'Hm?'

'I said, seems like a good place to make the tests right here.'

Jasper agreed. Taking a wooden post and a sand shovel from the rear of the truck, he walked about twenty yards and planted the post. Then he took readings with a number of the miniature compasses, scribbling the results in his notebook. 'Let's drive on and try to relocate this spot, shall we?'

They drove another mile and stopped again. Jasper hopped out of the cab and took bearings. He made his notations, but then turned to the right and stared quizzically into the distance. Finally, he shook his head, as if dismissing some inexplicable thought, and began taking a new set of readings.

Watching him, Hill felt the first twinge of nervousness. In that instant all of his romantic notions about the desert disappeared and he saw it as it was, a brutal, lifeless plain. As he climbed out of the Fordson to check the problem with Jasper, a load of sand that had collected between the truck's cab and rear bed cascaded down his neck. He tried to wriggle it out of his shirt as he walked over to Maskelyne. 'Anything wrong?'

Jasper watched Hill's sand dance for a moment, without comment, then waved his notebook. 'I'm not sure. These readings don't seem to gel.' If they followed the compass bearings, he explained, they would drive north to find the stake, when it was obviously directly behind them, west of their current location.

Hill took a set of readings and got the same result.

'Let's head back to the stake,' Jasper suggested. 'We'll try it again.'

Hill turned around and dead-reckoned back to the stake. Once again, Jasper took their bearings. 'Strange,' he said when Hill joined him, 'now these've changed.'

The private looked full circle around, but saw nothing except sand, brush and rocks. Absolutely nothing stirred.

'Let's have one more go at it,' Maskelyne decided. There was no obvious reason for the discrepancy in readings. All the compasses couldn't be wrong.

They drove two miles east and took new bearings. This time they seemed to be accurate. Instead of Maskelyne being cheered, he was perplexed. What caused the problem? he wondered. 'Let's push on a bit. I want to try it one more time.'

As they went deeper into the western desert, Jasper speculated on what might have gone wrong. The intense heat rising from the desert floor, a swirling sandstorm creating electrical energy, some unusual magnetic event...

Hill barely listened to Maskelyne's theories, instead trying to determine their position. He wasn't completely confident he knew where they were, and was scanning the desert for some landmark to navigate by when he saw it coming at them. 'Shit,' he said.

Jasper glanced past him and saw it. Just then, as if some wizard had cursed the sun, the bright day turned black and vicious. The wind swelled, and sand pebbles began peppering the windscreen. The air became dense and breathing was suddenly difficult. Mike stomped the accelerator to the floorboard, and the Fordson careered across the flats, but there was no escape.

A towering wall of reddish dust rolled toward them. The Khamsin.

Like a battalion of howling witches sweeping across the desert, it hit. The truck lurched sideways and almost tipped, but Hill held it, and turned its rear into the wind. The gale swirled into the canvas-covered bed and threatened to lift the truck back over front, but did not.

'Stop here!' Jasper screamed, and Hill, sitting only inches away, could barely hear him above the roar of the storm.

The Khamsin. The Wind of Fifty Days. This was the great cannon in nature's arsenal. War stopped in its path. Planes dared not fly. Tank forces cowered.

It hit them full blast, and there was nothing they could do but huddle inside the truck and try to keep sand out of their eyes and ears and wait, and pray it would end soon. The wind was unpredictable: it could blow for a week or die in an hour.

Once, Jasper sat up and opened his eyes. He was stunned. The desert had disappeared and he was trapped in a tunnel of whirling red dust. It was as if he was surrounded by moving-picture screens, each of them showing reddish sand racing past at light speed, while dozens of speakers broadcast incredibly loud and threatening sounds. Sand flowed down the windscreen like water, it rushed past the side windows, it poured through every minute crack in the cab.

After two hours the storm suddenly abated, then passed. The sun again shone brilliantly, and layers of rising heat shimmered on the horizon. A few small sandspouts twisted by in the distance, but otherwise the desert was uncomfortably still.

Maskelyne and Hill took turns digging the truck's wheels out of the sand that had piled around them, and emptying sand out of the bed, and it was midafternoon before they were able to move. Mike gripped the steering wheel, stared straight ahead, and finally asked the question both of them had carefully avoided. 'Which way?'

Jasper checked his miniature compasses, but their strange variations had made him doubt their accuracy. 'East, I should think,' he declared with as much confidence as he could muster. 'Put the sun to our back.'

'East it is, sir,' Hill said smartly. The desert had been transformed by the storm. All vehicle tracks had been erased. Dunes had been knocked flat and built up in other places. Rocks had been carried away. Nothing looked familiar.

Neither man spoke, but they shared the same fear. They were out on the desert with inadequate provisions and did not know where they were. But neither of them dared admit, even in their own thoughts, that they were lost. So they drove on the edge of that fear, searching the desert for a main track or an oasis or a landmark or even a spray of sand thrown up by something else alive and moving. The sun was just beginning to set on the day.

Suddenly, Hill made a sharp cut to avoid a half-buried rock, and drove the truck into a sand-filled wadi, or gully. Its rear left wheel sank into soft sand and churned wildly, splashing sand and digging an even deeper hole. 'Shit, shit, shit,' Hill screamed, pounding the wheel angrily. Then he turned off the engine and leaned back. 'I'm sorry, Jay,' he said.

'It's my fault, Mike,' Maskelyne replied, glad to finally face up to reality. 'This is a bit of a rough spot, though, isn't it.'

They made a halfhearted attempt to dig out the truck, although both of them felt that would be impossible. The Fordson sloped into the sand up to its tailboard, its left wheel completely buried.

They stopped working just after dark and made ready for their first night in the desert. They rolled down the legs of their antimalarial shorts to their ankles to keep their legs warm in the bitter cold. They rubbed Flit and flea powder on their exposed skin to keep the night biters away. Hill collected a few rocks still warm from the day and put them around his blanket. After a discussion, they decided not to brew up, afraid their night fire might attract a Jerry patrol or, more frightening, Arab bandits. They debated eating a full meal and finally decided to split a single tin, which they washed down with two swallows of lime juice and water. Then they lay down and failed to sleep.

In the full light of the morning their situation felt less desperate, and they made a second effort to free the truck. They dug out the tyre and shoved rocks and blankets under it to give traction, but it spat them right out. The Fordson was stuck; they were just going to have to wait to be rescued. 'Today, you think?' Hill asked.

'Soon,' Jasper told him.

Hill stiffened his upper lip. 'Five quid says today.'

'Bad shot, Mike. I don't bet against myself.'

They got through the day quite well, keeping themselves busy doing all those things they had been taught at desert survival school: they stayed out of direct sunlight except for the half-hourly occasions when one of them climbed on top of the cab and waved a blanket to attract attention. They took stock of their supplies and proportioned them into four equal parts. They drained the water from the truck's radiator into a can and buried the can in the sand so it wouldn't evaporate, and put the gasoline and oil into other cans so they could make fires when necessary. They scraped long arrows in the sand pointing to the truck in case search planes flew overhead, and prepared an oil fire that could be quickly ignited to attract anyone driving or flying within their range. They even held their ears to the ground to detect movement on the desert within twenty or so miles. They sang cheerful songs to keep their spirits high and avoided excess activity and spoke of rescue and never of fear. Jasper spent the afternoon jotting down thoughts about the speed-launch conversion as calmly as if he were sitting in the riverside gardens of Zamalek. It was only when the night turned cold and they had no more small tasks to keep their minds occupied that their bravado began to fade and reality set in.

They split their last chocolate bar and a tin of bully beef for dinner. 'How long you think we should stay with the truck?' Hill wondered.

The First Rule of desert survival was, Stay by your vehicle, the theory being that it was easier to spot a car or truck from the air than one or two men. But desert veterans felt differently, and most had set their own limits. To abandon the vehicle made the search more difficult; but to wait too long made a man too weak to survive a rigorous trek.

In this case, Maskelyne knew, they had no choice. 'We can't walk out of here,' he said. 'We haven't got the supplies to make it.' As the ranking officer, this was his fault. He had ignored the Second Rule of survival: carry adequate provisions. Like almost everyone else who had been living for so long on the lip of the desert, he had simply taken it for granted. They were unprepared for this trip. All they had in the

truck were four tins of assorted rations, a quart-plus of lime juice and
water, a sidearm and one dozen shells, some gasoline and oil, a
flashlight, Flit and flea powder, a spade, Jasper's suspect compasses
but no sextant, a pouch of tobacco, a pipe and matches, a spare wheel,
a fire extinguisher, blankets, a street map of Cairo, and the truck.

They settled down next to the truck. Hill clasped his hands beneath
his head and gazed into the starlit sky. One silver night cloud drifted
lazily eastward, toward the Nile, and he closed his eyes and imagined
it had steel handles and envisioned himself carried to safety. 'How far
do you think we are from Cairo?'

' 'Bout a hundred miles, I should say.'

'Long walk,' he replied, 'a long bloody walk.'

They curled up and tried to keep warm, but the chill got into their
bones and made it difficult to sleep. After a long silence, Jasper said,
'There's a whole army and air force mucking about this place. They'll
stumble over us, don't worry about it.'

In fact, an entire day passed before a search began. Kathy Lewis was
the first to miss them. When Michael was more than his usual half
hour late to pick her up she went to his quarters to give him what
for. Bill Robson was just leaving for dinner when she got there, and
he told her Hill hadn't been around all day. 'He drove out on the Blue
with Jay to test some new gadgets. Actually, I thought they'd be back
by now.'

'Shouldn't we alert someone?'

'I don't think so. You know Jay, once he gets his mind into
something he loses all track of time. This is probably good for him.
You know, since Frank ... well, you know.'

She nodded. 'I guess you're right. If you see him, though...'

'Soon as they come in I'll make him ring you up. But don't be
surprised if they camp out there tonight.'

When Maskelyne and Hill had not returned by high noon the next
day, Robson raised the alarm.

Standard search and rescue procedures were immediately put into
effect. All regular patrols and units operating in the desert were alerted
to look for the missing Fordson. RAF search-and-rescue teams were
informed the men were overdue and presumed lost. Maskelyne,
unfortunately, had committed still another error by failing to tell
anyone his planned route.

Search-and-rescue maps divided the desert into quadrants, allowing for an orderly and systematic operation. But the process was

time-consuming, and one thing that men who were lost on the desert
did not have was time. To complicate matters, preparations for the
summer offensive were in full swing and only limited equipment was
available.

The Magic Gang organized its own search. All other work ceased
at the Valley. Graham, Robson and Townsend each took responsibility
for a wide area, directing teams comprised of Magic Valley workers
using equipment supplied by Barkas. Fuller coordinated the effort from
Maskelyne's office. Although Regular Army search-and-rescue units
frowned on this type of amateur participation, there was nothing that
could be done to stop it.

The Gang did everything possible to reassure Kathy Lewis, but she
refused to be mollified, demanding of Townsend, 'The truth, what
chance do they have?'

'A good one,' he said emphatically, but without looking directly at
her. 'We're doing everything possible. We've got thirty vehicles and a
hundred and fifty men out there looking for them, plus all the regular
patrols. We've even contacted the caravans and posted a reward for
information. But it's going to take some time. The idiots didn't even
take a radio with them.'

'You're saying?'

'I'm saying we'll find them. As long as they stay with their truck
and conserve their resources we've got time, and that's really all we
need.'

The massive hunt began the morning of Maskelyne and Hill's second
full day lost in the desert.

By midafternoon that day the sun had begun baking the hope out
of the two men, and that void was quickly filled with fear. The night
had been a hard one. The temperature went down near freezing, and
the bugs had crawled out of the ground and made their attacks. Most
of the Flit and the flea powder was gone and both men had been bitten
and stung repeatedly. Grains of fine sand had got under the bites and
irritated the tiny sores. Hungry flies came at them in the morning.

Waiting was torturous, and the urge to take off across the sands, to
take their salvation into their own hands, was overwhelming. But they
resisted, understanding that it was just another illusion in the desert's
killing repertoire.

The oppressive heat was the worst of it. In the afternoon the desert
became a furnace. Both men sweated the moisture out of their bodies,
but it evaporated even before it could stain their shirts. Their skin

dried out and their lips chapped, then caked, and they couldn't produce enough saliva to keep them moist.

They agreed to cut their remaining ration in half and limited themselves to a single swallow of lime juice and water every few hours. Hill tried to distil the radiator water, but it tasted metallic and gave him a bad headache.

To conserve energy they signalled with the blanket only once each hour. During the torrid part of the day, when the truck became too hot to touch, they lay in its shade and tried to sleep away reality. There was too much time to think, and it was impossible to think about anything except rescue and death. Both of them knew the terrible way men died on the desert, tongues swollen out of their mouths, their minds cooked senseless, killed by dehydration and sunstroke and, finally, loss of the will to live, and both silently vowed it would not happen to them and prayed that was true.

The heat made their tempers smoulder and they argued about firing Maskelyne's sidearm. Hill wanted to fire a shot every few hours to attract attention, Jasper felt they should conserve their ammunition until the last possible moment. 'Dammit,' Hill said, 'we'll rot here if we don't do something.'

'Dammit yourself,' Maskelyne yelled, 'we'll need every bullet we've got once we've run out of food,' then stalked angrily away from the truck. He knew he couldn't blame Hill for being bitter; he'd got them into this hole and wasn't doing a blasted thing to get them out of it. Hill was right about one thing, they had to do something.

Marching back to the truck and examining their resources, he came up with a novel idea. After filling an empty gasoline can with sand and motor oil, he began unscrewing the two side mirrors from the truck, being careful not to burn his hands on the hot metal.

Hill watched him curiously. Finally he broke the strained silence. 'Need some help?'

'No, thank you,' Jasper answered. 'I can manage.'

'Ah, cripes, Jay, I'm sorry. I didn't mean to yell at you.'

Maskelyne stopped working to accept the apology. 'That's all right, I know you didn't. We're both a bit cross. Look, I could use some help getting these mirrors off.'

Michael stood up and shook the sand off his clothing. 'Tell you one thing,' he said, 'it'll be a long time before I go to the beach again.'

As soon as the mirrors had been removed Jasper lit the oil fire, and thick black smoke streamed into the air. Then, carefully adjusting the two mirrors, he projected a black smudge onto a linen-white cloud.

'It's a bloody picture show!' Hill shouted with delight.

'More of a magic lantern, actually,' Jasper admitted proudly. 'The family's been doing it for promotion since the turn of the century.'

He began tilting the second mirror up and down, causing the smudge to appear, then disappear, thus flashing a crude code onto the cloud.

The cloud floated out of range in a quarter of an hour. By the time another suitable puff glided close enough it was too dark to continue signalling. Michael began to extinguish the fire.

'Let it burn,' Jasper said.

'But what about Jerry? And the bandits?'

'Let it burn,' he repeated, and walked away.

They shared half a can, a gulp of water and their fantasies for dinner. Hill imagined himself preparing for a big supper with Kathy at one of the better dance clubs. 'I've decided to wear my dress uniform tonight, to please her. She's always asking me to wear it; don't know why I fight her so much about it. Anyway, she looks beautiful and we go to this place and as we walk in I can hear the steaks sizzling over the pit and this smell hits me...'

Jasper saw himself with Mary on Portobello Road on a cool, sombre Sunday afternoon. She was pulling him from stall to stall, pointing out curios and antiques, asking his opinion of them and then stating hers without waiting for his response. He followed her with a man's reluctance, dutifully agreeing when she wanted him to, standing quietly while she dickered for a price, and finally taking out his wallet when she looked at him with pleading eyes. Inevitably, he'd end up carrying home an armload of things that would be put away and rarely seen again.

As Jasper described this afternoon to Hill, he could feel the coolness of the day and the weariness of his arms, and his warmth. 'Once,' he said, smiling as he recalled the incident, 'I tripped over something, my foot I think it was, and dropped a mantel clock we'd just bought. The bloody thing smashed into fifty pieces. "That's all right," she said before I could apologize, "I really didn't care for it very much anyway." "But we just bought it," I said, "I don't understand." She smiled at me in that impish way of hers that would have excused anything silly she could have ever done, and said, "I know, but it was such a good price."'

'Women,' Hill said, shaking his head in admiration.

Jasper raised his empty hand as if it held a toasting glass. 'Women.' But he spent the rest of that brutal day in the desert reliving an ordinary Sunday afternoon in London.

After they had settled down for the night, Hill strained to hear the music of Cairo's nightlife drifting on the desert breeze. Once, he actually thought he heard some music, but realized it was being played by his imagination. It seemed incredible to him that he could be so hopelessly alone and lost less than one hundred miles from the bright, gay, vibrant city. Just before he fell off to sleep he decided to marry Kathy when he returned.

Phil Townsend spent part of that afternoon at GHQ's search command centre to ensure that the Gang did not duplicate their effort. There had been a glimmer of hope earlier in the day when an RAF pilot spotted movement near a truck, but investigation showed it to be a nomad group stripping a rusted hulk. 'What do you think?' Townsend asked Captain Franklin George Bruce, who headed the operation.

Captain Bruce shrugged.

'What I mean is,' Townsend prodded, 'they couldn't just disappear, could they?'

'Look here,' Bruce replied bluntly, 'I've been at this job almost two years and I still don't know what to tell you. Some of them are found, some aren't. Some walk in from fifty miles out, some die ten miles away. Strange things happen out there, things you just can't explain. People vanish and nobody ever finds hide nor hair of them. Maybe Jerry finds 'em, or the Arabs. Maybe it's just the desert. But don't ask me to make any predictions, okay? I've seen too much to know anything.'

The first three days in the desert had softened up Maskelyne and Hill for the real pain, and now the desert began to kill them slowly and cruelly.

The sun had blistered their skin and lips, and a steady rain of fine dust and sand rubbed them raw. Their infected bites had turned an ugly red and were full of pus. Their parched throats were swollen, and swallowing even a drop of water was like trying to force a coin into a slot just slightly too small. The great temperature range between day and night made them dizzy and both of them got colds, and each tiny cough grated their throats as if they were being rubbed with sandpaper.

The relentless sun gave them terrible headaches in the day.

The freezing night made them shiver and cough up blood.

Their arms and shoulders ached from signalling the empty desert with a blanket, an exercise they abandoned on the fourth day.

It was impossible to get even a second's relief from misery. Sand had penetrated every part of their bodies and clothing. Their teeth ground on it, their eyes burned from it, and particles of it were embedded in their feet and their desert beards and lodged in their throats.

Jasper's feet had swelled, making it painful for him to move about in boots, but he knew that if he took off the boots he would never be able to get them back on.

Most of the time they just lay in the shade of the truck, moving with it as the sun shifted. A thin layer of dust had already settled over the Fordson, and Hill figured the entire truck would be buried in a year or so. Him and Jay too, he knew, buried forever, if they weren't found soon. He began wondering what other marvels lay hidden beneath the sands. Maybe just more sand, clear through to the centre of the earth, or maybe there was a dirt floor, or the glistening bones of a thousand lost travellers, or maybe I even an entire city. Covered up. He thought about asking Jasper about it, but just didn't have the energy.

Maskelyne brushed the sand off the truck so searching aircraft would be able to see it, and spent the rest of the fourth morning projecting spots onto clouds. He rested during the torrid afternoon.

For dinner, they split the last two bites of hard beef. Afterward Hill said, 'Jay, if you've got any tricks up your sleeve, now's the time to use them.'

Jasper fired off a shot at dusk.

Blowing sand, which pecked at their skin like a billion needles, forced them to sleep in the rear of the truck that night. It was too hot and buggy to get any real sleep, but both of them managed to catch brief snatches of rest before the flies buzzed them awake. Just as Jasper was about to fall into one of these naps, Hill asked in a rasping voice, 'Was it worth it, Jay?'

Maskelyne wasn't sure he understood.

'You didn't have to come out here. You could've stayed back home.'

Was it worth it? He reflexively ran his dry tongue over his salty lips. His lips stung. The choice had been made so long ago he hardly remembered there being an option. Was it worth it? What had he accomplished? 'I had no choice,' he replied in a choked whisper.

Hill made a doubting sound.

'It's true. Had to do it. For myself.' He coughed, and his chest ached, and an inferno blazed in his throat. 'Don't think like that, Mike, we're not done yet. They're looking for us.'

After a prolonged silence, Hill said decidedly, 'They better hurry.'

At Magic Valley, tempers got short among the Gang. The pressure of time slipping by without any progress being made magnified each small problem and left everyone frustrated and cranky. An afternoon storm had grounded the search planes and had most certainly obliterated any tracks left by the Fordson.

During the evening hash-over, Graham wondered aloud if they were going about the search in the proper way. Fuller took offence and snapped, 'If you've got any complaints about the way I'm doing my job you're welcome to it. I wouldn't mind riding around out there all day instead of sitting here arguing with–'

'I didn't say I could do better. I was just wondering...'

Robson shouted them quiet. 'Let's just keep at the job, shall we, gentlemen?'

Fuller had spent a futile morning at Q Branch, the supply and transport people, pleading for more vehicles. Over a hundred additional volunteers were ready to join the effort, but there was no way of utilizing them. Some consideration had been given to working a second shift through the night, in case Maskelyne and Hill were lighting signal fires, but was finally dismissed. 'We've already got two men lost out there,' Barkas told them. 'Let's leave it at that.' Some Desert Rat teams took it on their own, however, and didn't bother coming in at night.

Kathy Lewis confided to Graham her certainty that Michael was still alive. 'I've got this ability to feel things,' she explained. 'I don't talk about it too much, but I just know certain things to be true. And I know he's all right. I do.'

Nails held her in his protective arms and allowed her to cry.

It had been a difficult time for Phil Townsend too. He hadn't slept much since the search started. When he wasn't actually on the job, he was trying to figure out what else might be done, or searching for some path that hadn't been followed, or trying to read Maskelyne's mind and determine where on the bloody burning sandbox they had been headed. It had been a long time since he'd given himself over so completely to anything except himself.

At first, he'd been relieved he wasn't in their boots. But later, as he became absorbed in the drama of the search, he found himself identifying with them, and wondering what they were doing and thinking, and soon after that imagined himself in their place and wondered what he would be doing and thinking. Inevitably, this tragedy had forced him to be dead honest with himself, and he wasn't rightly pleased with the reality he confronted. In the middle of the third night he sat alone in his clean, warm quarters and wrote a long letter to his wife. But it was really for himself. 'I have loved you more than I have ever loved anyone or anything before,' he admitted,

> and I still love you in many ways ... I know I was not an easy person to be with. There is this thing inside me that makes me distrust people. I don't know why this is, except perhaps I don't like myself too much, but I know it has made me unhappy and I hope to do something about it. When I come home, I'd like to see you. Not to patch things up, we've gone too far on different roads for that, but to try to learn more about myself. It's selfish of me to ask that of you, but you know me better than anyone, and it's terribly important that I learn these things.

He started to add some chatty items but decided the letter was fine as it was, and honest, so he signed it, with love, and sealed it.

Jasper was awakened from his restless sleep the next morning when a bug crawled inside his mouth. He instinctively moved his arm to swat it, and a sharp pain ripped through his shoulder. He grunted, and remembered, and puffed the bug out of his mouth.

He slowly climbed to his feet, each movement causing its own pain. He knew there was no food left, but checked anyway. His stomach was just beginning to distend from hunger.

Leaning against the truck for support, he scanned the corrugated desert like Robinson Crusoe surveying his island. Then he took the spade and began scraping another long mark in the sand. The work was not difficult, but he was weak and dehydrated and he had to rest three times before completing it.

Hill was awake by the time he finished. His face was sunburned crimson, and large sores had opened on his lips. ' 'Ning,' he mumbled.

'Morning,' Jasper replied. There was nothing for them to do except stay out of direct sunlight and wait, wait for whatever happened, and pray that it happened soon.

Having worn them down physically, the elements now attacked their minds. Hill began to slip in and out of delirium; one moment he would be totally rational, telling Jasper how much he'd give to hear one more gharry driver screaming at one more lazy camel, and a moment later he would be speaking to his parents, or friends Jasper did not know, as if they were sitting with them.

Throughout the morning they dipped their bandannas in the tepid radiator water and wiped their brows, but even that filthy water evaporated almost immediately. Around noon, Maskelyne sprayed the fire extinguisher into the air and both of them showered in its cooling solvent, which burned their skin, but provided some relief.

During one of Hill's lucid periods he asked Jasper what he would do if he spotted a German patrol.

'Crawl to them on my knees,' Maskelyne said. The desert had imposed its own perspective.

'Right-o,' Hill said, and slipped away.

For the first time, Jasper faced the probability that he would die on the desert. There was still hope, there would be hope until the very last second, but if they weren't found in the next two days, three tops, they would die. Lost in the desert testing a compass. How ironic, he thought, how wasteful. He wondered what the memorial service for him would be like, and soon imagined Mary sitting at home.

It would be very difficult for her. She wasn't the most independent woman in the world; his fault, probably, and starting over again would be impossible for her. She wouldn't marry again, but would live out her life doing good deeds for others.

He despised that thought. He wished he could reach her and tell her that life must go on, that it doesn't end with the death of a loved one. And as he thought about that, he realized he had allowed part of himself to die in the burning aircraft with Frank Knox. Since Frank's death he had struggled indifferently through life, as if his suffering were somehow keeping Knox alive.

Knox. He glanced at Hill, who was mumbling something unintelligible. It would have been the professor who was out here with him if ... He caught himself. No more ifs. Frank was dead and he was alive. That was it. He was still alive and desperate to survive. No more ifs.

At that moment he decided he was going to live. The desert would not kill him so easily. Now, he thought, today, this minute, the real fight begins. All of his defences had been stripped away one by one, except his will to live, and now that would be tested, and he would learn of what mettle he was made.

Survival is what matters, he finally realized. To the desert snakes and the flies, to Hill, even to Jerry, survival is all that matters.

He shook Mike Hill awake and dragged him into conversation. Each word, each breath, was agony, but he forced himself to speak and forced Hill to answer. They tried playing word games, but Hill wasn't much good at them, so Jasper made him tell stories about the girls he'd known on the streets.

Michael's ego made him respond, and he spoke in a gravelly whisper. The stories he told were crude, but Jasper was in too much pain even to blush.

When Hill finished, Maskelyne told him about the Egyptian Theatre, and about magicians, then about anything else he could think of to hold his mind. When they tired of stories they started singing, painfully croaking 'South of the Border,' 'Run Rabbit Run,' 'We're Going to Hang Out Our Washing on the Siegfried Line.' Anything to stay awake, anything to keep their minds working.

Both of them sang with their eyes shut, so Jasper thought his mind had introduced a new torture when he heard a chipper voice ask if brew was up. He opened his eyes a slit and the sun attacked them, but a hulking figure moved in front of him and blocked it out. In a heavy Australian accent, the man said, 'Say what, this is hardly the way to treat a guest, you know.'

He started sobbing, and from somewhere deep inside his body came tears.

FIFTEEN

Jasper opened his eyes, and shafts of sunlight stabbed them, blinding him, but a prim nurse kindly adjusted the window louvres.

'Something to drink?' she asked.

The glare slowly faded. He blinked his eyes into hazy focus and began looking around the room, trying to get his bearings.

'You're in Number Four General Hospital, Captain,' the nurse explained as she served him a glass of warm water. 'You had a bit too much desert, remember?'

'Yes ...' he started to say, but his throat felt as if he had been breathing fire. The pain shocked him into reality.

'Take a small sip of this,' she said, holding the glass to his dry lips. As he did so, she read his mind. 'Your friend is fine. We've just had him under close observation. I suspect they'll be bringing him in here with you this afternoon.'

He swallowed a few droplets of water. 'How long?' he croaked.

'Well, you've been here almost two days. You'll probably be with us another week or so, just till you get your strength back. You've got some nasty throat blisters and some infected sores, but it doesn't appear you've suffered any real damage.'

An overhead fan cooled him deliciously. A vase of red roses sat on his night table. He tried to push himself up into a sitting position, but sharp pains shot through his shoulders and he relaxed back into the pillows.

'Your friends've been by a few times to see you,' the nurse said as she rearranged the flowers. 'They asked me to give you a message.'

'Um?'

She paused, holding a rose in her right hand, and smiled. 'Stay out of the sun.'

Hill was brought in later that afternoon, looking chipper with his desert beard neatly trimmed, but frustrated by his doctor's orders not to speak for the next few days. He wrote up a storm on a clipboard. Townsend, Graham and Fuller came to the hospital directly from work and told Jasper and Mike how their lives had been saved. An Australian tank crew in an old Matilda had busted a track in the morning and was taking a shortcut to catch up with their group when they came upon the truck. They hadn't even known the men were missing.

'Just bloody good luck,' Townsend said respectfully.

'The joker in the deck,' Graham added. 'There's no figuring it. Half the men in North Africa are looking for you, and if this tank doesn't throw a track ...' He shook his head.

Kathy Lewis came by every lunchtime and evening. She fussed over Mike Hill like a mother, wiping his brow, fulfilling his whims, apologizing for imagined mistakes, agreeing with everything he wrote down. He did not write down a proposal of marriage, having decided that could wait until he was feeling better.

Jasper watched Hill slip easily back into normal life, flirting with the nurses, writing jokes on his clipboard, fighting with the doctors, and wished he too could pick up where he had left off. But it was not so easy for him. There had been damage done.

He had brushed too closely with death to dismiss it casually. When he wasn't sketching, or reading, or writing letters, he thought about what had happened out on the desert and tried to separate the reality of it from the illusion.

He finally concluded that the difference didn't really matter at all. Life was all that mattered.

He lived; Knox died. It wasn't any more complicated than that. Townsend called it luck. Graham said it was the joker. Jasper felt most comfortable thinking of it as fate.

Above all, he felt cleansed. Renewed. He would mourn his friend forever, but he was determined to burst back into life and live the hell out of it. He would never forget Frank Knox, but now he would put his memories on a shelf in his mind, where he could get at them once in a while, and go on with his own life. For Mary. For their children. But mostly for himself.

Each day he grew stronger. He had Jack Fuller bring his magic kit to the hospital, and as soon as he was permitted to walk, he entertained the other patients with the minor sleights. His hands were in poor condition, but his timing was good and his patter was warm and he derived tremendous satisfaction from performing.

One afternoon Richard von Glehn, the burned rescue man, hobbled into his room. He used a cane for support, and the lower half of his face was still bandaged, but his voice was clear and his mind was sharp. He'd had two operations thus far, he told Jasper, and surgeons were optimistic they could repair most of the facial damage. 'They told me they could make me look like Douglas Fairbanks if I wanted, but I told 'em nah.' He hesitated, then punched, 'I told 'em, Clark Gable or nothing.'

Before he returned to his own wing he said, 'Don't hold any blame for what happened that day. I was so excited I just forgot to get the suit wetted down.' He shook his head in disgust at the memory. 'You just can't take the basic stuff for granted, you know, you just can't.'

The one thing that continued to rankle Maskelyne in the hospital was the failure of his compasses in the desert. There had to be a logical reason why they malfunctioned, but he couldn't figure it out. He didn't believe it was the sandstorm. He gave a set to an Engineer mechanic for inspection, but in shop tests the man found nothing wrong with them. Jasper recalled his movements on the desert a thousand times trying to work out his mistake, but without success.

The prim nurse unknowingly provided the answer when she placed a metal water pitcher on the nightstand next to Maskelyne's bed. As soon as she put it down, the compass needles started dancing as if they had fleas. 'Of course,' Jasper said aloud in his scratchy voice, instantly remembering the schoolboy's rule for using a compass: never stand near a large metal object. Like a truck, he thought.

That was it. That had to be it. Some readings had been taken next to the Fordson; others had been taken yards away. Just like von Glehn, he thought, he had taken the basics for granted.

There was only one other thing that kept his mind occupied during his stay in Number Four General Hospital. At high tea on May 26 Rommel's army had attacked, a highly impudent hour to begin the final battle for North Africa.

The battle at the Gazala Line was a clash of military doctrines. Auchinleck, perhaps looking into history when knights in armour died storming castle bastions, believed the Germans would be smashed to pieces trying to overrun the formidable boxes of his defensive line. But Rommel had no such intention. An advocate of speed and surprise, he was certain the British had boxed themselves in with this strategy. Eighth Army was forced to stand firm to defend the vast supplies in these positions, forfeiting its mobility. Thus the fight would be made when and where he desired.

The Gazala Line ended at the fortified box of Bir Hacheim, and south of that stronghold was open desert. On May 26 Rommel launched Operation Theseus, sending part of his force directly into the line to keep the British occupied, while personally leading a force of ten thousand vehicles around that southern flank. He was so confident that his army would be in Tobruk in four days that he issued only limited quantities of food and water to his men.

Rommel's daring plan almost worked. Afrika Korps successfully made the turn around the Bir Hacheim horn the first night, but this flanking manoeuvre was spotted by Desert Rat patrols, and Auchinleck rushed his armour there in time to spoil Rommel's surprise. The German advance was stopped cold only ten miles behind the Gazala Line. In brutal fighting Rommel lost a third of his panzer force. He ordered his surviving tanks to regroup in a one-hundred-square-mile patch of open desert bounded by Eighth Army's boxes and deep minefields, an area Egyptian newspapers began referring to as 'The Cauldron.' Rommel's gamble for blitzkrieg victory had failed, and his underequipped army had taken refuge behind a screen of British minefields.

'If his relief column can't break through the minefields to supply him he's done,' Graham said flatly. Most of the Gang gathered in Jasper's hospital room each night to keep Maskelyne and Hill abreast of the latest news and rumours.

Townsend was reading the *Gazette*. 'Says here the Eyeties are trying to get to him.'

'Goodbye, Erwin,' Gregory, the navy man, said, drawing soft chuckles. Townsend cautioned him, 'Don't be so sure. That Fox has more lives than a whole family of cats.'

'Well, I say throw in everything we've got right now,' Gregory replied. 'We've got him surrounded there. We can wipe him out if we move quickly.'

'And if he breaks out?' Fuller wondered. 'What stands between him and the Nile?'

'He won't get out.'

Robson laughed out loud. 'Some general you'd make.'

Jasper said very little, being content to lie back and enjoy the good feelings of the moment. He had done his part. The desert had wrung the Quixote out of him. The battle could be won without his contribution and he wouldn't feel he was a slacker or had been cheated. That dreadful gnawing that had caused such dissatisfaction was gone, as if a hole in his stomach had been patched. He was willing to accept his bit part in the great show without complaint. It wasn't necessary to present the grand illusion.

By dusk on the twenty-ninth, Rommel's survival was dependent upon pluck and myth. His battle plan had been shattered. His men were out of water, and their tanks had little fuel. Only by driving through the night and personally navigating a supply convoy around Bir Hacheim did he put his divisions back into minimal fighting condition. But his army was still in a highly vulnerable condition.

Losses had been much greater than he had anticipated. More than a third of his tanks had been destroyed or had broken down. In addition, his trusted subordinate, General Crüwell, had been captured, and his chief of staff, General Gause, had been wounded. Afrika Korps was caught in a nest of minefields and was under constant attack from British armour and Tedder's Desert Air Force. Rommel admitted to a captured 3rd Indian officer that he would be forced to ask for terms if the Italians could not get a supply convoy through the minefields. An all-out British attack, he knew, would wipe him out.

But Eighth Army held back.

General Ritchie did not press his advantage. Instead of recognizing that the Fox was at bay and striking him in his lair, he hesitated, possibly intimidated by Rommel's legendary resourcefulness. Wary of charging into a trap, he refused to attack until he had overwhelming numerical superiority. That lost opportunity turned the battle.

On June 1, Italian sappers finally hacked through the minefields and opened a supply line to the desperate Afrika Korps. The moment he was resupplied, Rommel attacked, destroying the 150th Brigade box in seventy-two hours, then turned south toward the suddenly isolated Bir Hacheim box.

By the time Ritchie ordered his tanks into the Cauldron it was too late. His small groups of armour, penny-packets, were torn apart by Rommel's heavily concentrated tank force.

On June 7 Jasper checked out of Number Four, a day later Hill followed. Magic Valley had been humming all the while, but when Maskelyne got back it had the air of a buggy factory after the invention of the motorcar. The battle was being fought inside the Cauldron at point-blank range and there was little need for deception.

The Free French troops defending Bir Hacheim, under the command of 'the Old Rabbit,' Brigadier General Pierre Koenig, fought to their last bullet and managed to hold out until June 10. Once Bir Hacheim fell, giving Rommel a secure supply line in the south, his army turned north. One by one the 'impregnable' British boxes were overrun as Afrika Korps, now fat with captured supplies, rolled relentlessly toward Tobruk. On June 10, 'Black Saturday,' an Eighth Army armoured convoy was ambushed by dug-in 88s outside the scrub town of El

Adem. Two hundred British tanks were destroyed. The next day a general withdrawal to the Egyptian frontier was ordered.

The rumour in the Delta was that GHQ was preparing to evacuate Egypt, but no one really believed that. Tobruk would hold. Eighth Army would regroup. There would be a successful counterattack. There was no need to panic.

But soldiers and civilians began making 'worst case' plans. 'If they do evac,' Hill told Kathy, 'I want you to go straight away. Understand?'

'And who appointed you general?' she replied. 'At least I don't go getting myself lost in the desert.'

'Please,' he asked, 'no lip this time. Just do what I say.'

She did not want to be his possession, but she felt good knowing how much he cared. 'We'll see,' she told him.

Fortress Tobruk was considerably weaker than it had been during the previous siege. Many of its perimeter guns had been siphoned off to strengthen the Gazala Line, its vast carpet of minefields had been reduced, and it was being defended by 35,000 mostly untested troops led by South African Major General H. B. Klopper. The massive German assault began on June 20.

One hundred and fifty Luftwaffe bombers flew 580 sorties against the city that day. German and Italian artillery kept up a constant barrage. Rommel's shock troops attacked under this curtain of fire. His panzers came right behind.

In the afternoon, Klopper began blowing up his supply dumps to deprive Afrika Korps of this plunder and accidentally knocked out most of his own communications lines, thereby losing control of his troops. The battle for Tobruk was over in one day. At 9:40 A.M. June 21, Klopper surrendered his 33,000-man garrison to Rommel. 'Fortress of Tobruk has capitulated,' Rommel announced to his troops. 'All units will reassemble and prepare for further advance.'

On June 22 Adolf Hitler named Rommel 'beloved of the nation,' and made him, at age forty-nine, the youngest field marshal in German history.

The road to the Nile was finally open. For the first time in the desert war Rommel enjoyed a superiority of armour. Germany prepared to celebrate its great victory in North Africa. The Reichsbank began printing occupation currency. Campaign medals were struck for the gallant desert army. Songs commemorating the liberation of Egypt were written and recorded to be broadcast when the English surrendered.

Prime Minister Churchill was conferring with President Roosevelt in Washington when Rommel entered Tobruk. Calling the news 'rather disconcerting,' he nevertheless put up a bold public front. Actually, he was badly shaken. Even Roosevelt's agreement to ship 250 powerful new Sherman tanks to North Africa did not ease his despair. After two years of bitter fighting, the western desert had been lost.

British headquarters in Cairo tried to maintain calm. But while official agencies reported 'temporary adjustments to straighten the line' and 'withdrawal of some advance units,' Radio Roma prepared Egypt for the invasion. 'The Axis does not make war on the Egyptian people,' its announcers proclaimed. 'It means merely to liberate Egypt from the domination of the British. Don't worry! Lay in one week's supplies and remain indoors. No harm will come to anyone.'

Axis sympathizers readied a mansion on the Rue des Pyramides to serve as Rommel's official residence. Road signs were printed in German. Leaders of the Muslim Brotherhood prepared to rise up against the British at the appropriate moment.

In the midst of all the hullabaloo Maskelyne was summoned to Gray Pillars. Senior officers briefed him. Although Rommel was still half a desert away, preparations had to be made for the defence of Cairo and Alexandria. 'We mean to be ready for him,' one cocky young major swaggered, but it soon became apparent to Maskelyne that the Army was anything but ready. Beyond changing street signs and placing 'dragon's teeth,' pyramid-shaped metal tank obstacles, on major roads, there was no comprehensive plan for defending the Delta cities.

The Gang was ordered to design and produce suitable camouflage. 'You know,' explained Lieutenant Colonel Farber, an officer most renowned for his smart polo game, 'do up those things that make it difficult to move about easily.' He grinned, exposing a space between his two front teeth. 'Let's confuse the hell out of them.'

Jasper gritted his teeth. The greatest juggernaut in military history was marching toward them, and this polo-playing colonel thought it would be good sport to confuse them. 'Yes, sir,' he snapped, 'do our best, sir,' and saluted. As he drove back to Magic Valley on a motorbike he began to think Rommel had been correct in telling a group of British prisoners they had fought like lions but been led by donkeys.

The Magic Gang plunged into work. Maskelyne and Townsend sketched plans, Hill and Graham supervised the workshops, Fuller provided transportation, Robson scraped up materials. The camouflage and concealment plan was loosely based on the old plans for the defence of London and other English cities after Dunkirk. Real and dummy machine-gun pillboxes were produced. Permanently shadowed canvas 'walls' that hid gun emplacements were turned out by the score. Jasper devised a system of mirrors that could be adjusted to make streets appear to continue or end. 'Top floors' were added to buildings to shield gunners' nests. Townsend's team of artists painted long alleys on canvas flats that would be suspended by buildings to lure German vehicles into the walls. The workshops turned out canvas dragon's teeth, plywood traps and dummy guns.

And sophisticated booby traps. Real mines were disguised as camel dung or broken car parts or common street debris, while harmless replicas of real mines were produced in quantity to be strewn about the streets. High explosives were packed inside dead rats as they had once been stuffed into sheepskins. Plans were made to wire public toilets.

'You know,' Barkas said as he inspected plans in Maskelyne's office, 'we're getting pretty damn good at preparing for invasions.'

'Certainly,' Jasper replied. 'Practise makes perfect.'

Great piles of finished dummies were concealed beneath tarpaulins while Jasper made a master blueprint for their placement in Cairo and Alex. Other camouflage officers were drawing up similar plans in Suez and Port Said and the rest of the cities of the Delta. Maskelyne knew that these gimmicks wouldn't stop the Germans, but they might give Eighth Army time to make good its escape.

On June 25 Auchinleck sacked Ritchie and took personal command of Eighth Army. It had been generally believed since Wavell's time that if it became necessary, the British Army would make its last stand at Mersa Matrūh, a small port city midway between Tobruk and Alexandria. But the Auk did not feel he had sufficient time to dig in there, particularly since Rommel had feasted on Tobruk, capturing two thousand tons of fuel, five thousand tons of provisions, vast quantities of ammunition and two thousand vehicles. So he decided to withdraw Eighth Army to the way station of El Alamein, a scant fifty miles west of Alex. It was there the Army of the Nile would make its fight.

Obviously, he did not publicly announce this plan, so it appeared to everyone in the Basin that when Rommel drove past Matrūh after a brief, bloody battle, the army had collapsed. Thousands of civilians raced to escape the Panzerarmee, and 'The Flap,' the panicky evacuation of Alexandria and Cairo, began.

The first evacuees from Alex arrived in Cairo in limousines, holding the leashes of pure-bred dogs in one hand and clutching jewel boxes in the other, but as the panic spread others streamed into the city crammed in buses and trucks, carrying their possessions in cloth sacks.

Mostly, though, what they brought to Cairo was hysteria.

On July 1, 'Ash Wednesday,' it snowed charred scraps of paper and Cairo's streets were turned white as embassies and military offices burned confidential documents. The Royal Navy fled Alexandria harbour, steaming to the Red Sea. The roads out of the city were choked by every type of vehicle capable of moving under its own power. Every railway carriage was packed and thousands rode on their roofs. Aircraft shuttled in and out of Heliopolis carrying maximum loads to safer Middle Eastern and African cities. Many of those who couldn't find rides walked out with their belongings on their backs. Even those people who had nothing to fear from the Germans joined the lines of refugees, as if it were a lemming run.

Cairo was in organized chaos. Policemen and traffic controllers did their normal duties. The stock market fell, but remained open. Barclays Bank calmly paid out nearly one million pounds to skittish depositors in a single day. The value of a year-old car plummeted by 80 per cent, while the cost of luggage and trunks skyrocketed. Prostitutes lowered their prices and worked around the clock. People preparing to evacuate piled everything they couldn't carry with them in front of their flats and accepted whatever cash was offered.

Scores of American civilians descended on the United States Legation to demand transportation, and Minister Alexander Kirk struggled to arrange for planes and large vehicles.

The British government put up a confident front. Ambassador Sir Miles Lampson attended the afternoon races in Alexandria while his wife shopped for trinkets in Cairo's souk. At Heliopolis, the cricket matches were played as scheduled, and there was the usual long waiting list for a starting time at the Gezira Island golf course.

Mussolini confidently had his favourite white charger flown to Libya so that he might properly lead the victory parade into Cairo.

Nightfall calmed the city like a cloth laid over a screeching bird's cage. Although a curfew was imposed, the best restaurants and dance clubs were crowded. The Moselle was chilled and the strawberries were fresh. People dressed in their finery and wined and dined and danced to the music of the big bands at Shepheards and the Continental and all the other grand hotels and clubs. Lord Lampson hosted a dinner party for eighty guests at the Mohammed Ali Club and remarked, 'When Rommel gets here he'll know where to find us.' The only intrusion into this party mood was the occasional wail of air raid sirens and the choking white smoke of burning secrets billowing out of embassy chimneys.

Maskelyne and the Gang worked feverishly, finally feeling as if they were in the war. As Jasper had joked so long ago, it had finally come to them.

On July 2 GHQ ordered the evacuation of all dependants and female personnel as soon as transport could be arranged. It was believed that blondes would be perfectly safe with the Germans, so dark-haired women were put at the front of the lines. There was, however, a run on bleach at the chemists' as the women soldiers fought to stay at their posts as long as possible.

Kathy was ordered to pack her kit and stand by. Having no idea when she might be shipped out, she forged a curfew pass and went to Michael's room at the Valley to tell him what had happened. There was no one in the Gang's quarters. She went into the loo to wash up and instinctively bolted the door behind her – and the bolt snapped off in the lock. She was trapped.

In an instant the spunky façade she'd maintained as the Germans smashed toward Cairo dissolved, and she started screaming frantically and pounding on the door. She yelled herself hoarse, but there was no one nearby to hear her. By chance, Hill had decided to return to his room to collect a clean uniform for the coming hard stretch and found her there.

He booted out the lock and freed her, then kissed away her fears and said he loved her. He was quite surprised how good it felt to say that and truly mean it. They talked for a while, and kissed some more, and it got very late, and so it seemed entirely proper she stay the night.

Meanwhile, Eighth Army dug in at El Alamein. On June 30, Auchinleck tried to boost morale, telling his soldiers, 'The enemy is stretching to his limit and thinks we are a broken army ... He hopes to take Egypt by bluff. Show him where he gets off.' The Auk had picked the ideal place to stand fast. The Alamein Line was the shortest distance between two impassable points in the entire desert. Only forty miles separated the Mediterranean and the salt marshes and quicksand of the Qattara Depression. There were no traversable flanks, so the German attack had to be made directly into the passage. General Auchinleck stuck every man, gun and mine he could muster into these forty miles. Rommel would pay in blood for every inch of rock-studded sand he captured.

Rather than pause to reconnoitre, thus giving Eighth Army time to firm up, Rommel pushed his exhausted soldiers into the gap. The lack of intelligence information proved costly as his men ran into unexpectedly heavy concentrations. Both sides took heavy losses on July 1, but the British line held through a long day of close combat. That night German Supreme Command in Berlin prematurely announced, 'In Egypt, German and Italian divisions, supported by strong formations of dive bombers, have broken through the Alamein positions.'

The scent of total victory in Africa seduced German leaders to cancel Operation Herkules, the invasion of Malta, and assign those strike troops to Rommel. This gave him desperately needed reinforcements, but allowed the RAF and the Royal Navy to begin operating from Malta again, and they hammered Axis supply convoys.

Rommel attacked again on July 2, but achieved no more success. Mussolini waited impatiently at Comando Supremo headquarters in Cyrenaica to make his triumphant march.

On July 3 the tide of battle turned. The elite Italian Ariete Division was trampled by 13th Corps, New Zealanders. The Desert Air Force flew an incredible nine hundred sorties. By dusk, Rommel was reduced to twenty-six combat-ready tanks. Realizing his charge had been blunted, he decided to fortify his present position and resupply.

The heroic stand of Eighth Army at El Alamein bolstered public confidence in the Delta, and the panic subsided. Prices immediately returned to pre-Flap levels, and restaurateurs again put away their German-language menus. The Army's position was still precarious, however, and preparations for an orderly withdrawal from Egypt continued. Supplies not immediately needed at the front were shipped east of the Suez Canal to cover the retreat, and British agents in Damascus kept careful track of the Imam of the Dervish to make sure he was not up to his old tricks.

The evacuation of dependants proceeded, although female military personnel were permitted to remain pending further developments. Contingency headquarters facilities were set up a safe distance from the city.

The Gang worked steadily to turn Cairo and Alex into deadly traps for the Axis invaders. Once the basic deceptions were in production, Jasper began creating more esoteric devices, including soupy mists to hide big guns, artificial quicksand pits, flat lighting to make weapons-spotting more difficult and elaborate mirror mazes that channelled directly into ambush positions.

The fighting raged through early July without either side establishing an advantage. Rommel repeatedly stabbed at the Alamein Line, probing for a weak point through which to drive his army. He successfully concealed his own shortage of artillery by interspersing wooden tanks and dummy 88s among his armoured divisions.

Eighth Army met each thrust with a counterattack as Auchinleck tried to lure Panzerarmee Afrika into a battle of attrition which he knew he could win.

On July 20 Mussolini returned to Rome. Rommel's great drive to the Nile had been stopped. Once again, Afrika Korps would be summering in the desert.

By the end of July Cairo had settled into an uneasy calm. But luggage remained packed and vehicles juiced for a quick getaway in case the Desert Fox had one last surprise up his sleeve.

On August 3, Prime Minister Churchill arrived in Cairo to meet with his African and Far Eastern commanders. General Sir Alan Brooke, Chief of the Imperial General Staff, arrived a few hours after the Prime Minister. South Africa's Field Marshal Smuts and General Wavell from India came in later. Auchinleck, living in the field with his troops, was the last to make an appearance, still dressed in khaki drill and the familiar forage cap.

The bigwigs immediately disappeared into day-long meetings, but no announcement of their purpose was forthcoming. Speculation was that Churchill intended to name a new Eighth Army commander, freeing Auchinleck to concentrate on his duties as C-in-C of the entire Middle Eastern theatre.

Everyone had his own opinion about the reason for Churchill's visit, however. 'He's heard about the local bints,' Hill decided, 'that's all. Think it's so easy to get any, what with the whole bloody Empire watchin' you all the time?'

Fuller sighed. 'Michael, is sex all you think about?'

Hill made a big show of thinking about that.

Actually, Churchill was there to supervise an extensive shakeup of command. He was furious that the army upon which so much care had been lavished had performed so poorly in the field. The disaster at the Gazala Line had sparked renewed questions about his leadership. A desert victory was needed to restore lost confidence, and once again he pushed his commanders to give him that triumph. 'Rommel, Rommel, Rommel,' he fumed. 'What else matters but beating him?'

General Auchinleck had a much better appreciation of the tactical situation and knew he could field an overwhelming number of men and arms by early autumn. He wanted to hold the line at El Alamein until then, and argued that strategy forcefully with the Prime Minister.

Churchill and Brooke decided that the popular leader of XIII

Corps, General William 'Strafer' Gott, would assume command of Eighth Army. Much more shocking, they announced that, effective from August 15, General Sir Harold Alexander would replace Auchinleck at the head of Middle Eastern Command.

On August 5, the Prime Minister made a morale-building tour of the front and created a stir as he plodded along in his pith helmet, wearing dark goggles and carrying a parasol. Photographers snapped away to get full propaganda value from this show of bravery.

Two days later General Gott took precisely the same route Churchill had taken on his return trip from desert headquarters. But this time two Luftwaffe Me-109s materialized, as if they had been waiting for Gott's plane, and shot it down over the desert. The General scrambled out safely, but courageously returned to assist some of the men trapped inside. He was killed when the Germans made a second pass.

The terrible news sent Jasper into a dizzy spin. The similarity between this tragedy and Knox's death was uncanny. This time, though, rather than allowing his depression to catch hold and turn him inside out, he fought it. He went by himself to the military cemetery and stood on the gentle rise overlooking the trim rows of identical white crosses. Its size and symmetry gave the cemetery a tranquil beauty, and the great number of markers seemed to make the death of one man less significant. Once, Jasper might have listened to the winds, hoping to be told the good reason that the men resting here had died. But that was no longer necessary. The place calmed him, as it had been made to do, and he paid his respects to all the souls there and returned to the Valley.

Churchill selected General Bernard Law Montgomery to replace Gott. Montgomery was a bit of a mystery to the veterans of Eighth Army. He'd been training troops in England since Dunkirk, and about all that was known of his character was that he neither smoked nor drank, that he was a practising evangelical churchman and a fanatic about physical fitness. Jack Fuller thought the choice was a splendid one and recalled attending a Montgomery lecture in London at which 'No Smoking' and 'No Coughing' signs had been posted.

Hill shuddered. 'Sounds like he's got a great sense of humour.'

Monty immediately made his intentions known by burning a set of withdrawal plans and announcing, 'We stay here alive or we stay here dead.' Accustomed to a spit-and-polish army, he was rather rudely introduced to the realities of desert life. While visiting General Freyberg at the New Zealanders' headquarters, he commented drily, 'I notice your soldiers don't salute.'

'Oh, just wave to them,' Freyberg suggested. 'They'll wave back.'

Montgomery knew that Rommel would attack as soon as he could prepare his army, for each hour that passed allowed the British to further entrench at El Alamein. If he blitzed soon enough he might find a weak point in the line; if he waited too long a reinforced and resupplied Eighth Army would crush him. It was therefore imperative he be stalled as long as possible.

'There are two ways to do this,' Barkas told a hastily convened meeting of his senior camoufleurs, 'truth and lies. The RAF and Desert Rat commando teams are pecking at his supply lines. That's the truth. The lies are up to us.'

He paused, and looked around the room at the men who had been serving with him in the desert almost since the glory days of Wavell's triumphant march. 'Gentlemen,' he said in a low voice, 'they are finally taking us seriously. It has fallen upon our shoulders to convince Rommel that we are stronger than we actually are, to force him to hold back until we are strong enough. Specifically, our task is to create an army in reserve, complete to the smallest detail. We've been waiting a long time for this opportunity, let's not blow it.'

The objective of 'Operation Sentinel' was to buy time until the 51st Division arrived in Egypt with its complement of twenty-five American-made Sherman tanks. Military Operations described the sort of buildup that would most impress German Intelligence, then gave the camoufleurs access to as much labour and materials as they needed. Jasper worked closely with Barkas's second, Tony Ayerton, in drawing up plans.

For the first time, the graduates of Buckley's classes at Farnham would have the chance to put into the field all the techniques and tricks they'd mastered during two years in the desert. No longer would they have to scrounge for equipment and improvise from scrap heaps. Montgomery was a student of military history, and knew that war magic had been used successfully even before the Greeks penetrated the walls of Troy inside the Trojan horse. All he wanted from Barkas's men was that they make two motorized divisions appear on the barren sands north of Cairo.

The phantom cities that had fooled the Germans in England and Alexandria could not pass muster during daylight. Entire dummy bivouacs had to be created and had to look real enough to fool Jerry's low-level spotter aircraft.

Three days later a campsite large enough for two divisions was established. Rows of field tents were staked, and smoke began rising from cookhouses and refuse piles. Dust clouds raised by heavy construction equipment and supply trucks obscured large sections of the encampment, and a web of tracks crisscrossed the entire area. Day after day more tents were set up. Brand new heavy cannon appeared, often still in transport wrapping. Storage dumps grew rapidly. Footprints of thousands of soldiers in the hard sand offered proof that the NAAFI canteens were doing a brisk business. Individual campfires burned through the night. German reconnaissance photographs showed thousands of soldiers busy at their daily tasks, drilling, listening to lectures, even stealing winks behind a pile of unserviceable gasoline cans.

Only the field tents were real. The busy British soldiers were Maskelyne's dummies propped into every conceivable position, including sitting in the dummy latrines. The guns and dumps and most of the trucks were produced by Magic Valley workshops. The garbage was trucked in every morning. The buildings were hollow frames. The tracks were made by a few real trucks driving about the camp all day, raising dust clouds on cue for the benefit of enemy spotters. About a hundred men actually lived in the camp and made the footprints, stoked the fires, moved the 'Chinese' soldiers around and created some real waste. Compared to the hazards of driving a division of cardboard tanks into combat, this was considered country-club duty.

The camp expanded each day as more and more 'troops' and 'weapons' arrived. Then, after reaching the assigned strength of two motorized divisions, it began to thin out as the 'men' and 'guns' were trucked forward to bolster the Alamein Line.

To complete the deception, additional gun pits, dummy tanks and 'Chinese' soldiers were added to the Alamein defensive positions, carefully integrated among existing fortifications. 'How does it look?' was the question of the day.

'It'd fool me,' was the usual answer, 'but then again, I'm only a private.'

The factories at Magic Valley turned out 'soldiers,' 'guns,' 'tanks' and even 'trucks' by the truckload. To animate the 'soldiers' at Alamein the pop-up Tommy was invented. This was simply an ordinary dummy weighted at the bottom and held in a horizontal position by a string fastened to a spike in its helmet. When movement was desired, the string was released and the weight dropped into a previously dug hole, causing the dummy to pop up.

Maskelyne and Union Jack Fuller practically lived in a jeep. On a normal day Jasper would inspect the work being done at the Valley, arrange transportation for the finished props, supervise installation of the dummies at the campsite and examine procurement lists. At least once every day he met with Barkas or Ayerton and some of the other Farnham alumni, and somehow managed to put in some time at his drawing table. He was usually so exhausted by nightfall that he put off writing to Mary. She would understand. He'd finally got into the war.

Montgomery utilized other clever ploys to deceive Rommel. In order to slow Panzerarmee's attack, when it did begin, he had his cartographers create a desert map incorrectly identifying areas of impassable 'soft sand' and desirable 'hard going' on the Alamein Line. The coded map was carefully wrinkled and coffee-stained and entrusted to a British officer who had been disgraced by his intimate association with the belly-dancing Axis spy Hekmeth Fahmy. This officer drove gallantly into German minefields and was killed. As British Intelligence anticipated, his map case was discovered and sent to Rommel's headquarters.

Axis Intelligence took the bait. Deciding that this map was genuine, they plotted their attack corridors based on the terrain information it provided. The panzers would thus be driving into soft sand, becoming inviting targets for the RAF.

Rommel held back his army through the brutal desert heat of August. Both armies suffered the hardships of the desert, but Monty was able to provide his men with some relief.

Everyone in Cairo awoke each morning certain Jerry would attack that day. It was inconceivable that Rommel would wait until the autumn. Eighth Army was steadily growing stronger. Rommel had to come at them. He had to.

Mike Hill was going through a difficult time during this period, trying to keep his mind on his work while making a decision about Kathy Lewis. He knew he just couldn't let things go on too much longer; he'd either have to pop the question or break it off. His inability to make that decision was slowly driving him crackers.

He spoke to Jasper about it. He didn't think of Maskelyne as a father figure, but he respected him more than he'd ever respected his other friends. Maskelyne was old, and he had been married for so long, and he had been around the whole bloody world. 'So,' Hill asked bluntly one afternoon, 'what do you think, Jay? Should I marry her or what?'

'I suppose that depends,' Jasper teased. 'What's the what?'

Hill squirmed uncomfortably. 'You know what it is. It's ... that. That's what what is.'

Maskelyne thought he understood. 'I don't know, Mike. Seems to me the two of you are old enough to make your own decisions. You love her, right?'

'Yeah, course. But seems like there's more than that that's necessary.'

'There is, but that's a pretty good start.'

He finally bought a diamond ring, just in case. The stone was not very large, but he knew she wouldn't care about that. She wasn't the type who lusted after a man's purse. If she was, she wouldn't be with him.

He finally decided he would surprise her with it on her birthday, August 31. He arose early that morning, still determined to take the plunge. But just as he was climbing into the jeep to meet her at Clarke's office, Graham came running up to him. 'I wouldn't be going anywhere,' the carpenter told him. 'Rommel's jumped.'

Hill exhaled, and grinned, then laughed and laughed.

Nails did not understand how the news of battle could make a man so happy.

The night before, while Hill was turning restlessly in his bunk, the steel heart of Rommel's African army had moved south, leaving in its place an impressive display of wooden tanks and guns. The Field Marshal intended to duplicate his success at El Gazala by breaking through the reportedly weak southern tip of the Alamein Line near the Qattara Depression, then turning north and meeting the British defences piecemeal. Once again, he was depending on speed and surprise to compensate for his shortages of gasoline and ammunition.

But this time Eighth Army was waiting for him. British Intelligence had intercepted his wireless communications and knew his plans. This time the Fox would receive the nasty surprise.

The routes designated 'hard going' or 'firm ground' on the bogus map had been densely seeded with mines. Rommel's armour drove right into these fields and was trapped. Surprise had been lost even before the battle began. Now the element of speed had been taken away from him. As soon as Rommel's tanks bogged down in the soft sand, waves of RAF bombers lit the night with parachute flares, then rained tons of high explosive on the mired columns.

By daybreak, the attacking force had not reached its initial objective and had already suffered unacceptably heavy losses. Dozens of tanks had been knocked out. 21st Panzer Division commander Major General von Bismarck had been killed by a mine, and General Nehring was badly wounded in an air attack. Rommel abandoned his original plan and made an immediate right hook, ordering his troops to occupy the high ground of the Alam Halfa ridge.

Monty was waiting for him there.

The only safe route out of the British minefields funnelled the Axis force into soft sand. The column was temporarily saved by a sandstorm that grounded Desert Air Force, but when Rommel's armour finally broke free of the beachy terrain it drove right into Eighth Army's next trap. Scores of American-made Grant tanks and antitank guns had been secretly dug into position at the Alam Halfa ridge and opened up on the Germans. Relays of bombers and fighter aircraft relentlessly attacked.

By the afternoon of September 2 Rommel realized that his situation was desperate. His fuel had been exhausted slogging through the minefields and soft sands, and the thousands of gallons of reserves he had been promised had been sunk en route by destroyers and aircraft operating from Malta. He began a cautious pullback, still looking for an opening, still looking for a place to make a good fight. But Montgomery made no mistakes.

The first volley had made the dummy campsite obsolete. No hard evidence was available to evaluate its impact on Rommel's planning, but during the unexpected, and welcome, August lull, the 51st Division had arrived and been hurried into the Alamein gap.

On September 1 Jasper drove with Hill and Phil Townsend to the deserted and suddenly depressing campsite. Two days earlier the place had seemed alive and exciting, its existence allowing the Gang to believe they were playing an important role in the battle for North Africa. But overnight it had become dismal and shoddy, its cardboard weapons had become embarrassments, painful reminders to each of them that their greatest battle had been fought against cameras.

Looking over the silent camp, Townsend grumbled, 'Right now, I feel about as useful as a ticket for the *Titanic*'s second voyage.'

'Oh, I think you'll feel differently about that soon,' Jasper said in a surprisingly chipper voice. 'We've been at it awfully hard and we're all a bit let down. But we did a damn fine job. Damn fine. And we can be proud of ourselves.'

'Well, we'd better be,' Hill said disgustedly as he booted a cloth head into the side of a plywood truck, ''cause no one else knows we're bloody well alive.'

The encouraging reports from the battlefield lifted the Gang's spirits, but it was difficult to shake the depressing feeling of being left at home on the night of the gala ball. Jasper refused to admit he shared those feelings, repeatedly insisting that he was satisfied with his own contribution and that of his Camouflage Section. He said it so often, in fact, that even he began to believe it.

A few times he thought about his early dreams and felt foolish. He had been so headstrong, so confident. He was going to win the war by applying the techniques of magic to the battlefield. He was going to part the seas and invent Trojan horses. So naive. Back then, he hadn't had the faintest notion of what real war was about. He'd never seen the wounds of war up close. Well, he'd learned the lesson. All one man can do is his part, and do it as well as he is able.

He was proud of the role he'd played, even if he was not able to crown his performance with a grand illusion. That didn't matter anymore. He wasn't putting on a magic show, he was at war. And in that war he wasn't a magician, he was a King's soldier.

On September 4 Rommel began withdrawing his armour behind a screen of levelled 88mm antiaircraft guns. Montgomery resisted the strong temptation to chase him and finish him off, an urge that had proved disastrous to the commanders who had preceded him.

Panzerarmee had been badly knocked about. Without gaining an inch, it had taken four thousand casualties and lost fifty tanks. Eighth Army had lost a third as many men and sixty-eight tanks, but Monty was only fifty-five miles from his supply depot and could sustain such losses.

Most importantly, Eighth Army finally had a commander who had proved himself to be the tactical equal of Field Marshal Rommel. Panzerarmee's attack had proceeded precisely as he had predicted and the enemy had fallen in turn into each of his carefully prepared snares. The Battle of Alam Halfa, popularly becoming known as the Six-Day Race, had rejuvenated the exhausted Eighth Army.

The initiative now belonged to the British. For the first time in the seesaw desert campaign that army victorious in the last battle remained in range of its own supply areas. Within weeks Monty would be able to attack with an overwhelming force. Rommel's last best effort had failed.

The coming battle would be decisive. Rommel's army lacked the fuel to retreat or the resources to meet Eighth Army on the open desert, so it would fight for survival on the forty-mile-long Alamein Line. The defensive advantages of the position that had served Monty now worked for Rommel. Any attack would have to be made straight into German lines. The Field Marshal had massed the remnants of his army behind a wall of 500,000 buried mines, and organized mobile strike groups. Wherever the main thrust of the British attack took place, his tank concentrations would move to that point. Afrika Korps was wounded, but its claws were still deadly.

Montgomery began preparing for that offensive, code-named 'Lightfoot,' as soon as the enemy began retreating. Unhappy with the 'old boys' network' of commanders who continually questioned his directives, he made it absolutely clear that his orders were not to be debated, simply carried out. Those officers unable to accept this doctrine were replaced.

Monty was also displeased with the slapdash training his soldiers had received. Taking advantage of his favourable circumstances, and knowing that the desert was eating at the Germans and Italians, he began withdrawing units from the front and sending them to rear training schools. When Lightfoot began, his army would be better equipped, trained and disciplined than ever before.

Churchill again pleaded for the killing blow to be struck, but Monty refused to attack until he was absolutely ready. He warned the Prime Minister that he would resign rather than commit an unprepared army to battle. Churchill had to accede to the new hero's demands. It was agreed that the largest Allied attack of the war would be launched on October 23.

Jasper Maskelyne did not know it, but this was his moment to take centre stage. Montgomery was about to ask him to perform the greatest bit of legerdemain in the history of warfare. This was to be the grand illusion.

SIXTEEN

Everywhere in the Nile Basin preparations for Montgomery's Lightfoot offensive were in progress – everywhere except Magic Valley. Lacking a specific assignment, the workshops continued turning out the sets for the defence of the cities, although it was confidently held that they would never be employed.

Monty had imbued Eighth Army with a recharged fighting spirit. Units drilled in close formation. The colourful 'gypsy-dress' uniforms disappeared and soldiers wore issue khakis – with the shirts tucked into the shorts or trousers! Some troops even took up saluting again. There was the usual good-natured grumbling from the ranks, and Monty was described as 'in defeat, indomitable; in victory, insufferable,' but a feeling that final victory was at hand was in the autumn air.

It had been so long since Maskelyne had enjoyed any free time that he did not know what to do with it. He sketched a few ideas for Montgomery and wandered around the Valley making a nuisance of himself. One afternoon he played a sloppy round of golf on Gezira Island. Another time he decided to finally visit the Cairo Museum to see the gold of King Tut, but most of the collection had been buried in the desert for safekeeping. Those pieces left behind did not interest him.

He strolled slowly back to the Valley that day, browsing in the stalls, sipping coffee at a café. The pitiful army of Egyptian peasants was still camped outside Magic Valley's front gates to see the wizard who lived inside, but they'd been there so long they had lost connection to their original purpose. Those who had been there the longest competed for respect and power by claiming to have seen the wizard perform miracles, and the greater their stories the more respect they received. Gradually, the Sorcerer of the Valley had been given a supernatural form to match his abilities, which had grown more prodigious with each competing tale. Jasper could walk through the gates without being bothered, for these people were waiting for a god.

Actually, he sort of missed the attention.

Maskelyne's own period of inactivity ended on September 16. In the morning a dispatch rider delivered a note from Barkas requesting he stand by. At noon, Barkas and Tony Ayerton collected him in a Chevrolet staff car. 'Where to?' Jasper asked as they drove off.

'A meeting,' Barkas replied.

Instead of heading into town as Maskelyne expected, they drove west, past the Pyramids, past the tank repair depots jammed with damaged hulls, past Monty's training schools and gun ranges and bivouac areas, past the filthy Arab villages and out onto the desert.

This was Jasper's first trip onto the Blue since his trip with Hill, and he sweated with fear. During the drive the men avoided speculating about the meeting, and instead exchanged the latest Monty jokes and Shepheards gossip. There was talk of an Allied landing in Northwest Africa, an invasion which would squeeze Rommel like an egg in a vice.

Three miles northwest of the Burg-el-Arab way station, hard on the banks of the turquoise Mediterranean, Eighth Army had transformed a speck of barren desert into a sprawling, mobile command centre. Protected by an outer ring of tanks and heavy artillery, hundreds of office and supply trucks, staff cars, caravans and communications vehicles had begun gathering there in late August. Miles of telephone lines and power cables had been strung. Tents of all sizes had been staked among the dunes.

A military city had been born there, and as Maskelyne arrived it hummed with the motorized activity of a confident army preparing for battle. Dispatch riders on bikes roared through the perimeter, raising dust trails. Officers from all the Commonwealth armies scurried about clutching briefcases. From a nearby airstrip, Desert Air Force Spits rose into the air at precisely timed intervals to patrol the skies, working in conjunction with Long Range Desert Group observers out alone on the plain.

Security was extremely tight. Barkas had to show his pass at three different points before being permitted to park. An armed guard escorted them to a large marquee and handed them over at the flap door to another guard. The situation made Jasper wildly curious. Obviously something big was on tap. But what? he wondered.

Dudley Clarke had arrived earlier, and greeted them warmly. They took seats and small-talked while waiting. Another dozen officers had preceded them, and during the next hour four more straggled in. Coffee and tea were served.

Finally, a military policeman stepped into the tent and called them to attention.

Everyone stood and snapped to. An instant later General Bernard Law Montgomery materialized out of a glare of sunlight, followed precisely one step later by his chief of staff, General Francis de Guingand.

'Seats.' Everyone sat. The tent was absolutely silent.

Montgomery took off his black tanker's beret and had a few private words with de Guingand, then faced the small group. He was framed by a large situation map showing two great armies facing each other across the Alamein Line. 'Here it is, gentlemen,' he began crisply. 'The front line stretches across forty miles of open desert, bounded on the north by the sea and the south by the Qattara Depression. There are no passable flanks. So General Rommel is aware we must charge straight into his teeth and he will be waiting for us. It's going to be quite a scrap, but I do not believe I am overestimating the situation to say that the entire war will turn on what happens here. What I am about to ask you to do is impossible. It can't be done; but it must be done.' He paused, and his steel-blue eyes searched out Maskelyne. 'I hope you've brought your magic wand with you. We're going to need it now.'

Montgomery then turned the meeting over to his second. In a forthright manner, de Guingand laid out the top-secret plan of attack. Under the full moon of October 23, Eighth Army's tanks were going to smash through enemy minefields in the northern sector of the line, then fight south to cut off Afrika Korps' supply lines. Since the railhead and the only good road in the entire desert ran along the northern coast, the enemy would expect the attack to begin there. But with imagination, cunning and luck, tactical surprise might be achieved, and that was the reason this group had been assembled. Montgomery wanted to somehow convince Rommel's Intelligence that the main thrust of Eighth Army's attack would be made at the southern end of the Alamein Line, and that the clamour in the north was simply a loud diversion. If this ploy was successful, Rommel would be forced to hold back his reserve divisions until he was certain Monty was attacking in the north, giving Eighth Army vital time to breach Panzerarmee's vast minefields. If complete deception could not be accomplished, General Montgomery hoped to at least confuse the enemy about the date and magnitude of the attack.

'Well, there it is,' de Guingand concluded. 'You must conceal one hundred and fifty thousand men with a thousand guns and a thousand tanks on a plain as hard and flat as a billiard table, and the Germans must not know anything about it, although they will be watching every movement, listening for every noise, charting every track. Every bloody wog will be watching you and telling the Germans what you're doing for the price of a packet of tea. You can't do it, of course, but you've bloody well got to.' After pausing to let his impossible charge sink in, he asked for questions.

Eight hands shot into the air, and de Guingand took the questions in turn, but Jasper's thoughts drifted to the heart of the problem. Simply put, Monty was demanding the slickest bit of legerdemain in history. An entire army in full battle-dress was to be concealed in the open palm of one hand, while the enemy was to be made to believe it was in the other. Short of mass mesmerism, the General was correct, it couldn't be done.

Then how would they do it?

After the meeting was adjourned Jasper strolled around the area with Barkas and Ayerton, finally settling down on the crest of a high white dune. A few thousand yards in front of them the Mediterranean began its climb up and over the horizon. They smoked. 'Quite an assignment,' Barkas said.

'Quite,' Jasper agreed, and wondered why General Montgomery hadn't requested something reasonable, like splitting the Red Sea or calling down the plagues. His stomach was churning, but this time he knew it was not caused by fear of failure, this time it was the excitement of opportunity. Finally, here it was, the grand illusion! An illusion so important that it would alter the course of the war. An illusion of far greater magnitude than anything else ever attempted on a battlefield. An illusion much more difficult than anything performed by his grandfather or his father. Finally, he was being called upon to do precisely what he had set out to do three years earlier – perform the greatest magic trick in history.

He watched a set of gentle waves roll up the beach, then scurry back to the safety of the ocean. Jasper Maskelyne at war. The magician Maskelyne at war. Lives would depend on his ability. If this bit was properly presented the legendary Rommel would be left holding the deck – or, more precisely, holding his reserve armour in check long enough to allow a massive British tank force to break through his minefields. But if the bit failed, if he was not up to it, thousands of brave Englishmen and Australians and New Zealanders and Indians would be hung up in those minefields and ripped apart by Panzerarmee's machine guns, mortars and artillery.

His life in the theatre had brought him to this telling moment, and it would take everything he had ever learned to pull it off. 'It can't be done,' Monty said. 'You can't do it,' de Guingand said. Jasper took a deep breath of the ocean air, and smiled his broadest and most dazzling smile. 'Hey presto!' he whispered to the breeze.

Temporary workspace had been assigned to the camoufleurs in the third-class waiting room of the El Alamein railway station. Ayerton went off to scout the northern sector for natural features which might be incorporated into the plan, while Clarke, Barkas and Maskelyne set to work.

Each man saw the problem differently. Clarke, the civilian solicitor, approached it as an exercise in logic. 'Our intention is to make the enemy believe that the thrust of our attack will be made at his southern defences. To accomplish this, we've got to conceal troops, weapons and supplies in the northern sector while simultaneously creating the impression that a major buildup is taking place in the south.

'Failing that, we've got to at least confuse him as to the moment of attack.

'The enemy will gather information from his own observations, from interception of wireless communications and from paid informers. He'll be paying particular attention to the main desert tracks for any sign of increased activity. He'll be watching for our buildup and keeping a sharp eye on our water sources. He knows we can't go too far without adequate water supplies.' He paused, and sighed, 'It's a bit of a tough one, I'm afraid.

'We've got to take each of these areas into consideration, perhaps one at a time, and then work out a unified plan of action.'

Barkas, who had spent his civilian life between world wars making documentary films about smaller wars around the world, saw it as a classic problem of concealment and decoy, and gave an expert summation of the resources available to this massive camouflage effort. Then he looked at Jasper and said, 'I expect your dummies will be quite useful in the south. We can mount an entire decoy advance, complete with dummy tanks and guns and what-have-yous, similar to what we've done before but on a much greater scale, of course. It might not accomplish everything Monty asked for, but it should definitely help.'

Jasper listened intently as Clarke and Barkas laid out the problem. The complications appeared insurmountable. Rommel's army was waiting behind a screen of half a million mines with machine guns, 88s, mortars, artillery and all the other killing devices of modern warfare. His spies were privy to every breath Eighth Army took. Yet somehow he had to be deceived. 'You can't make a camel fly,' Frank Knox had once told Jasper. Well, of course he could. As he had often claimed, given the proper equipment anything was possible. 'It's a trick, is all,' he said aloud.

'Hmm?' Barkas asked.

'It's a trick, that's all. Look here, the situation absolutely begs for a classic misdirection. What we intend to do is make something that is in one place appear to be in another place. I've spent most of my life doing just that and I know how to do it. We've got to present Jerry with an array of evidence and allow him to draw his own conclusions as to what it all means. If we show him the proper evidence, he'll reach the conclusions we want him to. If we simply show him a finished product he's sure to question it closely, but if we show him our preparations he'll make his own decisions. Now,' he continued, growing excited as the possibilities became clear in his own mind, 'we're going to stage this just as we would present a theatrical illusion. First, we've got to prepare our props. These props are the key to everything that happens thereafter, and then we've got to put them on display. After he's had some time to see them, we transpose them, move them from one hand to the other, and finally we make our presentation. He smiled broadly. 'Spring the trap.'

Clarke and Barkas questioned Maskelyne closely, but he was able to sustain the analogy. 'My grandfather defined magic as causing something or somebody to pass mysteriously from one condition to another, and that's really all we're doing.'

'All right,' Clarke finally agreed, 'we'll pull this trick on Rommel.' Working on a battered old typewriter with sticky keys, they banged out a general plan of approach, a so-called 'appreciation of the situation.' This plan, as befitting its creators, was logical, practical and whimsical. It called for two military forces to be put in the field, one real and deadly, the other paste and cardboard. The enemy would be given an opportunity to become familiar with their disposition and make his own judgment regarding their purpose. Then, at an opportune time, under the black velvet curtain of night, these armies would be transposed. Other principles of stage magic were alluded to, including distraction, disguise and simulation, but the main plan of deception was simply a misdirection performed on a gigantic stage.

It was night by the time they finished drafting this 'appreciation.' Barkas read it over and got quite excited. 'If this works,' he boasted, 'it'll make the Trojan horse look like a merry-go-round fixture!'

The paper was submitted for approval the next morning. During the drive back to Abbassia Jasper told Barkas, 'If this is a go, I want an assignment for my people.'

Barkas chuckled. 'If this is a go, Maskelyne, your people won't even have time to catch a nap. A plan of this magnitude requires thousands of decoys, more than could possibly be produced at the Valley. We'll have to get help from Number Eighty-five Camouflage, from the Mechanics...'

'No,' Jasper asserted, 'I don't mean that kind of work. We've done that before. I mean a real assignment.'

Barkas tried to dismiss the request. 'If you mean assign your chaps to a field unit, I'm afraid we're quite well equipped.'

'I'm serious about this, Major,' Jasper said coldly. 'I can't go back to them and tell them they're going to be stagehands this time. They've worked too hard for too long not to be in on the big one.'

The major sighed, then nodded, 'Okay, I'll see what I can do.'

Operation Lightfoot details were 'most secret' and Jasper could discuss them only generally with the Gang. 'The success of the entire plan depends greatly on a camouflage operation larger than anything ever done before,' he explained, 'and we're right at the centre of it. Montgomery wants to put an entire decoy army in the field to convince Rommel his southern points are going to be attacked. To do this—'

Hill cut in singing the familiar chant, 'There once was a famous magician who...'

The other men joined in the heckling.

'No, not this time. This time it's our show. No one's ever done anything like this before. And—' Jasper started to tell them that Barkas was going to get them a piece of the action, but caught himself. There would be no more disappointments for his men. 'That's all for now.'

The plan drawn up in the El Alamein railway station was approved by Monty, with minor modifications, and code-named 'Bertram.' Barkas, Ayerton, Clarke and Maskelyne hammered out the specifics in a room at A-Force. The first working day Jasper hung a sign on the wall as a constant reminder. 'The supreme question must be,' this stage dictum read, 'what impression will the introduction of this detail produce upon the mind of the spectator?'

In theory, Bertram was relatively simple. A large group of seemingly harmless transport and supply vehicles would assemble in the north, while the armoured force would appear to be headed south. At the last possible moment a transposition, or switch, would be made and the attack would be launched in the north. All they had to do was figure out how to do it.

Like any magic show, Bertram, the most complex military deception ever attempted, began with the preparation of the stage. In the theatre, the apparatus had to be loaded. In the desert, long before the tanks and guns and soldiers came onto the scene, supplies had to be laid in for them. Lightfoot required two thousand tons of gasoline, six hundred tons of provisions, six hundred tons of ammunition and other ordnance and four hundred and twenty tons of Engineers' supplies. All of this had to be moved into position in the north without being detected by enemy observers and had to sit there for a month without being discovered.

Simultaneously, to imply that the attack would begin in the south, a similar cache of dummy supplies had to be laid in there.

The most difficult material to store secretly, particularly in the desert heat, was gasoline. Tens of thousands of four-gallon cans had to be stocked. This first of the countless problems the camoufleurs would face was solved by Tony Ayerton. During his tour of the Alamein area he discovered one hundred masonry-lined slit trenches that had been dug more than a year earlier. By this time, he reasoned, German Intelligence would have become used to seeing them on photographs and probably take them for granted. Experiments with similar trenches in the rear proved that gasoline cans could be stacked against their walls without appreciably changing the shape of the telltale interior shadows. The 'loading' of the stage began the night of September 23, one month before the offensive was scheduled to begin, when truckloads of gasoline cans were neatly piled inside these forward trenches.

In an important test the following day, British reconnaissance pilots failed to locate this storage dump. Lightfoot was fuelled.

On that same day, although Allied Intelligence would not learn of it for another month, a sick and exhausted Erwin Rommel flew to Semmering in the Austrian mountains for a desperately needed rest period, leaving General Georg Stumme in command of Panzerarmee. Rommel left the battlefield only after being assured by his Intelligence that the British offensive could not possibly begin without a minimum of two days' warning, since the required buildup of supplies would be detected by the Luftwaffe's hourly air observation of the battlefield.

Magic Valley's workshops strained to produce the props for Monty's decoy army. Sunshields, dummy tanks, dummy trucks, dummy cannon, millions of 'gun flashes' and thousands of cloth 'soldiers' were needed. Civilian labourers were recruited to work in the factories and were assigned to make specific parts, rather than complete dummies, to prevent enemy agents from figuring out what was in progress.

From his tiny office in the War Rooms beneath Whitehall, Prime Minister Churchill tracked the preparations in the desert with great anticipation. This was the offensive he had been urging on his commanders since Wavell, an all-out attack that would smash the Nazis once and for all.

Never had there been a better time to strike. Hitler's European armies were brutally slugging it out against the Russians at Stalingrad. The Japanese were battling the Americans in the vicious South Pacific campaign. Total victory in the desert would free elements of the North African army to reinforce troops in India and the Far East, as well as deprive Hitler of the vital canal supply route and the oil of the Middle East.

In Cairo, Jasper had no time for such international reflections. For him the battle was to be fought a few miles away, and his role would be pivotal. He was constantly on the prowl: pushing and prodding, demanding, cajoling, threatening, and enjoying every minute of it. 'We are engaged in preparations for the final battle,' he wrote to Mary, carefully avoiding facts that would be censored.

> What a wondrous show it will be. There appears to be a real need for my services this time, and I am extremely busy. This time the Germans will never know what hit them. The men seem quite confident; Montgomery has won their respect. You will be reading about our campaign in the coming months.
> Don't fret, dearest, I will be fine.
> With all my love,
>
> JAY

The actual setting of the stage began on September 26. In an attempt to mislead the Germans concerning the date and sector in which the attack would be made, soldiers from Army Troops Company 578 began extending an existing water pipeline from the large El Imayid supply depot toward the southern strongpoint of Samaket Gaballa. Of course, the entire pipeline extension was an elaborate hoax.

Common fuel cans had been cut open and flattened, then laid end to end to simulate lengths of pipe. Each day five miles of this 'piping' was laid out on the desert while hundreds of soldiers dug trenches for it. Each night the trenches were filled in and the same flattened cans were picked up and laid down alongside the following day's five-mile stretch. 'If nothing else tells them we're going south,' Jasper explained to Fuller, 'this pipeline points it out like a bloody arrow. They can't possibly miss it.' Even more importantly, at the five-mile-per-day rate the pipeline couldn't reach Samaket Gaballa until early November, and German Intelligence would undoubtedly assume that the offensive wouldn't begin until it was completed.

In addition to the 'pipe,' that was laid, three dummy pumphouses were built along the route. They 'serviced' a few real trucks which were ordered into the area to create tracks in the sand, as well as the usual dummy trucks.

The stockpiling of real provisions in the vicinity of the El Alamein station began at just about the same time. Since it was not possible to hide the tons of preserved meat, tea, biscuits, cigarettes, flour, sugar, powdered milk and similar items on the featureless plain, some means of disguising them had to be found. Prolonged discussions centred around the fact that ordinary transport were the most common vehicles found on the desert. Concentrations of trucks were so much a part of the everyday scene that neither side paid them much attention. Camoufleur Brian Robb suggested that supply cases be stacked and concealed beneath camouflage so that they resembled ordinary three-tonners under protective netting. It proved as simple to do as it was effective.

Additional supplies were hidden under 'bivvies,' or individual soldiers' tents, staked among those of a resident Australian unit. RAF crews regularly took snaps of the site for inspection, and necessary modifications were then made.

German spotters frequently nosed around the 'truck concentration,' and once it was strafed by a lone Messerschmitt, causing an Australian trooper to run naked through the camp shouting, 'They've shot my biscuits, they've shot my biscuits.'

Much of the ammunition and ordnance was added to the established supply dump at El Imayid, twenty miles behind the front line. This depot had been in operation long enough for the Germans to have carefully inspected it, and the new stores were dispersed among existing piles. Although the original stacks of boxes had been left uncamouflaged, the new supplies were draped with netting and covered with sand to hide the buildup. Desert breezes continually swept away the sand cover, but for the most part the six hundred tons of Lightfoot supplies were successfully blended into the area.

In six days and nights the provisions for the offensive were put into place. Operation Bertram was gradually taking shape directly under the watchful eyes of the Germans, but they seemed not to notice.

To reinforce the impression being given by the 'pipeline' that Eighth Army would not be ready to launch its offensive until November,

Monty's staff decided to delay the buildup of dummy supplies in the south for a few weeks.

Meanwhile, the full-scale display of transport vehicles in the north was scheduled to begin the night of September 30. During the following week four thousand real trucks drawn from reserve units and service companies, and seven hundred dummy trucks, Magic Valley sunshields, were to be deployed under camouflage in an eight-mile-by-five-mile rectangle designated 'Martello.' Since such an assembly of support equipment was quite normal before a major attack, it was believed the Germans would examine it thoroughly, then watch it for movement, but would not feel threatened by it because it included no tanks or heavy weapons.

Martello, in fact, was the military equivalent of the stage magician's production table, for at the snap of General Montgomery's fingers seven hundred tanks and twenty-five-pounders would emerge from this seemingly harmless concentration of transport vehicles. It was from Martello that Eighth Army would sally forth on October 23. If the Germans did not catch onto this display before that night, Bertram, and therefore Lightfoot, had an excellent chance of succeeding.

Preparations for the delivery and assembly of the sunshield 'hides' occupied most of Jasper's time. But on September 29, Fuller caught him between workshops and informed him that Barkas had to see him immediately on a matter of importance. Jasper tried to beg off, but Fuller wouldn't hear of it, reminding him, 'He is your superior officer, you know.' They drove toward Gray Pillars, but turned away near the river.

'Here now,' Jasper snapped, 'where are you taking me?' He was beginning to get a bit annoyed, as this was certainly not a time for games. Barkas knew that.

'Special conference,' Fuller replied, finally pulling up in front of the Blue Daze, a belly-dancing club.

Jasper hurried into the cabaret and stopped abruptly, completely stunned. The entire Gang was waiting there, and Gregory, and Kathy Lewis, Barkas, some camouflage chaps from as far back as Farnham, some Engineers and other friends he'd made in Egypt. Hill came up to him and stuck out his hand. 'Happy birthday, Jay!'

In the rush of preparation, he'd completely forgotten his fortieth birthday. He stammered in confusion, then blurted out at Fuller, 'You crafty old sod. You tricked me!'

Fuller accepted the compliment. 'Yes, I suppose we have. That's jolly good for our side.' Luncheon was served, toasts raised, and humorous gifts presented. By midafternoon the party was over.

As Jasper walked to Fuller's jeep, Barkas took him aside. His gift, he told him, was a field assignment for the Magic Gang. 'Your people have had good success with boats, so I thought something in the order of an amphibious invasion might tickle your fancy. Nothing spectacular, mind you, but Monty's asked Cunningham to stage some sort of diversion behind Jerry's lines in the northern sector when we push off, something to attract a bit of attention. Navy'll provide whatever equipment you need. I realize it's probably not the sort of show you had in mind, you may not even draw fire, but at least you'll be in on the opening act. Well, what do you say?'

'It's a splendid present, Major.'

'Good. Fine. Cunningham's people'll be in touch. They've got the particulars.'

Even Fuller's sluggish speed couldn't get Maskelyne back to the Valley fast enough. 'Admiral' Hill's fleet was going to sail again.

The next night, the thirtieth, the bluff at Martello got under way as scheduled. Seven hundred and twenty-two sunshields were set up beneath garnished nets, many of them balanced on empty tar barrels that would pass as truck tyres when observed from the air.

Eventually each of these 'hides' would house a tank or a heavy weapon. Once the dummies were in place among the real trucks, each one was given a serial number and its position was marked on camouflage maps. Tankers and gun crews would be issued a corresponding number and, on the night of the big switch, the transposition, would know precisely where their assigned shelter was located.

The Alamein Line remained reasonably peaceful while the stage was being 'loaded,' although Monty had ordered a series of probing attacks in the south to lend colour to the overall impression. One night Queens Brigade of 44th Division suffered 392 casualties during an assault on the heavily defended Munassib Depression, but it captured territory that would have been needed as a staging point if the offensive were actually to have been launched in the southern sector.

German spotters were particularly active in the south, causing the camouflage people to believe they had at least caught Jerry's attention.

'Brian,' the construction of the dummy supply dump in the south, began on October 7 near a place called Bir Mseilikh, under the supervision of its creator, Brian Robb. The stacks, which represented nine thousand tons of supplies, were made from palm-wood bed frames, pickets, dummy railway tracks, old fuel cans, wicker tomato cases, and a large amount of wire. They were camouflaged by open meshed cloth, dark-green steel wool or dark garnished nets. Over seven hundred stacks were built, although some of the false piles of ammunition were only two-dimensional.

To complete the phoney supply depot, dummy buildings were erected and bivvies staked. A resident squad drove three trucks around the area all day to create the track impressions of dozens of vehicles.

Once Brian was completed, the stage was set. 'Transport' vehicles were in the north and 'supply dumps' were in the south. Some time would be allowed to pass before the performers – the thousand tanks and guns of Eighth Army – took their positions on that stage, to give the audience an opportunity to become accustomed to the scenery. Only after enemy Intelligence had examined it thoroughly, just the way a sceptic would test the Linking Rings, could the subtle changes essential to the success of the performance take place.

To keep the audience entertained in the meanwhile, Monty ordered increased patrolling in the south, including occasional forays into mine-strewn no man's land, while things remained peaceful in the north.

German Intelligence examined the set very carefully. Air reconnaissance photographs were taken several times every day and scrutinized for the slightest indication of movement. There was no question that the British would take the offensive with a force much larger than Panzerarmee, but the important questions to be answered were when and where this would happen. Correct answers would enable the highly mobile African army to meet the thrust of the attack with a maximum force and blunt it.

From Rommel's point of view, all evidence indicated that an attack would be launched in the southern sector in early November. The stores being massed there made any other conclusion senseless, and the pipeline under construction could not possibly be completed until then. In any event, German Intelligence remained confident it could provide Rommel with at least two days' warning prior to the attack, more than enough time to allow him to return to the battlefield.

The work at Magic Valley lightened only slightly when the first dummies were put into position at Martello. Hundreds more of every type had to be provided for the actual transposition, the switch, or 'sting,' in American gangster terminology, and arrangements had to be made to move those currently in place to another spot on that night. It wasn't until October 10 that Jasper learned the details of the Gang's seaborne invasion.

Admiral Cunningham's office wasn't expecting too much. The Navy would provide three swift craft equipped with deck guns to shell the coastline behind Jerry's lines. 'We'd like to raise a bit of a fuss,' explained the project officer, Lieutenant David Fielding. 'Just create a minor diversion to catch their attention, then skedaddle. I'm sure you understand.'

Jasper did; he also had much bigger plans. 'As long as we're making the effort,' he politely suggested, 'let's do it right. Let's convince Jerry that a major landing is taking place.'

Fielding pooh-poohed the suggestion, pointing out that the Navy had neither the men nor the equipment for such a mission.

Jasper smiled confidently. 'What if I could pull it off with my men and your three boats?'

'By all means,' Fielding replied. Operation Knox was born.

The final piece of battlefield scenery was put into place the night of October 15 near the Munassib Depression in the south. Troops of 44th Division dug gun pits and set up dummy fieldpieces, dummy limbers, dummy trucks and 'Chinese' soldiers equivalent to three regiments of field artillery.

Here many of the lessons learned from the ill-fated *Houdin* were put to good use as desert camoufleurs made a half-baked effort to hide these props. Torn nets were used to 'cover' the dummy guns, and improperly tacked-down bits of cardboard and cloth fluttered beneath them in the breeze. One dummy three-tonner leaned to the side and cast an improbable shadow. The 'Chinese' soldiers were left in the same place for days at a time, including those in the dummy latrine. These errors were obvious enough to be detected by enemy Intelligence, but subtle enough to be considered unintentional. Once the camoufleurs were certain Jerry had spotted these defects they were corrected, as if Eighth Army had discovered its own mistake.

This was a classic double bluff. The enemy was encouraged to believe he had discovered a weak spot in Eighth Army's defences. At the opportune moment he would undoubtedly utilize this vital information – only to discover that even cardboard wasps have deadly stings.

Operation Knox, the Gang's naval operation behind enemy lines, received official approval on October 16. A communications code and a timetable were drawn up and all necessary equipment was gathered, although Fuller had more difficulty locating the hand-cranked gramophone than anyone had anticipated. At Maskelyne's request, the Navy provided three barges in addition to the speedboats.

Everyone in the Gang was beginning to get excited about the

mission, except Hill, who grumbled, 'They're really settin' us up for the big dump this time.'

The players in Maskelyne's grand illusion – one thousand tanks, two thousand guns and sufficient transport – came on stage on October 18. That morning, in full view of enemy observers, Montgomery's Armoured Corps rolled out of its rear training sites heading for the staging areas Murrayfield and Melting Pot. These assembly points were fifty miles, or approximately two days' drive, from the Alamein Line, and were situated alongside the main tracks leading south. No effort was made to camouflage this movement, leading Panzerarmee Intelligence to report that it was most probably a training exercise rather than preparations for the offensive, but these armoured concentrations were kept under surveillance from dawn to dusk.

Although General Stumme's Intelligence had guaranteed a forty-eight-hour cushion, this manoeuvre made him uneasy. After conferring by wireless with Field Marsh Rommel, who was still recuperating from the effects of the difficult desert campaign, he decided to split up his five hundred combat-ready tanks. 15th Panzer and the Italian Littorio Division remained in the north, while 21st Panzer and Ariete moved into defensive positions on the southern front. His reserves, the 90th Light and Trieste Divisions, were held at a swing point behind the lines.

British infantrymen had been gradually moved forward during the brisk nights of mid-October. Most simply melded into existing troop concentrations, but some huddled during the days in a complex of camouflaged trenches near the front line.

As a fine performance of stage magic is made up of a continuous chain of essential details leading to a single effect, so the many pieces of Bertram were falling neatly into place. But, as had occasionally happened to Jasper on stage, he had become so involved with the details that he failed to appreciate the whole. Now, with the stage set and the pieces displayed for inspection, he stepped out of his role and imagined himself sitting beyond the footlights.

The attention of this audience had been very carefully directed.

On view in the north was a large but apparently harmless assembly of support vehicles under camouflage. Although this formation of specks on the desert was curious, the trucks had remained in place for weeks and implied no threat. The eyes had become used to it, and the mind began overlooking it.

The hectic situation in the south required considerable attention. A twenty-mile thread of water pipeline had been stitched into the desert.

Pump stations had been built and were servicing numerous vehicles every day. Large supply caches had been laid in. Armoured-car patrols darted about on the desert, and air squadrons crisscrossed the skies. Three artillery regiments had taken positions on the front line – at least partially bolstered by phoney batteries.

In rear staging areas, sparkling in the sunlight, lay the real danger. The guns of Montgomery's Armoured Corps aimed south and waited for the overture to begin.

It was October 20. Time for the magician to seal the spiked mummy case with his brave assistant quivering inside. Time to throw the sheet over the distressed damsel and prepare to elevate her. Time to turn on the buzzsaw.

It was time to do the trick.

Early that morning the signal went out to All Concerned Personnel that the move forward, the transposition, would begin at dark. Maskelyne and his men spent the day loading Magic Valley cardboard tanks onto trucks – one dozen tanks fit snugly into a single five-tonner.

At a meeting in the Amariya Cinema, Montgomery revealed his entire battle plan to all Eighth Army officers above the rank of major. From that morning on, all soldiers having knowledge of Lightfoot details were restricted to secure areas. Troops patrolling near the Alamein Line were not told about it in case they were captured. The battle, Monty warned, 'will be a real roughhouse,' but he was supremely confident his well-trained army would 'strike the enemy for six.'

Minutes after the sun went down that evening the desert rumbled into life. The Eighth Army began its transposition from south to north.

To provide a distraction to cover the move, a skeleton crew of 10th Armoured wireless operators pattered on at great length about a training operation in progress. Thirteenth Corps in the south staged a series of phoney raids, 'accidentally' illuminating 'Chinese' soldiers who took considerable enemy fire in their cloth guts.

The tank groups and their support vehicles moved out of staging areas Murrayfield and Melting Pot and headed toward the assembly of harmless trucks at Martello. Farther back, through the entire Basin, hundreds of spare trucks and staff cars converged on Murrayfield and Melting Pot to replace them.

Maskelyne and the Gang were in the first group of trucks to arrive at Melting Pot with loads of dummy tanks.

As each armoured vehicle departed, one of the substitute trucks or cars drove into its position. The tanks were replaced by Magic Valley dummies which were camouflaged with ordinary netting. It had proved impossible to produce enough dummy tanks for Bertram, so in some cases palm-wood bed frames were laid on their sides and concealed beneath camouflage nets.

Tenth Armoured thundered forward at top speed to Martello. It was a difficult movement, because the tanks travelled with minimum lights and had to follow precisely in the tracks made by the convoy leaders.

Jasper proudly watched them pull out of Melting Pot in the silvery glow of a gibbous moon, the last group equipped with tank-track erasers to obliterate their trail. All around him two-and three-man camouflage teams were setting up an entire armoured corps made of paste, canvas and cardboard. As this army of Magic Valley tanks and guns came to life, he couldn't help thinking back to the early days at Farnham, when Buckley's boys had been kept away from the regular soldiers at Aldershot lest the real army somehow be tainted by their presence.

When each real tank or mobile gun arrived at Martello, it was taken in charge by another camouflage team and guided into the numbered sunshield specifically prepared for it. The dummy trucks that had been sitting at Martello for weeks were dismantled and loaded onto service company vehicles, then returned to Melting Pot and Murrayfield to be set up in vacated positions.

Once the tanks and guns were in position at Martello, their crews were not permitted to move about during the day. Fires were prohibited and sheets were not to be aired. The slightest flaw could give away the entire trick.

At Munassib, in the southern sector, a battery of real artillery replaced the poorly camouflaged dummies.

The transposition took two nights. By dawn on both October 21 and 22 the desert was quiet. Enemy reconnaissance aircraft making their early-morning runs above these areas reported that 10th Armoured was still in place fifty miles behind the Alamein Line. As usual, blankets and bedsheets were hung on the tanks to dry in the sun, and thousands of troops brewed up over smoky campfires.

The Germans were completely unaware that 1,500 replacement vehicles and 1,870 tanks and three-tonners – both real and cardboard – had been substituted for 10th Armoured at Melting Pot and Murrayfield in the south, while the real armoured division had moved forward to the truck assembly at Martello and was now poised just behind the northern sector of the front line.

General Stumme routinely wired headquarters on the twenty-first: 'Enemy situation unchanged.'

That same day General Montgomery had quietly cancelled all leave. All units were ordered to remain in their starting blocks. At El Alamein, foot soldiers lay hidden in the forward slit trenches, fighting off flies, just waiting.

The Gang held its breath throughout the day. The waiting was far more difficult than the work had been. 'Let's get it over with,' Hill whined. 'What the bloody hell is he waiting for? We're in position and we're ready to go. Let's go.'

'Soon,' Townsend said, 'soon.'

'I'm telling you, he's gonna blow the whole thing. You think you can fool Rommel so easy?' Hill shook his head. 'You can't.'

In the afternoon, Maskelyne and Gregory drove up to Alex to check the speedboats. 'Just one more day,' Jasper said.

'I'm not sure I'll last that long,' Gregory replied.

Cairo was on edge. The Shepheards basement storeroom was jammed with officers' luggage, stored at the daily rate of four pennies. Soon, everybody knew, soon.

Luftwaffe spotter planes followed their normal flight patterns. They noted that an antiaircraft battery had been installed near Murrayfield, but otherwise the situation remained unchanged.

On the evening of the twenty-second Jasper waited at Magic Valley and watched the scarlet sunset. There was nothing more to be done. The army was in place. The props were loaded. The Gang's mission wouldn't get under way until the next afternoon. All that could be done had been done.

He raised a glass of Italian wine to the last rays of the sun. One night from that moment the presentation of the greatest trick in history would begin. His trick. The grand illusion.

If the hands of Eighth Army had been quicker than Axis eyes, the audience would die in surprise.

SEVENTEEN

On the morning of October 23 a 'Personal Message from the Army Commander,' Montgomery, was read to each Eighth Army soldier about to go into combat:

1. When I assumed command of Eighth Army I said the mandate was to destroy ROMMEL and his Army and that it would be done as soon as we were ready.

2. We are ready NOW. The battle which is now about to begin will be one of the most decisive battles of history. It will be the turning point of the war. The eyes of the whole world will be on us, watching anxiously which way the battle will swing.

We can give them the answer at once. 'It will swing our way.'

3. We have first class equipment; good tanks; good anti-tank guns; plenty of artillery and plenty of ammunition; and we are backed by the finest air striking force in history.

All that is necessary is that each one of us, every officer and man, should enter this battle with the determination to see it through—to fight and to kill—and finally, to win.

If we do this there can be only one result—together we will hit the enemy for 'six,' right out of North Africa.

4. The sooner we win this battle, which will be the turning point of this war, the sooner we shall all get back home to our families.

5. Therefore, let every officer and man enter the battle with a stout heart, and with the determination to do his duty so long as he has a breath in his body.

AND LET NO MAN SURRENDER SO LONG AS HE IS UNWOUNDED AND CAN FIGHT.

Let us all pray that 'the Lord Almighty in battle' will give us the victory.

B. L. MONTGOMERY
Lieutenant-General, GOC-in-C, Eighth Army

The Gang awoke at 7 A.M., just as the night chill was beginning to lift, and brewed up. 'Lorry'll be here at 0900,' Jasper reminded them. 'Any last things, get to them now.'

Like most other soldiers in the shadow of battle, they passed the last hour writing just-in-case letters. These were sealed and left in a packet on Maskelyne's desk, to be posted only if the Gang did not return. Jasper wrote a happy letter, barely alluding to the offensive. 'Remember always,' he concluded, 'I love you all so very much.'

The truck didn't show until 9:30 A.M. 'Great way to start an invasion,' Hill complained, still convinced the Gang's amphibious assault was going to be scrubbed. They loaded six folded tanks, the gramophones and amplifiers, and cases of dummy shell flashes in the rear and by ten o'clock were on their way to Alexandria harbour.

Out on the Blue, 30th Corps infantry lay nearly motionless in cramped slit trenches. All unnecessary movement was forbidden and anything short of warding off a scorpion was deemed unnecessary. The men tried to sleep, but swarms of feasting bugs made that impossible. So they lay there and boiled in the sun, watching mirages perform for them and waiting. Within hours they would precede the largest armoured force in history through 'the Devil's Gardens,' Rommel's screen of half a million mines, machine guns, mortars, antitank weapons and artillery.

By the time the Gang got to Alex their nervousness had been overwhelmed by excitement. They were finally going to be smack-dab in the middle of it. After a hot meal mostly picked at they reported to the harbour to pack their boats. Three motor-torpedo craft were fuelled and ready, and three wooden barges floated nearby. A few hundred yards down the wharf four large troop transports were tied up.

'There they are,' Jasper said, nodding toward the four transports, 'just like we were promised.'

'Where's the rest of our gear?' Gregory asked.

Maskelyne pointed out a heavily guarded warehouse.

They split up into crews to unload the cardboard tanks and pack their gear aboard the launches. Robson paused at one point and started chuckling. 'You mean this whole crazy thing is really going to come off?'

Hill lugged an air raid siren onto a barge. 'Don't bet on it,' he said.

At 1500 hours, eight hundred combat-ready soldiers arrived. They piled out of their trucks and formed ranks, then were smartly marched aboard the transports. Simultaneously, heavy-duty cranes lifted a total of thirty tanks on board, setting them down below deck.

This loading was witnessed by Egyptian labourers working in the yard quite a distance away, who reported it to their contacts for transmission to Panzerarmee Intelligence.

Maskelyne and the Gang watched this scene contentedly from their speedboats. The dummy invasion force was taking shape. The eight hundred 'combat soldiers' had been drawn from headquarters and quartermaster companies and repair depots in Cairo. The 'tanks' were Magic Valley dummies. As soon as they disappeared below deck they were dismantled and carried off the ships in pieces. Inside the guarded warehouse they were quickly snapped together, loaded onto limbers and again delivered to the transports.

By four-thirty the ships were loaded and their gangways were lifted.

Even Hill's resolve was beginning to crumble. 'It's a good show,' he admitted, 'I'll certainly give you that.'

At five o'clock the four troop transports sailed out of Alexandria harbour. Within minutes, news of this departure was on its way to Libya.

At five-thirty Luftwaffe surveillance aircraft over the desert made their final inspection of the day. They reported that the armoured divisions at Melting Pot and Murrayfield were settling in for the night.

The Gang began rechecking its equipment a bit after six o'clock. Jasper and Hill manned the first barge; Fuller and Gregory, the second; Graham, Townsend and Robson, the third. Gregory ran a mechanical and fuel inspection of the small flotilla. Checking with Maskelyne, he said, 'I make it six-thirty.'

Jasper synchronized his watch. 'Eighteen-thirty hours it is.'

A half hour later the three Royal Navy speedboats, each pulling a barge, glided into the twilight sea.

Just after dusk, like desert rats crawling out of their cool burrows, Eighth Army's infantry came to life on the Alamein Line. Thousands of soldiers crawled out of their slit trenches and tried to jangle feeling into their aching limbs. A hot meal, the last one they would enjoy for weeks, was brought up from the rear. Buddies checked each other's equipment: every trooper carried a weapon, fifty rounds of ammunition in a bandolier, two grenades, a pick or entrenching tool and four empty cloth bags that could be filled with sand to provide protection, and a backpack marked with a white Saint Andrew's cross that would make him easier to follow in the dark. The pack contained a ground sheet, shaving cream and a straight razor, one day's bully beef, biscuits and iron ration. Each man double-checked his own water bottle.

Some of the men hung in groups while waiting for the whistle to move to the start line, others sat by themselves and wrote letters or had a final word with God.

Refrigerated blood trucks, with giant vampire bats painted on their sides, stayed just out of sight. In the rear, doctors and medics checked supplies for the expected rush.

Safe in German field headquarters west of Tel el Eisa, General Stumme and his staff prepared for dinner. It was hoped the special treat of the night, fresh gazelle, might help them forget the distressing situation at least temporarily.

Only that afternoon, Intelligence had reported that the British could put approximately 200,000 men, 1,000 tanks and 1,000 guns into the field, nearly double the Germans' own strength in each category. In addition, Panzerarmee fuel reserves had been reduced to three days' issue, the water supply was low, and provisions were close to exhausted.

Intelligence also noted, however, that Eighth Army would not be capable of mounting a full-scale offensive for at least two more weeks. Stumme was confident the supplies promised by Hitler would arrive within that period. The fact that his troops were outnumbered did not in itself concern him, for the men of Afrika Korps were the finest soldiers in the world. And Rommel, their commander, who would return to the desert at the first hint of attack, had proved himself a military genius. Victory was a matter of supply.

Dinner began promptly at 8 P.M. with a fresh garden salad, complemented by a golden Moselle.

The Mediterranean was a bit choppy and quite chilly that night, and the three speedboats laboured under their heavy tows. Gregory reassured Maskelyne that they would reach their destination by 1 A.M., zero hour.

Five miles out of Alex they passed the four transports riding at anchor. 'They'll all be home in their bunks three hours from now,' Graham commented to Robson.

'What's the matter, Nails? Jealous?'

The carpenter grinned at him. 'You crackers?'

Even Hill no longer doubted that their mission was a real one. 'Watch now,' he told Jasper ruefully, 'we're gonna get lost out here and blow the whole show.'

Jasper barely heard him above the din of the speedboat's inboard engines. The sea spray matted down his hair and droplets of salt water fell from his moustache, and occasionally he wiped his mouth and brow dry with the back of his wrist, but rarely had he felt more alive than at that moment.

He glanced at his wristwatch every few minutes. Ordinary intervals of time suddenly took on new meaning. The second hand took an hour to make a single circuit. Five minutes became an eternity. His heart was thumping like a swing band's percussion section. Once, as he sat on a crate of dummy ammunition flashes, he caught his left foot tapping away to some racing rhythm. He rested his hand on his knee to stop it, but a few minutes later that independent foot was at it again.

'Some night,' Hill shouted to him, and grinned a mile-wide grin.

'Some night,' Jasper shouted right back.

At 7:30 P.M., near El Alamein, military policemen wearing white gloves and red caps laid down a white-tape start line on top of nearly invisible piano wire that had been put down days earlier to mark the path forward. The MPs were to direct traffic into six twenty-four-foot-wide lanes. Huge Scorpion minesweepers and courageous Engineer sappers carrying metal detectors would lead the way, followed in strict order by water carts sprinkling the sand to hold down the dust, the infantry, and finally the tanks and armoured cars.

General Montgomery spent the twilight hours walking among his troops. Sometimes he would climb up on a tank and, with troops sprawled informally around him, run down the strategic situation. At eight o'clock he retired to his trailer. Alone. On the wall above his bed he had hung a flattering photograph of his opponent, Rommel, and beneath it he taped a quote from Shakespeare's *Henry V*: 'O God of battles! Steel my soldier's heart.'

At precisely 8:30 Martello awakened. The tranquillity of the night desert was shattered by the full-throated roar of a thousand engines. Tanks and mobile guns emerged from their cocoons. Support transport assembled to the rear. Platoons began forming up.

General Montgomery's army was going to work.

At nine o'clock the soldiers of XXX Corps infantry hefted their packs, fixed bayonets and walked up to the start line. Within moments they would learn whether Maskelyne's greatest illusion had been successful. Their lives were staked on it.

Mike Hill glanced at his watch. It was 9:15 P.M. 'Getting a bit nippy out here,' he said to Maskelyne.

Jasper's throat was as dry as it had been on the desert. He nodded.

At 9:30, forty-eight Wellington bombers flew over the front lines en route to known German gun positions. British artillery gunners on the ground were ordered to 'Take post,' and did so, most of them putting on gloves and sticking rubber plugs or cotton wads into their ears. On the start line the troops shook hands and wished each other well and shifted about nervously. Sergeants went down the line reminding their men, 'Keep your distance, don't bunch up, watch out for trip wires, and, whatever happens, keep moving forward.'

At 2140 Egyptian Summer Time, 9:40 P.M., artillery commanders the length of the Alamein Line gave the command, 'Fire by order, five rounds gunfire.' Then, after a breath-long pause, crisply ordered, 'Troop, fire!'

As have battles for a thousand decades, the Battle of El Alamein began to the thunder of war drums. The heavy artillery of Eighth Army pounded the earth with the ancient rhythm, thus making firm the connection between the warriors of history.

The barrage made the desert tremble beneath the feet of the infantry. It rattled teacups sixty miles away in Alexandria. Eighth Army's artillery fired nine hundred shells per minute. Exactly ninety-six shells hit each known German position.

At sea, eighty miles from the firing line, Jasper saw a slice of the horizon turn pink, and a few seconds later heard the unmistakable staccato *thumpthumpthumpthump* of twenty-five-pound shells blasting their targets.

He tried to imagine the scene as the thousand tanks of Eighth Army burst free of their sunshields, grinding forward hull-down, guns spitting into the night. 'Hey presto!' he whispered, then said aloud, 'Hey presto!' Then Jasper looked at Mike Hill and shouted it as loudly as he could, 'Hey presto!'

Hill took it up, raising his fists high over his head and shouting it with Maskelyne, over and over and over...

The incredible artillery barrage raised a hellish cloud of smoke and swirling dust on the desert, obscuring the battlefield. Troopers tied bandannas under their eyes as they awaited the command to go forward.

In a rear headquarters station, a skeleton crew of 10th Armoured wireless operators began reading from prepared scripts, mimicking the chatter relevant to a major tank invasion in the southern sector.

West of Tel el Eisa, General Stumme and his staff were just finishing dinner when the first shells crashed into their forward positions. They looked at one another in astonishment, then absolute horror. Colonel Büchting went to the window and watched the world disintegrating in front of him. 'It's not possible,' he murmured in disbelief.

Stumme's first thought was of Rommel sitting peacefully in the Austrian mountains. Then he sighed, took a final sip of wine, and calmly walked across thirty yards of open desert to his command post.

The initial shelling had torn apart his communications network, cutting him off from his army. After informing Berlin that the British offensive was under way, he waited calmly for brigade messengers to report so that he could make some sense out of the situation.

Montgomery's artillery 'walked' across the Devil's Gardens in measured increments, detonating scores of mines and ripping huge gaps in the barbed-wire defences. Scores of Panzerarmee soldiers keeled over and died without being marked, victims of concussion and shock, while numerous others were buried alive when their forward trenches, dugouts and observation posts collapsed.

General Stumme waited patiently in his bunker for the barrage to subside, quite confident the British could not break through his defences. Every square inch of the forward line was protected by mines or gunners.

The Gang sailed toward Sidi Abd el Rahman, charged by the drums of Lightfoot. On the second boat Gregory wondered what the infantrymen were thinking at that very moment. 'If you were out there ready to go,' he asked Union Jack, 'what do you think would be running through your mind?'

'Remember to duck,' Fuller answered sensibly.

Scorpion minesweepers led Eighth Army into the minefields, tailed closely by Royal Engineer sappers carrying 88,000 lamps and 120 yards of white tape to demarcate cleared lanes. The anachronistic hand-drawn water carts followed them.

Directly behind the carts, rifles held at high port, bayonets sharpened, the infantry walked into battle at a pace of fifty yards per minute. Row after row of them, each exactly three yards behind the last, disappeared into the cloud of churning sand like spirits fading into a dusky dream. Tracer shells, fired just a few feet over their heads, sliced white paths into the cloud to guide them toward their initial objectives.

In the north, four divisions of XXX Corps infantry advanced

over a seven-mile span, while in the south XIII Corps began their diversionary attack on Rommel's southern defences.

Bertram had caught Panzerarmee by surprise. By the time a defence could be mounted, Eighth Army had already smashed into the minefields. Even then, the German response was sporadic and disorganized. But Stumme still had good reason to be confident – getting through the Devil's Gardens had proved to be much more difficult than Montgomery had anticipated.

Within the first hour of the attack most of the Scorpion mine-sweepers had broken down or overheated and were abandoned. Five hundred sappers using personal metal detectors took the lead, aided by Tommies who got down on their hands and knees and probed for mines with their bayonets. Still, numerous mines were 'deloused' when soldiers stepped on them. A 250-pound emplanted aerial bomb ripped apart a thirty-man platoon. Antipersonnel S-mines the size of ration cans caused severe damage. But given the sizable force making the Lightfoot assault, this was an acceptable means of clearing the Gardens.

Reports filtering into Panzerarmee headquarters indicated that the British were attacking over the entire forty-mile expanse of the Alamein Line. Stumme decided to keep his armour split between the northern and southern sectors, holding his key armoured reserves in check until the situation was clarified. But XIII Corps' ferocious attack at Hime-imet Ridge reinforced his firm belief that the main thrust of the offensive had to be made in the southern sector.

Eighth Army's murderous artillery barrage ended exactly four hours after it had begun. Thirtieth Corps was still trying to fight through the minefields, its once orderly march having become a mad scramble. It was taking much longer to sweep the tank corridors than Montgomery had allowed, and intense German small-arms fire began taking an incredible toll.

When the shelling ended, the Gang was sitting off the coast approximately twenty miles behind enemy lines, a short distance from the important airfield at Fuka. Even before the last echoes of the barrage had faded, Maskelyne blinked his signal lamp three times and the Magic Gang launched its invasion.

Smoke cannisters were lit on each barge, and the three boats echeloned and swept past the beach, drawing a thick curtain of smoke between their position and observers on land. After a half-mile run parallel to the shore, the boats turned around and came back for a second pass, now safely hidden behind a smokescreen.

During this second pass the navy crews manning the deck guns began lobbing shells onto the beach. On the barges the Gang cranked up the gramophones and blasted the sounds of an amphibious landing at the few isolated German defenders.

These coast watchers were stunned. Thick smoke obscured their vision but they could see incoming shells blasting craters into the beach and multicoloured signal flares lighting the night sky, they could hear ships' guns firing, anchor chains dropping and orders being shouted. They could smell burning naval engine oil in the air. There could be no doubt a major amphibious assault was being made, presumably on the airfield. They frantically began signalling head-quarters.

On the lead barge Jasper was racing about at full pelt, igniting strings of dummy artillery flashes, shouting phoney orders at nonexistent men, restarting the barrage recording every two minutes, clanking a ship's bell. Hill was cranking the air raid siren and heaving harmless smoke grenades toward the beach. He was as excited as a schoolboy at term's end, bravely cursing the enemy with each toss. 'Up yours, Hitler!' he screamed, and 'Take that, you bloody Nazi bastards!'

Fuller and Gregory on the second barge had charge of the oil pots – which emitted an acrid smell similar enough to that of engines running at power – and the flares that coloured the beach, as well as their own recordings. On the third barge Graham, Townsend and Robson tossed smoke grenades, flashed incomprehensible lamp signals, and played a ship's horn as well as a recording.

The coast watchers pleaded for immediate reinforcements, describing their situation as untenable. 'An enemy landing is in progress,' they reported, having to scream into their radio to be heard above the din. 'Repeat, a full-scale enemy landing is in progress at map coordinates...'

Amid the incredible confusion caused by Eighth Army's artillery barrage and the widespread attack on the Alamein Line, such an assault on the Fuka airport seemed credible. Stumme's aides, who had seen the brief communiqué from Alexandria harbour reporting the loading of four troop transports, logically assumed this force was attempting the landing. After brief deliberations, 90th Light's reserve element was ordered to meet the invasion, and Luftwaffe bombers and fighters were diverted from the front lines to the beach.

Meanwhile, the single Panzerarmee battery within range of the coast began blindly shelling the 'invasion fleet.'

The first German shells landed a few thousand yards in front of the boats as the Gang's 'fleet' began its third run down the beach. As a series of harmless waterspouts erupted, Hill started screaming victoriously, 'They're shootin' at us! We're in the bloody war!'

Another artillery salvo landed off the starboard side, much closer than the first rounds, rocking the barges and shocking Hill. 'What the blazes ...' he complained, surprised and seemingly offended. 'They're *really* shootin'. at us!'

The Gang made four runs down the beach in the allotted forty minutes. A few German rounds exploded close enough to the barges to dampen their jollity, but there were no injuries. At Maskelyne's amplified command to embark, they detached the barges and scrambled aboard the speedboats. As Jasper abandoned his barge he lit a delayed fuse, and the Gang's getaway was highlighted by a tremendous dummy barrage that sent German spotters ducking.

Ninetieth Light's reserves got to the beach and deployed to meet the landing only minutes after the Gang's top-speed departure. Luftwaffe Junkers dropped tons of bombs into the smokescreen, but when it lifted – the entire invasion force had vanished! At dawn, German pilots spotted the three drifting barges and realized they'd been duped.

The Gang raced the sunrise home. On board each of the speedboats there was much handshaking and back-pounding, as well as rowdy speculation as to the German reaction. Hill was practically delirious, recounting each second of the assault many times over, his role in it already assuming the colours of a lifelong legend. 'I'd love to have seen their bloody faces when they heard us out there,' he shouted. 'They didn't know what hit 'em. Pow! Right out of the night and there we were.'

Jasper's joy was much more subdued. He laughed at Hill's antics, but spent most of the journey home in the ship's cockpit, listening to whatever snippets of information could be picked up concerning the progress of Lightfoot. The Gang's invasion had been an enjoyable sleight, Lightfoot was the illusion. Inside, though, in his gut, he felt a great glowing warmth. Only his maturity prevented him from dancing.

The others reacted in predictable ways. Fuller stood in the prow of his boat, staring straight into the night. Finally, he had made it to war. He had served under enemy fire and never flinched. Union Jack let the sea spray wet his face, and no one ever knew that some of the large drops of water were tears of satisfaction.

'We did it, by golly,' Graham repeated over and over, 'we did it. Can you believe that?' The apparent success of the mission had him flabbergasted beyond intelligent conversation.

Robson sat on the rear deck, watching the lightning of artillery battle over the desert. Every once in a while, though, he laughed out loud.

Townsend was almost as excited as Hill. His reaction was so totally out of character as to be almost embarrassing, as it verged on a sort of hysteria.

When the three boats reached Alex the entire 'invasion fleet' climbed onto the dock and simply stared at one another for a few seconds. Then, to Hill's *whoop!* they fell over one another in a jumble. Even Maskelyne, who found himself in the middle of this pile, was screaming with joy.

A respectful decorum had been imposed by the time they got back to Magic Valley. They had played their parts well, but the real battle was being hard fought on the desert. They took their places around the radio in the dayroom and waited impatiently for the victory to be declared, for this time they would celebrate it as fighting men.

First reports from the BBC were optimistic, but it was much too soon to determine how successful the Bertram ploy had been. German resistance had stiffened after the initial shock had worn off, and Panzerarmee was counterattacking at several points. General Montgomery claimed to be satisfied with the early progress, although 10th Armoured's tanks had failed to break through Rommel's minefields the first night and had withdrawn at daybreak to less-exposed positions.

General Stumme had been unable to obtain sufficient information on which to plan his defence, so sometime in the middle of the night he decided to visit the battlefield. Accompanied by Colonel Büchting, he left his headquarters at sunrise in an open staff car. They drove right into an ambush. Australian machine-gunners opened up at close range, killing Büchting in the first fusillade. Stumme stood up and desperately tried to get out of the car. His driver, Corporal Wolf, began twisting out of the trap. The General held on to the open door as the car careened wildly about the desert. Finally he was thrown out and fell into the dust clutching his heart. Unbeknownst to driver Wolf, Stumme died there of a heart attack.

Throughout the rest of the day Panzerarmee had no commander, but fought with the courage and tenacity that had been instilled by Rommel.

In response to Adolf Hitler's urgent request, the Field Marshal immediately made plans to return to North Africa.

When Major Barkas arrived at Magic Valley late in the morning for a firsthand account of the 'invasion,' Jasper pressed him for Lightfoot details. 'No question but that we caught Jerry with his knickers down,' Barkas replied, 'but keep your fingers crossed. It looks like he isn't sure what we're going to do. Twenty-first Panzer is standing firm in the southern sector, and it's a good thing, too. Most of the Scorpion minesweepers broke down right away and, no matter what Monty says, if Rommel'd caught us in his minefields with his full strength we'd be packing our kits right now.'

'Well, what is Montgomery saying?'

The major frowned. ' "Everything's fine and dandy. Push on, push on." ' He shrugged his shoulders. 'What else could he say?'

They strolled in step around the usually bustling yard. Now, at the height of the battle, it was quiet. None of the materials produced in Magic Valley's shops could help at this point. It was a duel of steel and will.

After listening to Maskelyne describe the events of the evening, Barkas told him there had been some excellent reports. 'Intelligence intercepted some transmissions during your attack. Seems they really believed you were a large force. They sent part of Ninetieth Light and most of an air squadron to find you. I'd love to have seen their Nazi faces when they found your barges.'

Jasper nodded at the amusing thought, but continued walking with his hands thrust into his pockets and his head down.

'You don't seem very pleased.'

'Oh, I am,' Maskelyne insisted, 'I am. Just a bit fagged.'

Barkas was sympathetic. He'd learned that the afterglow of battle is often depression. 'How do you feel?'

'I don't know. Surprised, mostly, I think.'

'Oh?'

Jasper was having a difficult time understanding his feelings, much less describing them. 'I just ... It's like ... I don't know, it's not like I thought it would be, that's all.' He'd finally got into the real war, finally served under fire. He'd passed that test. And yet he felt no differently than he had before. The experience hadn't relieved his self doubts or exorcised the ghosts of his father and grandfather, it hadn't provided that cleansing of spirit he had hoped for. He wasn't depressed, just terribly disappointed. There should have been more to it. That was the big surprise.

Barkas seemed to understand. 'It's rare, you know, you more than anyone should know, that reality ever lives up to expectation. Even the reality of something as magnetic as combat.'

Jasper stared at his dust-covered shoes as they walked along. 'It just seems so anticlimactic. I don't know what it was I expected to happen. But something more ...'

'Sounds to me like you were out there looking to find something that doesn't exist. Look here, I don't mean to sound like some snooty university type, but perhaps the answer you're looking for isn't found on the battlefield. It would seem to me the place to start looking is within yourself.' Barkas paused to light a cigarette and gather his thoughts. 'I learned a very important lesson in the Great War. Just risking your life won't make it better. Actually, I discovered, you really don't need much to become a target. All it takes is incredibly bad luck.'

Jasper chuckled. 'I know it's silly to feel the way I do, particularly with the fighting on the line ...'

'Be proud of what you've done, Jay! Dammit, you've done some things that not one man in a hundred out there on the Blue right now would've done. If risking your life is the whole thing, well, you've done that. You walked straight into a fire without a protective suit. Paste or no paste.'

'But I knew it was safe,' Maskelyne protested.

'No,' Barkas corrected, 'you *believed* it was safe. That is a very different thing. Now, I'm sorry you're in a funk, but you simply weren't trained and shipped out here to be cannon fodder. You were given a job to do and you've done it to the best of your ability. The results of our little Bertram aren't in yet, but at first glance it appears to have been a rousing success. That might not mean too much to you, but it absolutely thrills me.'

Jasper found himself nodding in agreement with each point Barkas made. The major was right, he knew, he had contributed to the best of his ability. Somehow, though, that knowledge did not relieve his disappointment.

Panzerarmee managed to hold the line throughout that entire first day, though both sides suffered heavy casualties. Because 10th Armoured failed to break through the minefields in the north, it was vital that Rommel's 21st Panzer be kept in the south until a second attempt to break out of the Devil's Gardens could be made. To help keep them there, 4th and 8th Hussars sped toward 'January,' the southern minefield, dragging with them two squadrons of Maskelyne's cardboard tanks. Enemy reconnaissance aircraft spotted them almost immediately and reported an armoured attack under way in the south. After dark, the Hussars, led by armoured cars broadcasting the sounds of a tank force moving forward, and revving their own engines at high speed to aggrandize the deception, proceeded into partially cleared corridors with the dummies.

Twenty-first Panzer met this attack with great fury.

In the north that night, 10th Armoured again tried to push through. This time a Luftwaffe strafing attack turned a column of twenty-five transport vehicles into an incredibly bright torch lighting the entire area. 15th Panzer's artillery sighted on the blazing trucks and battered the sector. Twenty-seven British tanks were destroyed in an hour.

Appalled at the rapidly mounting losses, Montgomery's generals appealed to him to halt the attack. At an emergency conference held at 3 A.M. on October 25, Monty pointed out that nine hundred tanks remained in action, and threatened to replace any commander who did not push forward aggressively.

Maskelyne hung near the radio all day the twenty-fifth. It was apparent that Lightfoot was bogging down in the minefields. Although it did not seem possible that the Germans had the resources to wage such savage battle, somehow they had managed to meet each Eighth Army thrust with brute force.

Graham said he'd heard that ten thousand men had been killed or wounded in the first two days' fighting. 'Those poor blokes are taking a beating out there,' he said sorrowfully. 'Monty just can't keep throwing them in the chopper like this. It's madness.'

'It's just a rumour,' Jasper said. 'It's exaggerated.' Only two days had gone by since the Gang's return to Alex, but waiting helplessly in front of the radio made it seem like two years. Their brief scrimmage no longer seemed to have any direct connection to the horrific battle being fought on the desert. Jasper felt like a relay team member who had run his leg and now could do nothing but cheer his side on. 'I'm sure it's exaggerated,' he reiterated.

'Well,' Nails sighed, reflecting the same frustration that plagued Maskelyne and the rest of the Gang, 'I'd sure like to be out there doing somethin'. This sitting around can drive a chap bonkers!'

Late in the afternoon of the twenty-fifth, a German tank force tried to counterattack through the 'dummy artillery battery' at Munassib. The real guns, which had lain doggo for two full days of fighting, opened up at nearly point-blank range and devastated the attackers.

Field Marshal Rommel returned to his desert headquarters that night to take command of the battle, and was greeted with distressing reports. In the northern sector XV Panzer had lost 88 of its 119 tanks and could fuel its surviving armour only three more days. The potentially most dangerous British gains had been made near the coast road in that sector, where 9th Australian was almost out of the minefields and threatening to cut off Panzerarmee's supply lines to Libya.

To meet this immediate threat, Rommel reluctantly brought 90th Light in from reserve and ordered 21st Panzer to strike north. Bertram, and the French diversionary attack, had kept these two elite units out of the heart of the battle for two full days, thus making possible the northern gains.

In Abbassia, the Gang spent most of their days pacing the dayroom at a quickstep. Having had a small taste of action, they were hungry for more. But their special talents weren't required at this stage of battle. They had no choice but to sit by, strumming their fingers on table tops and tapping their feet, living for the quarter-hour battle reports, and gradually going insane.

Panzerarmee fought its way north during the next few days, successfully containing Eighth Army in the minefields. At the end of five days' close combat, many British units had still not achieved the first day's objective. Montgomery refused to retrench, as his senior staff desired, instead proposing to counter Rommel's movement north by shifting the brunt of Lightfoot farther south. This major attempt to break through enemy lines, code-named 'Supercharge,' was to be launched the night of November 1.

Thirtieth Corps, led by General Freyberg's 2nd New Zealanders, was to smash through at a seam in Rommel's defences, a point at which German and Italian Forces abutted. Monty knew his opponent would resist this 'real hard blow,' as he described it, with every available gun, but he was willing to accept the necessary large losses. Freyberg, told that some of his field commanders were predicting fifty per cent casualties, responded tersely, 'It may well be more than that. The Army Commander has said he is prepared to accept one hundred per cent.'

At Magic Valley, the Gang struggled under the incredible weight of unfilled time. Having no suitable outlet for their frustration, they started snapping at one another. Jasper did his best to maintain the peace, sending his men off on contrived missions as often as possible, but the tension was thick enough to chop up and pack into boxes.

Once again, it was the imperturbable Barkas who broke the mood. He came racing into the Valley on the twenty-ninth full of energy. Although Jasper guessed he hadn't had a decent sleep in at least a week, he presented his usual professional appearance. 'I do hope you're not too busy,' he began facetiously.

Jasper was chewing on the tip of his pencil. 'Depends,' he replied. 'The grass around this place has grown dangerously long. It's going to require some serious attention.'

'Pity,' Barkas continued, 'because I've got a job for you.'

Townsend was napping on the daybed. He opened one eye and said softly, 'Well, we didn't care too much for the grass anyway.'

In an armoured riptide, Barkas explained to the Gang, Rommel's 21st Panzer was flowing north while Monty's XXX Corps went south to prepare for Supercharge. To cover the XXX Corps movement, the General wanted to let the enemy see as many small tank groups, 'penny-packets,' in the northern sector as possible. 'He wants as many camouflage people in the field with dummy tanks as we can muster. You people know the drill, you've done it before.'

The Gang waited expectantly for their detailed orders. Where should they go? When were they expected? Would they be joining other outfits? How long might they be out there? What fuel was to be provided?

Because of the pressure of battle there would be no official orders, the major replied. 'It's a bit slapdash,' he admitted.

Nails was perplexed. 'That's the bit? Just go out somewhere on the desert and set up some cardboard tanks?'

Barkas nodded. 'Yes, I'm afraid that's it. This isn't a formal party. Find a good spot and set up, let them have a good look at you, then pack it in and do it again somewhere else down the line. Otherwise, try to stay out of the way of the armoured chaps and remember to keep your heads down.'

Townsend snorted contemptuously, 'Some funny way to run a world war, if you ask me.'

A search of the workshops turned up four serviceable dummy tanks, hardly enough to make a threatening show. The remainder had been abandoned at Murrayfield or Melting Pot and perhaps destroyed, or picked up by other outfits, or were still in place. 'Then there's the five up in Alex,' Union Jack remembered.

'If they're still lying around,' Robson said. 'Who knows what the Navy's done with them or where they've left them.'

Hill looked at Jasper. 'We could bang out a few more lickety-split.'

Jasper shook his head. 'We used everything we had for Lightfoot. I don't think we've got two yards of canvas or a pint of paint left. But,' he added, 'there's another way to make our tanks appear.'

Hill closed his eyes. 'Here we go again.'

'Look here, even if we had the canvas, it'd take two days for the paint to dry. And then we could still fit seven or eight dummies in the truck with all of us. But suppose, just suppose, we could create an entire brigade. Suppose we could carry fifteen of them. Or maybe twenty.'

'That'd be lovely,' Townsend responded. 'And while you're at it, would you mind turning some of the rocks in the yard into gold nuggets?'

'We can do it,' Jasper insisted. 'We can do it just as I'd do it on stage.' He hesitated, and glanced around the dayroom, looking at each of the men in turn. The Gang. The men with whom he had fought his most unusual war. His men. And then he smiled, his broad and dazzling smile, the smile that had lit theatres around the world and charmed countless audiences. The smile of the magician at work, unfolding wonders. The smile that had not been seen since Frank Knox went down at Heliopolis. 'We'll do it with mirrors, naturally.'

'What!' Hill blurted.

Nails looked at Mike as if he were mad. 'Didn't you hear what the man said?' he asked. 'He said we'll do it with mirrors. Naturally.' Then he looked at Maskelyne, and frowned. 'You'd better have a bloody good one up your sleeve this time,' he warned.

EIGHTEEN

'Mirrors?' Bill Robson repeated, as if it were a foreign word.

'Mirrors,' Phil Townsend repeated, making sure he had heard correctly.

'Mirrors,' Jasper repeated firmly.

Hill found the concept utterly amazing. 'Sounds like a smashing idea,' he said sarcastically, ''cept for one slight problem. We don't have any mirrors.'

'Oh, that's no problem,' Jasper replied, then added, with perfect stage timing, 'we don't really need them.'

'That's it,' Hill snapped, throwing up his hands in surrender. 'The man's crackers. Somebody take his temperature. First he says we'll make tanks we don't have appear with mirrors we don't have, then he says we don't need the mirrors to do it. I give up! Quits!'

Jasper tried to explain. 'Now, just wait a bit, that's not what I—'

Robson finally broke into hysterics, laughing so hard he had to take off his glasses to rub the tears from his eyes. 'Too bloody much,' he managed to get out, 'too bloody much. Can you imagine, can you just imagine what people are going to say when we try to tell them what we did during the war?' He shook his head in disbelief, then mimicked an aged veteran speaking in stentorian tones. 'First we moved Alexandria harbour and then we hid the Suez Canal. After that we made our own navy, and then Maskelyne walked into an inferno without wearing a safe suit, and then we used mirrors that we didn't have to make tanks that we didn't have appear ...' Finally his laughter fizzled out, and he took a deep breath and sighed. 'Hookay, boss, please let us in on it. All of us would really like to know how we're going to pull this one off.'

While getting the dummy tanks from the workshops, Maskelyne explained, he had noticed a pile of rectangular plywood boards. In the paint shop, he knew, was a large cache of bright silver paint left over from various aircraft and nautical projects. 'Put 'em together and what've you got?' he asked.

'Plywood painted silver,' Townsend answered, 'but not mirrors.'

'Not yet,' Jasper corrected, 'but wait and see.'

In unison, the Gang tramped to the shops to make mirrors. The boards were laid out in the yard and splashed with silver paint. The paint was spread with rags as evenly as possible. Mike Hill got on his hands and knees and practically drowned in the silver paint, but whether he spread it thick or thin he could not see his reflection. 'I know he's gone daft this time,' he muttered, but continued spreading the paint.

The job was completed in a few hours. While the boards were drying in the afternoon sun each man went to his quarters and packed a five-day kit.

They were on their way before dawn the following morning. Twenty-five painted plywood boards and four folded tanks had been crammed into the rear of a five-tonner. Jasper and Fuller rode in the cab, while the rest of the Gang squeezed uncomfortably into the back.

The sun rose on the devil's sideshow. Lightfoot had turned the desert into a black carnival. The Gang's good humour vanished as they drove past hundreds of smashed and burned trucks and jeeps and vans and staff cars and armoured cars and tanks, some of them still smouldering, and some of them still containing the charred lumps of flesh that had died inside them. As the Gang drove closer to the front they came upon more corpses. One soldier had been killed while eating a meal, and a swarm of flies feasted on the ration tin that he still held in his lap. Another man had died on his motorbike and driven into a barbed-wire fence that held him upright in his seat. Four men sat dead in a jeep as if they were dozing. The breeze carried an awful stench. Jasper closed the cab windows and lit his pipe to cover the smell of death in the air.

Six miles from the front lines they bumped into Freyberg's 2nd New Zealanders moving south. They had to wait ten minutes for a gap in the convoy before they could slip through and be on their way.

All Eighth Army seemed to be working near the battlefield. Tanks were being loaded on limbers or receiving field repairs or being cannibalized for parts. Canteens were serving food. The Postal Service was delivering emergency mail. Field Security had set up interrogation posts. Lines of troopers moved in and out of mobile hospital tents. It was as if entire sections of Cairo's military establishment had been picked up whole and laid down in the desert. 'About all that's missing,' Robson noted, 'is the Turf Club. And I'll bet if you brought that up here, you'd probably even be able to find some colonels and generals!'

But then, as if it were all a mirage, the Gang would drive over a ridge and be alone in a seemingly empty desert. Only the sounds of battle were inescapable. The desert resounded with the clatter of machine guns, the popping of rifles, the *thumpthump* of a big shell landing and, incongruously, the clanking of hammers banging metal into shape.

During the first water break in the morning, Jasper instructed the Gang to take the silver-painted boards out of the truck and rub them down with sand. After complaining about doing unnecessary work in the heat, they followed his orders. Astonishingly, as they rubbed, the plywood boards actually began to reflect light and shadow. It was not possible to make out any sharp details in these makeshift mirrors, no matter how hard the men rubbed them with fine sand particles, but they did reflect vague shapes.

'Well, I'll be ...' Graham said with delight.

'Who are these things supposed to fool?' Hill wondered.

'Rommel,' Robson told him. 'Didn't you know?'

Hill chortled.

The Gang set up its four dummy tanks when they stopped near a dry wadi for lunch. 'I suppose you'll want the mirrors put up, too?' Fuller asked.

'Not yet.'

They sat in place for an hour. Some friendly traffic passed nearby, but the only sign of the enemy was a surveillance plane that stayed at a good distance.

'Some show,' Hill grumbled.

'At least we're near the action,' Fuller reminded him.

They finally broke down the dummy tanks and moved a few miles down the line and slightly westward. On their drive to this position they ran into a team from Number 85 Camouflage Company coming from that direction. 'Nothing going on back there, mates,' one of the men of Number 85 yelled as their truck bounced past.

This time they set up in a shallow depression between two gentle ridges, the perfect spot for a tank group to rest, or hide. Graham stood watch on the top of the rise. 'Mirrors?' Fuller asked.

'Not yet.'

The Gang spent the entire day setting up the tank dummies, then breaking them down, five times in all. Maskelyne never employed the plywood mirrors. Around the campfire that evening, Hill wondered what they were being saved for.

'Beats me,' Graham answered. 'I only work here. But I'm sure he knows,' he added, nodding in Maskelyne's direction. 'Least, I hope so.'

October 31 was a repeat of the previous day. While Lightfoot was being fought in front of them and support troops were hard at work behind them, the Gang roamed up and down the line putting together and then taking apart its four cardboard tanks and beginning to feel foolish about the whole operation. 'Haven't we done this whole bit before?' Nails suggested.

Hill kept busy trying to outguess Maskelyne. 'He's got a special plan for the mirrors,' he said knowingly. 'He knows just what he's gonna do with them, but he doesn't want us to know.'

'Why is that?' asked Fuller.

''Cause it's a secret,' Hill explained.

From their position in the midst of the battle it was not possible to get any feel of its progress. The entire desert seemed to exist in a state of confused flux. No one, except the 10th Armoured tankers who rumbled forward every night and retreated just before dawn every morning, seemed to have any particular destination. Truck drivers just rolled from one point to the next, picking up, dropping off, carrying wounded, bringing up water. One truck jockey was even operating a mobile card game that had been in progress since the day before the battle had begun.

From the news the Gang managed to pick off the grapevine, Lightfoot had become a stalemate. Rommel was strong enough to prevent Eighth Army from breaking out of the Gardens, but lacked the resources to mount an offensive of his own. As with most other western-desert campaigns, this had become a battle of attrition.

Both sides fought the sun and the heat. Every once in a while Jasper would see a familiar movement on the flats, or pick an odour off the breeze, or hear a natural sound, and he would shiver in fear, remembering the days he had spent dying on the desert. Hill mentioned it only once, asking him if he ever thought about it. 'Sometimes,' he admitted.

'Me too, and it gives me the willies. One good thing, though. With half of bloody England traipsing about out here it isn't likely we're going to get lost again.'

While heading north on November 1 the Gang paused alongside a small transport convoy evacuating wounded from the battlefield, to catch up on the latest rumours. A group of the less seriously injured had brewed up, and Maskelyne suddenly recognized the ranking officer among them, an exceedingly proper major he had met at Hobart House, the reserve officers' recruitment centre in London. The major had turned him away, pointing out rather brusquely that the Army was a place for soldiers, not aging magicians.

The man's right arm was being held rigid in a sling by wooden slats and his head was partially bandaged, the result, Jasper learned, of having taken one round square in the shoulder and being winged in the scalp by another. The major remembered him immediately. 'I saw one of your shows in Cairo,' he said in a surprisingly cheerful tone. 'What in the blazes are you doing out here? I thought you'd be back there entertaining the boys.'

'Actually,' Jasper explained, 'I've been trying to get forward since I got to Egypt.'

The major was astonished. 'Whatever for?'

'To be part of it, I suppose. Do my share.'

'You're not serious,' the major scoffed.

'Absolutely,' Jasper said. This once formal officer had been transformed since their meeting in London. His beard was thick, his uniform irregular, his entire attitude slack. All traces of the quintessential British officer had disappeared.

'The old spirit, eh, Maskelyne?' The major shook his head in amusement. 'I should've thought you were too old to believe that rubbish.' He hoisted his strapped arm a bit. 'This isn't a medal, you know. It's a damn painful wound. I know, we've all got our jobs to do, but I'll tell you, Maskelyne, no matter what you think, I tried to do you a favour back at Hobart House.' He sipped his tea and collected his thoughts. 'Now tell me, have you played your tricks on Jerry?'

Maskelyne told him about Magic Valley. 'We've designed most of the dummies being used out here,' he said proudly.

'Good for you, good for you. I'm glad one of us did some good out here.'

Jasper still did not understand. 'But you certainly seem to be in good spirits, Major.'

The officer smiled broadly. 'And why shouldn't I be? I'm out of it alive.'

Later, as the Gang proceeded further north, Maskelyne repeated the conversation to Jack Fuller. 'Sounds like a queer duck, if you ask me,' the sergeant said.

'Perhaps,' Jasper agreed, but the meeting left him more confused than ever. Maybe Barkas was right, maybe he was looking in the wrong place for fulfilment.

Late in the afternoon of November 1, like a cleansing wind sweeping across the desert, a resilient mood took hold of Eighth Army. The malaise of the past few days seemed to evaporate. The lines suddenly looked straighter, the orders sounded more certain, the soldiers seemed grimly determined. The word raced down the line: Monty's Supercharge was to be launched that night.

At dusk, the Gang settled down with some squaddies from a Tank Recovery outfit. The night started out regularly enough, and by ten o'clock each of them had dug a shallow trench in the still-warm ground, pulled his blanket over his shoulders, and fallen asleep to the lullaby of sporadic gunfire.

Four hours later Jasper was shaken awake. An incredible guttural wave of thunder rose out of the south and swept over him and beyond him, and became a canopy of sound over the entire desert. The sky lit up like a flashing marquee on opening night. Supercharge had begun, and he was right in the middle of it.

Six miles away, near the Miteirya Ridge, the barrage stepped forward one hundred yards every three minutes. The infantry and the armour followed in its dust. Seventy tanks were lost in the first hour, but Monty fielded a hundred more to replace them, and eventually this steel army rolled over German gun positions, often crushing the gun crews to death beneath their treads. By morning the battlefield was a junkyard of bodies and wrecked vehicles, but the Devil's Gardens had been breached and men and armour were pouring through this thin corridor. After being held up for more than a week, Britain's Army of the Nile was slamming forward again.

Rommel desperately tried to close the gaps, ordering any units not directly engaged with the enemy into the sector. He knew that the Battle of El Alamein, and the desert campaign, would be decided on this morning.

The Gang had packed up and was ready to move by 7 A.M. With Montgomery's armour driving south, Jasper decided to take his dummy tanks north.

They had gone about nine miles up the battle line when a single truck came racing toward them at top speed. It spun to a halt almost directly in front of the Gang's truck, and a soldier in cook's whites leaped out of its cab. 'You chaps got a wireless?' he shouted.

'Sorry,' Jasper said. 'Why? What's up?'

The cook grunted as if punched in the stomach. 'There's a bunch of Jerry tanks comin' this way. They're zigzagging through their own minefields. They're going to try to hit the flank.'

Jasper grabbed hold of this opportunity and held it tightly. 'How many men've you got in your truck?'

'There's six of us, but we're just cooks. We haven't even got rifles with us. We just got a little lost and came over this ridge, and bam!–' the cook smacked his hands together '–they were comin' right at us.'

'All right, Sergeant,' Maskelyne ordered, 'I want you and your people to come with us. How far back d'you say they were?'

The cook wasn't sure. 'Three, four miles maybe. But it's slow going through those fields. I'd say they were a good twenty minutes away, probably more. But, look, Captain, see, we're just cooks and–'

'Good, we've got a little time.' The objective of this raiding force was obvious. By sneaking through their own minefields, these panzers could attack Eighth Army's corridor from the flank. With some luck, they would be able to inflict enough damage to clog it up with smashed armour and give Panzerarmee time to rush reinforcements into the area. Given a few extra hours, Rommel might be able to organize a counterattack and close the wound in his lines.

Hill leaned out from the rear of the truck. 'What's holdin' up the war?' he yelled.

Maskelyne jogged to the back of the truck and outlined the situation, concluding, 'I think we can stall them long enough for one of the cooks to drive back and get some help.'

Hill glanced at the rest of the Gang 'I don't know, Jay,' he finally said, 'those are real tanks out there. They've got real guns. And, no matter how real our dummy tanks look, we've only got four of them, and that's not enough to scare off Jerry if he wants to come.'

Jasper gritted his teeth. 'You were the one complaining about not being in the war, Mike. Now here's your chance. I say we can slow them down, and I'm going to try it. If any of you want to ride back with the cooks, go ahead. But make your decision right now, we haven't got any spare time.'

Hill looked at Robson. Robson hesitated, then waved a conceding hand. 'Ah, let's go. I've heard of more ridiculous things.'

'Like what?' Hill wondered. He couldn't imagine anything more ridiculous than trying to halt a panzer tank force with cardboard tanks and plywood mirrors.

They followed the tracks made by the cooks' truck for a little more than a mile, stopping at the base of a dune that rose gently to a height of twenty-five feet. The Gang parked behind it, while one of the cooks took their truck to find a wireless and call in air support. The other cooks helped the Gang set up the four dummy tanks. Maskelyne climbed to the crest of the dune and stared out at the empty desert. As he shaded his eyes from the morning sun, he thought he saw a dust cloud in the distance, but couldn't be sure it was not simply his imagination willing the enemy tanks toward him.

He marked positions for each of the dummy tanks about thirty yards apart. Slightly behind each placement, at an angle of about forty-five degrees to the left and then to the right, he drew additional marks on the ground. As soon as he finished, he ordered the men to place the tanks at the bottom of the dune near their designated positions and lay the plywood boards face up on the marks he had made. 'When I say so,' he explained, 'we'll push the tanks up into position. Then, one by one, we'll get the mirrors up. Remember, not until I give the word.'

The cooks looked around for the mirrors.

Jasper watched the horizon. The cloud was drifting closer.

The Gang waited anxiously next to the tanks. Graham looked at Townsend. 'Nervous?'

'Nah.'

'Better tell your foot, then,' Graham joked, pointing to the painter's rapidly tapping left foot.

'A little,' Townsend admitted.

One of the cooks looked at the silver plywood boards and declared flatly, 'Those aren't mirrors, you know.'

The German *Panzergruppe* consisted of five Panzer IIIs and three of the new Mark III Specials. The group commander stood in the cupola of the lead tank and scanned the desert through his binoculars. The Luftwaffe support he had been promised had not materialized, but that did not surprise him. The Air Force was obviously very busy at Miteirya Ridge. His tank force still enjoyed one major advantage: the element of surprise. The British would never expect an attack from the flank. If he remained very lucky...

'All set, Jay,' Graham yelled to Maskelyne. 'Just give us the word.'

Jasper estimated that the enemy tanks were still more than two miles away. When they got just a bit closer he would begin the illusion. Looking down from the crest to Nails, he shouted back, 'If they start shooting, we'll get out of here right quick.'

Hill cheered.

They waited. Occasionally, they could hear artillery shells thumping into the desert, or an air-sucking *whoomp!*, indicating that another tank had been hit somewhere down the line.

As he lay flat on the crest of the dune, watching the cloud of armour moving toward them, Jasper suddenly remembered lying flat inside a cramped machine-gun nest in the fields at Farnham, holding his breath as Lord Gort searched for his position. It seemed to have taken place such a long time ago.

'They're coming!' Townsend shouted to him.

'I got 'em.' The panzers were driving straight toward the dune line. Jasper chuckled to himself as he remembered Frank Knox pushing his broom handle through the slit. It was such an innocent time. He had been so determined then. So determined and so confident, and so naive.

The lead panzer finally picked up speed and raced out of its dust cloud. 'All right,' Jasper commanded, 'let's do it. Let's go. Now.'

The men lifted the dummy tanks and carried them up the gentle incline. One by one they were placed in position, their wooden guns aimed directly at the advancing *Panzergruppe*.

Jasper took his silver lighter out of his pocket and used it to deflect the rays of the morning sun onto the desert flats. He worked carefully with the lighter, moving it up and down, up and down, creating bursts of sunlight that might catch the attention of the panzer column.

'What's he doing now?' one of the cooks asked Graham.

'Just checking his makeup,' Nails replied.

The *Panzergruppe* commander spotted the flashes. At that distance it was not possible to determine what was causing them, but he immediately informed his individual tank commanders of their existence and ordered the column to reduce speed. It was difficult enough weaving a path through the minefield without having to wage a battle.

Jasper waited another minute, just watching, until he just couldn't wait any longer. 'Raise 'em,' he ordered. 'Get 'em up.'

Townsend and a cook picked up a board to Maskelyne's right. It bounced the sunlight toward the enemy tank column.

Nails raised a board by himself.

In quick succession the other boards were pushed upright, like tanks climbing to the top of the dune.

Hey presto! Jasper thought to himself.

The *Panzergruppe* commander asked over the radio if anyone could determine what was creating these bursts of light. But it was a perfunctory request. He knew, he knew.

Within moments, the boards were all in place.

The panzer column continued moving forward.

Hill scanned the skies, trying to wish a Desert Air Force squadron into existence.

Each tank commander kept his field glasses on the dune crest, but the reflected sunlight made it impossible to make out any shapes.

Desert experience had taught these tankers that such flashes were usually caused by vehicles, although these particular vehicles might just as easily be harmless transport as tanks.

The column finally halted, and sat motionless in the minefield. To continue forward, the commander knew, made no sense. Whether these flashes were being caused by British trucks or tanks did not matter, the element of surprise had been lost. Trucks would have radios. And if this was a tank force waiting for him at the end of the minefield, his small column would be decimated.

He peered through his glasses one final time. He thought he could barely make out the distinctive shape of an American Grant, but was not sure. It made no difference. 'Withdraw,' he ordered, thankful that the high morning sun had given away the British position.

'They're backing off,' one of the cooks yelled jubilantly. 'Look at 'em, look at 'em!'

'I told you,' Hill shouted. 'Didn't I tell you? Didn't I?' The Gang hugged one another and the cooks and danced in wide circles. The cooks thought they were crazy, but, having just helped beat off a panzer column with cardboard and plywood, they were in a dancing mood, too.

Twenty minutes later, while they were packing up the dummies for the next display, six Spits flew directly overhead in pursuit of the panzer column. Fuller watched them fly toward the sun, then was struck by an odd thought. 'Hey, Captain,' he asked Jasper, 'what would you have done if it was overcast?'

Maskelyne thought about that, then grinned. 'A disappearing act.'

By the end of that fateful day, Rommel's African army had been reduced to thirty-five German and one hundred ineffective Italian tanks. Disregarding Hitler's order to 'stand fast, yield not a yard of room and throw every gun and man into the battle,' the Field Marshal began retreating. His tattered column stretched forty miles on the coast highway. Hundreds of vehicles ran out of fuel during this withdrawal and had to be abandoned. In the battles at El Alamein, he had lost 32,000 men, more than 1,000 guns and 450 tanks. Only heavy rainstorms, which grounded the British air force, prevented even greater losses. 'The dead are lucky,' he wrote to his wife. 'It's all over for them.'

England's newest hero, Montgomery, called it a 'fine battle. Complete and absolute victory ... Boches are finished – finished!'

Brigadier Currie of 9th Armoured, a brigade that had been in the thick of Supercharge, had a difficult time sharing Monty's exuberance.

Asked by a fellow officer where his regiments were, he pointed to twelve battered tanks and replied, 'There are my armoured regiments.'

Rommel's retreat ended the battle for the western desert although British and American forces would pursue him through North Africa for many months before finally bringing his army to ground.

This time the Gang celebrated as fighting men. This time they didn't have to step silently to the back of the bar when the boasting began. The story of their incredible 'invasion' had quickly become a favourite tale in Cairo. 'It wasn't much of an invasion,' Hill modestly told a group of spellbound clerks who were paying for the drinks at the Melody. 'There we were on these three boats, but we had 'em convinced we were a full-scale landing force. You should've seen 'em running around that beach. There was this one Nazi–'

'Actually, we didn't really see them,' Robson interrupted. 'You know, it was dark.'

Hill was not one to let such details ruin a good story. 'See. Hear. What's the difference? They sure knew we were there. Half the bloody Luftwaffe came at us and we were dashing about behind this smokescreen–'

'Maybe not half their air force,' Fuller corrected, 'and certainly not until we'd already departed. Surprise was the key to the success of the operation.'

Hill frowned and shook his head. 'Are you going to let me tell the story or not?' he asked Union Jack.

'But the details are important, Mike,' Fuller replied.

'Well, I've got all the details, Sarge, but I just don't wanna get into specifics!'

Jasper sat with Major Barkas across the dark room. As he tried unsuccessfully to weave a coin through his fingers, they rehashed the Battle of El Alamein for the many-hundredth time.

'No question about it,' Barkas declared, 'they fell for Bertram completely. No question about it at all. Von Thoma said so himself.' General Ritter von Thoma, one of Rommel's top commanders, had been captured late in the fighting. He admitted to Montgomery that Afrika Korps had been led to believe the attack would be made in the south, opposite Munassib, and prepared for that.

'Then there was the report from their Intelligence, too,' Jasper reminded Barkas. While doing so, he dropped the coin again. His fingers felt like logs, so out of condition he doubted he'd ever be able to perform in public again. The Panzerarmee summary to which he referred had predicted Eighth Army would attack in the south, although suggesting that diversionary thrusts might take place in the north.

The Italians had also taken the bait. A captured map prepared by their Intelligence indicated that Montgomery's armoured divisions were staging in the south, and noted that the assembly in the Martello area posed no threat.

Maskelyne raised his glass. 'Bertram!'

'Bertram,' Barkas responded. The fact that Rommel had kept a substantial portion of his armoured force in the southern sector for the crucial first few days of the battle was proof that he had fallen for the greatest deception in military history.

Jasper put down his glass and snaked the coin through his fingers, caught it in his palm, made a fist, then turned his hand over and opened his palm to Barkas. It was empty. 'Hey presto!' he said.

'I'm so sorry,' Barkas complained, 'but that's my coin.'

On November 11, Prime Minister Winston Churchill addressed the House of Commons. After paying tribute to the leaders and men of the Eighth Army, he continued, 'I must say one word about ... surprise and strategy. By a marvellous system of camouflage, complete tactical surprise was achieved in the desert. The enemy suspected – indeed, knew – that an attack was impending, but when and where and how it was coming was hidden from him. The Tenth Corps, which had been seen from the air exercising fifty miles in the rear, moved silently away in the night, leaving an exact simulacrum of its tanks where it had been and proceeded to its points of attack. The enemy suspected the attack was impending, but did not know how, where or when, and above all had no idea of the scale upon which he was to be assaulted.'

The war magician took his bows.

On the morning of the December Sunday he was to join the Gang to celebrate the engagement of Michael Hill and Kathy Lewis, Jasper drove to Giza to finish some important business. As he had done once long before, he crawled on his hands and knees down the narrow passage into the King's Chamber of the Great Pyramid. He was alone there, although he could hear the electronic buzz of Eighth Army's headquarters communications centre at work in a nearby chamber.

He did not sit down on the stone floor, because he did not expect to stay there long. He would not wait impassively for the ancient magicians to commune with him. He was there to discover once and forever if he belonged with the great wizards of the ages, and he had realized that no one could tell him this. He would know.

He had performed all the illusions that had been required of him, illusions far more astounding than those of the men who had built these massive monuments. He had caused great armies to appear on the field of battle and conjured up their weapons. He had launched fleets of ships and had vanished waterways and had seemingly moved the land itself. He had done his grand illusion.

He stood there staring at the cold walls, thinking of his grandfather, the illustrious John Nevil Maskelyne, and his father, Nevil Maskelyne. He had tested himself in ways they would understand, and he had passed every test. He knew he could stand tall with them now.

He had learned so much in the desert. Real magic did exist in the world, he was sure of that now. But it had nothing to do with elaborate productions or crafty legerdemain. It was the simple wonder of love and loss and renewal and even death. Mary had taught him that, being at his side every moment though thousands of miles away. The Gang had taught him that. Frank Knox had taught him that.

Perhaps, he thought as he stood at the very centre of the kingdom of magic, there is one real magician.

Jasper took a deep breath of the pharaoh's air. His shoulders relaxed, his hands lay easily at his side, and he was comfortable. His search was over. He knew he could stay there as long as he pleased, for he had found what he was looking for.

Resolved, he turned around and left. He didn't want to be late for the engagement of his friends. There was to be magic in the afternoon.

EPILOGUE

The successful conclusion of the western desert campaign was hardly the end of Jasper Maskelyne's incredible exploits during World War II. By the time the Axis powers surrendered unconditionally he had been promoted to the rank of major and served in sixteen countries, among them Italy, the Balkans, India, Burma, Malaya and Canada. In Canada he established Station M – the 'M' standing for 'Magic' – where he created top-secret illusions to be used around the world. While serving at Station M he recreated the illusion he had used in Farnham to convince Lord Gort that the battleship *Admiral Graf Spee* was sailing down the Thames, this time making American FBI Director J. Edgar Hoover believe German cruisers were at work on Lake Ontario.

Although his wartime work was supposedly secret, his contributions became well known among the war planners. In Delhi, India, at a reception soon after his arrival, Maskelyne was introduced by Lord Louis Mountbatten to Lady Mountbatten as 'Jasper Maskelyne, in charge of all the camouflage and illusion inventions we're using.'

On the dark side of the battle lines, Hitler's Gestapo added his name to its infamous 'Black List,' and placed a large bounty on his head.

Much of his work after the western desert campaign was done for Allied secret services and remains classified. Among the numerous devices he invented was a means of communicating between aircraft and ground-control stations by infrared waves and a method of making aircraft invisible to searchlights at low altitudes. But perhaps most intriguing is a photograph that appears in his personal wartime album, of a miniature submarine hooked onto the bottom of the hull of a larger ship. 'This is the submarine we used to torpedo the German ship carrying the 'heavy water' needed for the creation of atomic weapons from Scandinavia to Germany,' reads the handwritten caption. A large *X* appears at the top of the page. No other information regarding this submarine is available.

Maskelyne's Magic Gang split up soon after the Battle of El Alamein, but Magic Valley's workshops, under Mechanical Engineer supervision, continued supplying dummies and decoys to Allied armies until the end of the fighting in the Middle East and Far East.

Michael Hill was transferred to India, rising to the rank of sergeant, and married Kathy Lewis in England in 1946. Union Jack Fuller resigned from the Army at the cessation of hostilities, but stayed on in the Middle East in the employ of a major exporting firm. He died there in 1965. Bill Robson returned to England after the war and became a successful fashion illustrator and teacher of fine arts at a London university. Philip Townsend eventually became a director of television commercials and remarried happily. Theodore Graham returned to his family trade, opening up a carpentry shop in a London suburb.

Jasper returned to Mary and his children in 1946. In those desperate postwar years there was little interest in England in stage magic, and an attempt to tour with *Maskelyne's Magical Mysteries* failed.

In 1948, the Maskelynes emigrated to Kenya. There, in the early 1950s, Jasper again picked up his magic wand and worked for the National Police in the war against the Mau Mau. During that war he managed to pull off an illusion he had often promised, projecting an image of Mau Mau leader Jomo Kenyatta in the sky above Mount Kenya.

After that war ended Maskelyne managed the Kenyan National Theatre and eventually settled on a small farm outside Nairobi.

He maintained contact with the members of his Magic Gang for a number of years after the war, but as wartime memories faded, this correspondence ended.

Jasper Maskelyne, the war magician, died in Kenya in 1973.